D0382428

PERCY GLOOM

by **CATHY MALKASIAN**

Fantagraphics Books

**MANY THANKS TO THE FINE PEOPLE AT FANTAGRAPHICS.
SPECIAL THANKS TO ROBERT GOODIN.**

Fantagraphics Books
7563 Lake City Way NE
Seattle, Washington 98115

Edited by Gary Groth
Design by Adam Grano
Promotion by Eric Reynolds
Published by Gary Groth and Kim Thompson

To receive a free full-color catalog of comics, graphic novels, prose novels, and other
fine works of artistry, call 1-800-657-1100, or visit www.fantagraphics.com.
You may order books at our website or by phone.

Distributed in the U.S. by W.W. Norton and Company, Inc. (212-354-500)
Distributed in Canada by Raincoast Books (800-663-5714)
Distributed in the United Kingdom by Turnaround Distribution (108-829-3009)

ISBN: 978-1-56097-845-9
Second Fantagraphics printing: July, 2007
Printed in China

CONTENTS

Part One:
BIRTH

MATE WITH ME, PERCY GLOOM! GIVE ME A SWEET AND PEACEFUL LITTLE BABY THAT IS MINE ALL MINE I INSIST I INSIST RIGHT NOW YOU WILL MATE WITH ME PERCY GLOOM—MATE NOW! I DON'T HAVE ALL (OVER) →

ATE NOW! MATE!! WITH ME MATE, MATE, ATE, MA— MATE MATE M MATE M

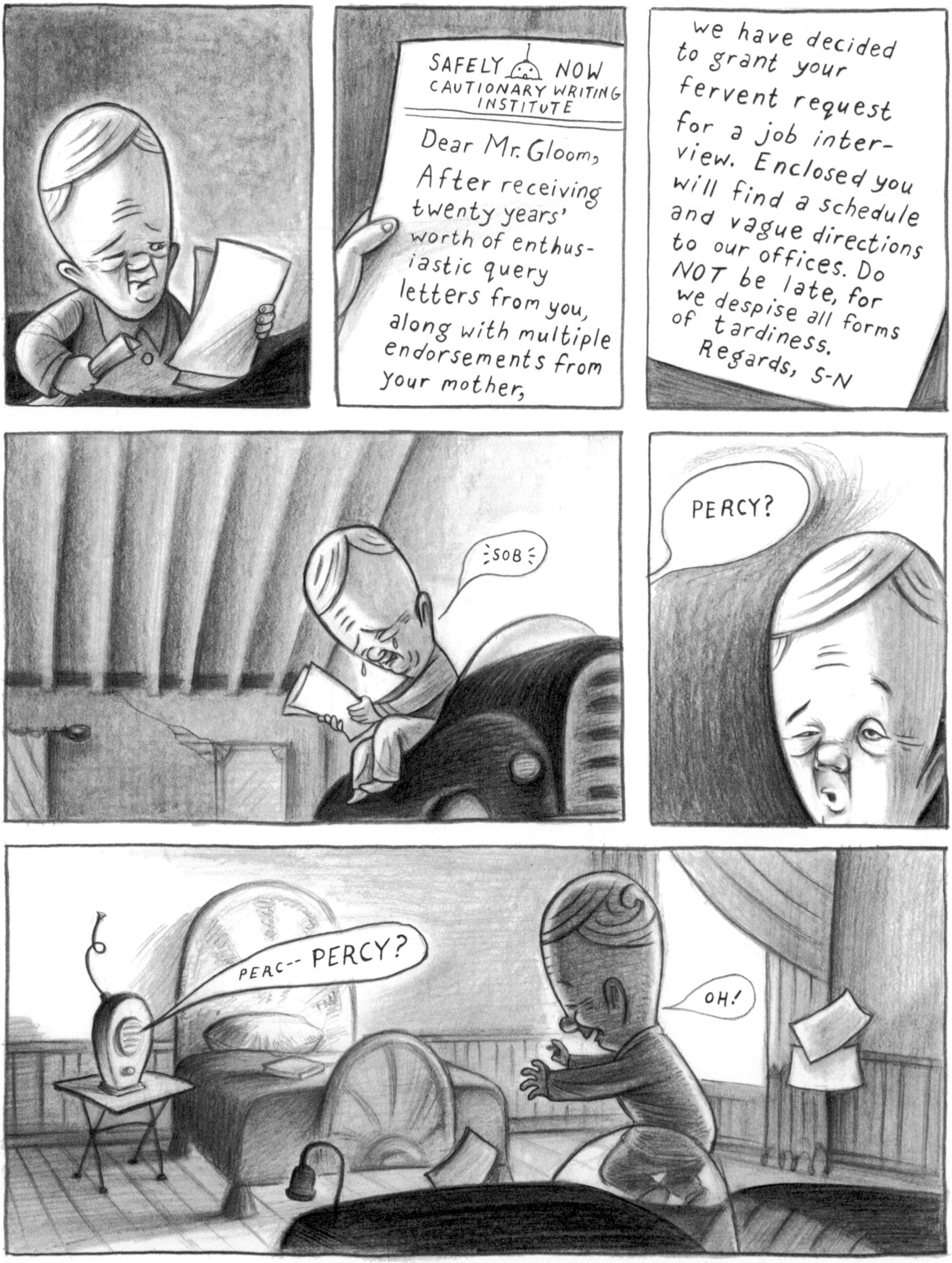
SAFELY NOW
CAUTIONARY WRITING INSTITUTE
Dear Mr. Gloom,
After receiving twenty years' worth of enthusiastic query letters from you, along with multiple endorsements from your mother,
we have decided to grant your fervent request for a job interview. Enclosed you will find a schedule and vague directions to our offices. Do NOT be late, for we despise all forms of tardiness.
Regards, S-N
SOB
PERCY?
PERC-- PERCY?
OH!

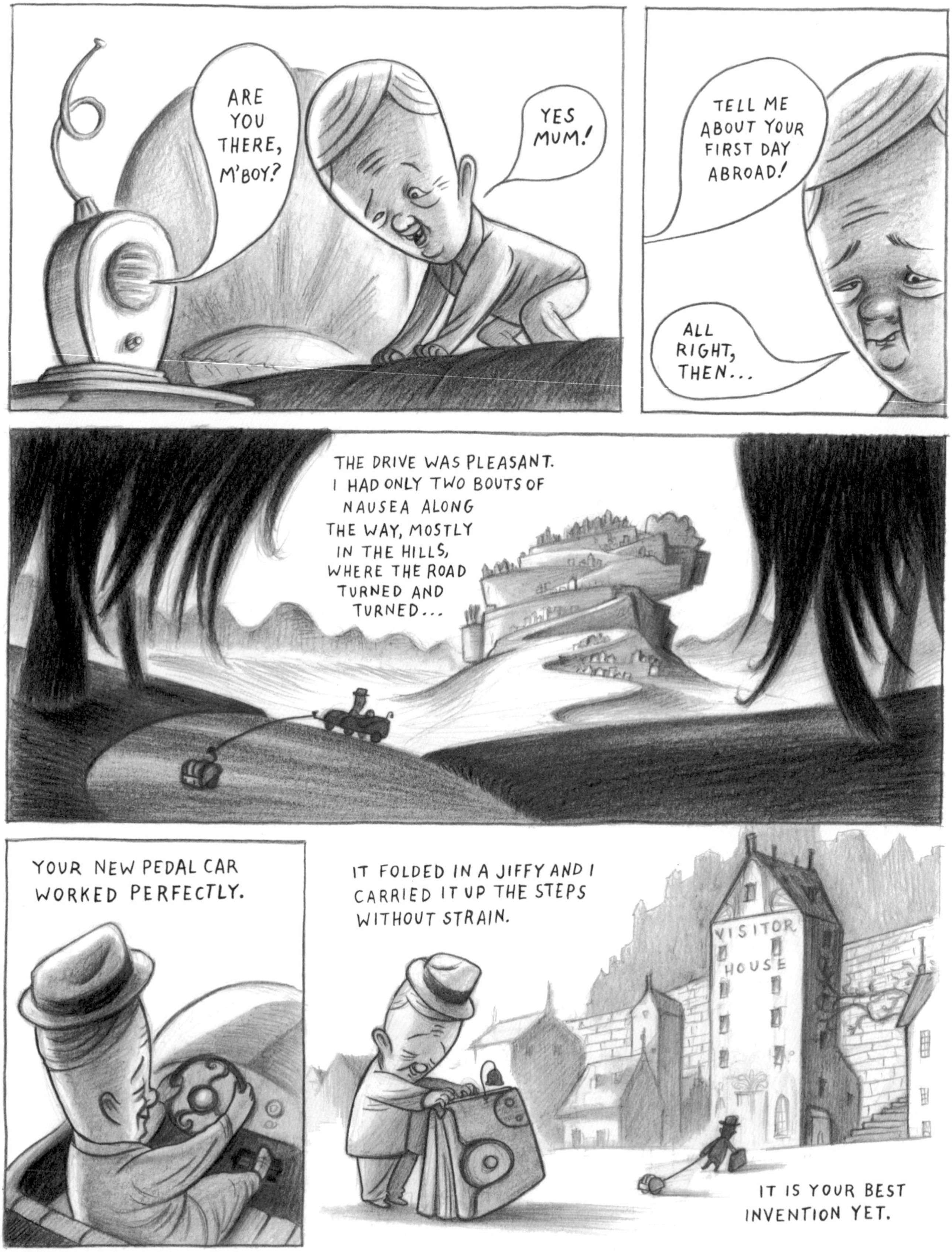
ARE YOU THERE, M'BOY?
YES MUM!
TELL ME ABOUT YOUR FIRST DAY ABROAD!
ALL RIGHT, THEN...
THE DRIVE WAS PLEASANT. I HAD ONLY TWO BOUTS OF NAUSEA ALONG THE WAY, MOSTLY IN THE HILLS, WHERE THE ROAD TURNED AND TURNED...
YOUR NEW PEDAL CAR WORKED PERFECTLY.
IT FOLDED IN A JIFFY AND I CARRIED IT UP THE STEPS WITHOUT STRAIN.
VISITOR HOUSE
IT IS YOUR BEST INVENTION YET.

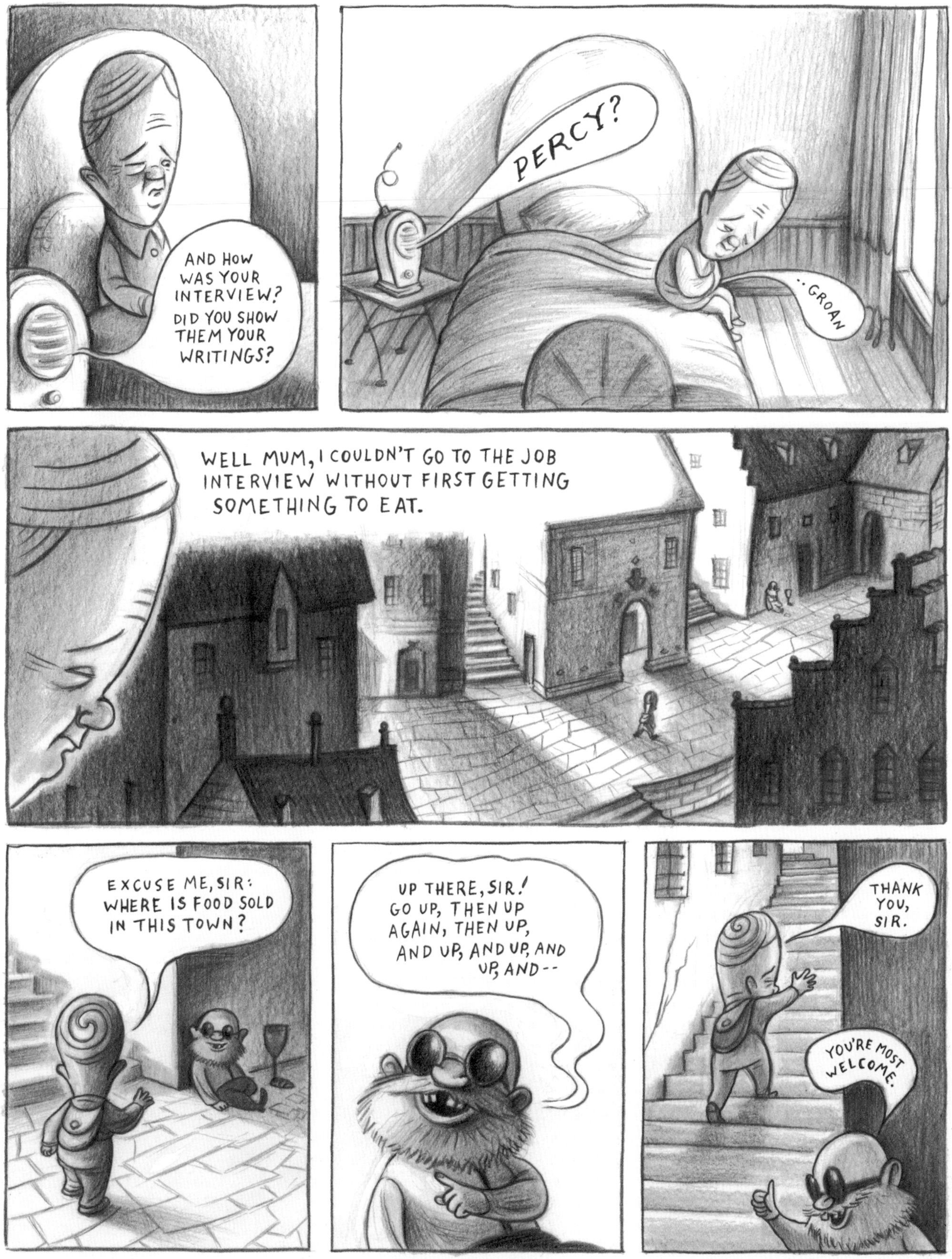
AND HOW WAS YOUR INTERVIEW? DID YOU SHOW THEM YOUR WRITINGS?
PERCY?
..GROAN
WELL MUM, I COULDN'T GO TO THE JOB INTERVIEW WITHOUT FIRST GETTING SOMETHING TO EAT.
EXCUSE ME, SIR: WHERE IS FOOD SOLD IN THIS TOWN?
UP THERE, SIR! GO UP, THEN UP AGAIN, THEN UP, AND UP, AND UP, AND UP, AND--
THANK YOU, SIR.
YOU'RE MOST WELCOME.

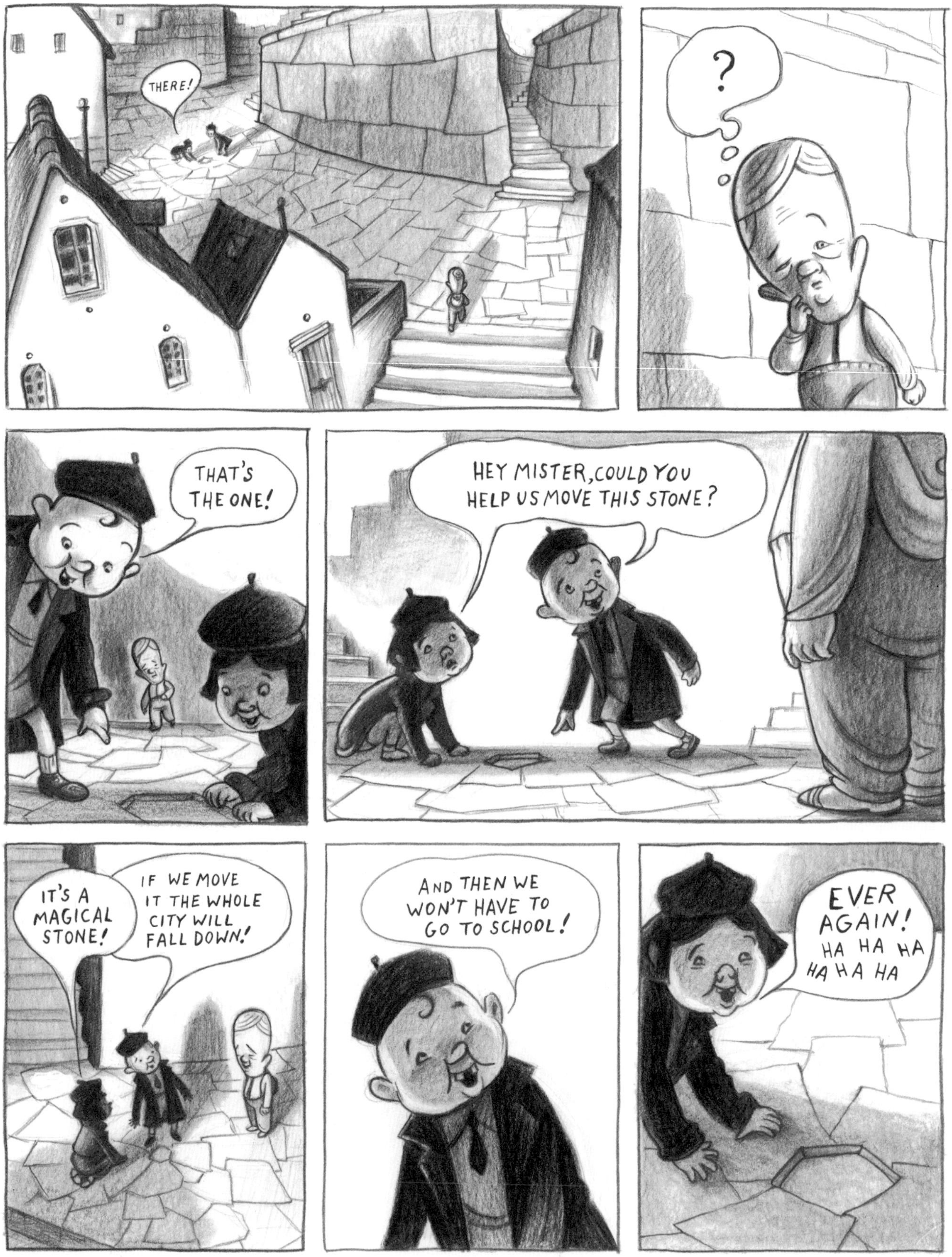
THERE!
?
THAT'S THE ONE!
HEY MISTER, COULD YOU HELP US MOVE THIS STONE?
IT'S A MAGICAL STONE!
IF WE MOVE IT THE WHOLE CITY WILL FALL DOWN!
AND THEN WE WON'T HAVE TO GO TO SCHOOL!
EVER AGAIN!
HA HA HA HA HA HA

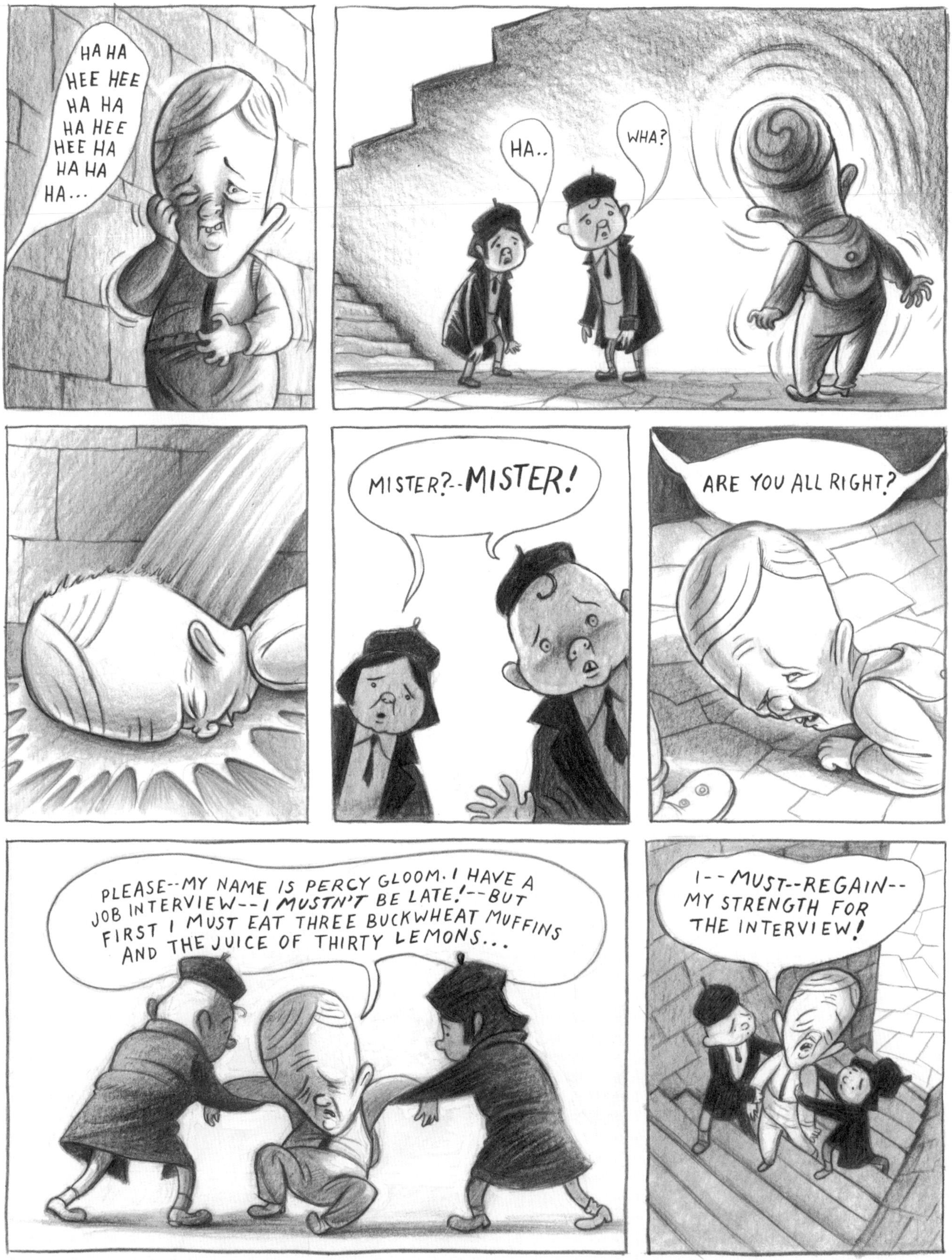

HA HA HEE HEE HA HA HA HEE HEE HA HA HA HA...
HA..
WHA?
MISTER?--MISTER!
ARE YOU ALL RIGHT?
PLEASE--MY NAME IS PERCY GLOOM. I HAVE A JOB INTERVIEW--I MUSTN'T BE LATE!--BUT FIRST I MUST EAT THREE BUCKWHEAT MUFFINS AND THE JUICE OF THIRTY LEMONS...
I--MUST--REGAIN--MY STRENGTH FOR THE INTERVIEW!

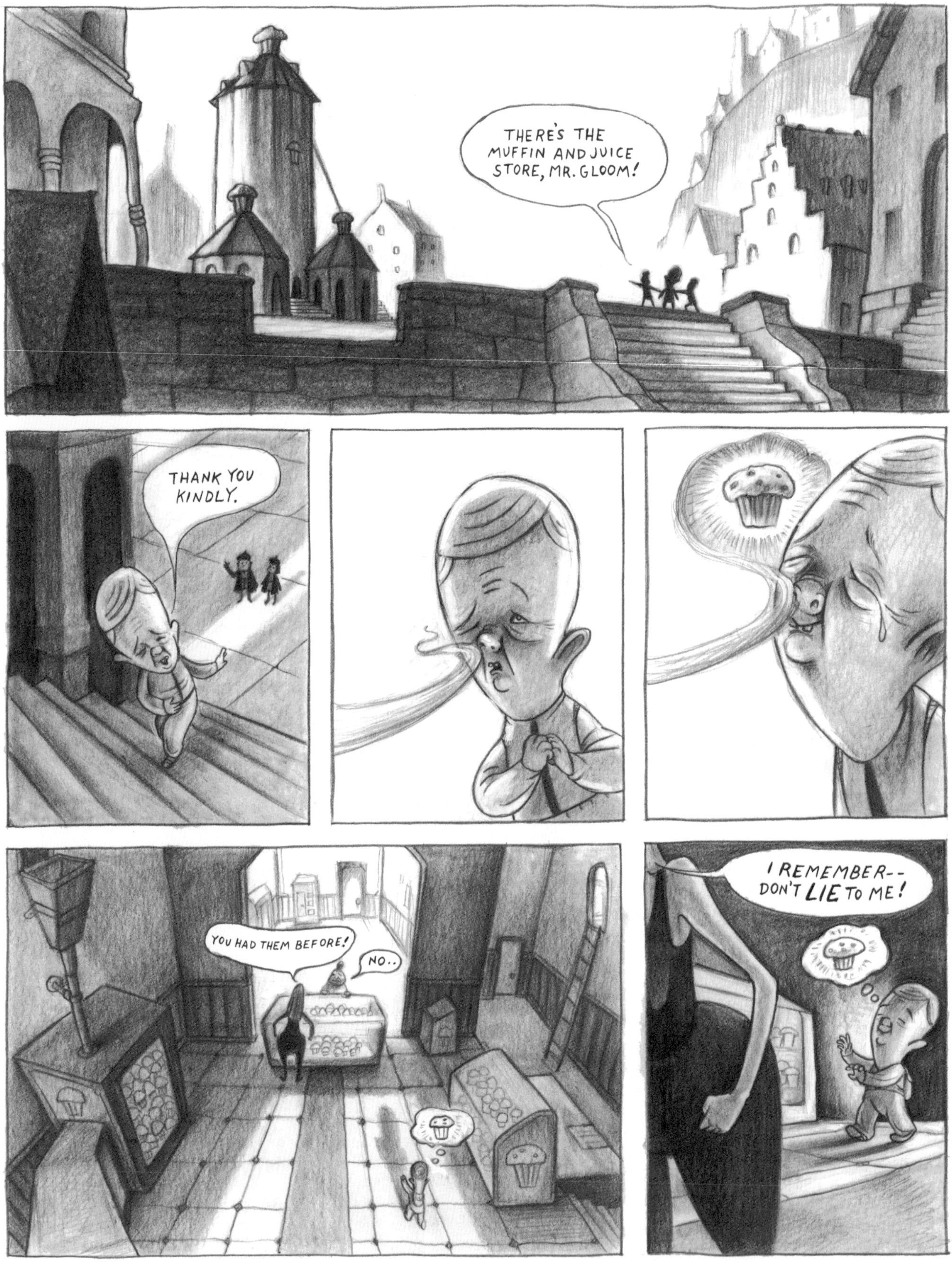
THERE'S THE MUFFIN AND JUICE STORE, MR. GLOOM!
THANK YOU KINDLY.
YOU HAD THEM BEFORE!
NO..
I REMEMBER-- DON'T LIE TO ME!

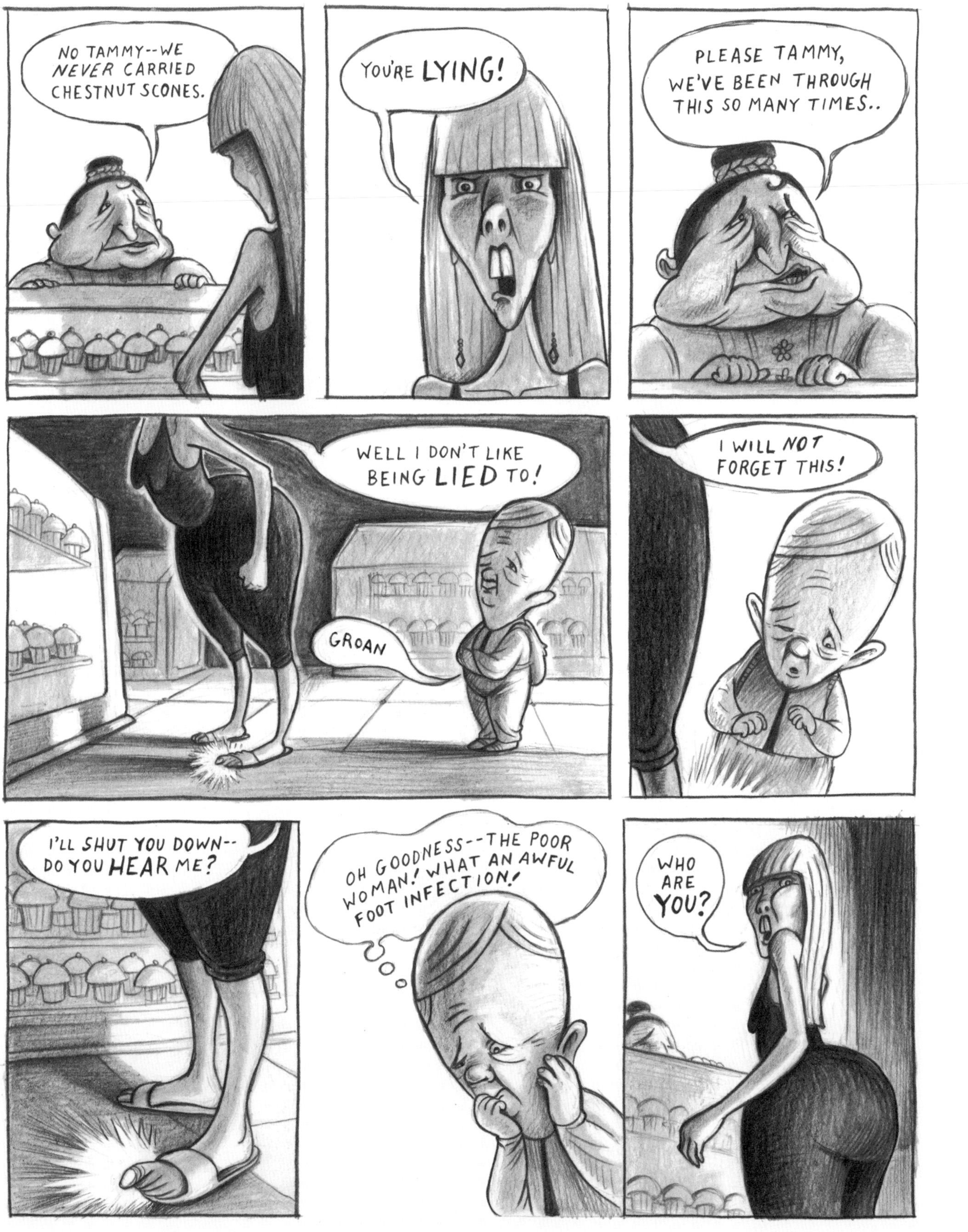
NO TAMMY--WE NEVER CARRIED CHESTNUT SCONES.
YOU'RE LYING!
PLEASE TAMMY, WE'VE BEEN THROUGH THIS SO MANY TIMES..
WELL I DON'T LIKE BEING LIED TO!
GROAN
I WILL NOT FORGET THIS!
I'LL SHUT YOU DOWN-- DO YOU HEAR ME?
OH GOODNESS--THE POOR WOMAN! WHAT AN AWFUL FOOT INFECTION!
WHO ARE YOU?

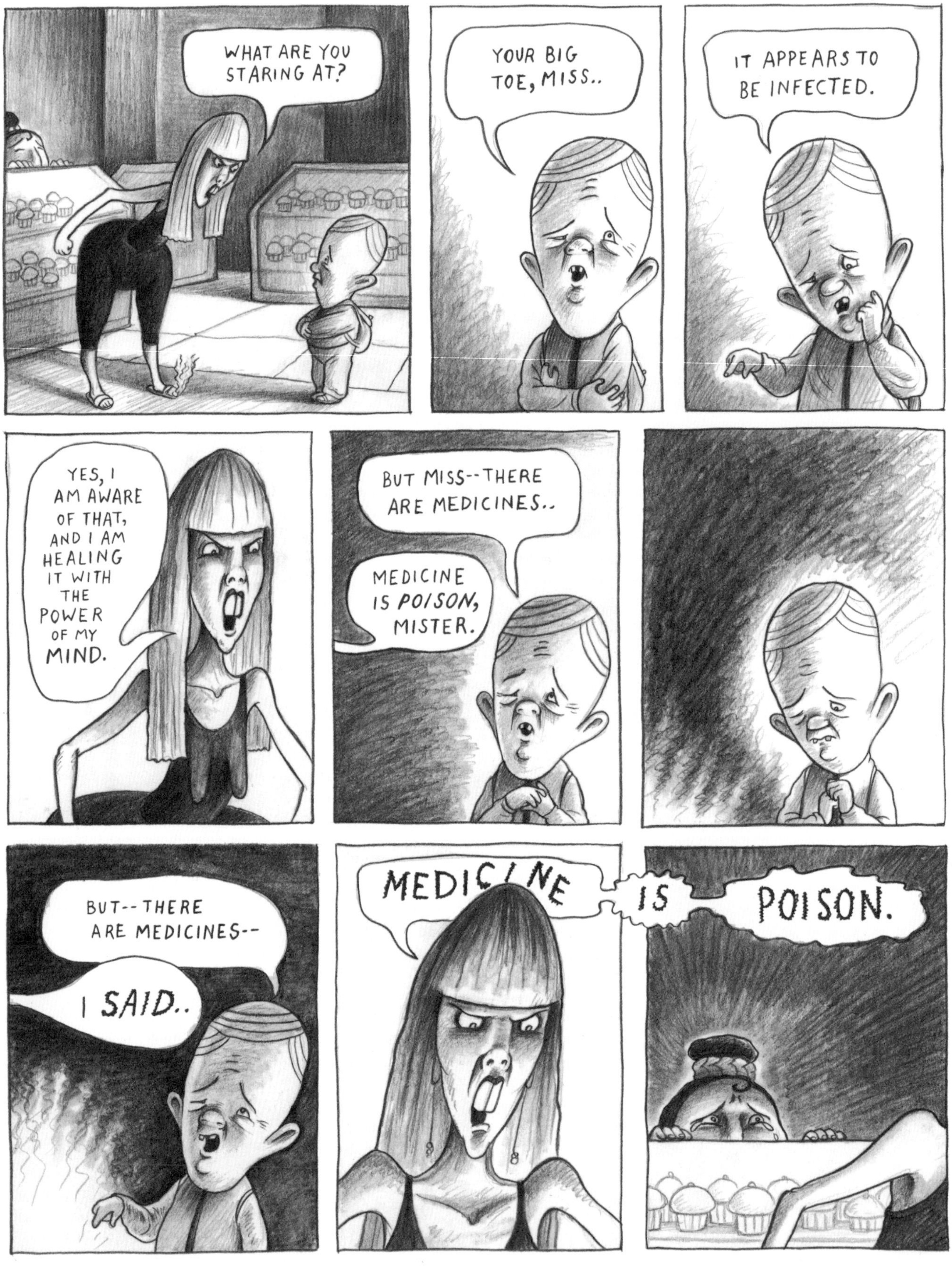
WHAT ARE YOU STARING AT?
YOUR BIG TOE, MISS..
IT APPEARS TO BE INFECTED.
YES, I AM AWARE OF THAT, AND I AM HEALING IT WITH THE POWER OF MY MIND.
BUT MISS--THERE ARE MEDICINES..
MEDICINE IS *POISON*, MISTER.
BUT--THERE ARE MEDICINES--
I *SAID*..
MEDICINE
IS
POISON.

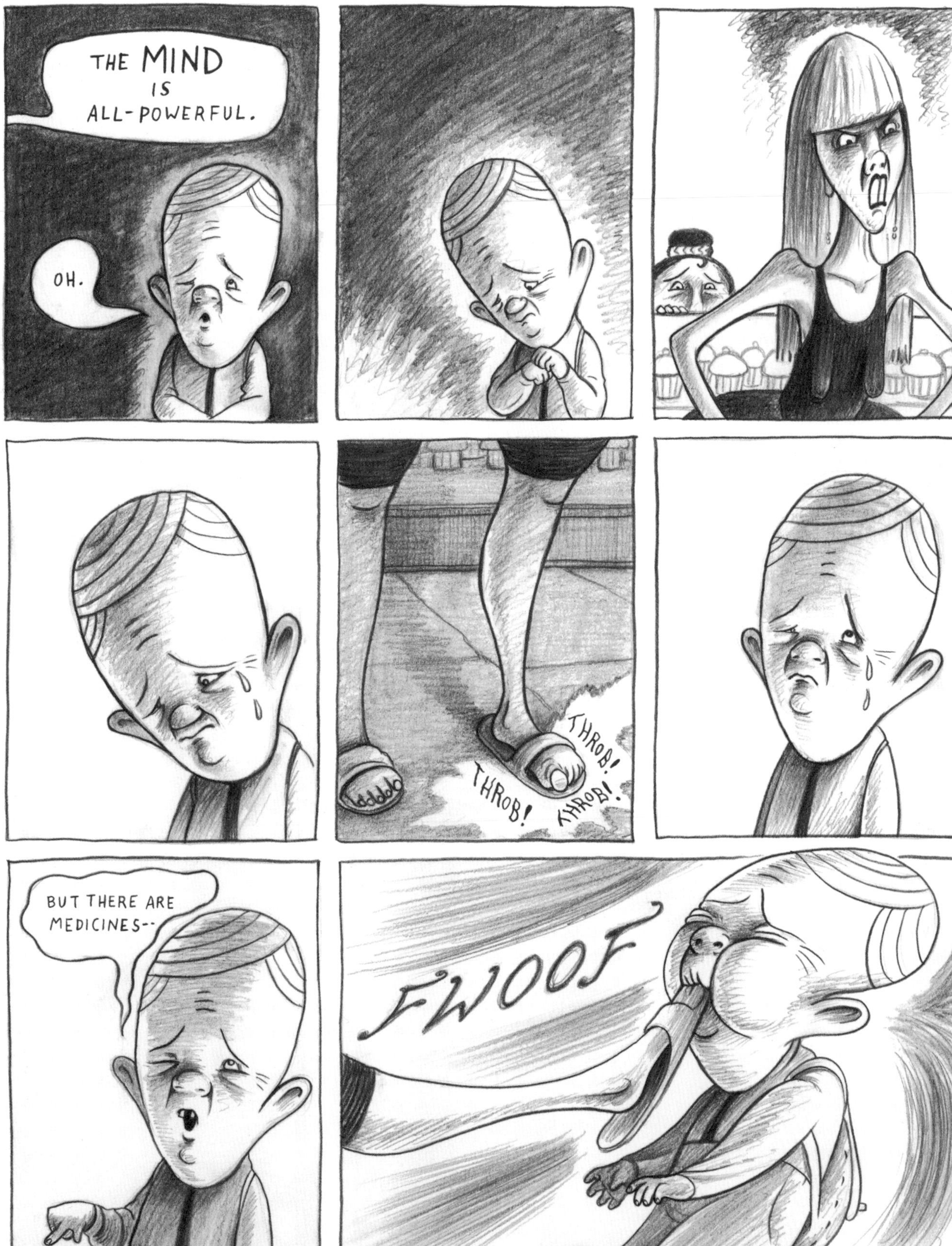
THE MIND IS ALL-POWERFUL.
OH.
THROB!
THROB!
THROB!
BUT THERE ARE MEDICINES--
FWOOF

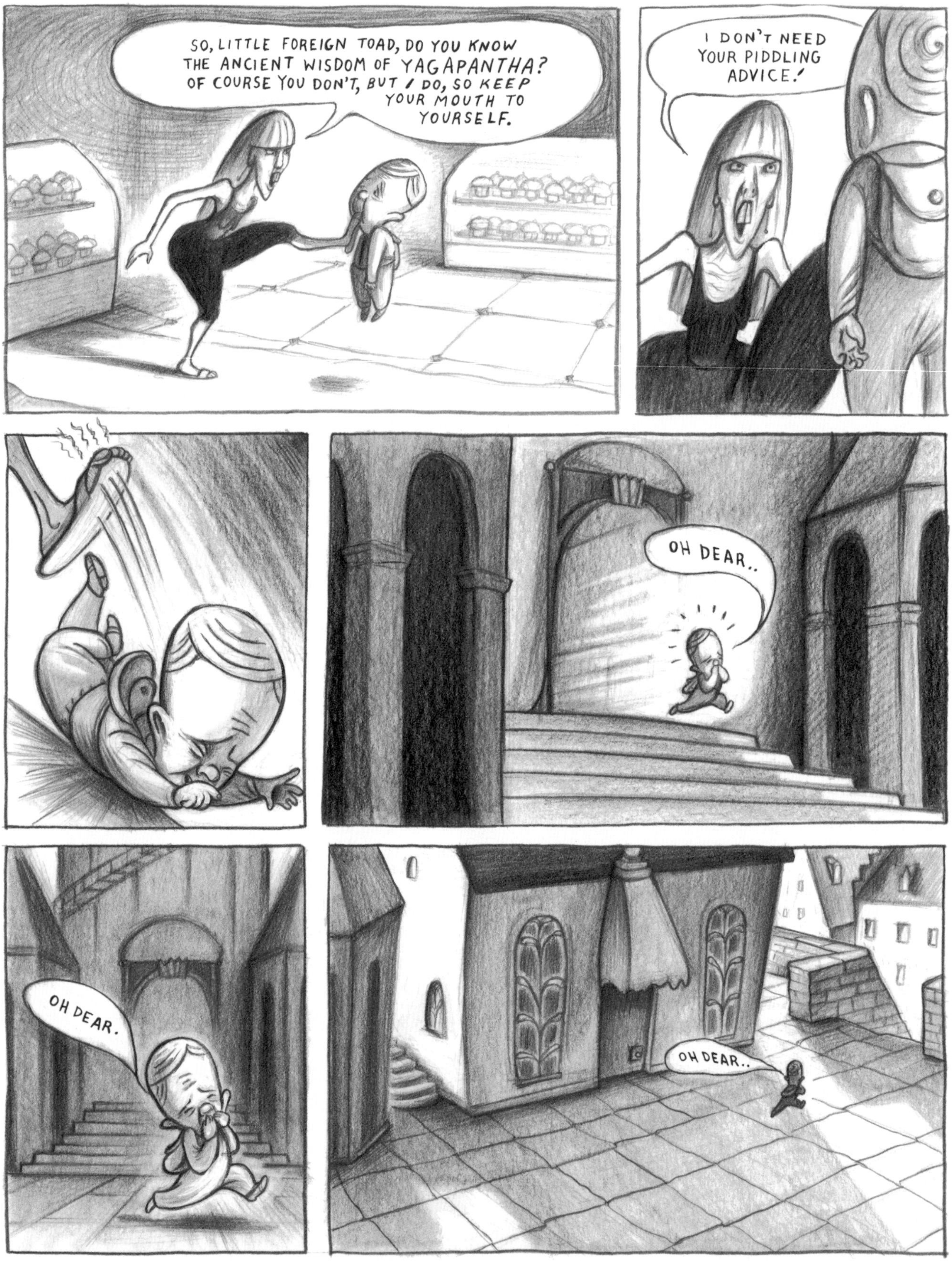
SO, LITTLE FOREIGN TOAD, DO YOU KNOW THE ANCIENT WISDOM OF YAGAPANTHA? OF COURSE YOU DON'T, BUT I DO, SO KEEP YOUR MOUTH TO YOURSELF.
I DON'T NEED YOUR PIDDLING ADVICE!
OH DEAR..
OH DEAR.
OH DEAR..

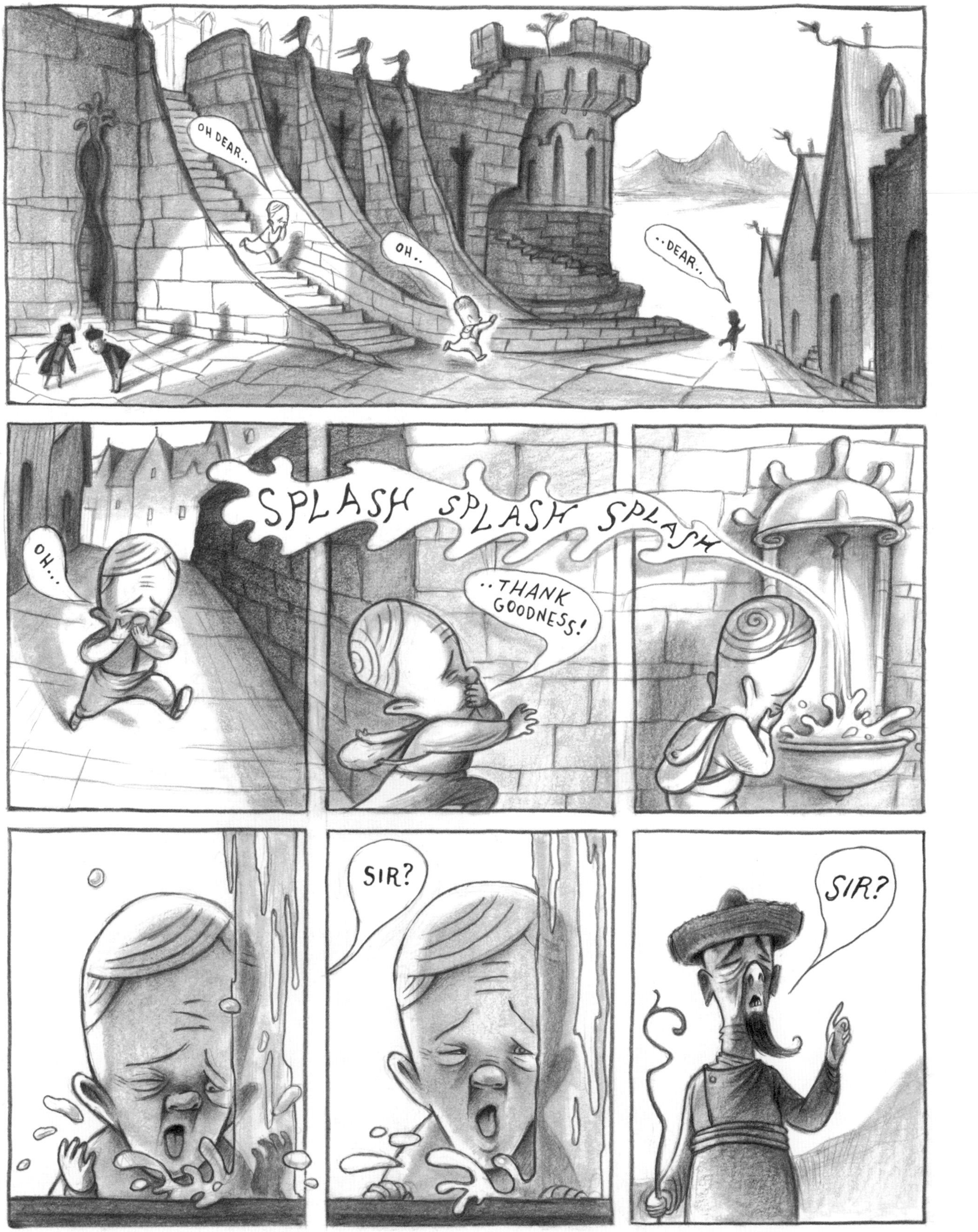
OH DEAR..
OH..
..DEAR..
OH...
SPLASH SPLASH SPLASH
..THANK GOODNESS!
SIR?
SIR?

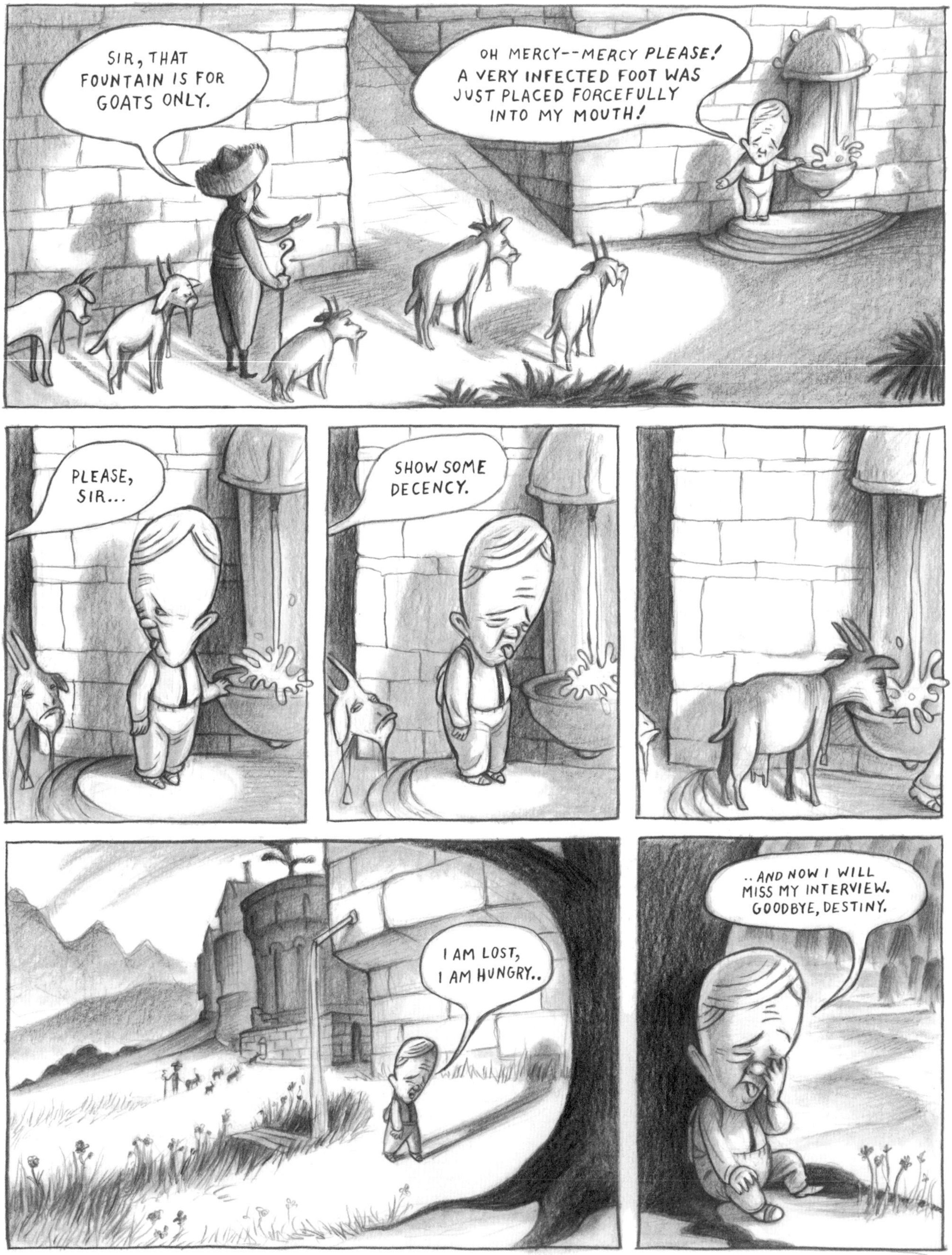

SIR, THAT FOUNTAIN IS FOR GOATS ONLY.
OH MERCY--MERCY PLEASE! A VERY INFECTED FOOT WAS JUST PLACED FORCEFULLY INTO MY MOUTH!
PLEASE, SIR...
SHOW SOME DECENCY.
I AM LOST, I AM HUNGRY..
..AND NOW I WILL MISS MY INTERVIEW. GOODBYE, DESTINY.

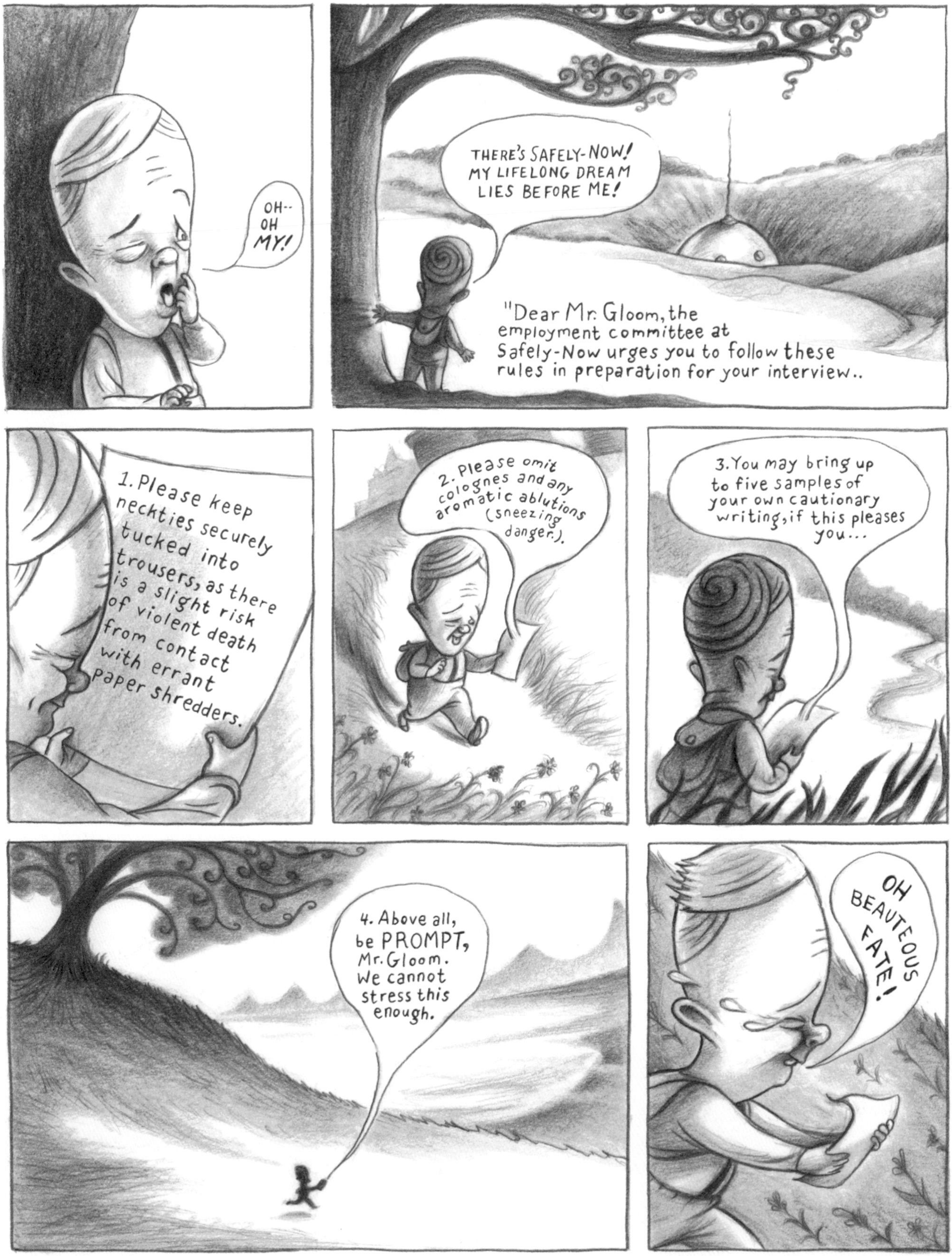
OH-- OH MY!
THERE'S SAFELY-NOW! MY LIFELONG DREAM LIES BEFORE ME!
"Dear Mr. Gloom, the employment committee at Safely-Now urges you to follow these rules in preparation for your interview..
1. Please keep neckties securely tucked into trousers, as there is a slight risk of violent death from contact with errant paper shredders.
2. Please omit colognes and any aromatic ablutions (sneezing danger.).
3. You may bring up to five samples of your own cautionary writing, if this pleases you...
4. Above all, be PROMPT, Mr. Gloom. We cannot stress this enough.
OH BEAUTEOUS FATE!

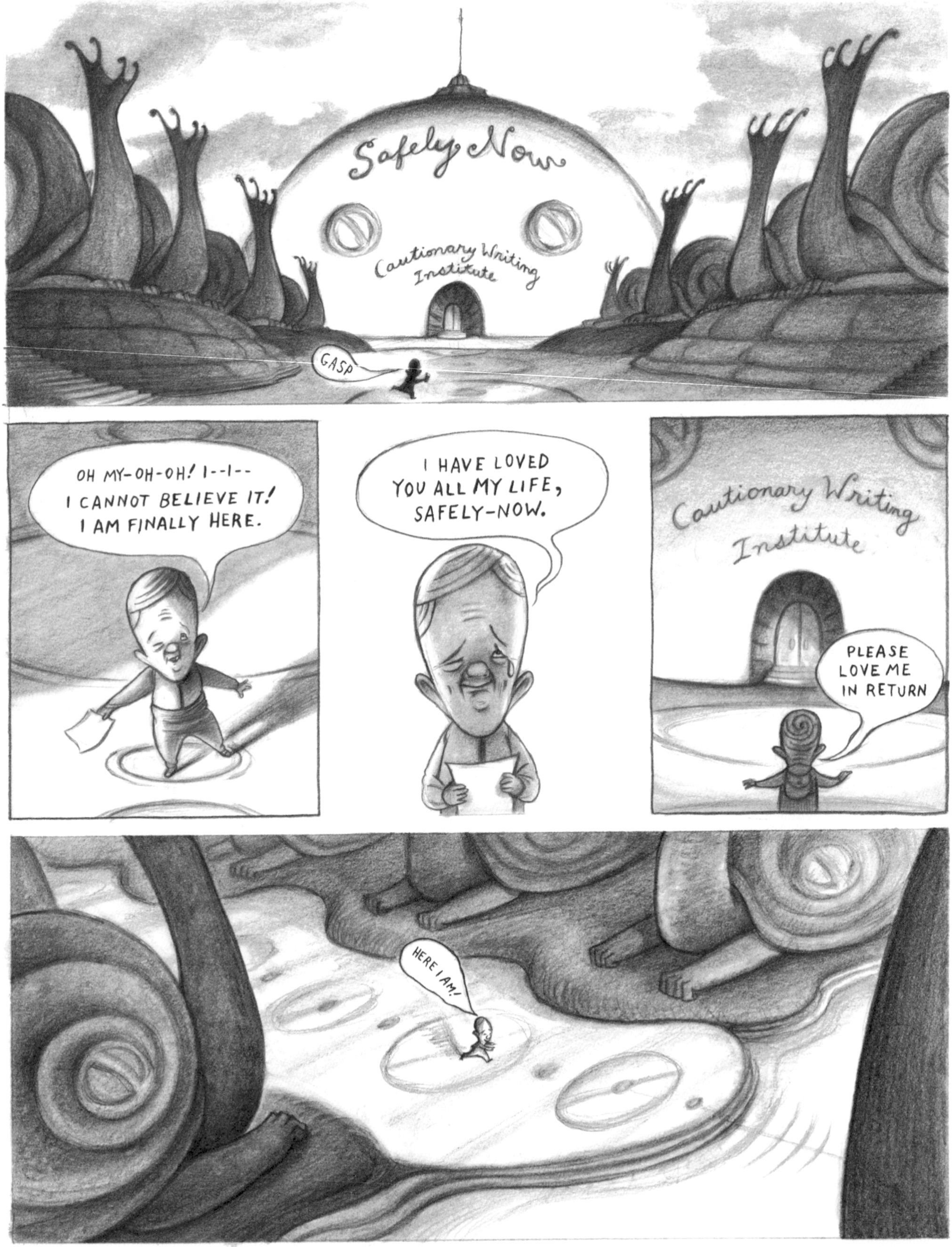
Safely Now
Cautionary Writing Institute
GASP
OH MY-OH-OH! I--I--
I CANNOT BELIEVE IT!
I AM FINALLY HERE.
I HAVE LOVED YOU ALL MY LIFE, SAFELY-NOW.
Cautionary Writing Institute
PLEASE LOVE ME IN RETURN
HERE I AM!

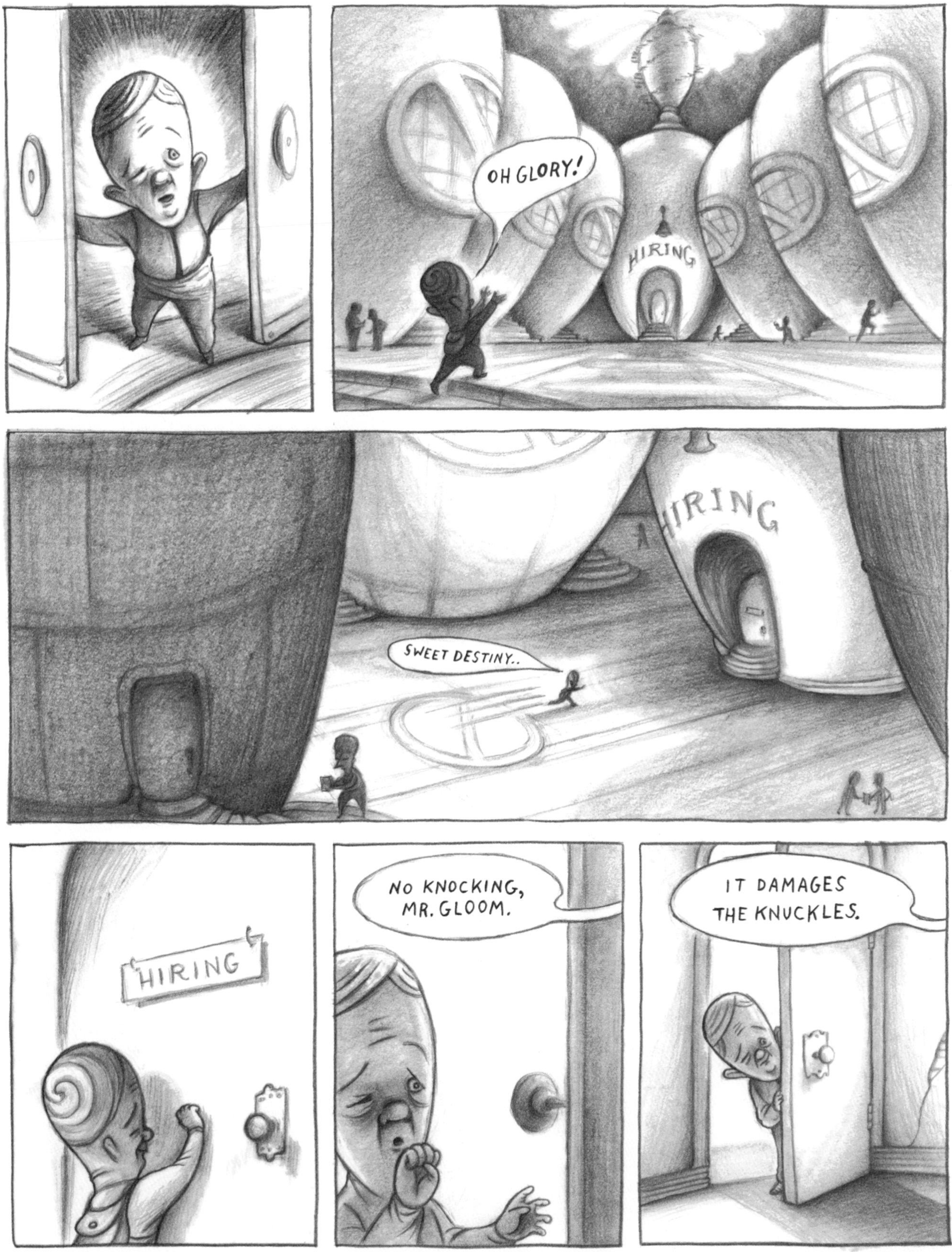
OH GLORY!
HIRING
HIRING
SWEET DESTINY..
HIRING
NO KNOCKING, MR. GLOOM.
IT DAMAGES THE KNUCKLES.

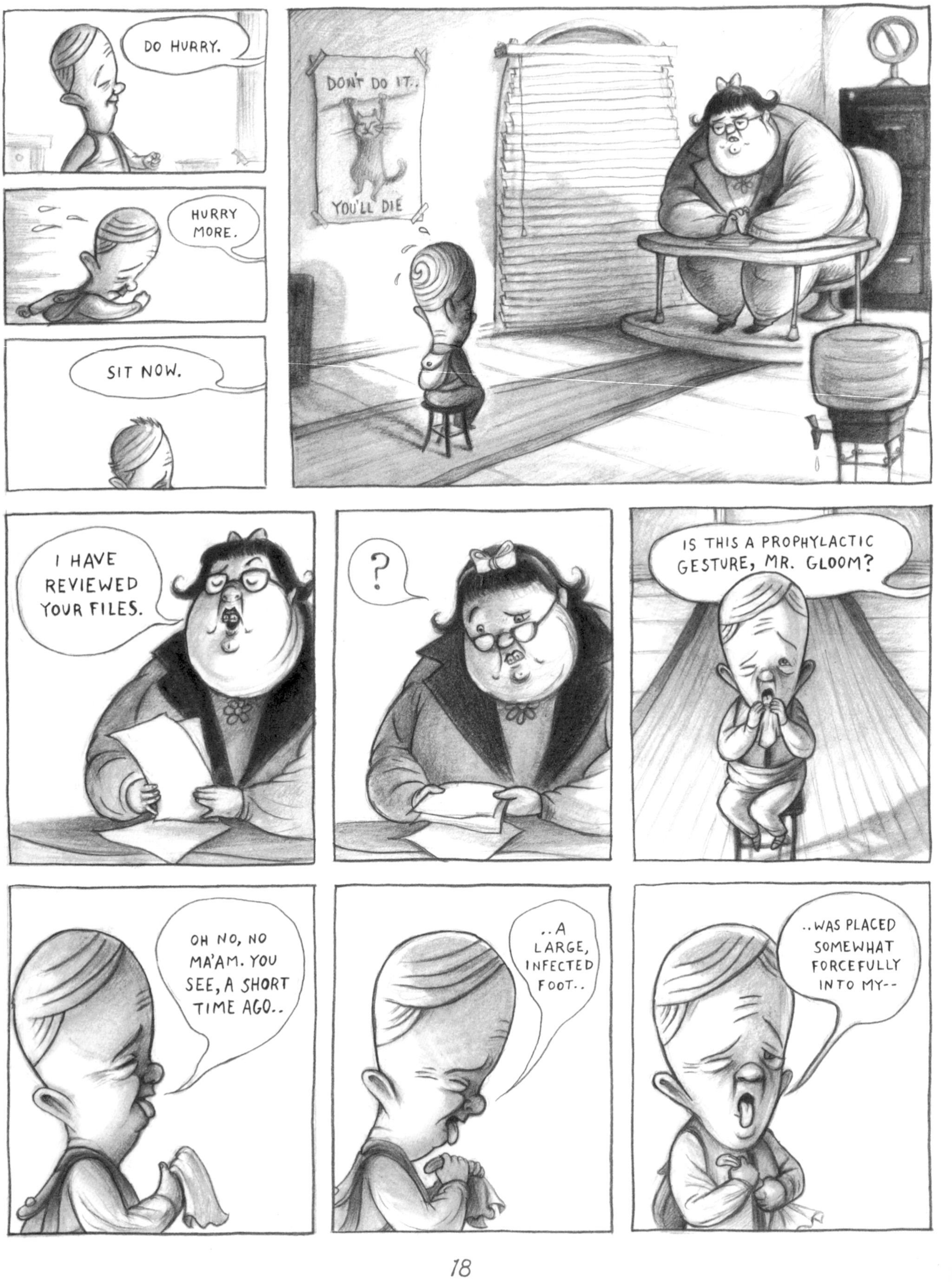
DO HURRY.
HURRY MORE.
SIT NOW.
DON'T DO IT..
YOU'LL DIE
I HAVE REVIEWED YOUR FILES.
?
IS THIS A PROPHYLACTIC GESTURE, MR. GLOOM?
OH NO, NO MA'AM. YOU SEE, A SHORT TIME AGO..
..A LARGE, INFECTED FOOT..
..WAS PLACED SOMEWHAT FORCEFULLY INTO MY--

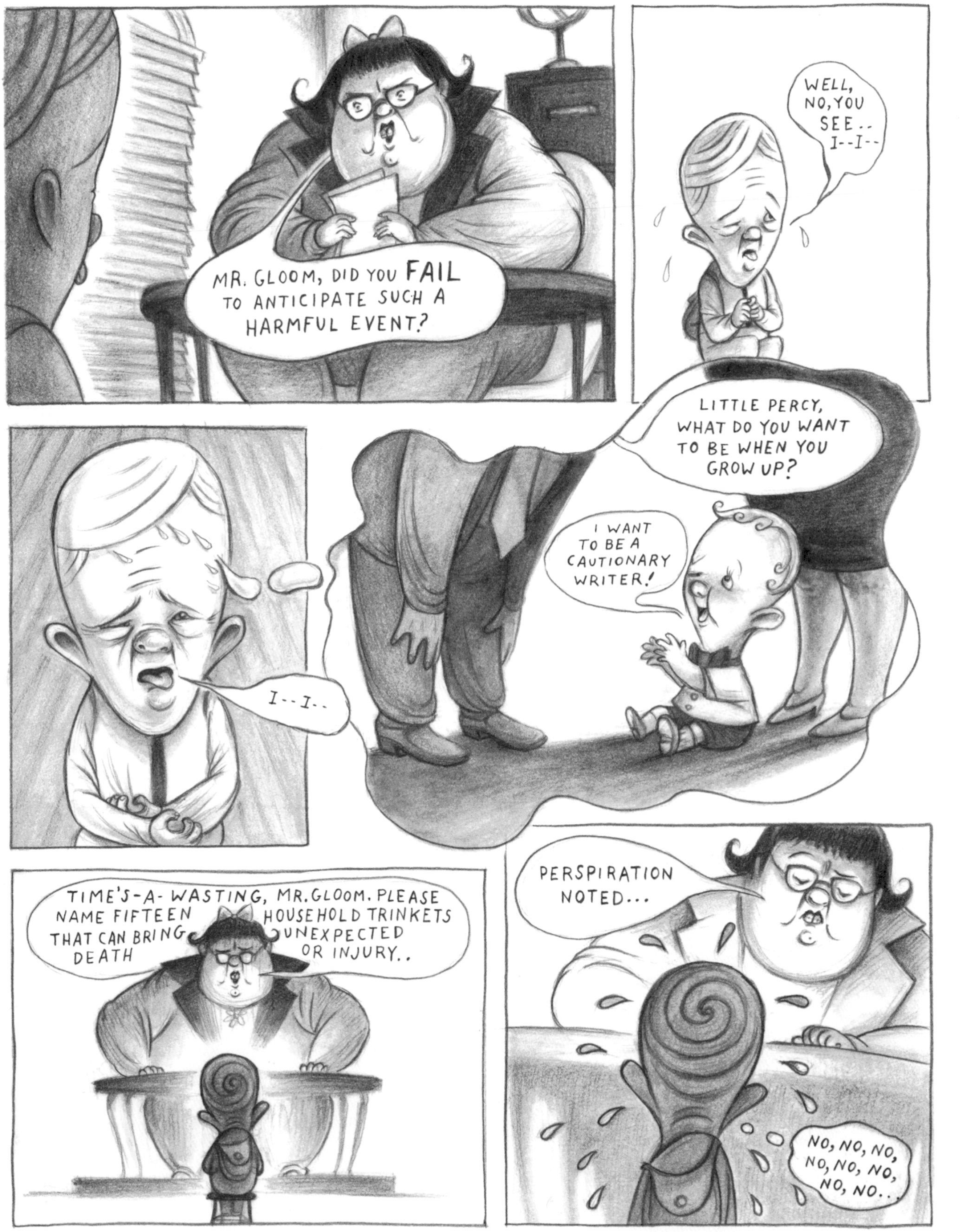
MR. GLOOM, DID YOU FAIL TO ANTICIPATE SUCH A HARMFUL EVENT?
WELL, NO, YOU SEE.. I--I--
LITTLE PERCY, WHAT DO YOU WANT TO BE WHEN YOU GROW UP?
I WANT TO BE A CAUTIONARY WRITER!
I--I--
TIME'S-A-WASTING, MR. GLOOM. PLEASE NAME FIFTEEN HOUSEHOLD TRINKETS THAT CAN BRING UNEXPECTED DEATH OR INJURY..
PERSPIRATION NOTED...
NO, NO, NO, NO, NO, NO, NO, NO...

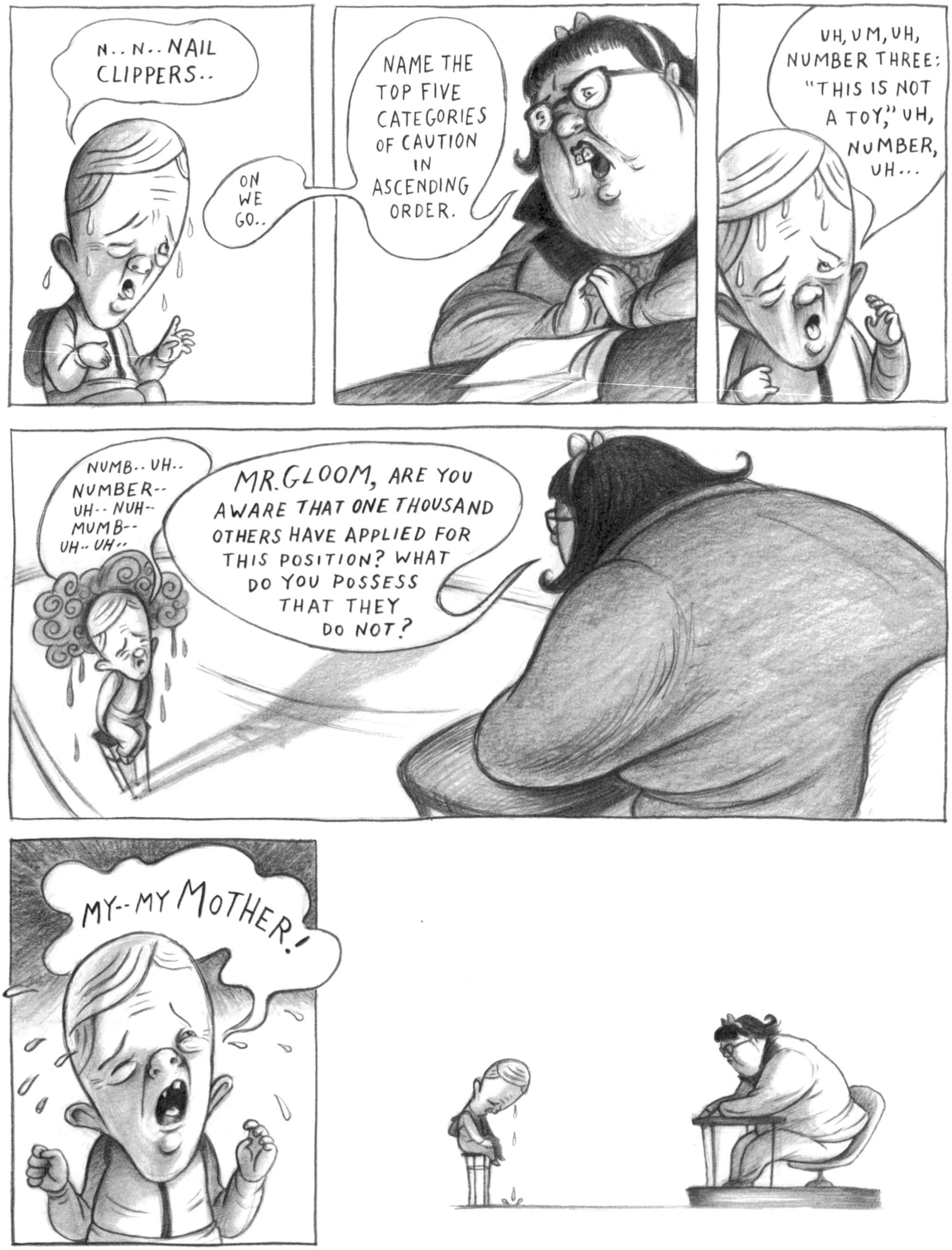
N.. N.. NAIL CLIPPERS..
ON WE GO..
NAME THE TOP FIVE CATEGORIES OF CAUTION IN ASCENDING ORDER.
UH, UM, UH, NUMBER THREE: "THIS IS NOT A TOY," UH, NUMBER, UH...
NUMB.. UH.. NUMBER-- UH-- NUH-- MUMB-- UH.. UH..
MR. GLOOM, ARE YOU AWARE THAT ONE THOUSAND OTHERS HAVE APPLIED FOR THIS POSITION? WHAT DO YOU POSSESS THAT THEY DO NOT?
MY-- MY MOTHER!

MY MOTHER IS AN INVENTOR, YOU SEE..

I SPENT YEARS IN HER LAB..

I ASSISTED HER.

SHE COULD BE A BIT ABSENT-MINDED NOW AND THEN--

..BUT I FORESAW EVERY DISASTER.

MR. GLOOM,

SOMEWHERE, SOMEONE MAY FIND YOUR HISTORY COMPELLING..

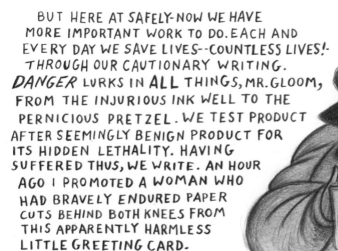

BUT HERE AT SAFELY-NOW WE HAVE MORE IMPORTANT WORK TO DO. EACH AND EVERY DAY WE SAVE LIVES--COUNTLESS LIVES!- THROUGH OUR CAUTIONARY WRITING. DANGER LURKS IN ALL THINGS, MR. GLOOM, FROM THE INJURIOUS INK WELL TO THE PERNICIOUS PRETZEL. WE TEST PRODUCT AFTER SEEMINGLY BENIGN PRODUCT FOR ITS HIDDEN LETHALITY. HAVING SUFFERED THUS, WE WRITE. AN HOUR AGO I PROMOTED A WOMAN WHO HAD BRAVELY ENDURED PAPER CUTS BEHIND BOTH KNEES FROM THIS APPARENTLY HARMLESS LITTLE GREETING CARD.

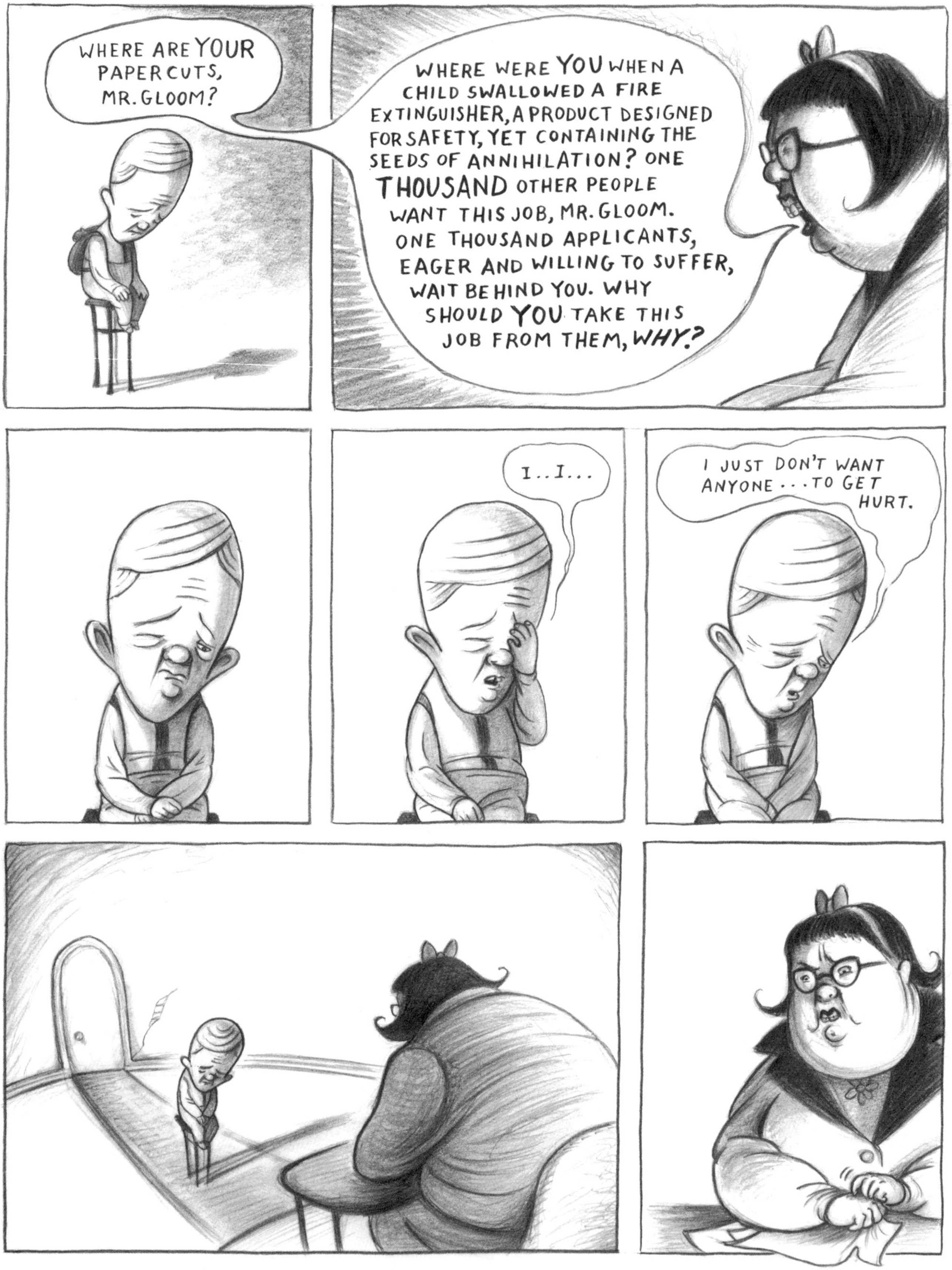
WHERE ARE YOUR PAPERCUTS, MR. GLOOM?
WHERE WERE YOU WHEN A CHILD SWALLOWED A FIRE EXTINGUISHER, A PRODUCT DESIGNED FOR SAFETY, YET CONTAINING THE SEEDS OF ANNIHILATION? ONE THOUSAND OTHER PEOPLE WANT THIS JOB, MR. GLOOM. ONE THOUSAND APPLICANTS, EAGER AND WILLING TO SUFFER, WAIT BEHIND YOU. WHY SHOULD YOU TAKE THIS JOB FROM THEM, WHY?
I.. I...
I JUST DON'T WANT ANYONE . . . TO GET HURT.

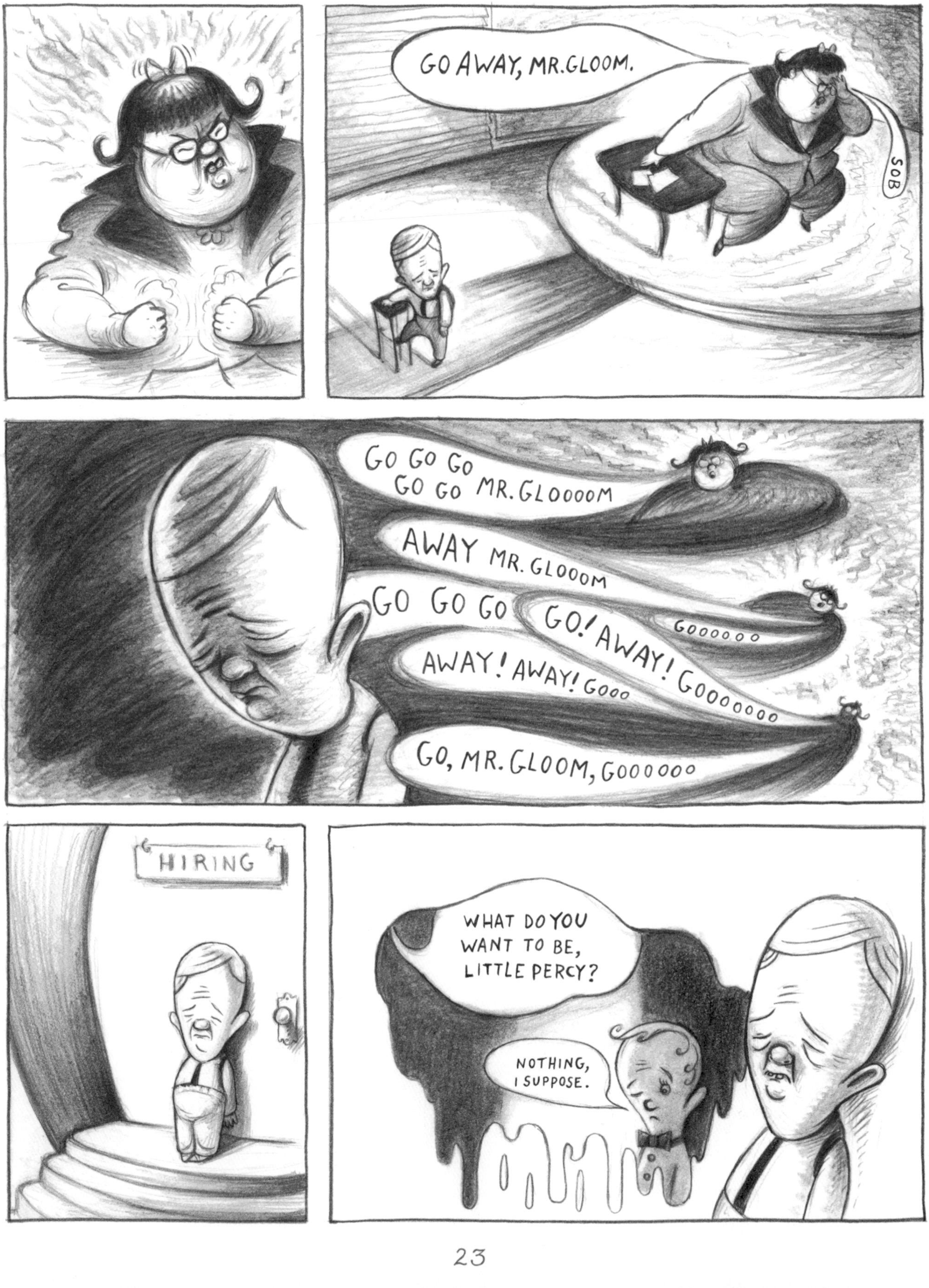
GO AWAY, MR.GLOOM.
SOB
GO GO GO
GO GO MR. GLOOOOM
AWAY MR. GLOOOM
GO GO GO
GO! AWAY! GOOOOOOO
GOOOOOO
AWAY! AWAY! GOOO
GO, MR. GLOOM, GOOOOOO
HIRING
WHAT DO YOU WANT TO BE, LITTLE PERCY?
NOTHING, I SUPPOSE.

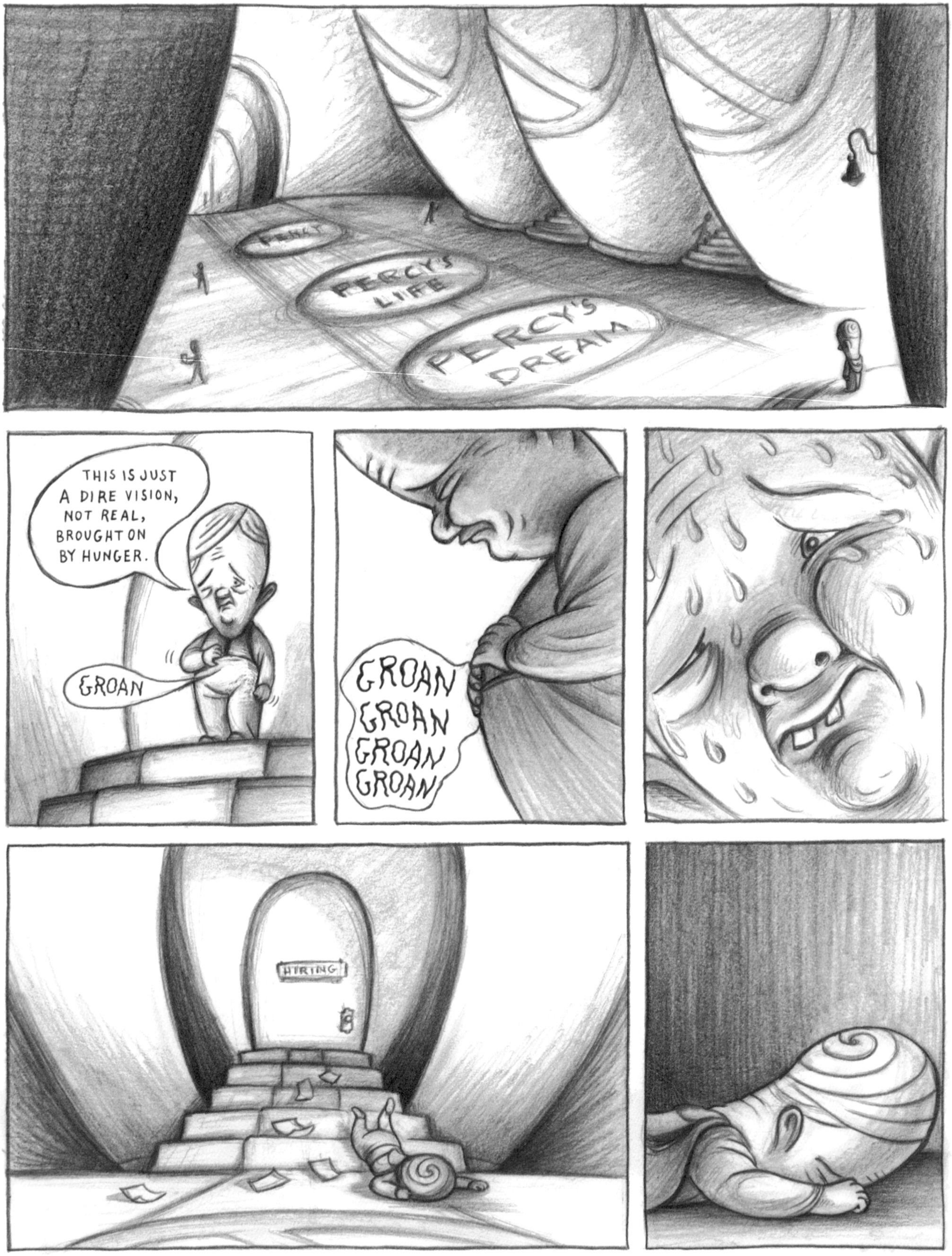
PERCY'S LIFE
PERCY'S DREAM
THIS IS JUST A DIRE VISION, NOT REAL, BROUGHT ON BY HUNGER.
GROAN
GROAN GROAN GROAN GROAN
HIRING

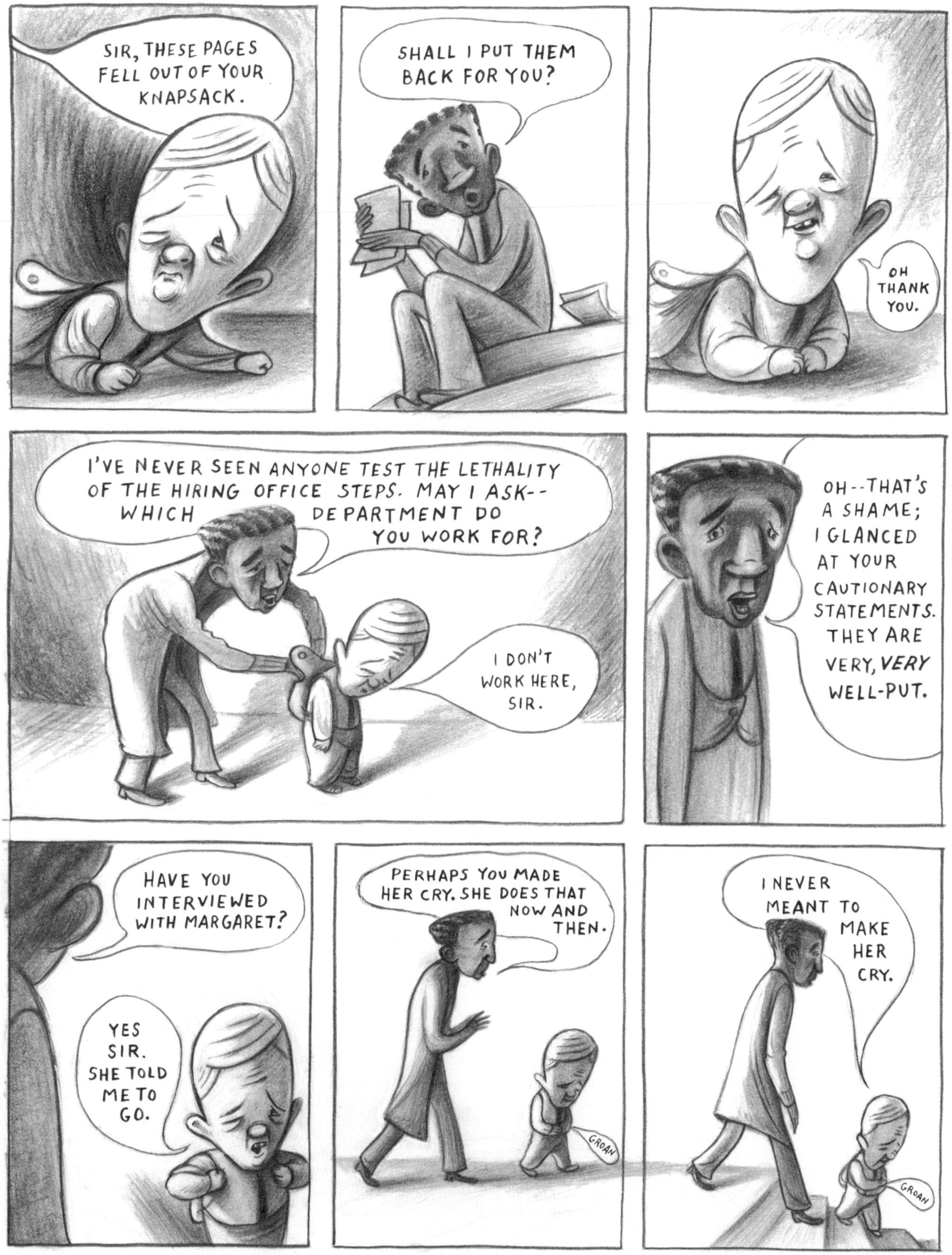
SIR, THESE PAGES FELL OUT OF YOUR KNAPSACK.
SHALL I PUT THEM BACK FOR YOU?
OH THANK YOU.
I'VE NEVER SEEN ANYONE TEST THE LETHALITY OF THE HIRING OFFICE STEPS. MAY I ASK-- WHICH DEPARTMENT DO YOU WORK FOR?
I DON'T WORK HERE, SIR.
OH--THAT'S A SHAME; I GLANCED AT YOUR CAUTIONARY STATEMENTS. THEY ARE VERY, *VERY* WELL-PUT.
HAVE YOU INTERVIEWED WITH MARGARET?
YES SIR. SHE TOLD ME TO GO.
PERHAPS YOU MADE HER CRY. SHE DOES THAT NOW AND THEN.
GROAN
I NEVER MEANT TO MAKE HER CRY.
GROAN

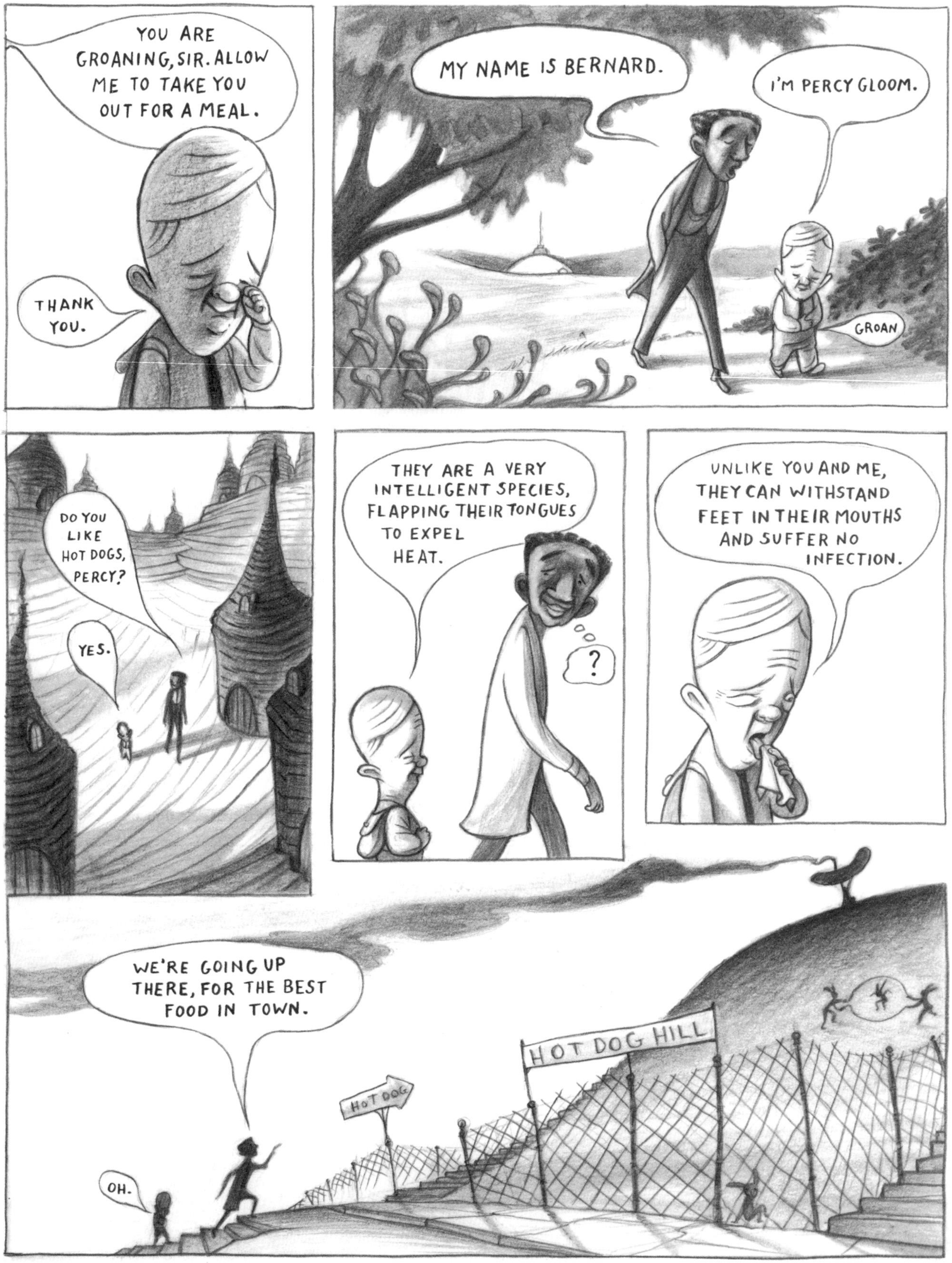
YOU ARE GROANING, SIR. ALLOW ME TO TAKE YOU OUT FOR A MEAL.
THANK YOU.
MY NAME IS BERNARD.
I'M PERCY GLOOM.
GROAN
DO YOU LIKE HOT DOGS, PERCY?
YES.
THEY ARE A VERY INTELLIGENT SPECIES, FLAPPING THEIR TONGUES TO EXPEL HEAT.
?
UNLIKE YOU AND ME, THEY CAN WITHSTAND FEET IN THEIR MOUTHS AND SUFFER NO INFECTION.
WE'RE GOING UP THERE, FOR THE BEST FOOD IN TOWN.
HOT DOG HILL
HOT DOG
OH.

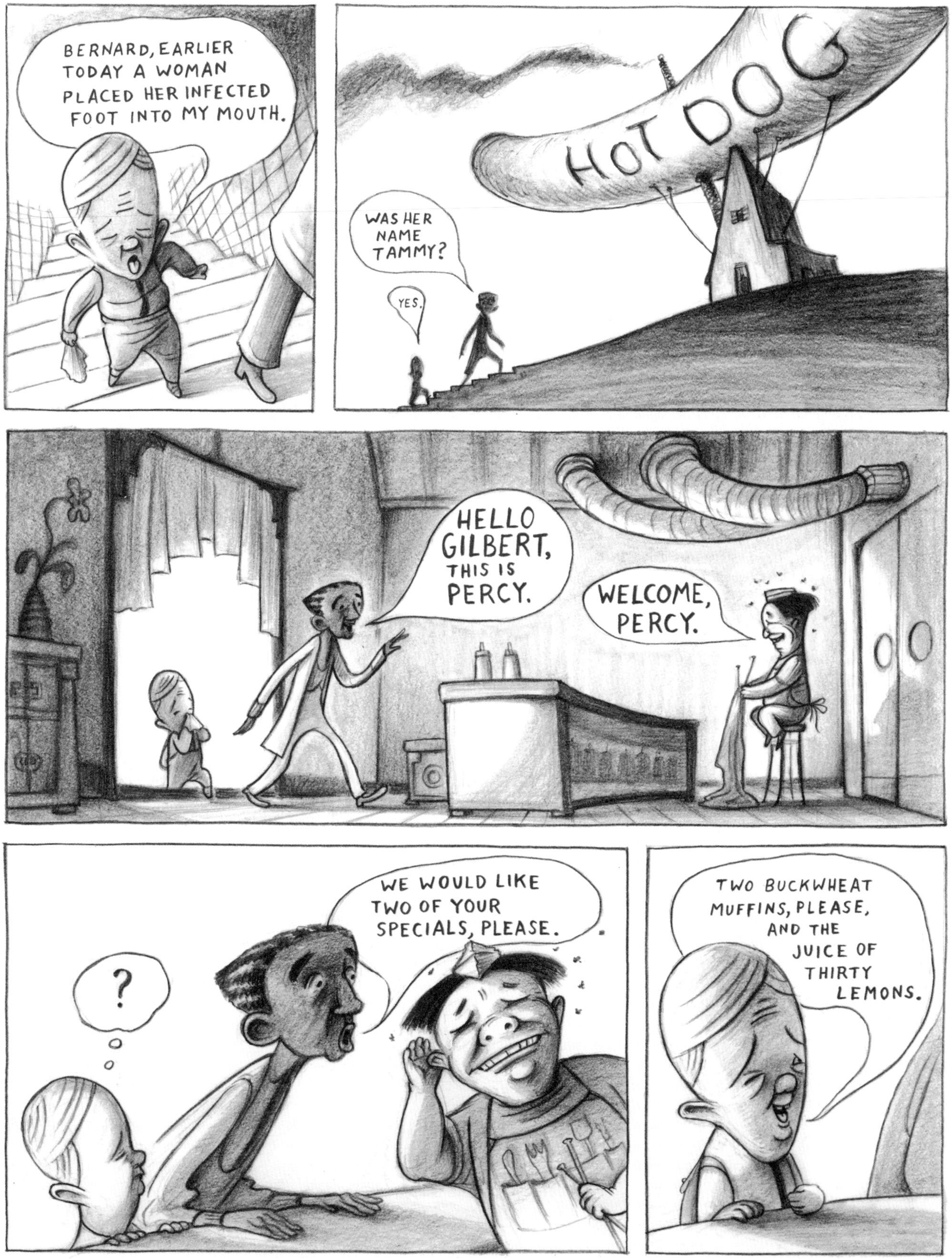
BERNARD, EARLIER TODAY A WOMAN PLACED HER INFECTED FOOT INTO MY MOUTH.
HOT DOG
WAS HER NAME TAMMY?
YES.
HELLO GILBERT, THIS IS PERCY.
WELCOME, PERCY.
WE WOULD LIKE TWO OF YOUR SPECIALS, PLEASE.
?
TWO BUCKWHEAT MUFFINS, PLEASE, AND THE JUICE OF THIRTY LEMONS.

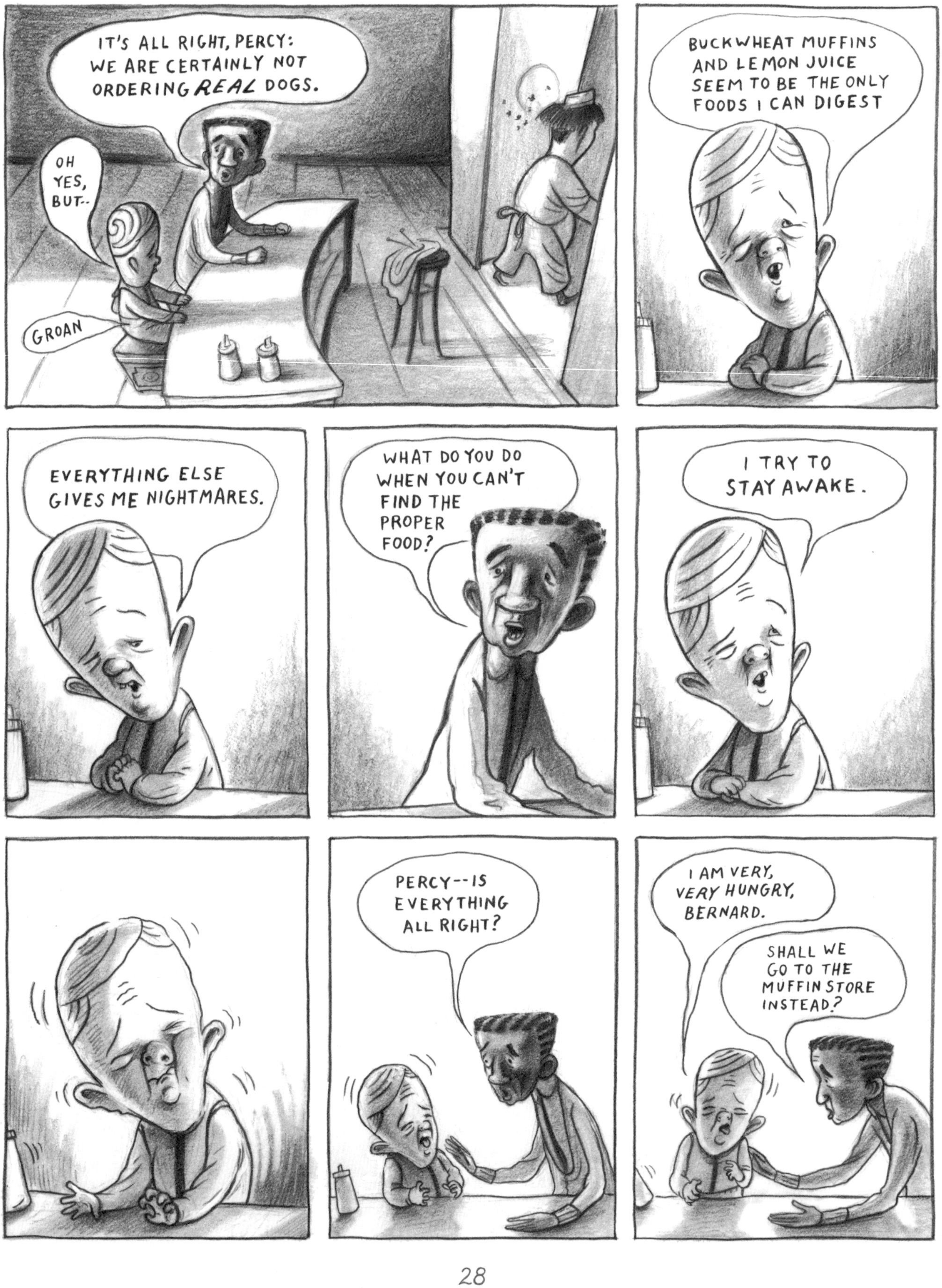
IT'S ALL RIGHT, PERCY: WE ARE CERTAINLY NOT ORDERING REAL DOGS.
OH YES, BUT--
GROAN
BUCKWHEAT MUFFINS AND LEMON JUICE SEEM TO BE THE ONLY FOODS I CAN DIGEST
EVERYTHING ELSE GIVES ME NIGHTMARES.
WHAT DO YOU DO WHEN YOU CAN'T FIND THE PROPER FOOD?
I TRY TO STAY AWAKE.
PERCY--IS EVERYTHING ALL RIGHT?
I AM VERY, VERY HUNGRY, BERNARD.
SHALL WE GO TO THE MUFFIN STORE INSTEAD?

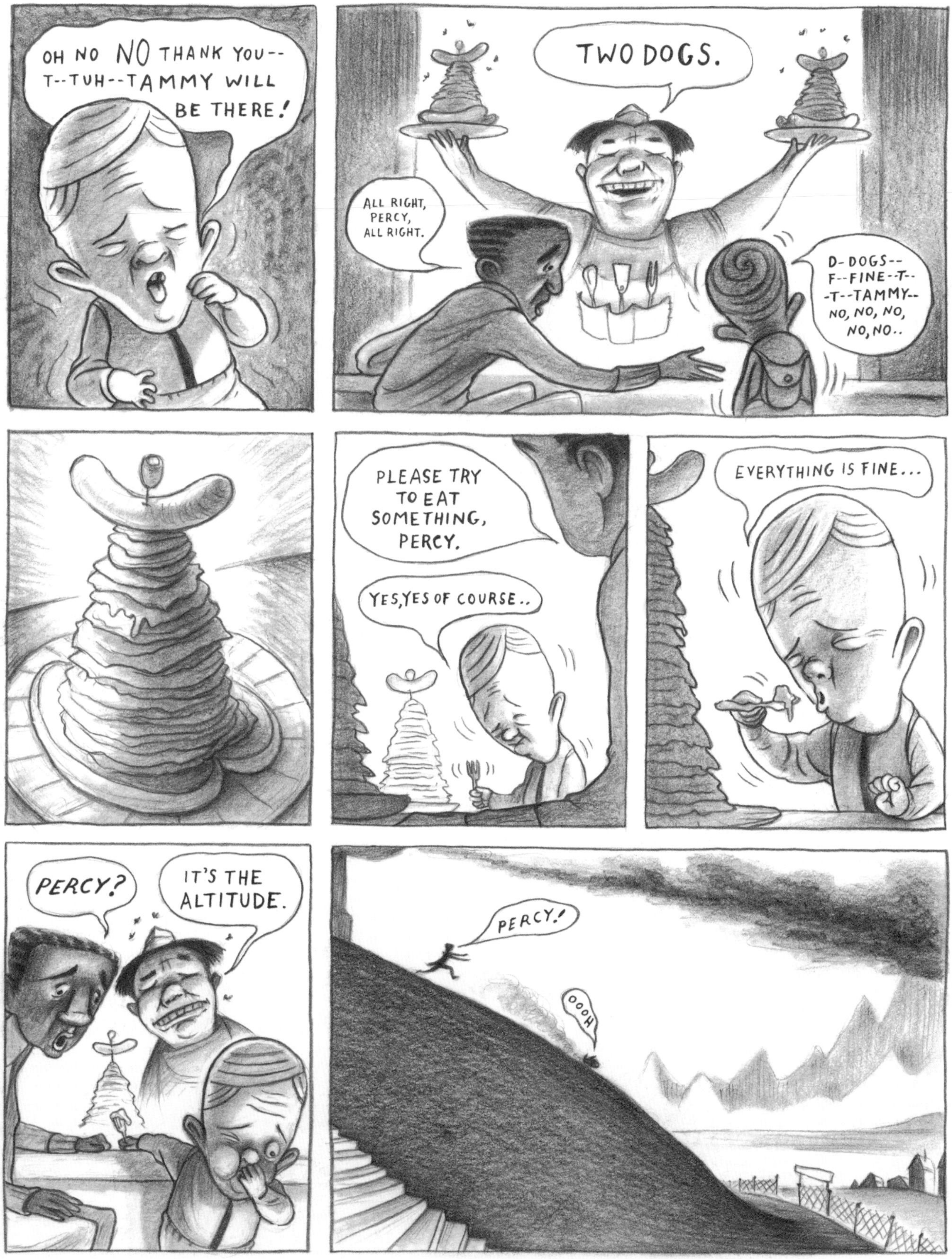
OH NO NO THANK YOU-- T--TUH--TAMMY WILL BE THERE!
TWO DOGS.
ALL RIGHT, PERCY, ALL RIGHT.
D-DOGS-- F--FINE--T-- -T--TAMMY-- NO, NO, NO, NO, NO..
PLEASE TRY TO EAT SOMETHING, PERCY.
YES, YES OF COURSE..
EVERYTHING IS FINE...
PERCY?
IT'S THE ALTITUDE.
PERCY!
HOOO

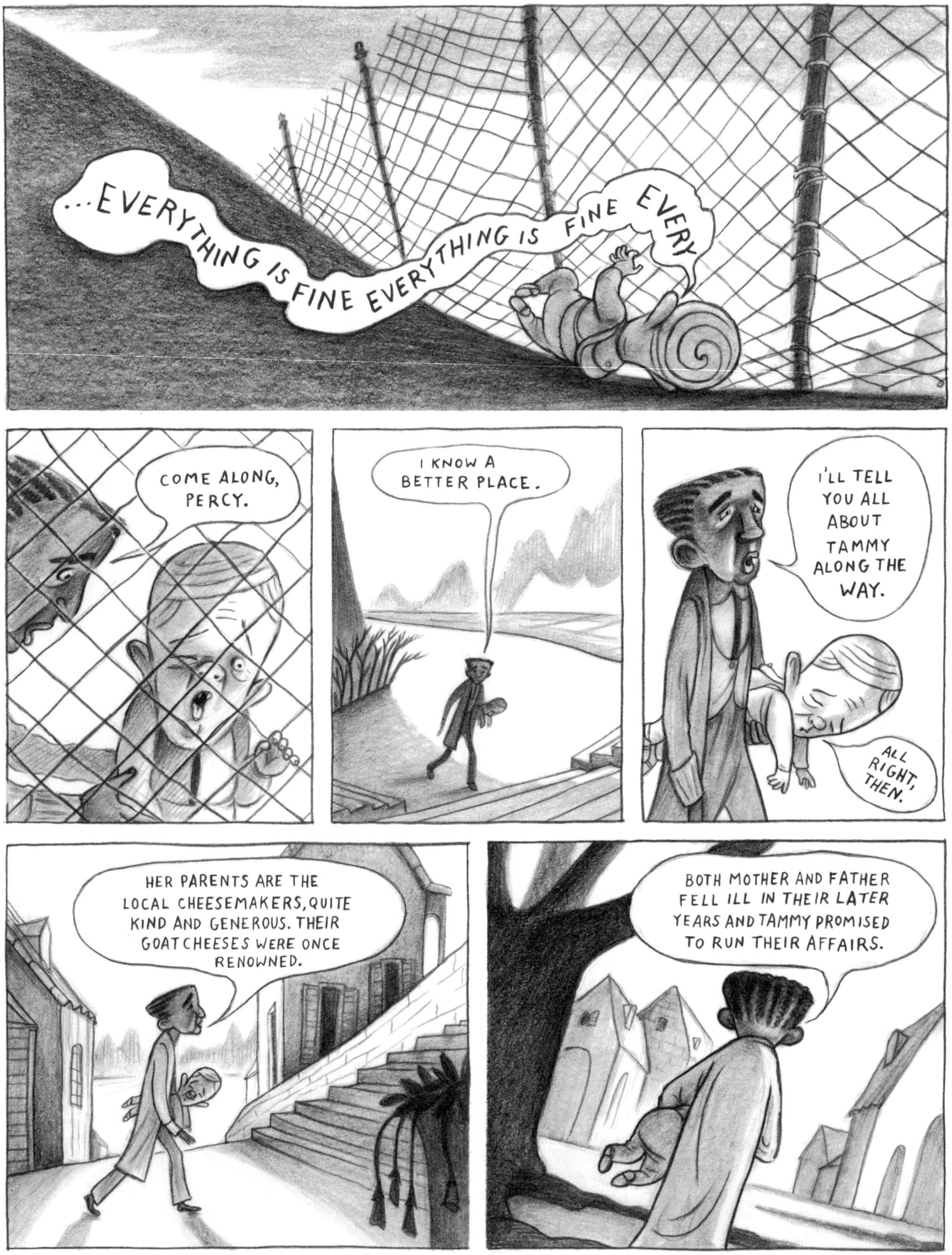
...EVERYTHING IS FINE EVERYTHING IS FINE EVERY
COME ALONG, PERCY.
I KNOW A BETTER PLACE.
I'LL TELL YOU ALL ABOUT TAMMY ALONG THE WAY.
ALL RIGHT, THEN.
HER PARENTS ARE THE LOCAL CHEESEMAKERS, QUITE KIND AND GENEROUS. THEIR GOAT CHEESES WERE ONCE RENOWNED.
BOTH MOTHER AND FATHER FELL ILL IN THEIR LATER YEARS AND TAMMY PROMISED TO RUN THEIR AFFAIRS.

SHE HAD NO SUCH INTENTION. INSTEAD, SHE SPENDS HER DAYS BULLYING EVERYONE IN TOWN..

EVEN HER PARENTS' MILKING GOATS.

OH DEAR..

I BELIEVE I'VE MET THOSE GOATS, BERNARD.

YES. THEY ARE THE MOST FORLORN CREATURES YOU'LL EVER SEE.

THEY FEEL USELESS AND, I DARE SAY, HOPELESS.

TAMMY'S PARENTS ONCE DOTED ON THOSE GOATS. TAMMY REJECTS THEM, AS SHE DOES WITH ANYTHING THAT ISN'T PERFECT IN HER EYES.

FOUNDER'S PARK

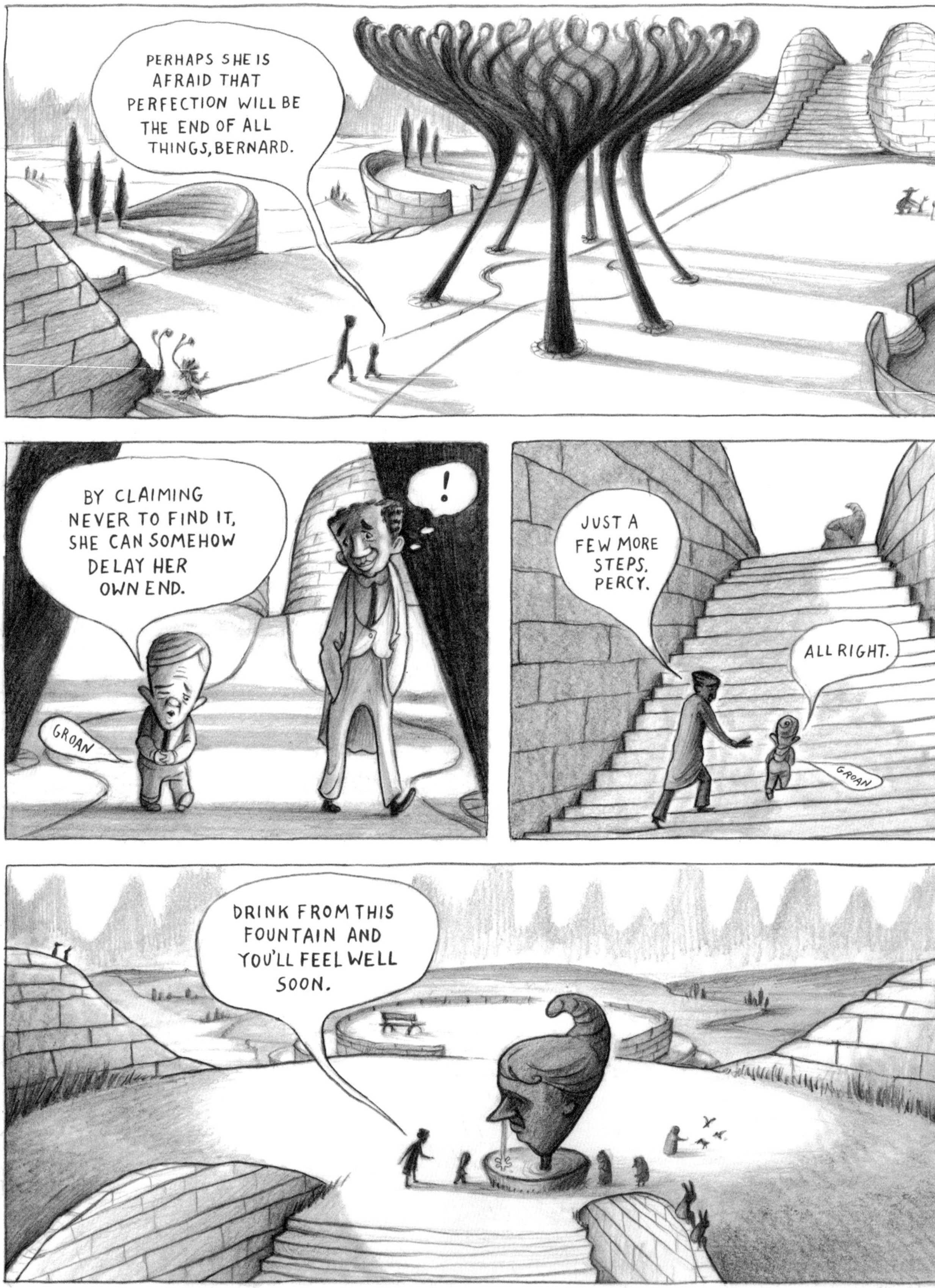
PERHAPS SHE IS AFRAID THAT PERFECTION WILL BE THE END OF ALL THINGS, BERNARD.
BY CLAIMING NEVER TO FIND IT, SHE CAN SOMEHOW DELAY HER OWN END.
GROAN
!
JUST A FEW MORE STEPS, PERCY.
ALL RIGHT.
GROAN
DRINK FROM THIS FOUNTAIN AND YOU'LL FEEL WELL SOON.

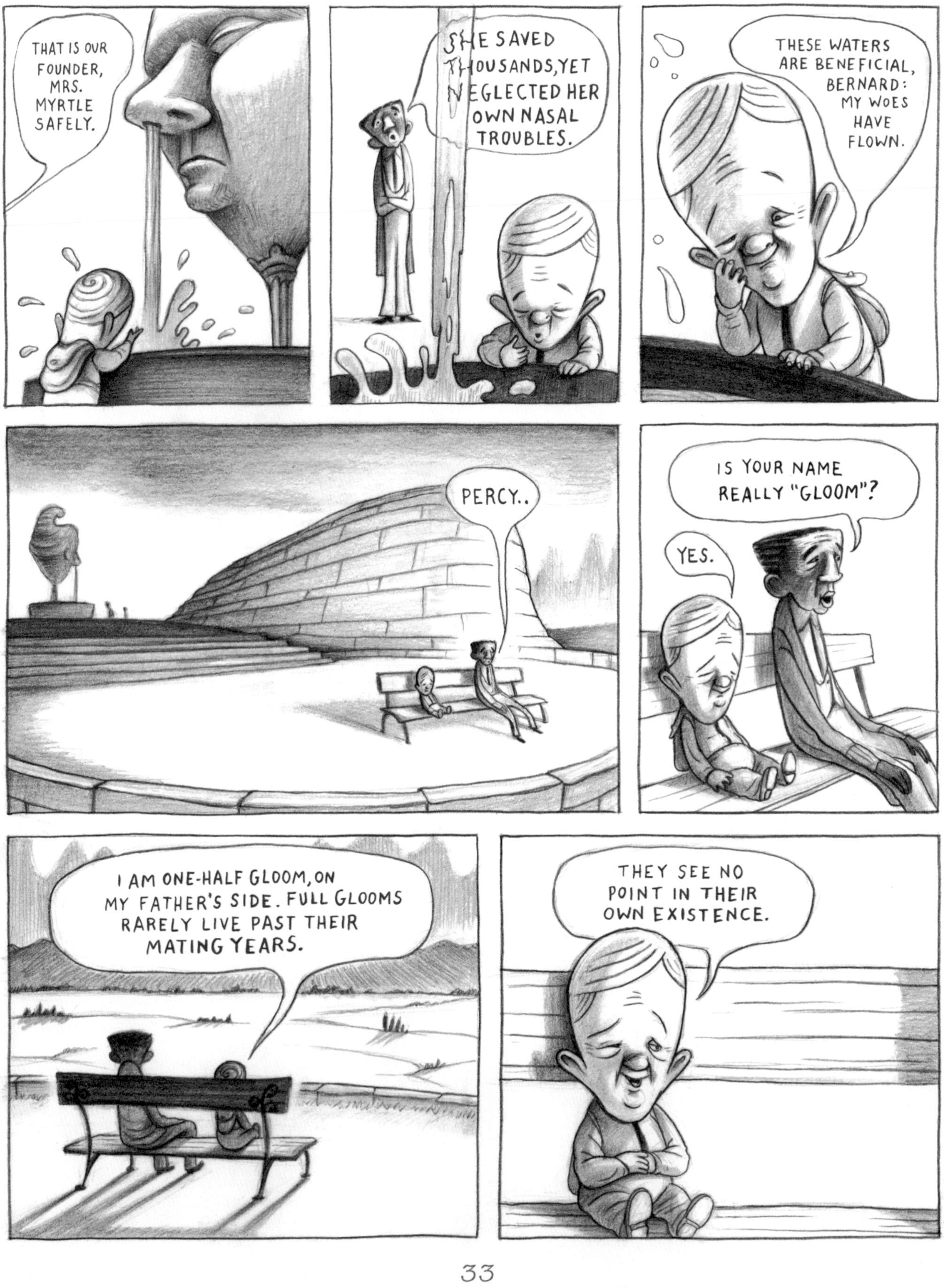
THAT IS OUR FOUNDER, MRS. MYRTLE SAFELY.
SHE SAVED THOUSANDS, YET NEGLECTED HER OWN NASAL TROUBLES.
THESE WATERS ARE BENEFICIAL, BERNARD: MY WOES HAVE FLOWN.
PERCY..
IS YOUR NAME REALLY "GLOOM"?
YES.
I AM ONE-HALF GLOOM, ON MY FATHER'S SIDE. FULL GLOOMS RARELY LIVE PAST THEIR MATING YEARS.
THEY SEE NO POINT IN THEIR OWN EXISTENCE.

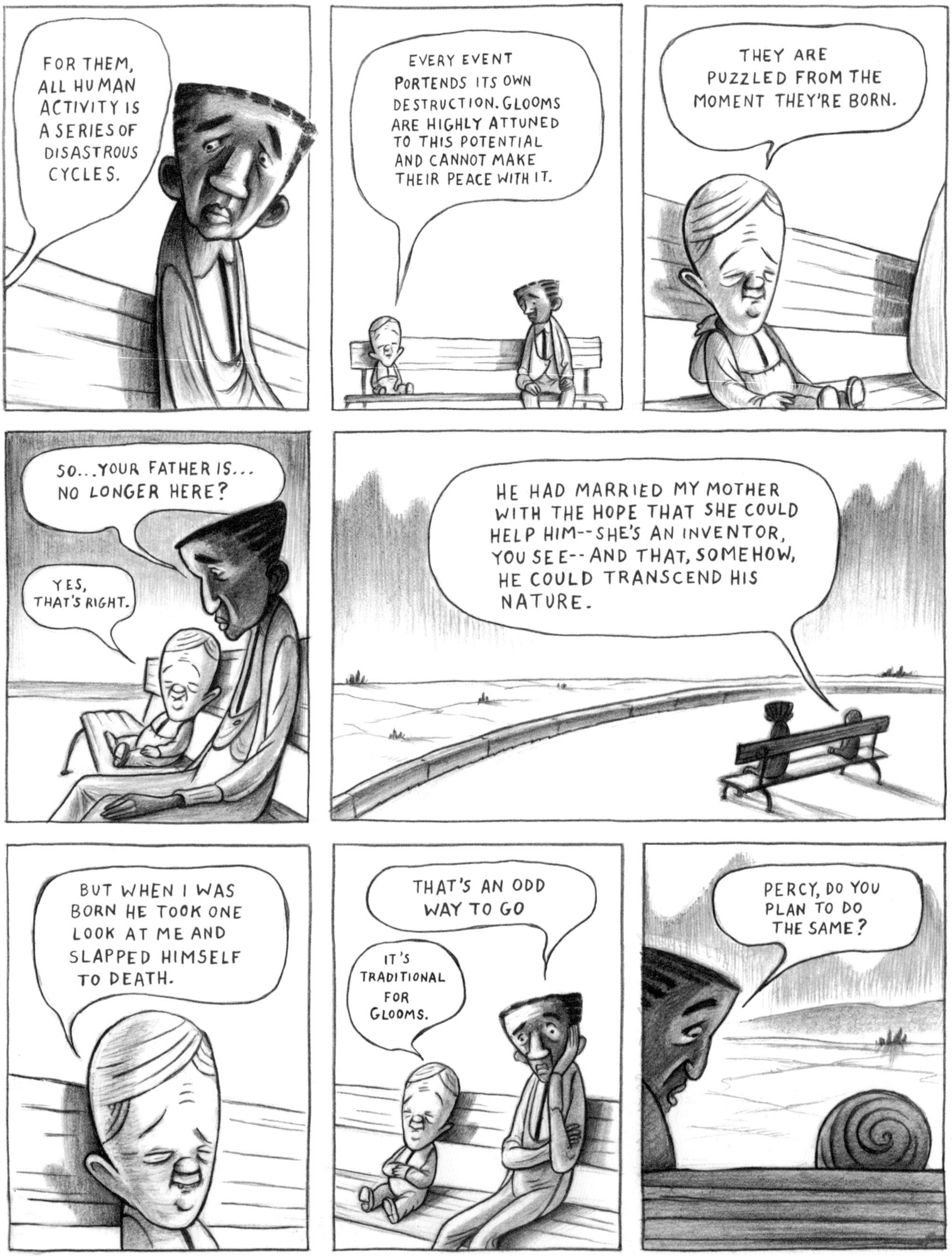
FOR THEM, ALL HUMAN ACTIVITY IS A SERIES OF DISASTROUS CYCLES.
EVERY EVENT PORTENDS ITS OWN DESTRUCTION. GLOOMS ARE HIGHLY ATTUNED TO THIS POTENTIAL AND CANNOT MAKE THEIR PEACE WITH IT.
THEY ARE PUZZLED FROM THE MOMENT THEY'RE BORN.
SO...YOUR FATHER IS... NO LONGER HERE?
YES, THAT'S RIGHT.
HE HAD MARRIED MY MOTHER WITH THE HOPE THAT SHE COULD HELP HIM--SHE'S AN INVENTOR, YOU SEE--AND THAT, SOMEHOW, HE COULD TRANSCEND HIS NATURE.
BUT WHEN I WAS BORN HE TOOK ONE LOOK AT ME AND SLAPPED HIMSELF TO DEATH.
THAT'S AN ODD WAY TO GO
IT'S TRADITIONAL FOR GLOOMS.
PERCY, DO YOU PLAN TO DO THE SAME?

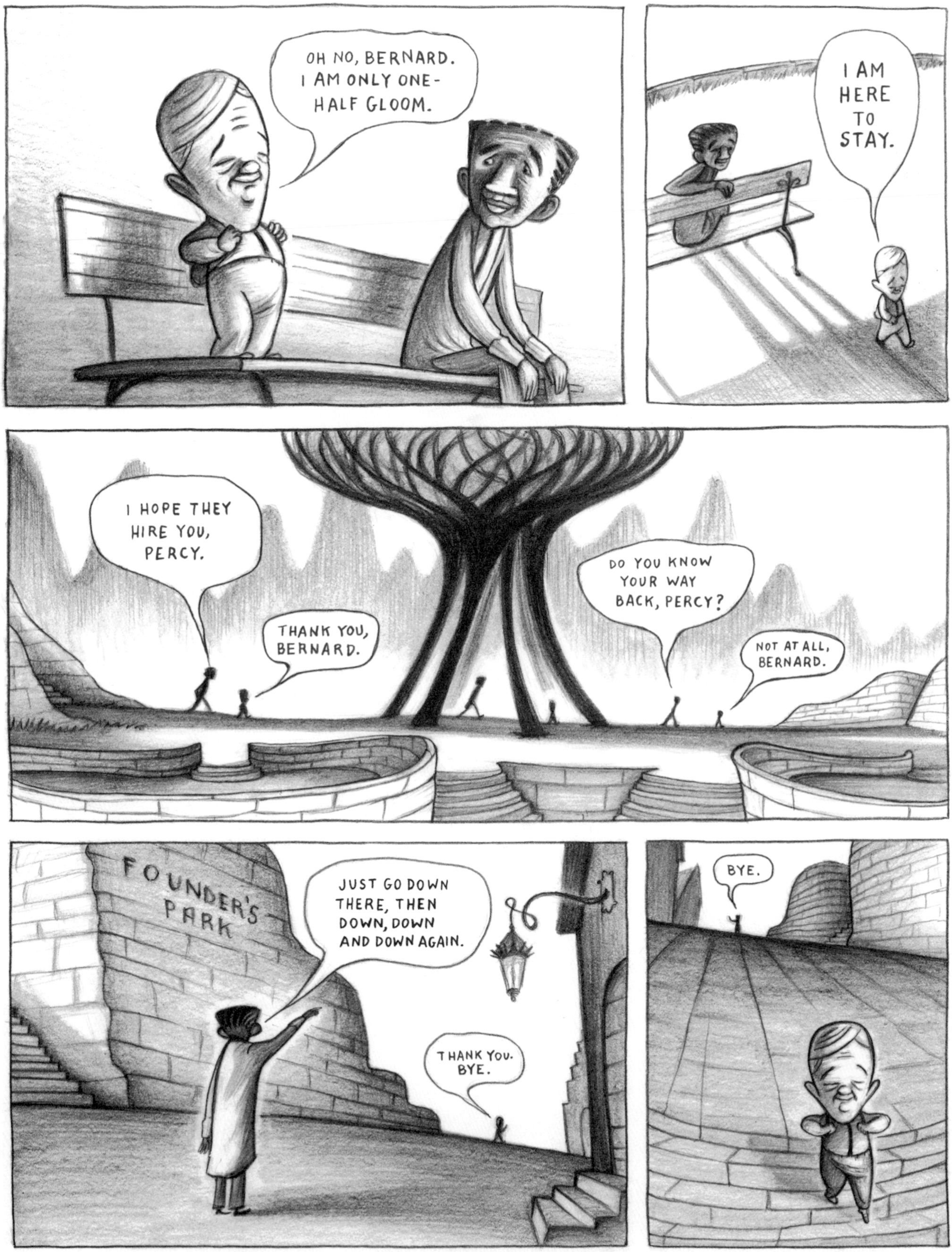
OH NO, BERNARD.
I AM ONLY ONE-
HALF GLOOM.
I AM HERE TO STAY.
I HOPE THEY HIRE YOU, PERCY.
THANK YOU, BERNARD.
DO YOU KNOW YOUR WAY BACK, PERCY?
NOT AT ALL, BERNARD.
FOUNDER'S PARK
JUST GO DOWN THERE, THEN DOWN, DOWN AND DOWN AGAIN.
THANK YOU. BYE.
BYE.

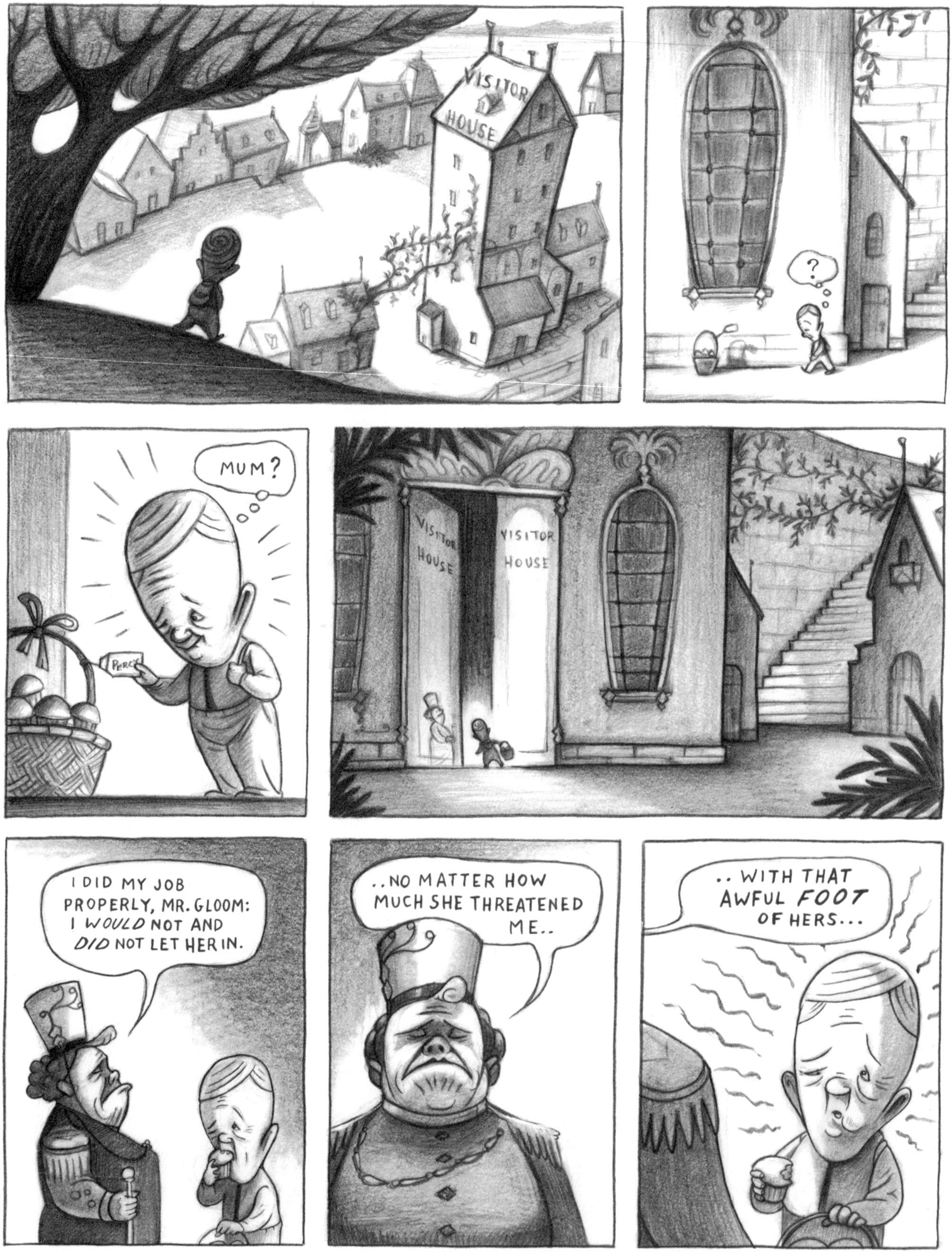
VISITOR HOUSE
?
MUM?
PERCY
VISITOR HOUSE
VISITOR HOUSE
I DID MY JOB PROPERLY, MR. GLOOM: I WOULD NOT AND DID NOT LET HER IN.
..NO MATTER HOW MUCH SHE THREATENED ME..
.. WITH THAT AWFUL FOOT OF HERS...

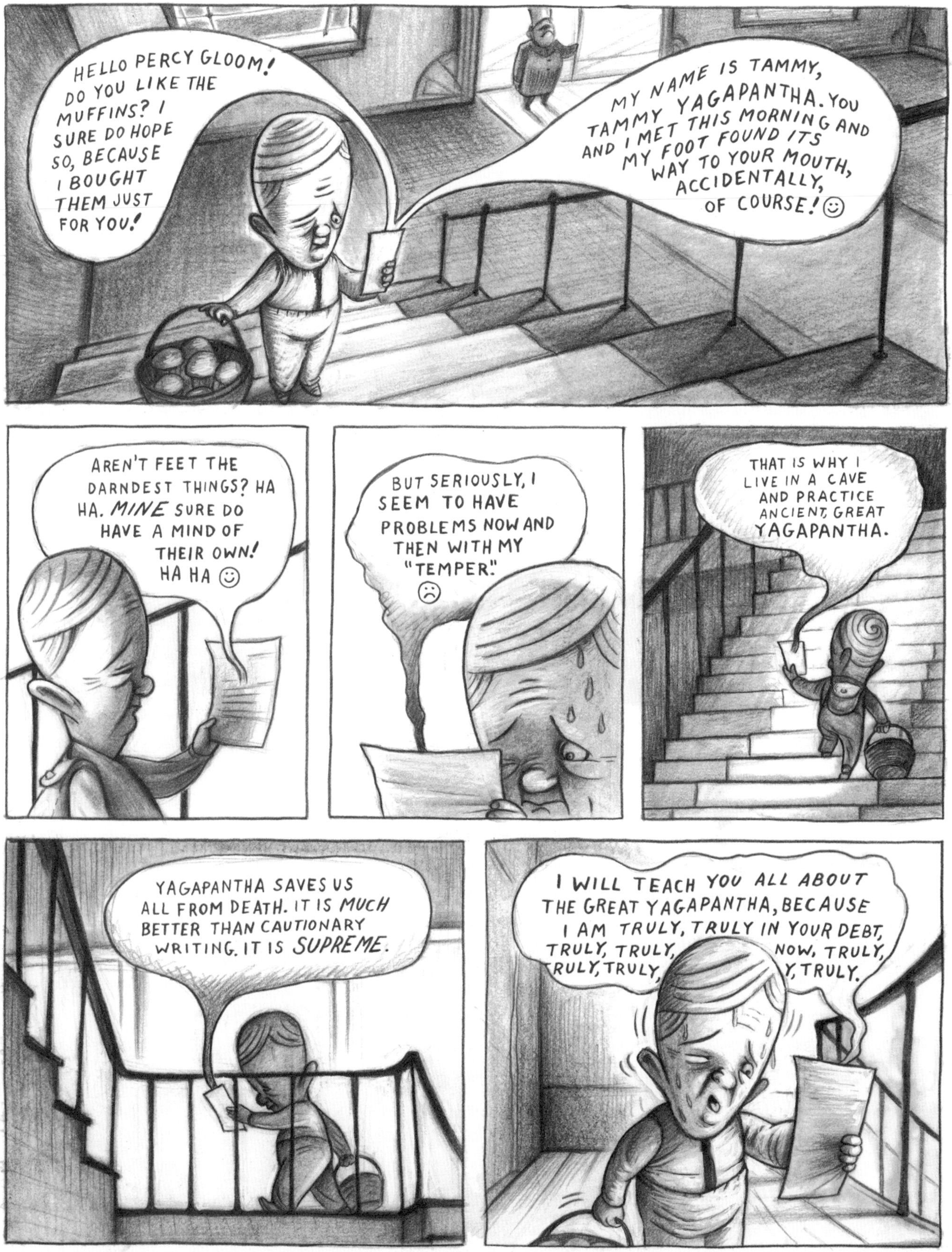
HELLO PERCY GLOOM! DO YOU LIKE THE MUFFINS? I SURE DO HOPE SO, BECAUSE I BOUGHT THEM JUST FOR YOU!
MY NAME IS TAMMY, TAMMY YAGAPANTHA. YOU AND I MET THIS MORNING AND MY FOOT FOUND ITS WAY TO YOUR MOUTH, ACCIDENTALLY, OF COURSE! ☺
AREN'T FEET THE DARNDEST THINGS? HA HA. MINE SURE DO HAVE A MIND OF THEIR OWN! HA HA ☺
BUT SERIOUSLY, I SEEM TO HAVE PROBLEMS NOW AND THEN WITH MY "TEMPER." ☹
THAT IS WHY I LIVE IN A CAVE AND PRACTICE ANCIENT, GREAT YAGAPANTHA.
YAGAPANTHA SAVES US ALL FROM DEATH. IT IS MUCH BETTER THAN CAUTIONARY WRITING. IT IS SUPREME.
I WILL TEACH YOU ALL ABOUT THE GREAT YAGAPANTHA, BECAUSE I AM TRULY, TRULY IN YOUR DEBT, TRULY, TRULY, NOW, TRULY, RULY, TRULY, Y, TRULY.

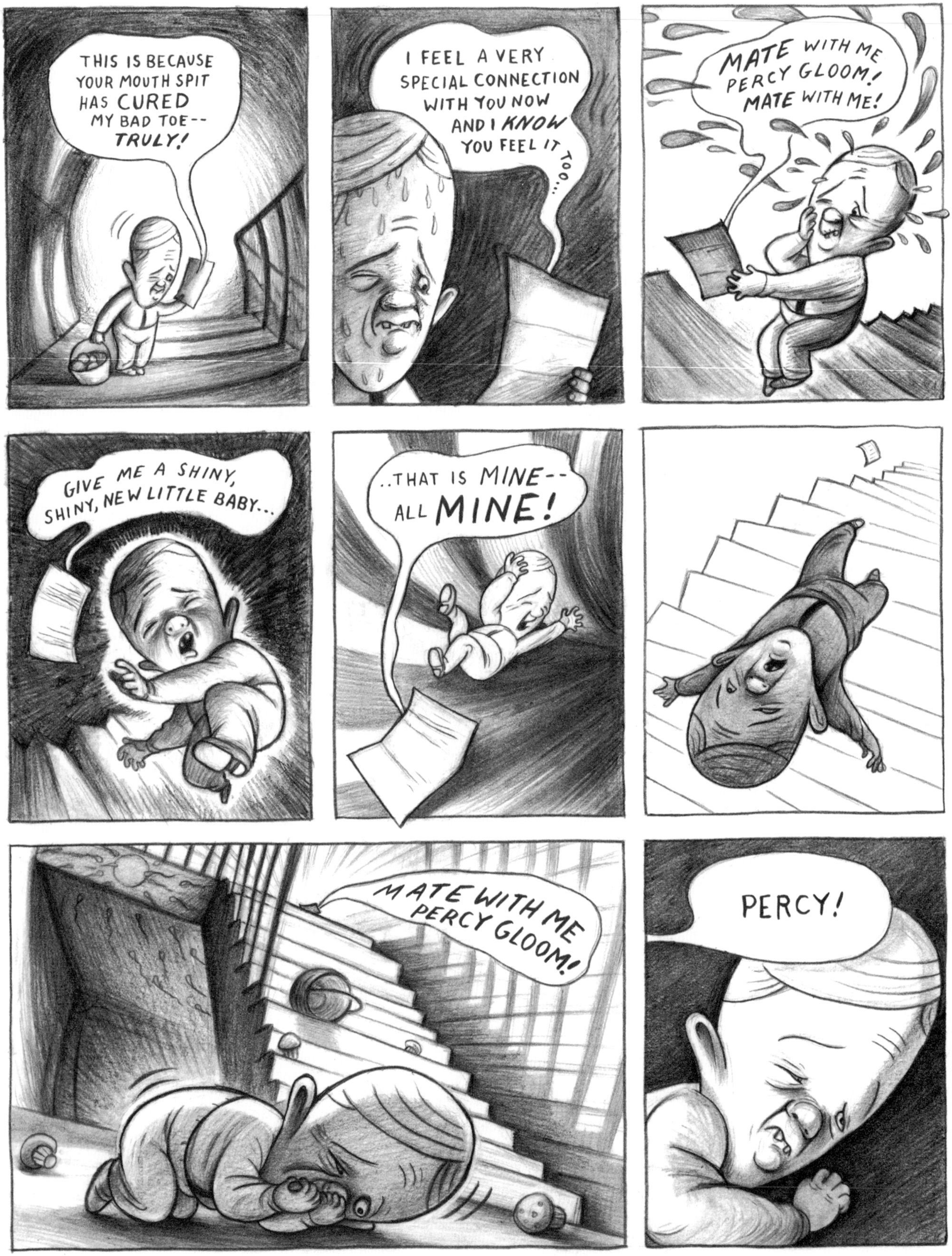
THIS IS BECAUSE YOUR MOUTH SPIT HAS CURED MY BAD TOE-- TRULY!
I FEEL A VERY SPECIAL CONNECTION WITH YOU NOW AND I KNOW YOU FEEL IT TOO...
MATE WITH ME PERCY GLOOM! MATE WITH ME!
GIVE ME A SHINY, SHINY, NEW LITTLE BABY...
..THAT IS MINE-- ALL MINE!
MATE WITH ME PERCY GLOOM!
PERCY!

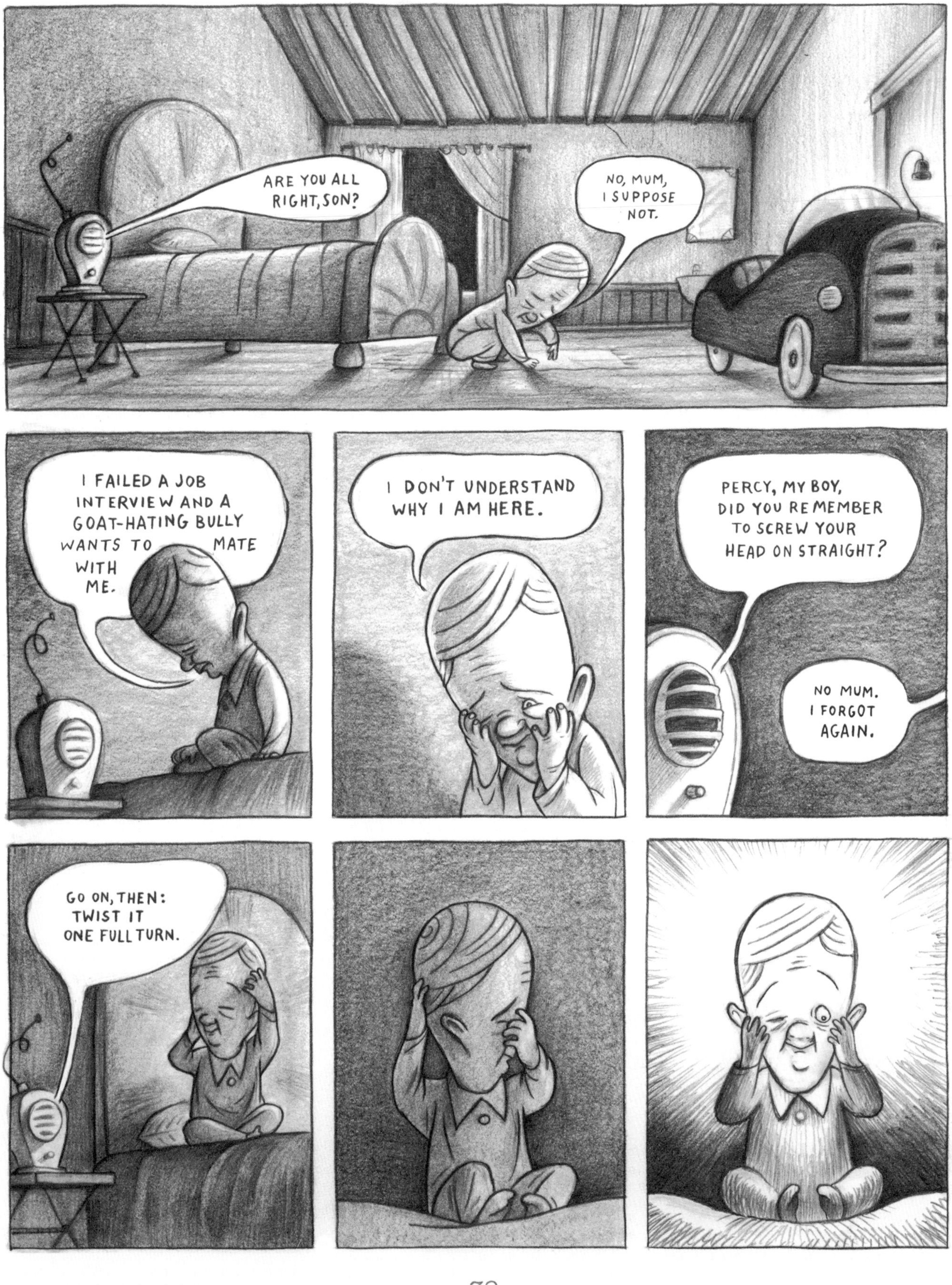

ARE YOU ALL RIGHT, SON?
NO, MUM, I SUPPOSE NOT.
I FAILED A JOB INTERVIEW AND A GOAT-HATING BULLY WANTS TO MATE WITH ME.
I DON'T UNDERSTAND WHY I AM HERE.
PERCY, MY BOY, DID YOU REMEMBER TO SCREW YOUR HEAD ON STRAIGHT?
NO MUM. I FORGOT AGAIN.
GO ON, THEN: TWIST IT ONE FULL TURN.

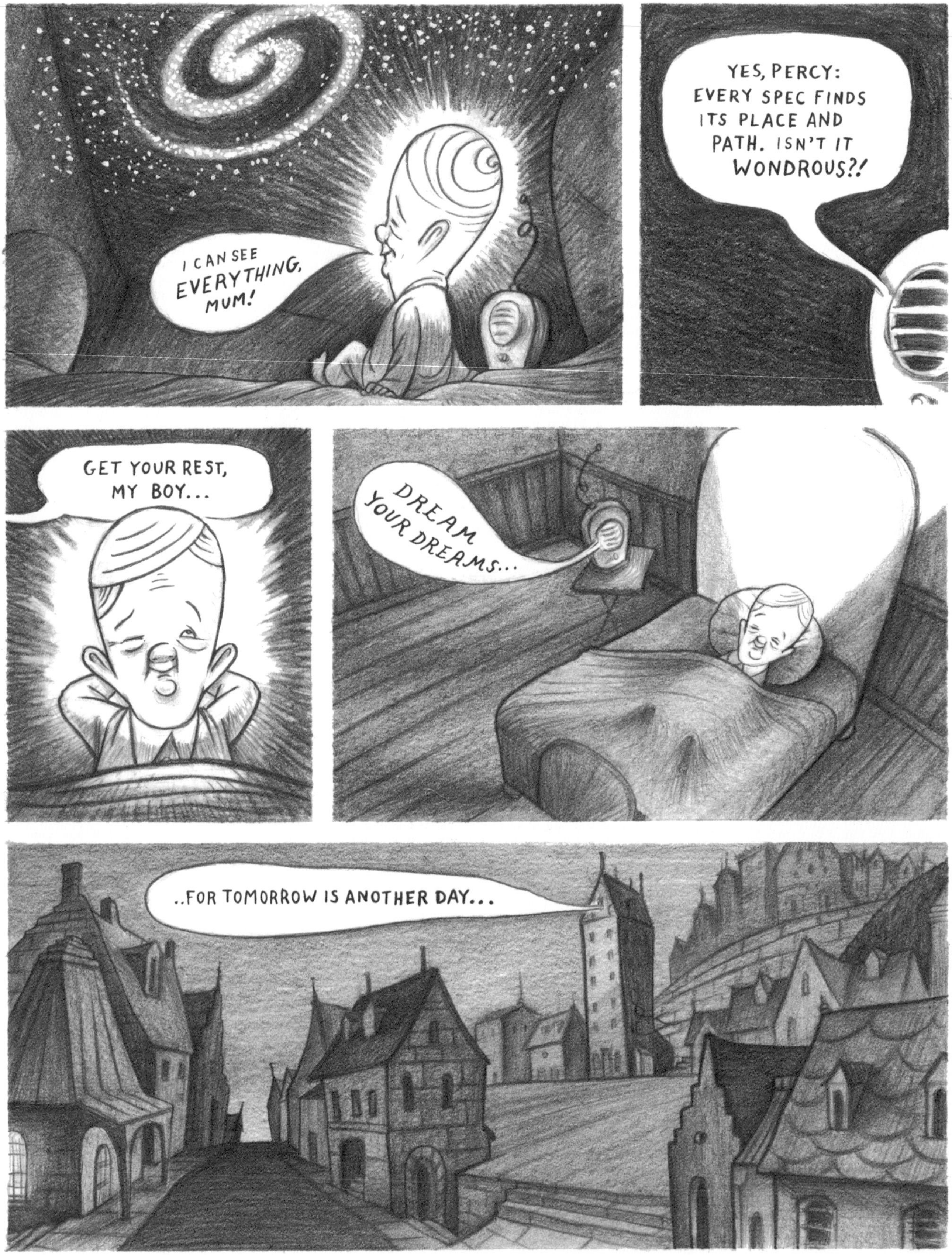
I CAN SEE EVERYTHING, MUM!
YES, PERCY: EVERY SPEC FINDS ITS PLACE AND PATH. ISN'T IT WONDROUS?!
GET YOUR REST, MY BOY...
DREAM YOUR DREAMS...
..FOR TOMORROW IS ANOTHER DAY...

Part Two:
AWAKE

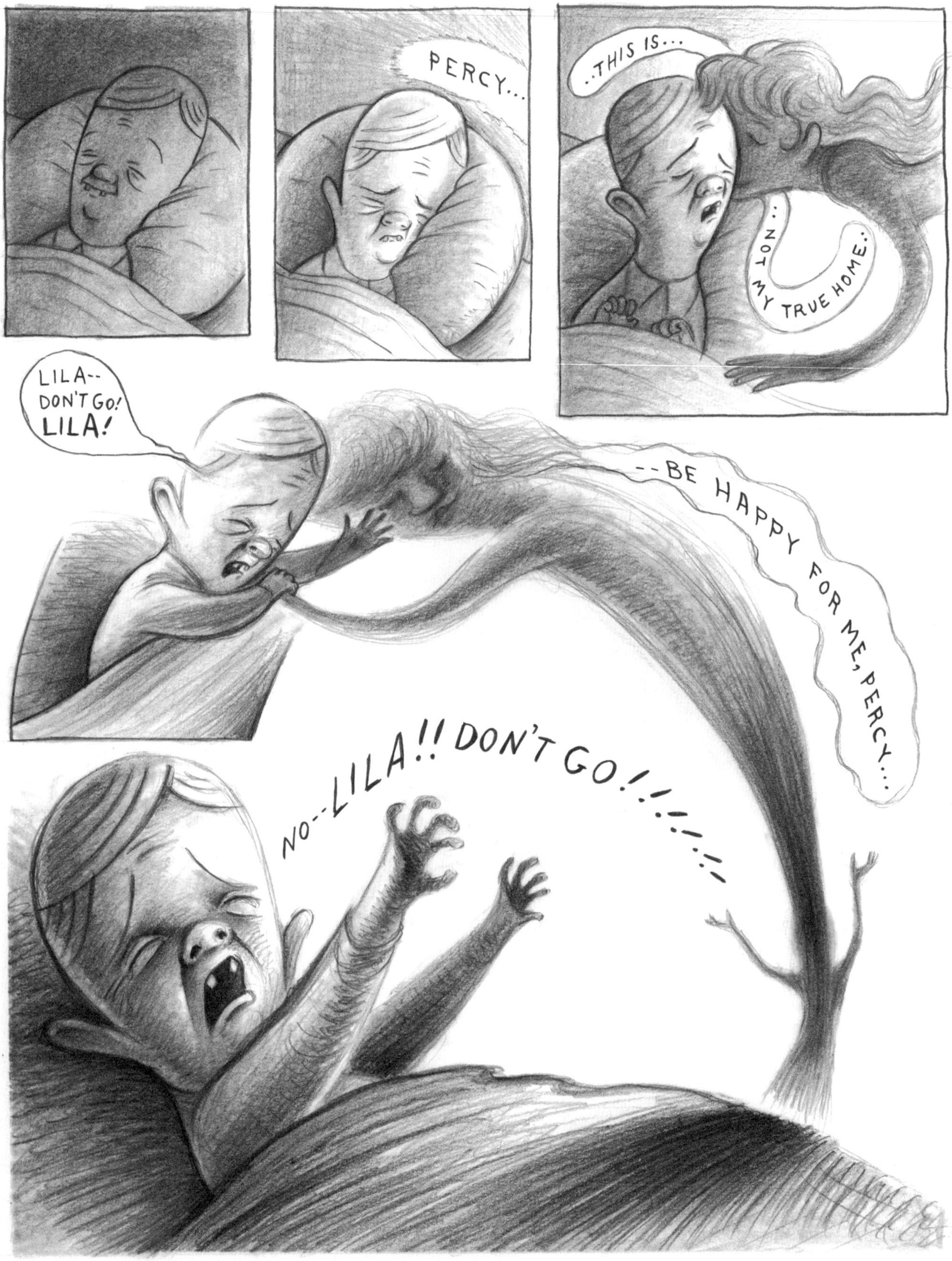
PERCY...
..THIS IS...
..NOT MY TRUE HOME..
LILA--
DON'T GO!
LILA!
--BE HAPPY FOR ME, PERCY...
NO--LILA!! DON'T GO!!!!!!!

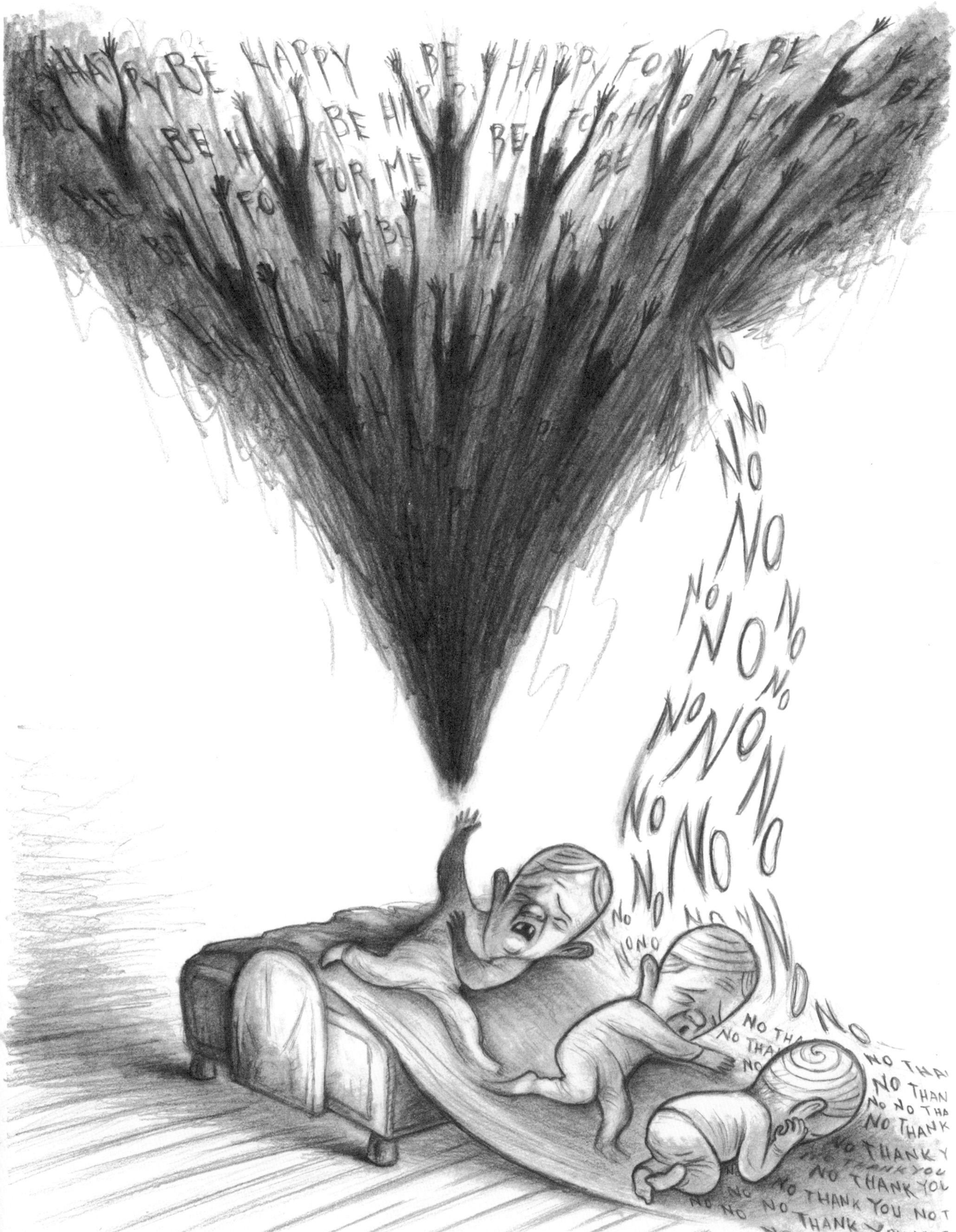
BE HAPPY BE HAPPY FOR ME BE
NO
NO THANK YOU

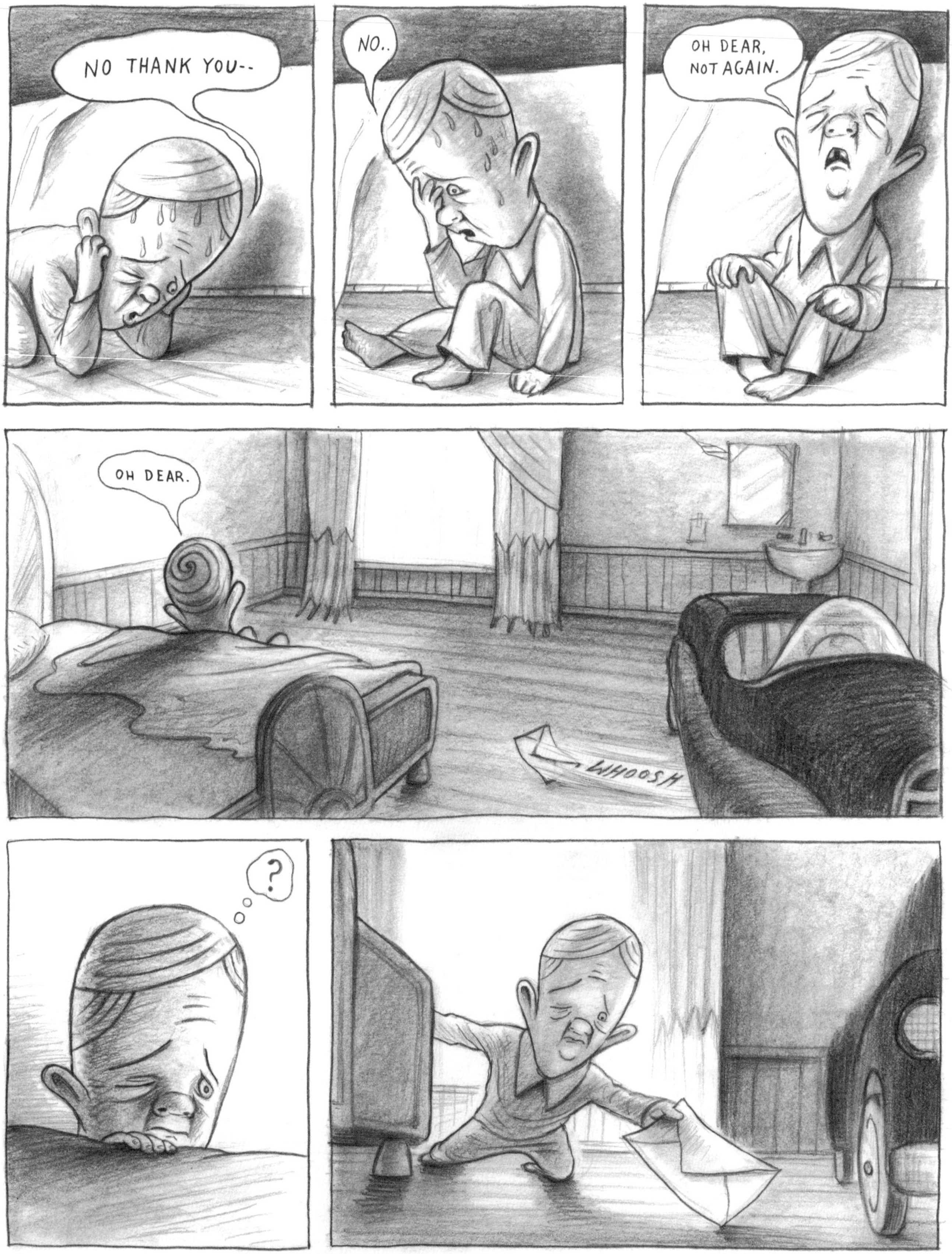
NO THANK YOU--
NO..
OH DEAR, NOT AGAIN.
OH DEAR.
WHOOSH
?

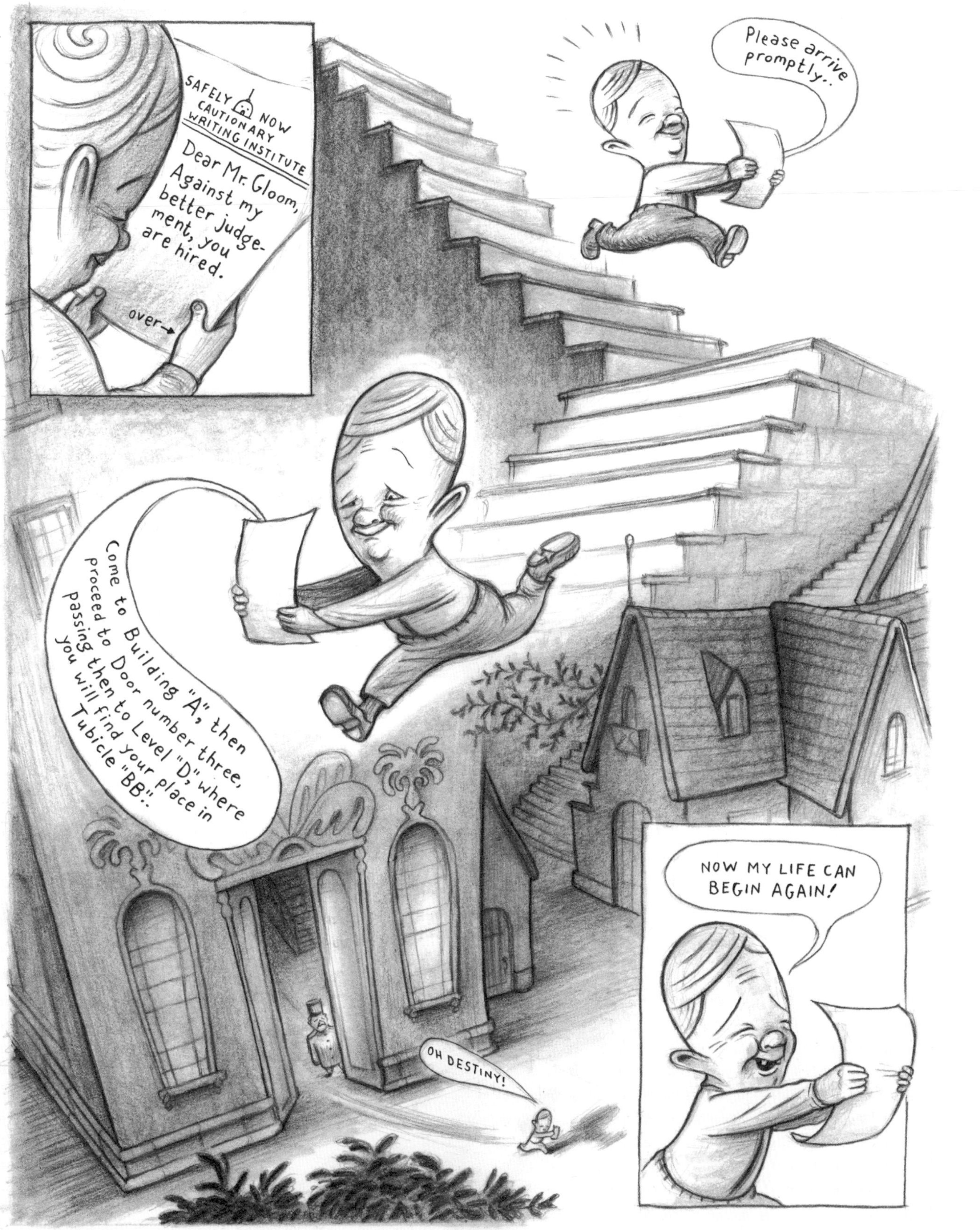

SAFELY NOW CAUTIONARY WRITING INSTITUTE
Dear Mr. Gloom, Against my better judgement, you are hired.
over→
Please arrive promptly..
Come to Building "A", then proceed to Door number three, passing then to Level "D", where you will find your place in Tubicle "BB"..
OH DESTINY!
NOW MY LIFE CAN BEGIN AGAIN!

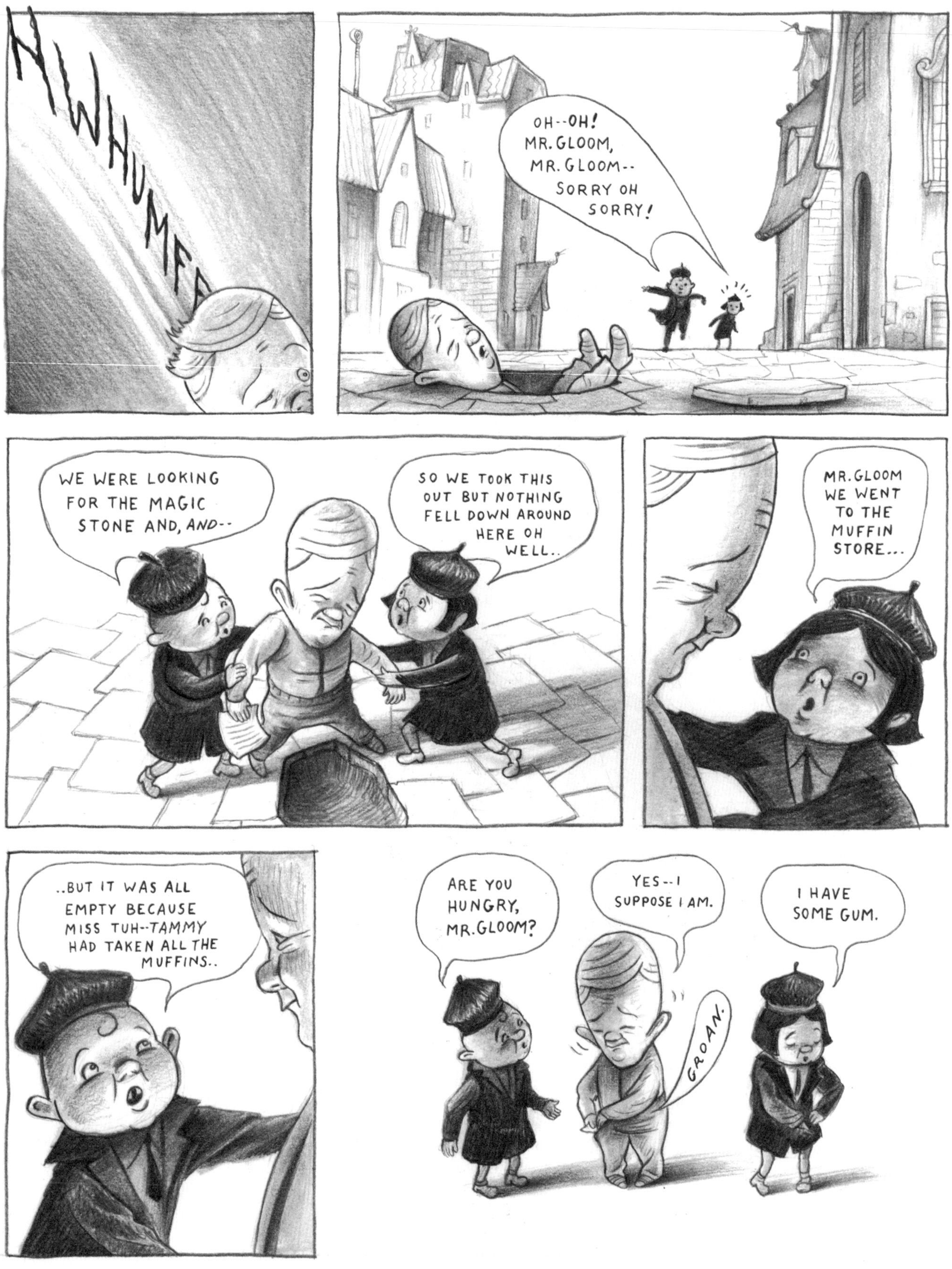
NWHUMFF
OH--OH! MR. GLOOM, MR. GLOOM-- SORRY OH SORRY!
WE WERE LOOKING FOR THE MAGIC STONE AND, AND--
SO WE TOOK THIS OUT BUT NOTHING FELL DOWN AROUND HERE OH WELL..
MR. GLOOM WE WENT TO THE MUFFIN STORE...
..BUT IT WAS ALL EMPTY BECAUSE MISS TUH--TAMMY HAD TAKEN ALL THE MUFFINS..
ARE YOU HUNGRY, MR. GLOOM?
YES--I SUPPOSE I AM.
GROAN.
I HAVE SOME GUM.

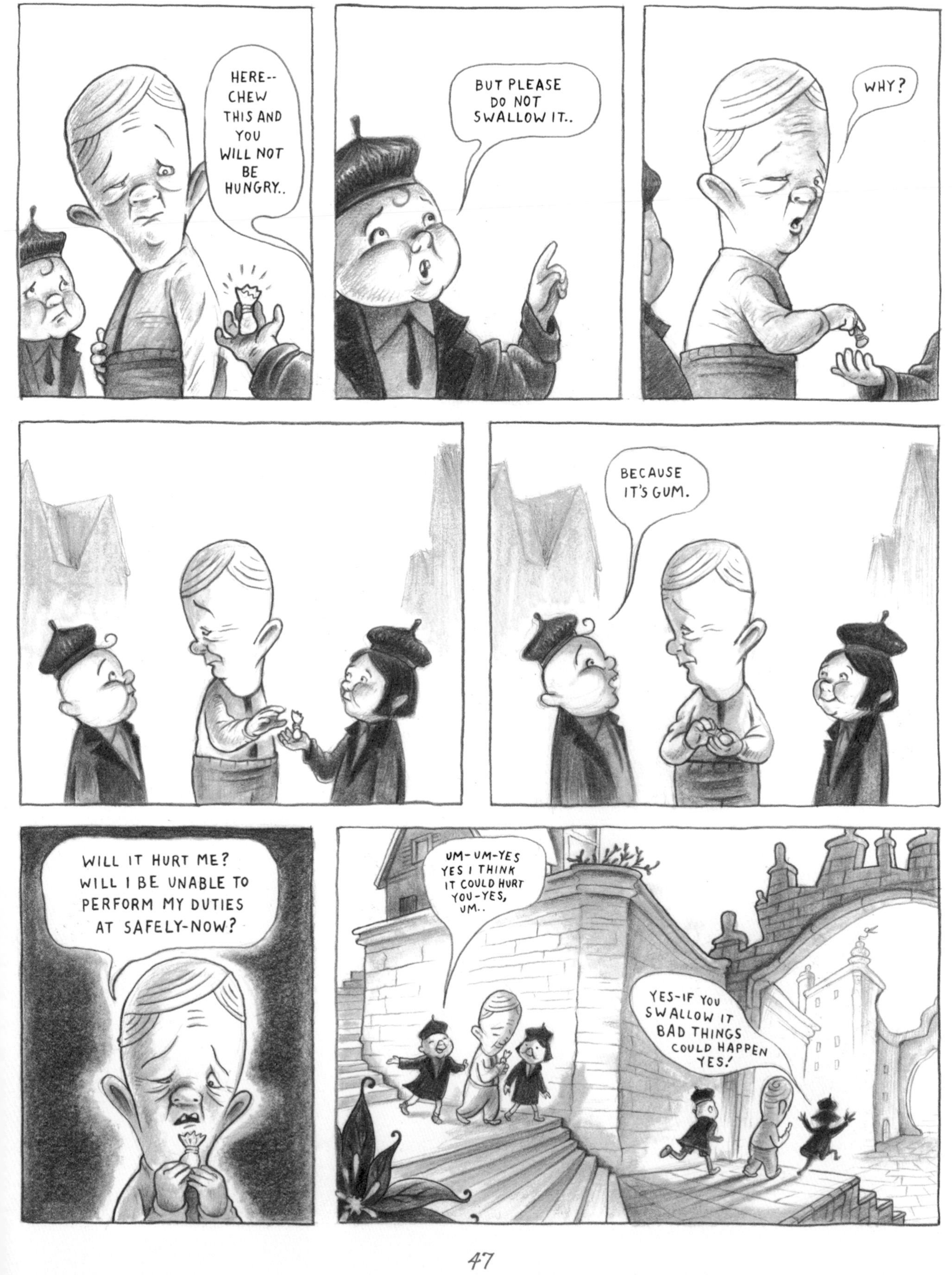

HERE-- CHEW THIS AND YOU WILL NOT BE HUNGRY..
BUT PLEASE DO NOT SWALLOW IT..
WHY?
BECAUSE IT'S GUM.
WILL IT HURT ME? WILL I BE UNABLE TO PERFORM MY DUTIES AT SAFELY-NOW?
UM-UM-YES YES I THINK IT COULD HURT YOU-YES, UM..
YES-IF YOU SWALLOW IT BAD THINGS COULD HAPPEN YES!

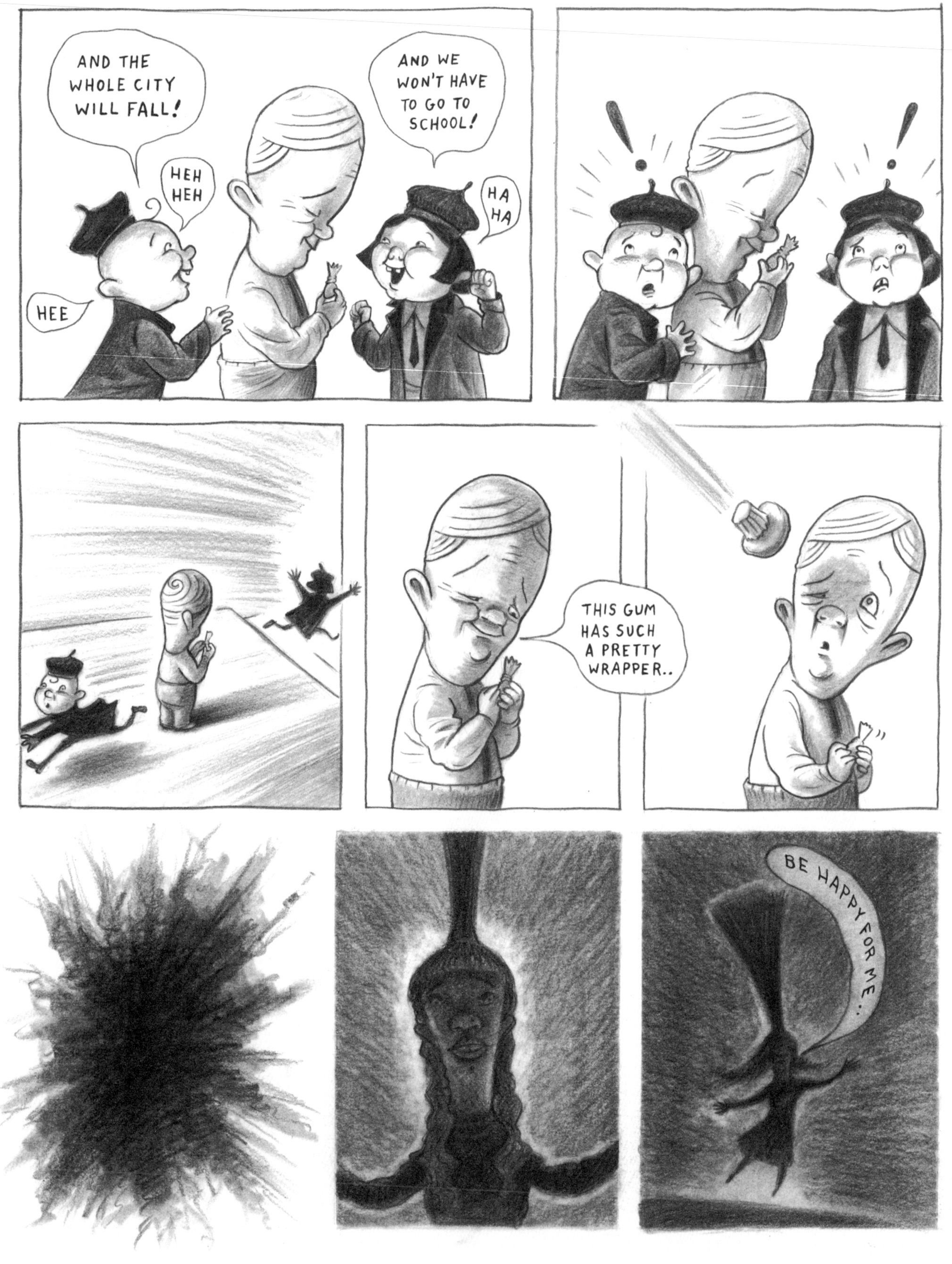
AND THE WHOLE CITY WILL FALL!
HEH HEH
HEE
AND WE WON'T HAVE TO GO TO SCHOOL!
HA HA
THIS GUM HAS SUCH A PRETTY WRAPPER..
BE HAPPY FOR ME..

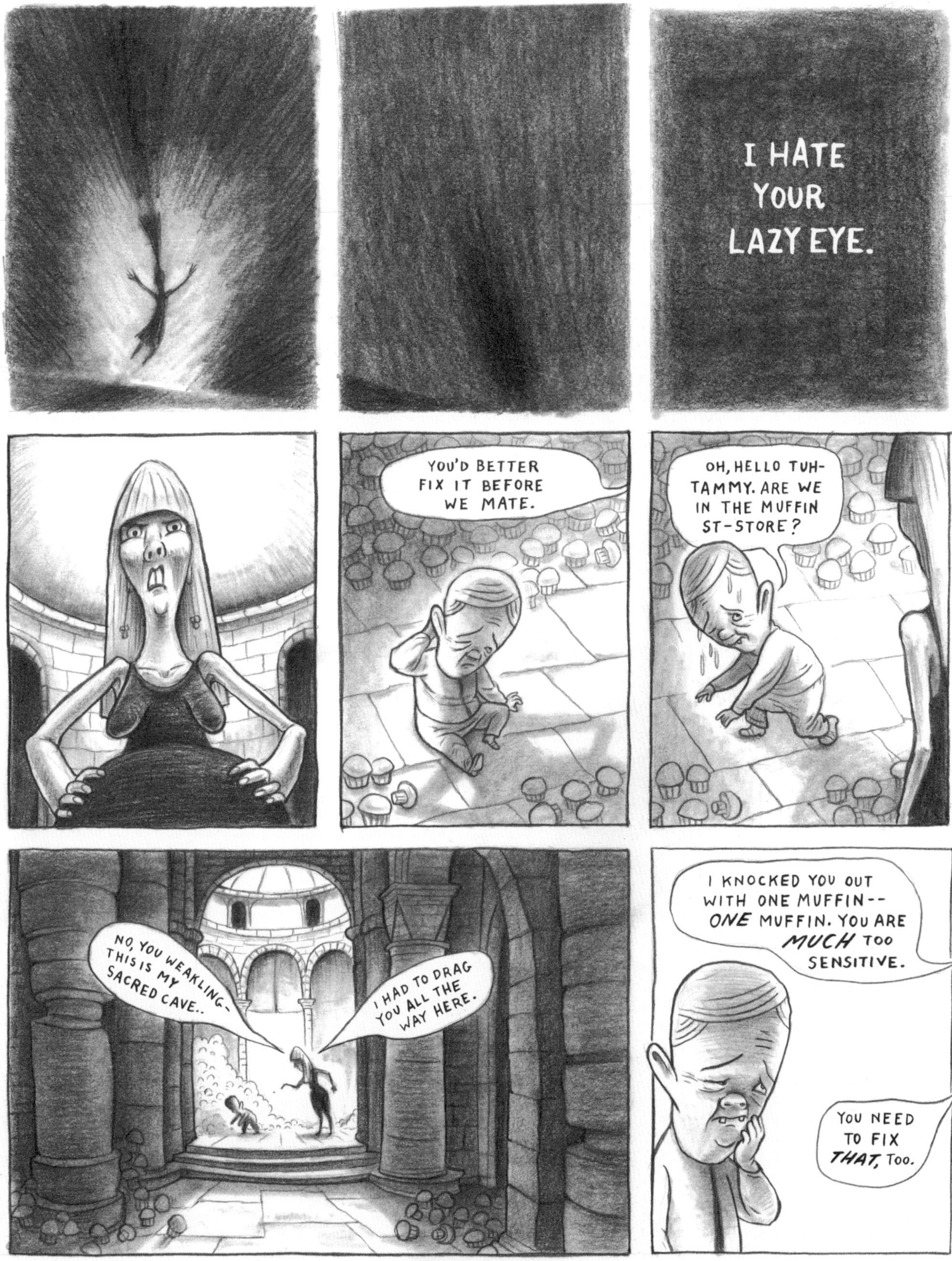
I HATE YOUR LAZY EYE.
YOU'D BETTER FIX IT BEFORE WE MATE.
OH, HELLO TUH-TAMMY. ARE WE IN THE MUFFIN ST-STORE?
NO, YOU WEAKLING-THIS IS MY SACRED CAVE..
I HAD TO DRAG YOU ALL THE WAY HERE.
I KNOCKED YOU OUT WITH ONE MUFFIN-- ONE MUFFIN. YOU ARE MUCH TOO SENSITIVE.
YOU NEED TO FIX THAT, TOO.

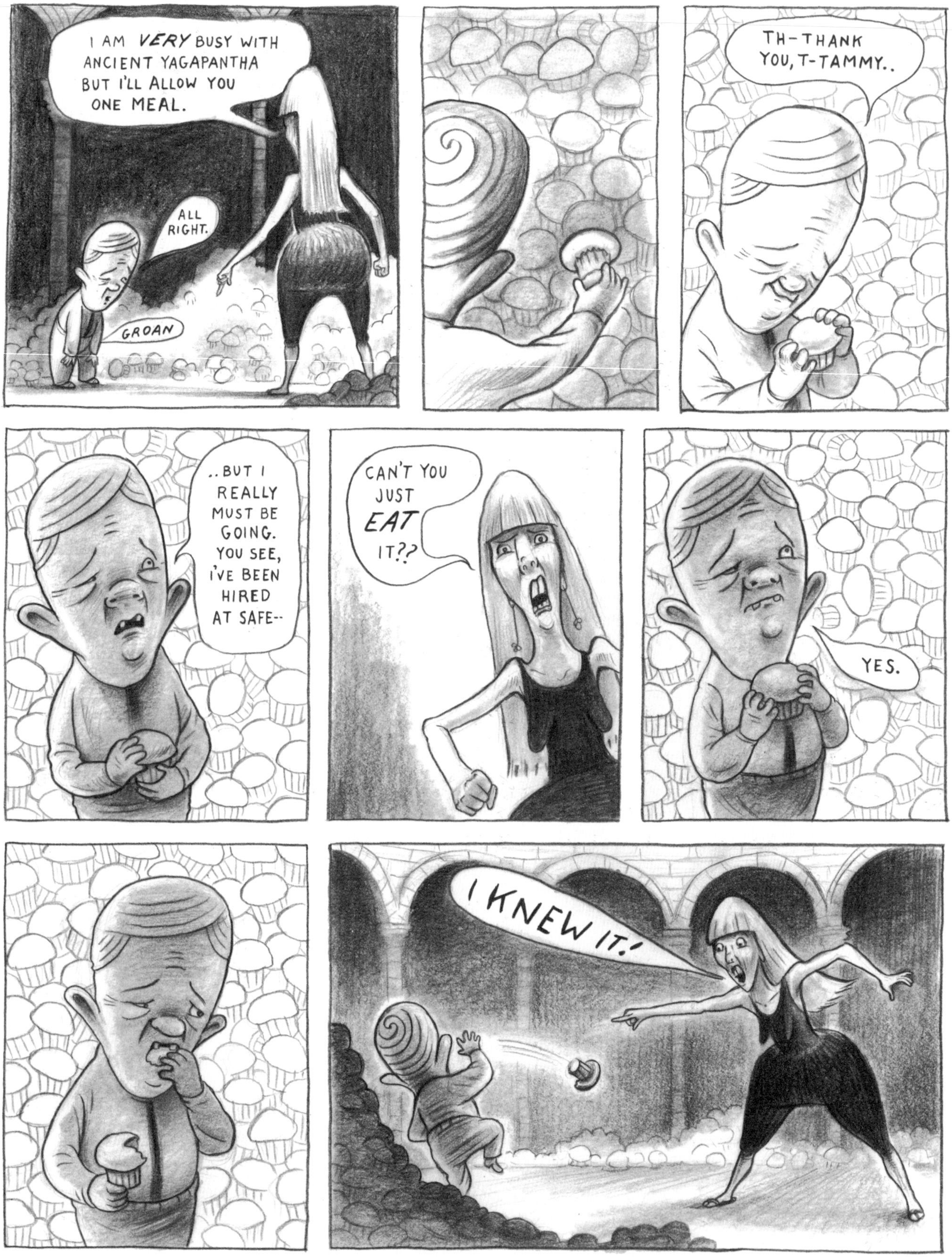
I AM VERY BUSY WITH ANCIENT YAGAPANTHA BUT I'LL ALLOW YOU ONE MEAL.
ALL RIGHT.
GROAN
TH-THANK YOU, T-TAMMY..
..BUT I REALLY MUST BE GOING. YOU SEE, I'VE BEEN HIRED AT SAFE--
CAN'T YOU JUST EAT IT??
YES.
I KNEW IT!

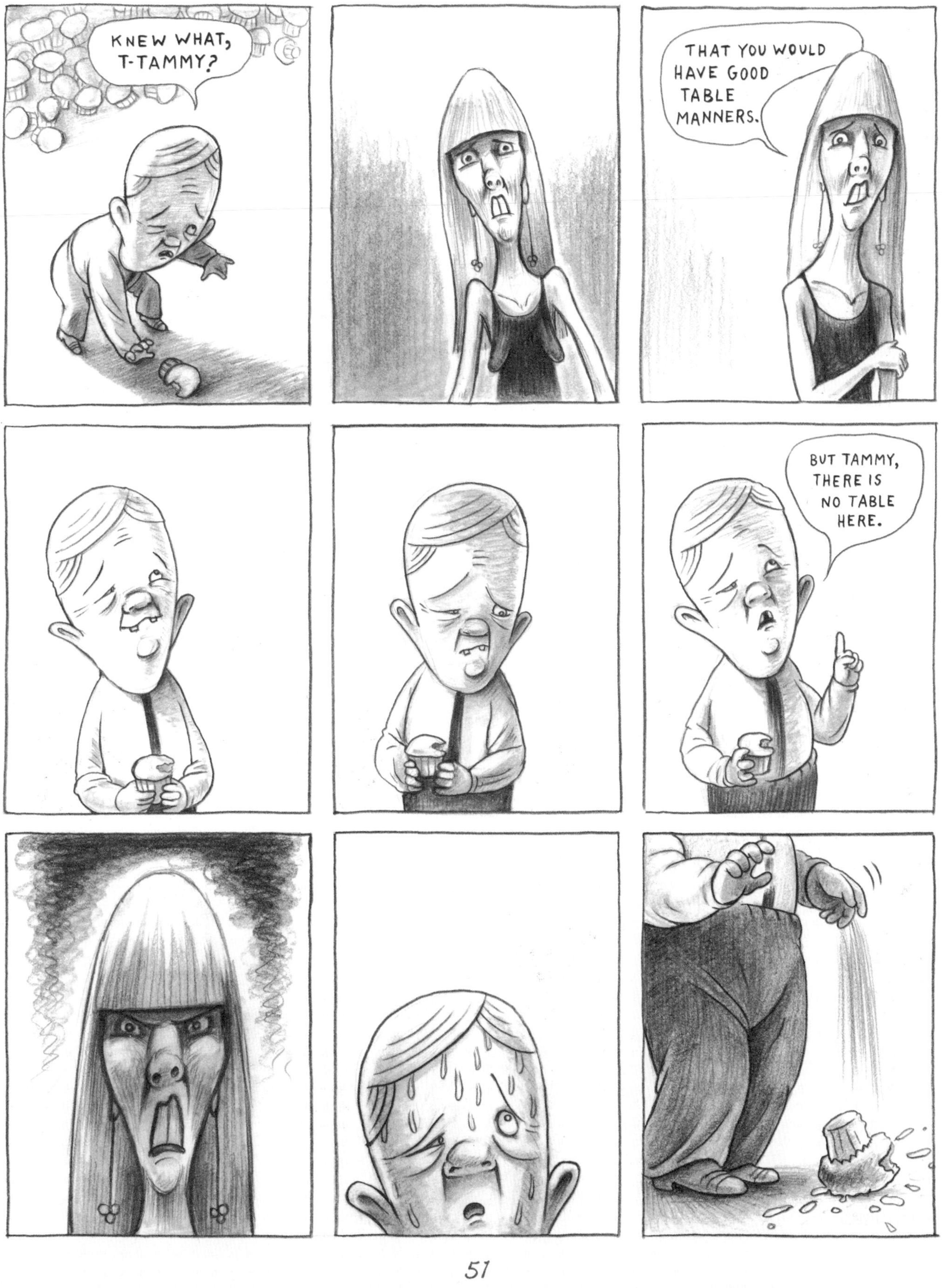
KNEW WHAT, T-TAMMY?
THAT YOU WOULD HAVE GOOD TABLE MANNERS.
BUT TAMMY, THERE IS NO TABLE HERE.

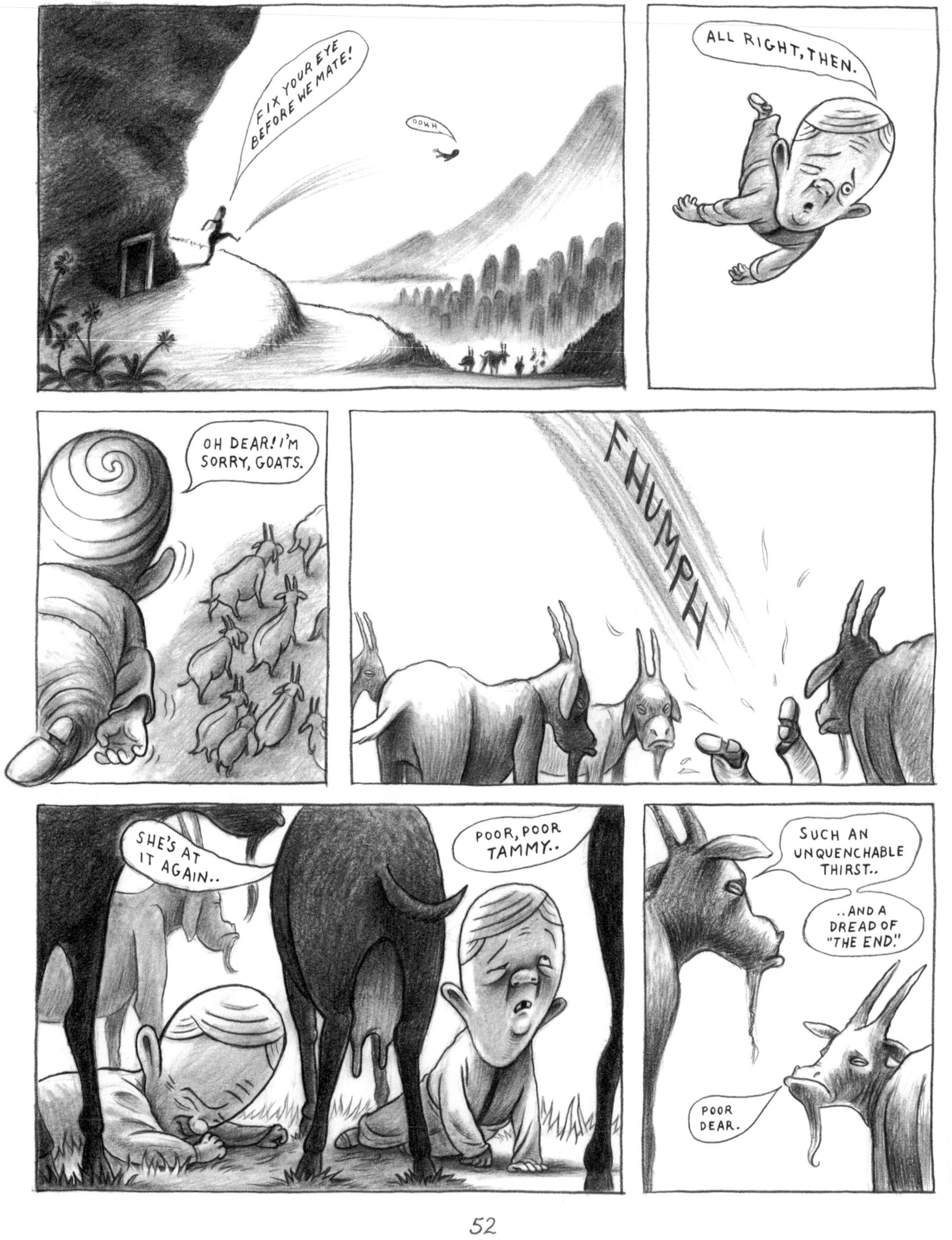
FIX YOUR EYE BEFORE WE MATE!
OOHH
ALL RIGHT, THEN.
OH DEAR! I'M SORRY, GOATS.
FHUMPH
SHE'S AT IT AGAIN..
POOR, POOR TAMMY..
SUCH AN UNQUENCHABLE THIRST..
..AND A DREAD OF "THE END."
POOR DEAR.

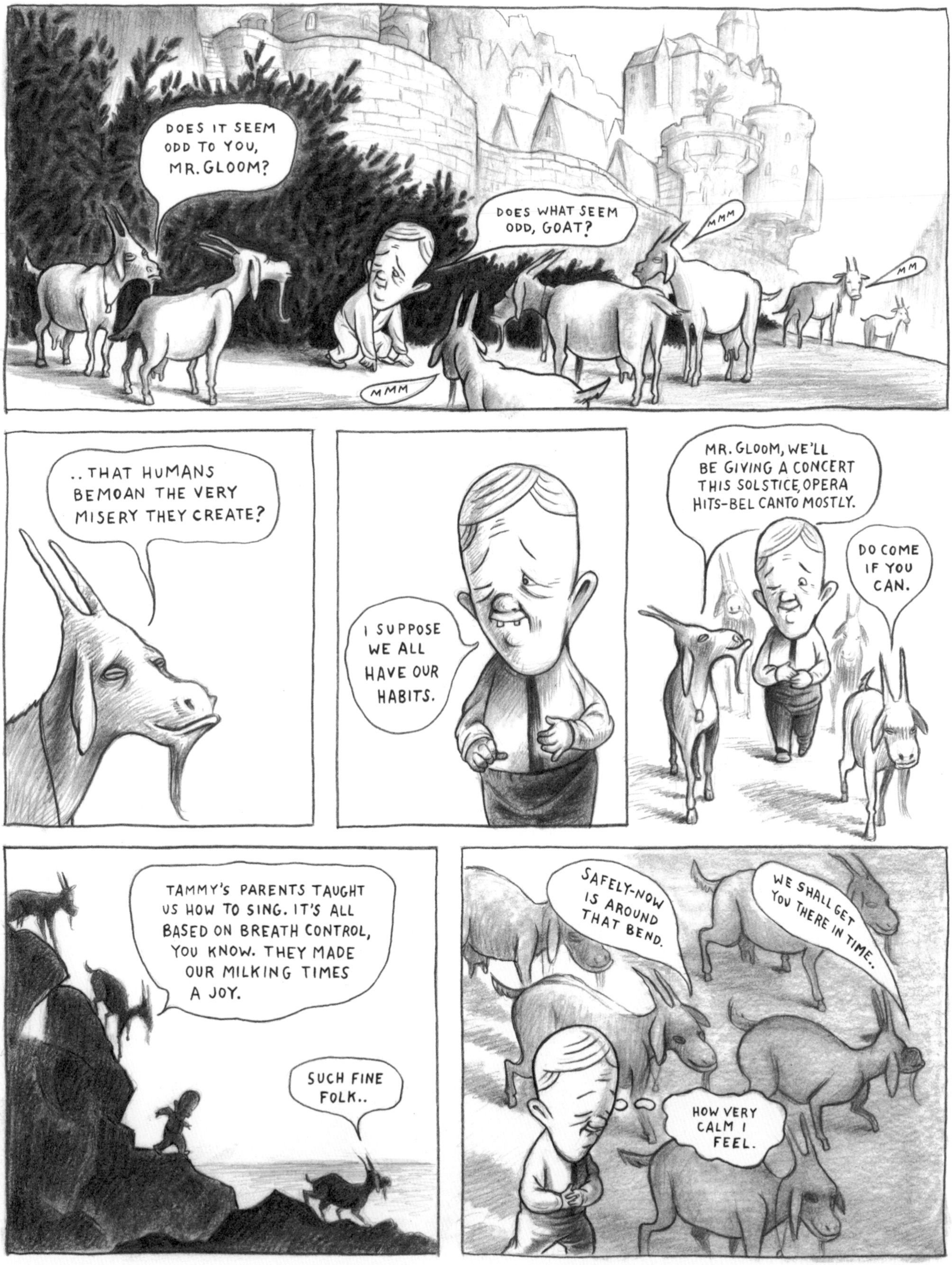

DOES IT SEEM ODD TO YOU, MR. GLOOM?
DOES WHAT SEEM ODD, GOAT?
MMM
MMM
MMM
..THAT HUMANS BEMOAN THE VERY MISERY THEY CREATE?
I SUPPOSE WE ALL HAVE OUR HABITS.
MR. GLOOM, WE'LL BE GIVING A CONCERT THIS SOLSTICE, OPERA HITS-BEL CANTO MOSTLY.
DO COME IF YOU CAN.
TAMMY'S PARENTS TAUGHT US HOW TO SING. IT'S ALL BASED ON BREATH CONTROL, YOU KNOW. THEY MADE OUR MILKING TIMES A JOY.
SUCH FINE FOLK..
SAFELY-NOW IS AROUND THAT BEND.
WE SHALL GET YOU THERE IN TIME..
HOW VERY CALM I FEEL.

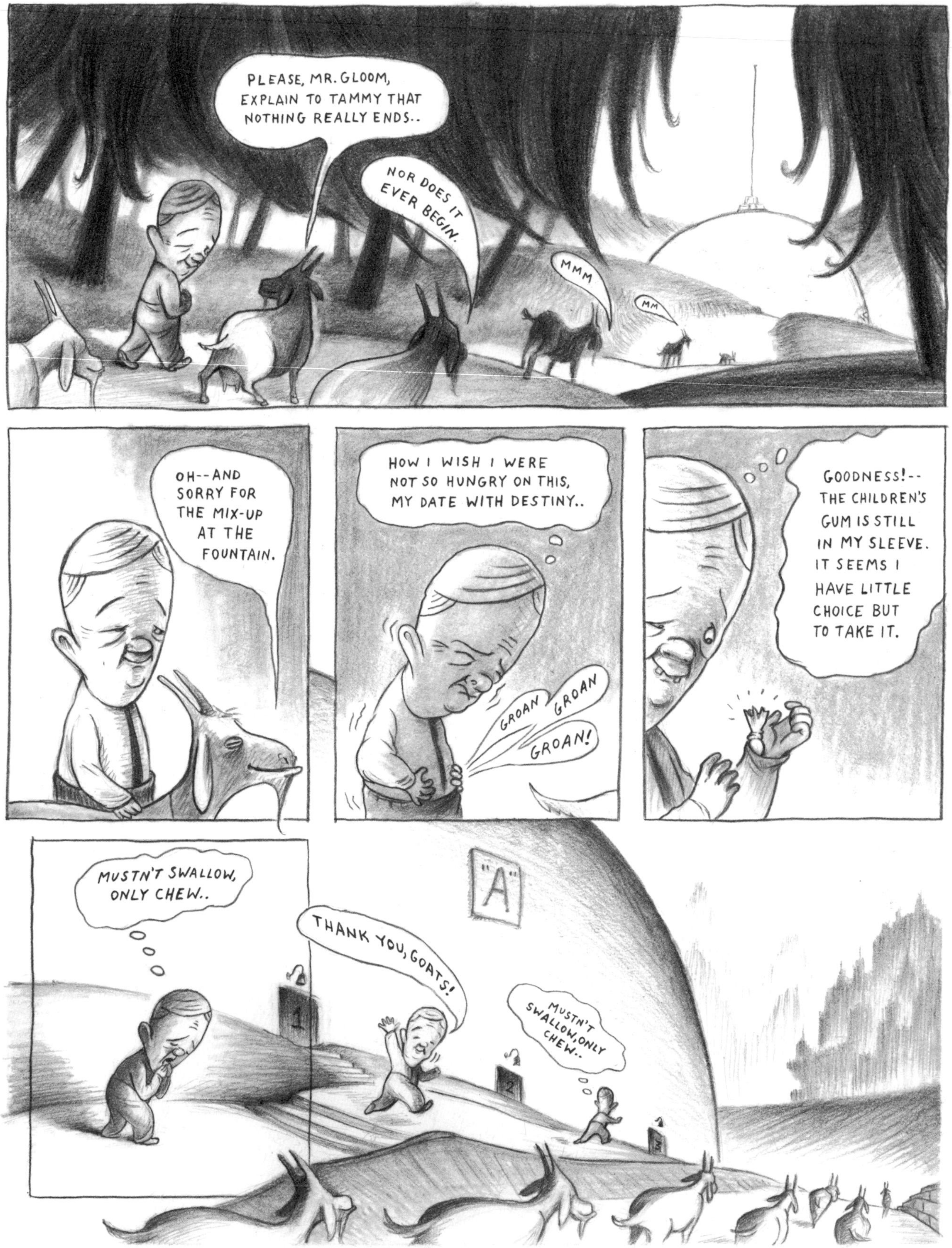
PLEASE, MR. GLOOM, EXPLAIN TO TAMMY THAT NOTHING REALLY ENDS..
NOR DOES IT EVER BEGIN.
MMM
MM
OH--AND SORRY FOR THE MIX-UP AT THE FOUNTAIN.
HOW I WISH I WERE NOT SO HUNGRY ON THIS, MY DATE WITH DESTINY..
GROAN GROAN GROAN!
GOODNESS!-- THE CHILDREN'S GUM IS STILL IN MY SLEEVE. IT SEEMS I HAVE LITTLE CHOICE BUT TO TAKE IT.
MUSTN'T SWALLOW, ONLY CHEW..
"A"
THANK YOU, GOATS!
1
MUSTN'T SWALLOW, ONLY CHEW..
2

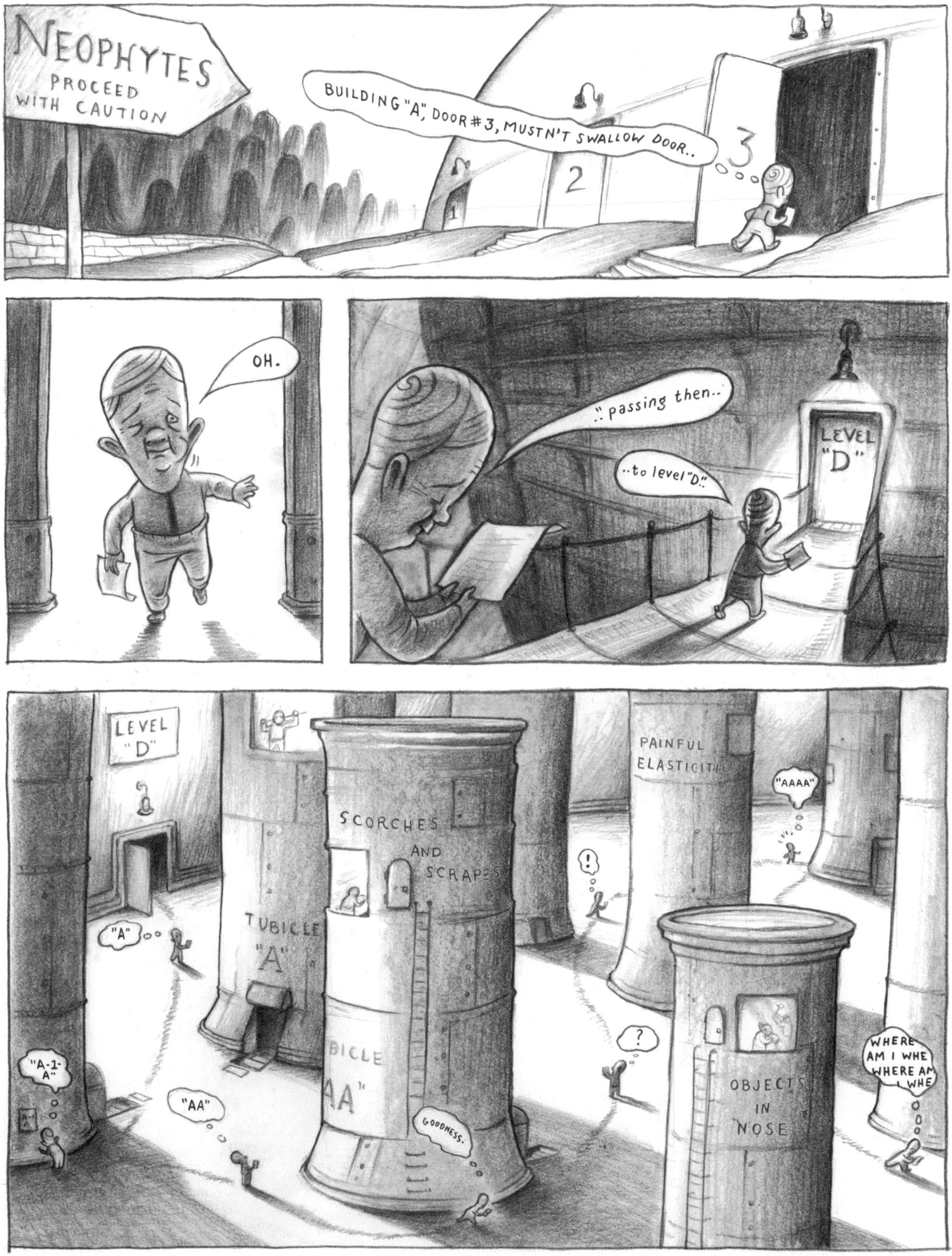
NEOPHYTES
PROCEED WITH CAUTION
BUILDING "A", DOOR #3, MUSTN'T SWALLOW DOOR..
1
2
3
OH.
..passing then..
..to level "D".
LEVEL "D"
LEVEL "D"
SCORCHES AND SCRAPES
PAINFUL ELASTICITIES
"AAAA"
!
"A"
TUBICLE "A"
"A-1-A"
"AA"
BICLE "AA"
GOODNESS.
?
OBJECTS IN NOSE
WHERE AM I WHE WHERE AM I WHE

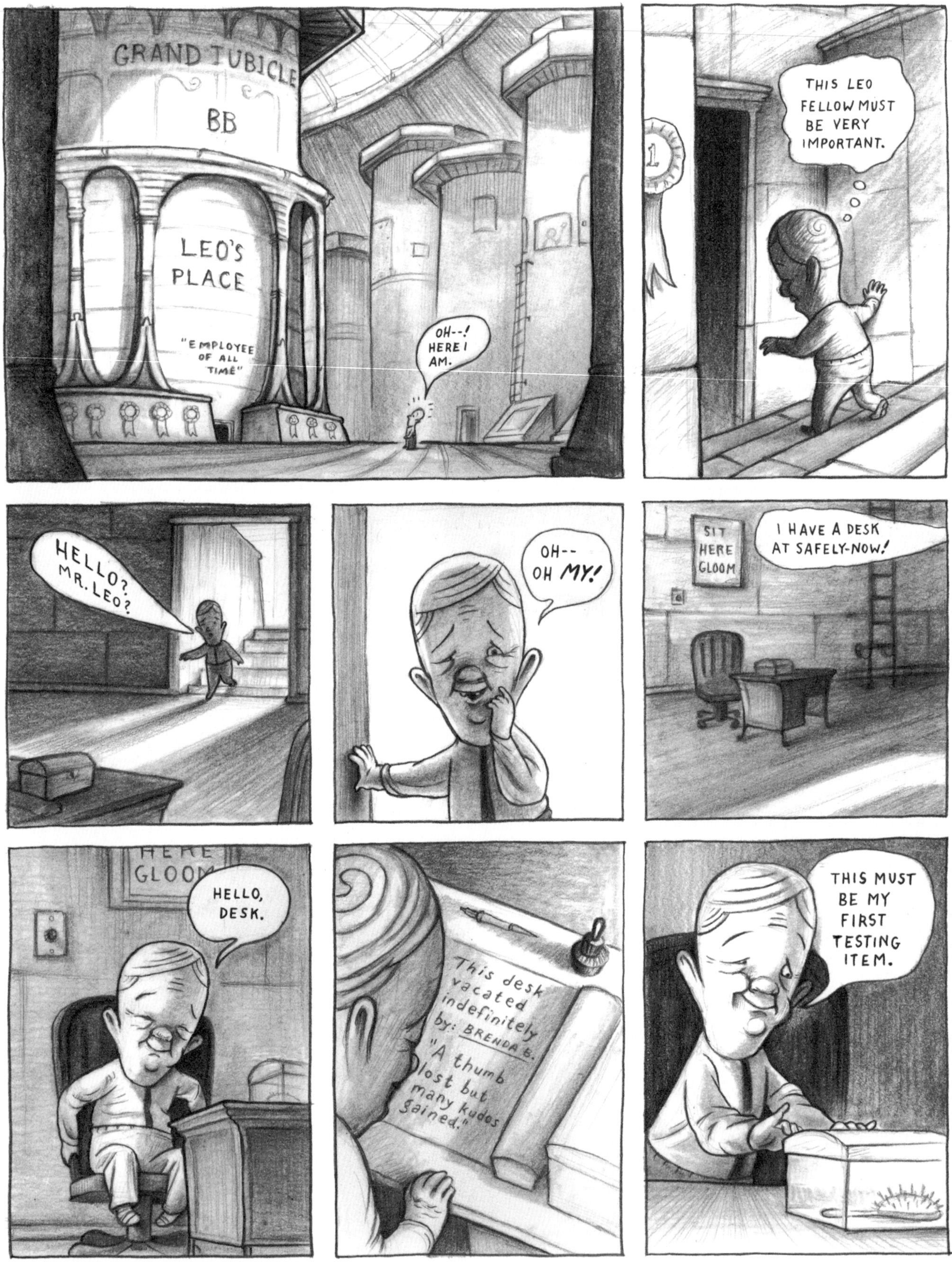
GRAND TUBICLE
BB
LEO'S PLACE
"EMPLOYEE OF ALL TIME"
OH--! HERE I AM.
THIS LEO FELLOW MUST BE VERY IMPORTANT.
HELLO? MR. LEO?
OH-- OH MY!
SIT HERE GLOOM
I HAVE A DESK AT SAFELY-NOW!
HERE GLOOM
HELLO, DESK.
This desk vacated indefinitely by: BRENDA B.
"A thumb lost but many kudos gained."
THIS MUST BE MY FIRST TESTING ITEM.

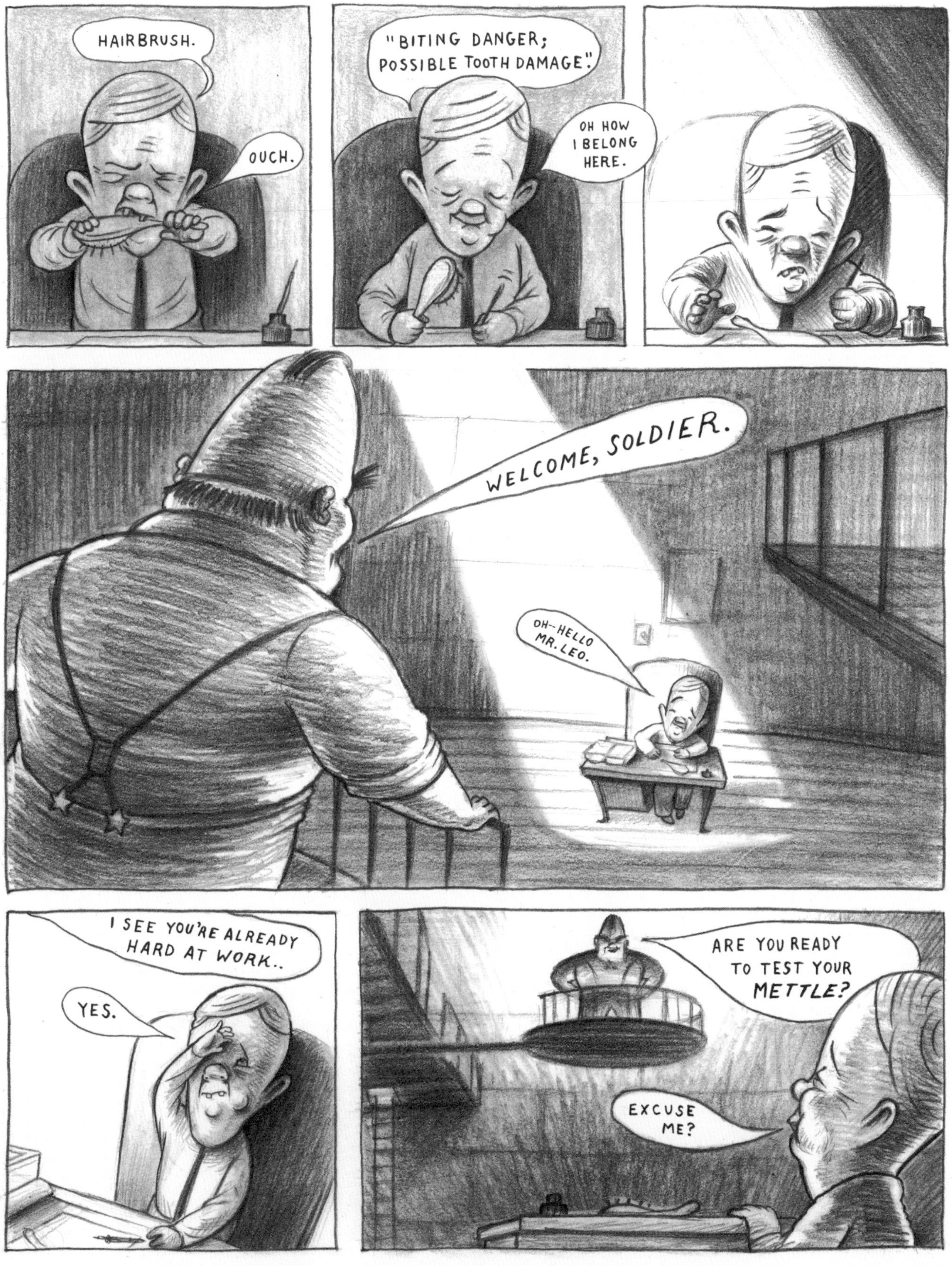

HAIRBRUSH.
OUCH.
"BITING DANGER; POSSIBLE TOOTH DAMAGE".
OH HOW I BELONG HERE.
WELCOME, SOLDIER.
OH-- HELLO MR. LEO.
I SEE YOU'RE ALREADY HARD AT WORK..
YES.
ARE YOU READY TO TEST YOUR METTLE?
EXCUSE ME?

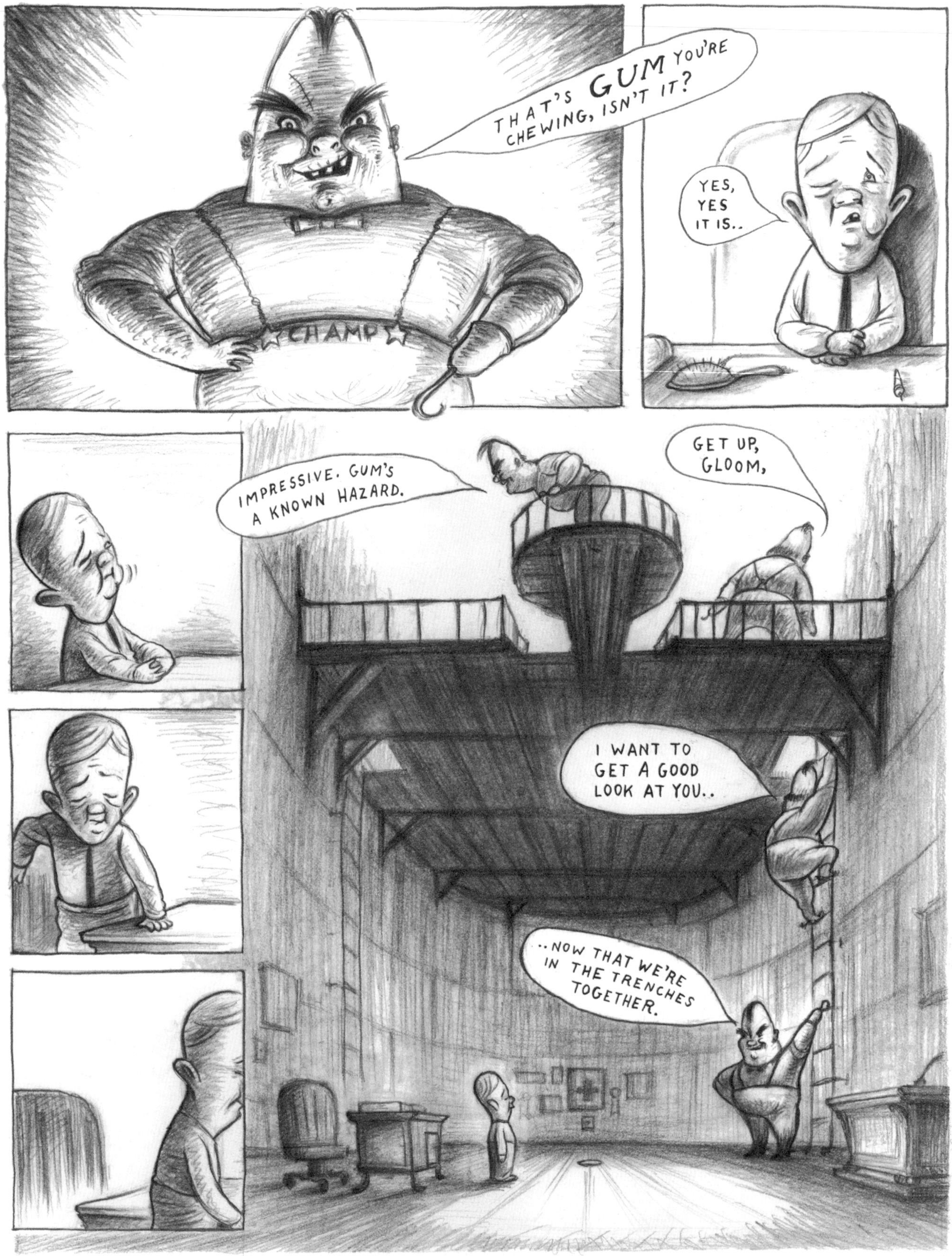
THAT'S GUM YOU'RE CHEWING, ISN'T IT?
YES, YES IT IS..
IMPRESSIVE. GUM'S A KNOWN HAZARD.
GET UP, GLOOM,
I WANT TO GET A GOOD LOOK AT YOU..
..NOW THAT WE'RE IN THE TRENCHES TOGETHER.

YOU HAVE VERY BIG EARS, GLOOM.

YOU'RE NOT FROM AROUND *HERE*, ARE YOU?

?

NO.

FOREIGN, EH? LUCKY FOR YOU..

?..?

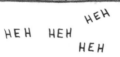

ELASTIC WAISTBAND-- VERY THOUGHTFUL..

BUT EVEN ELASTIC IS A *HAZARD*, YOU KNOW.

IT CATCHES ON THINGS.

HEH

HEH HEH HEH HEH HEH

WELL, WELL-- YOUR VERY FIRST TESTING ITEM..

..A ♡*LADIES'*♡ HAIRBRUSH..

?

?

?

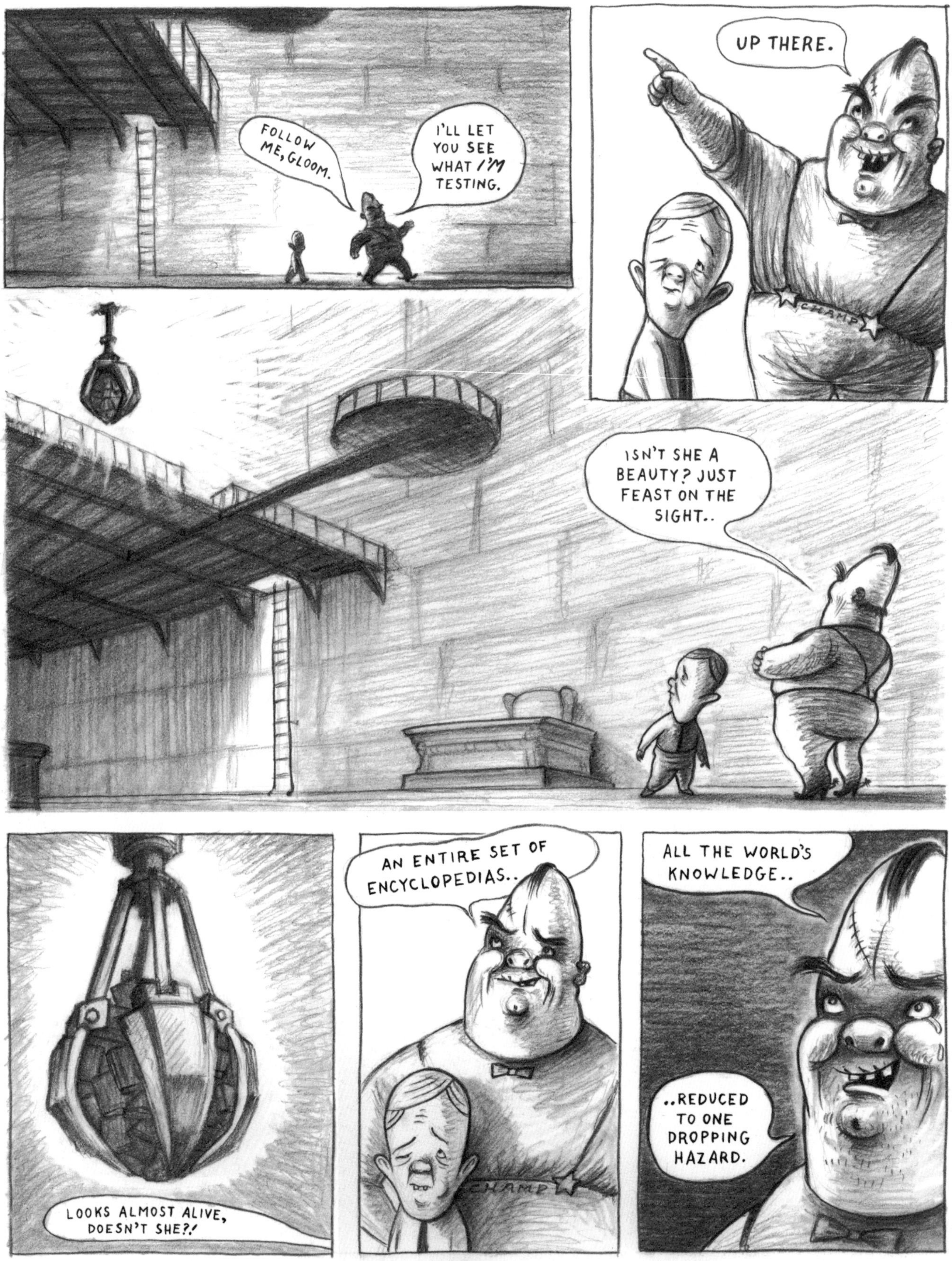
FOLLOW ME, GLOOM.
I'LL LET YOU SEE WHAT I'M TESTING.
UP THERE.
ISN'T SHE A BEAUTY? JUST FEAST ON THE SIGHT..
LOOKS ALMOST ALIVE, DOESN'T SHE?!
AN ENTIRE SET OF ENCYCLOPEDIAS..
CHAMP
ALL THE WORLD'S KNOWLEDGE..
..REDUCED TO ONE DROPPING HAZARD.

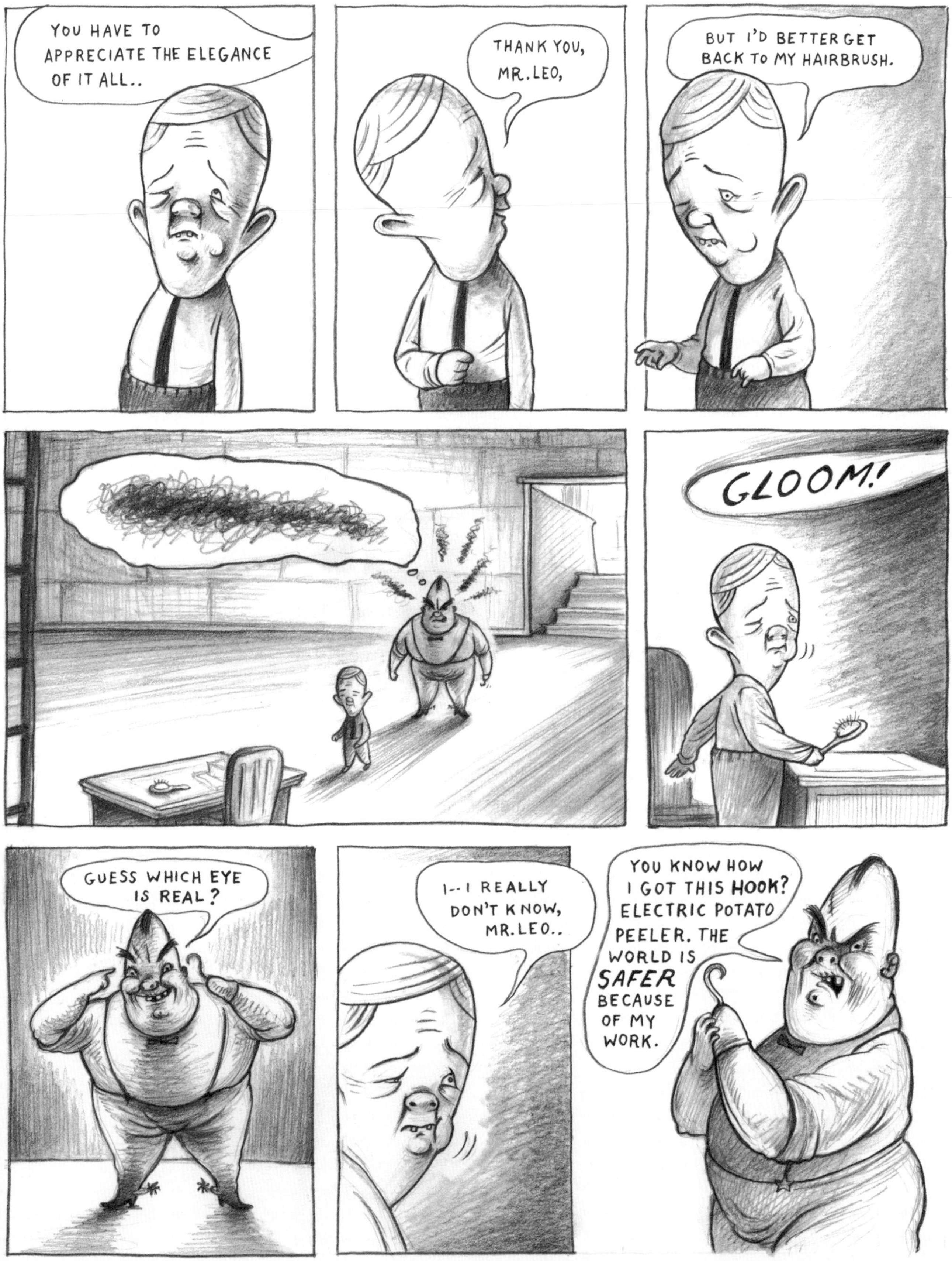
YOU HAVE TO APPRECIATE THE ELEGANCE OF IT ALL..
THANK YOU, MR. LEO,
BUT I'D BETTER GET BACK TO MY HAIRBRUSH.
GLOOM!
GUESS WHICH EYE IS REAL?
I-- I REALLY DON'T KNOW, MR. LEO..
YOU KNOW HOW I GOT THIS HOOK? ELECTRIC POTATO PEELER. THE WORLD IS SAFER BECAUSE OF MY WORK.

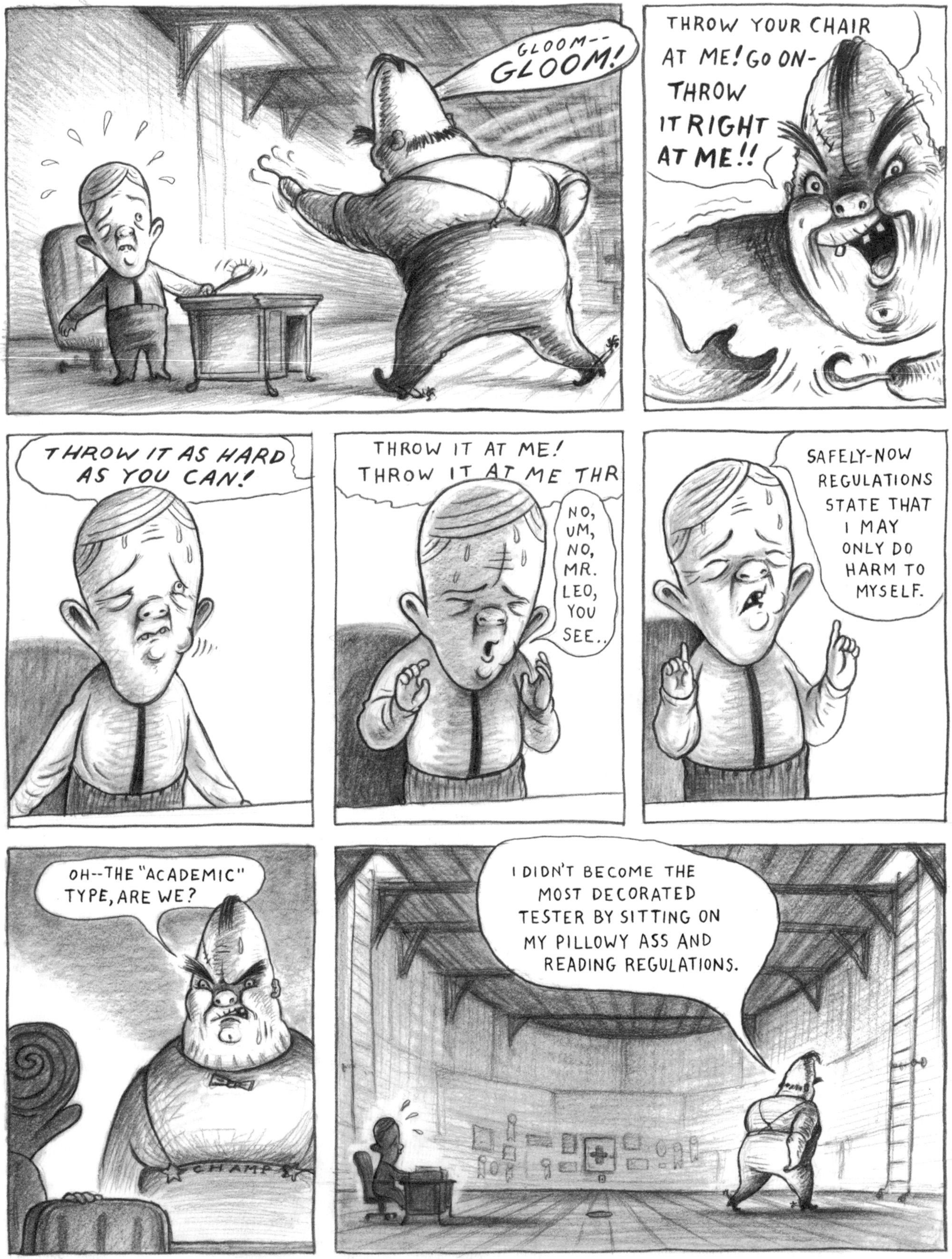
GLOOM--
GLOOM!
THROW YOUR CHAIR AT ME! GO ON- THROW IT RIGHT AT ME!!
THROW IT AS HARD AS YOU CAN!
THROW IT AT ME! THROW IT AT ME THR
NO, UM, NO, MR. LEO, YOU SEE..
SAFELY-NOW REGULATIONS STATE THAT I MAY ONLY DO HARM TO MYSELF.
OH--THE "ACADEMIC" TYPE, ARE WE?
CHAMP
I DIDN'T BECOME THE MOST DECORATED TESTER BY SITTING ON MY PILLOWY ASS AND READING REGULATIONS.

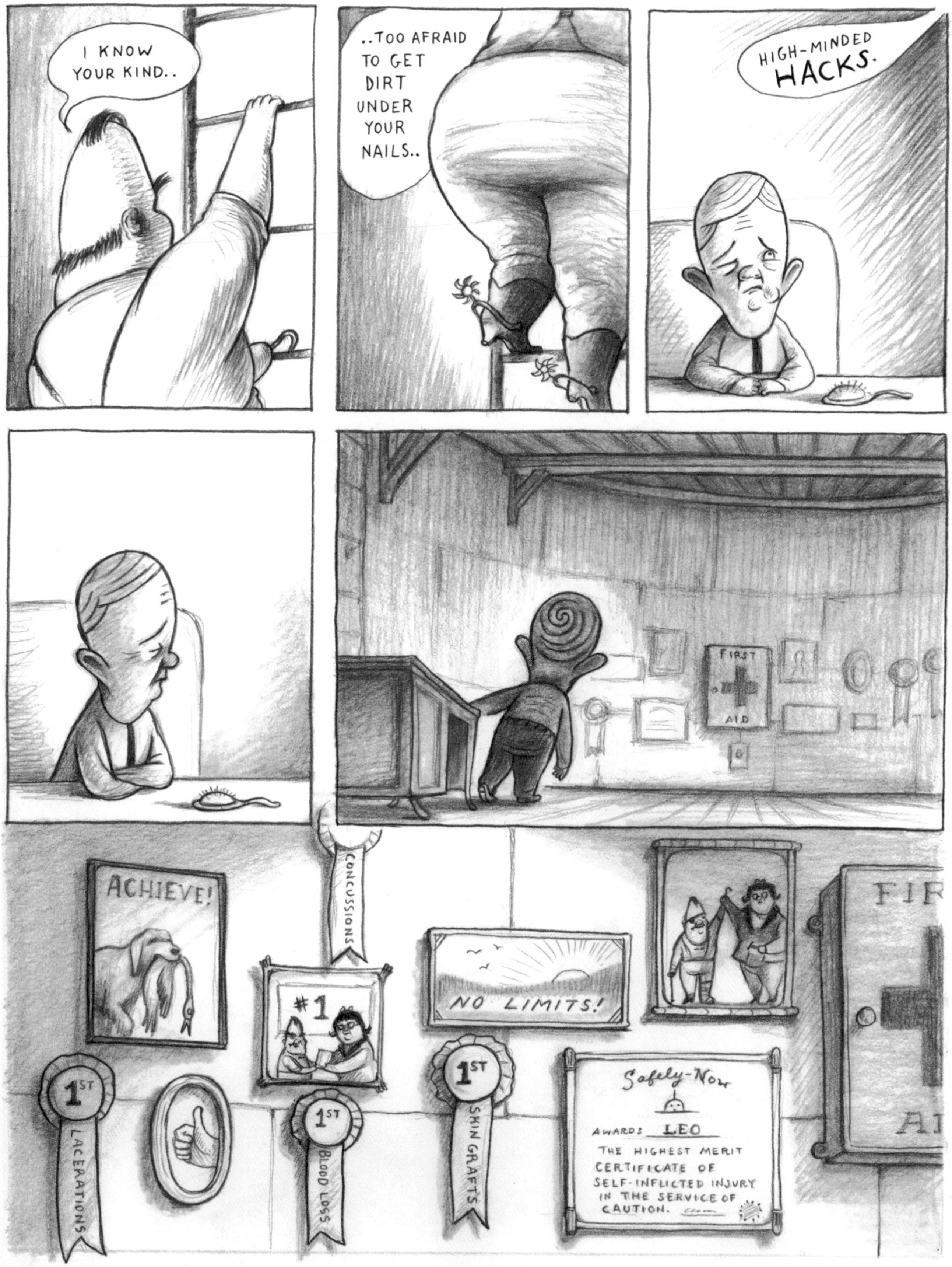
I KNOW YOUR KIND..
..TOO AFRAID TO GET DIRT UNDER YOUR NAILS..
HIGH-MINDED HACKS.
FIRST AID
ACHIEVE!
CONCUSSIONS
#1
NO LIMITS!
FIR
AI
1ST
LACERATIONS
1ST
BLOOD LOSS
1ST
SKIN GRAFTS
Safety-Now
AWARDS LEO
THE HIGHEST MERIT CERTIFICATE OF SELF-INFLICTED INJURY IN THE SERVICE OF CAUTION.

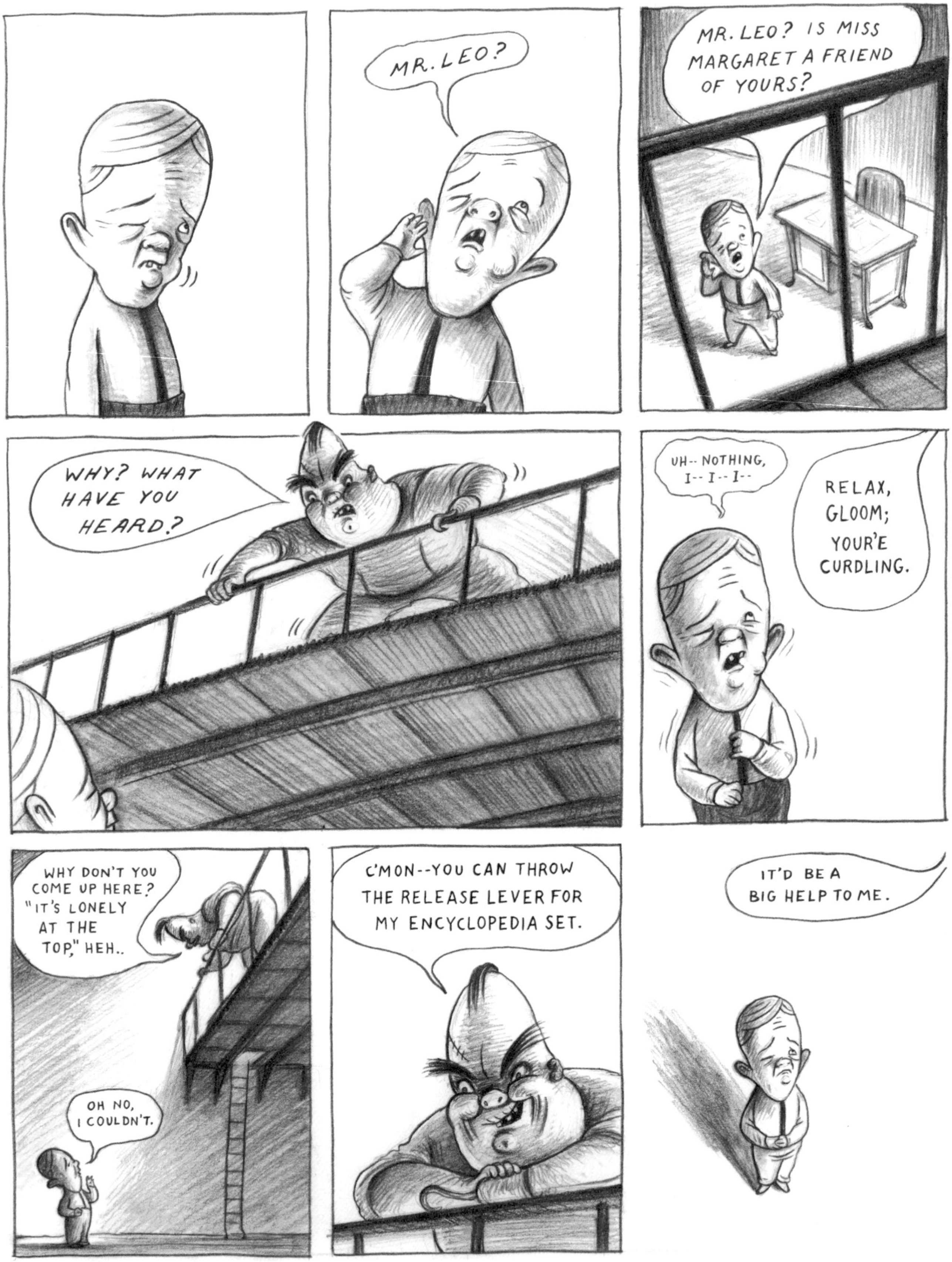
MR. LEO?
MR. LEO? IS MISS MARGARET A FRIEND OF YOURS?
WHY? WHAT HAVE YOU HEARD?
UH-- NOTHING, I-- I-- I--
RELAX, GLOOM; YOUR'E CURDLING.
WHY DON'T YOU COME UP HERE? "IT'S LONELY AT THE TOP," HEH..
OH NO, I COULDN'T.
C'MON--YOU CAN THROW THE RELEASE LEVER FOR MY ENCYCLOPEDIA SET.
IT'D BE A BIG HELP TO ME.

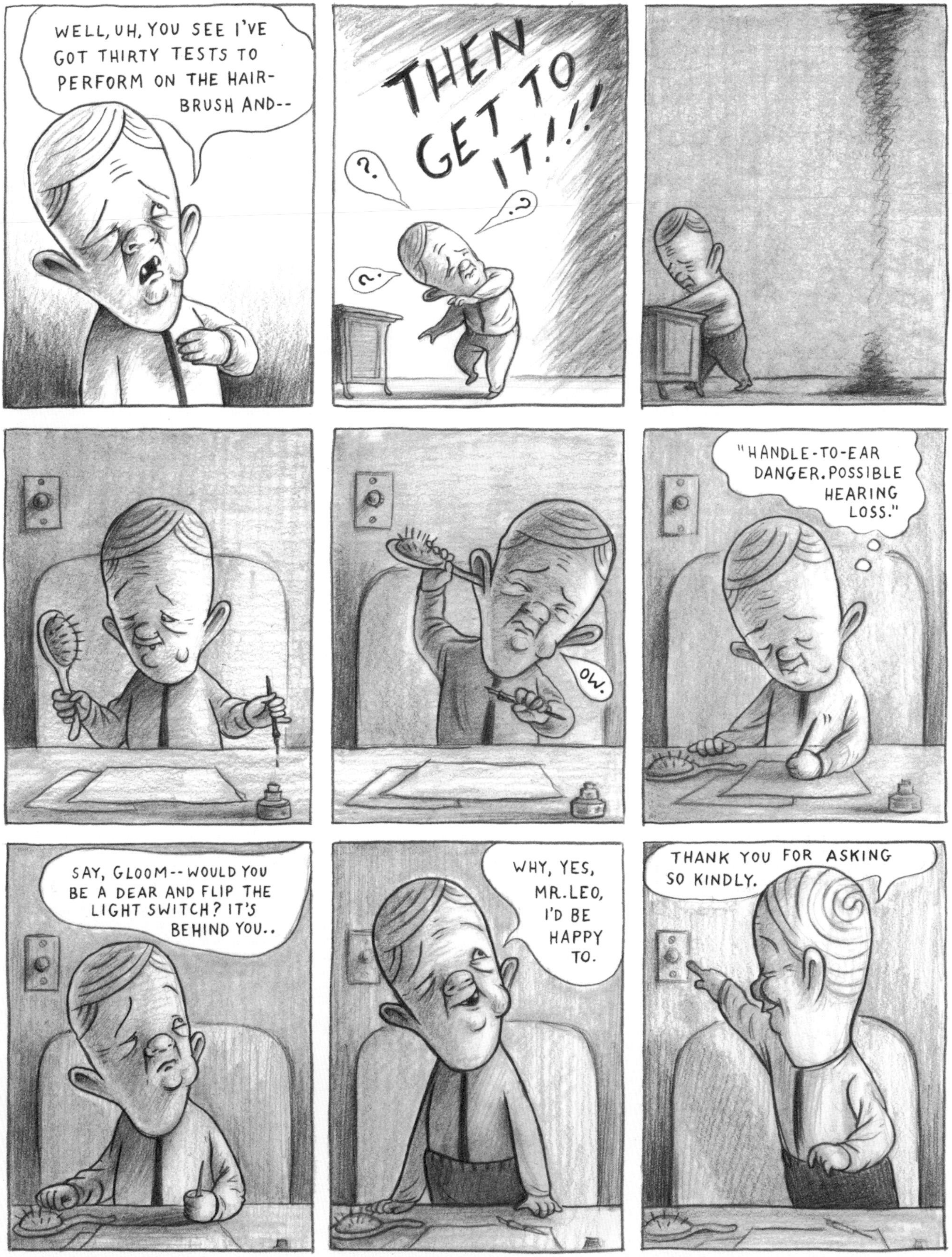
WELL, UH, YOU SEE I'VE GOT THIRTY TESTS TO PERFORM ON THE HAIR-BRUSH AND--
THEN GET TO IT!!!
?
?
?
"HANDLE-TO-EAR DANGER. POSSIBLE HEARING LOSS."
OW.
SAY, GLOOM--WOULD YOU BE A DEAR AND FLIP THE LIGHT SWITCH? IT'S BEHIND YOU..
WHY, YES, MR. LEO, I'D BE HAPPY TO.
THANK YOU FOR ASKING SO KINDLY.

TTHHHWEEEEZZZ ZRRUUUMMM

MMUU MMRRRUR RRMMUUK EEEEZZ

FOOLED YOU! HA HA. THANKS, GLOOM!

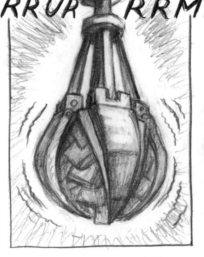

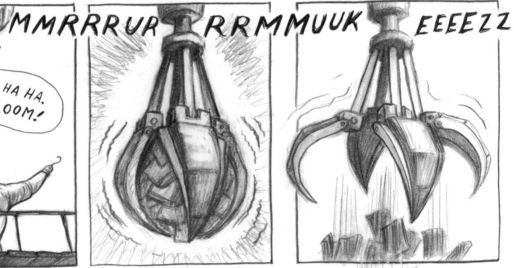

OH!

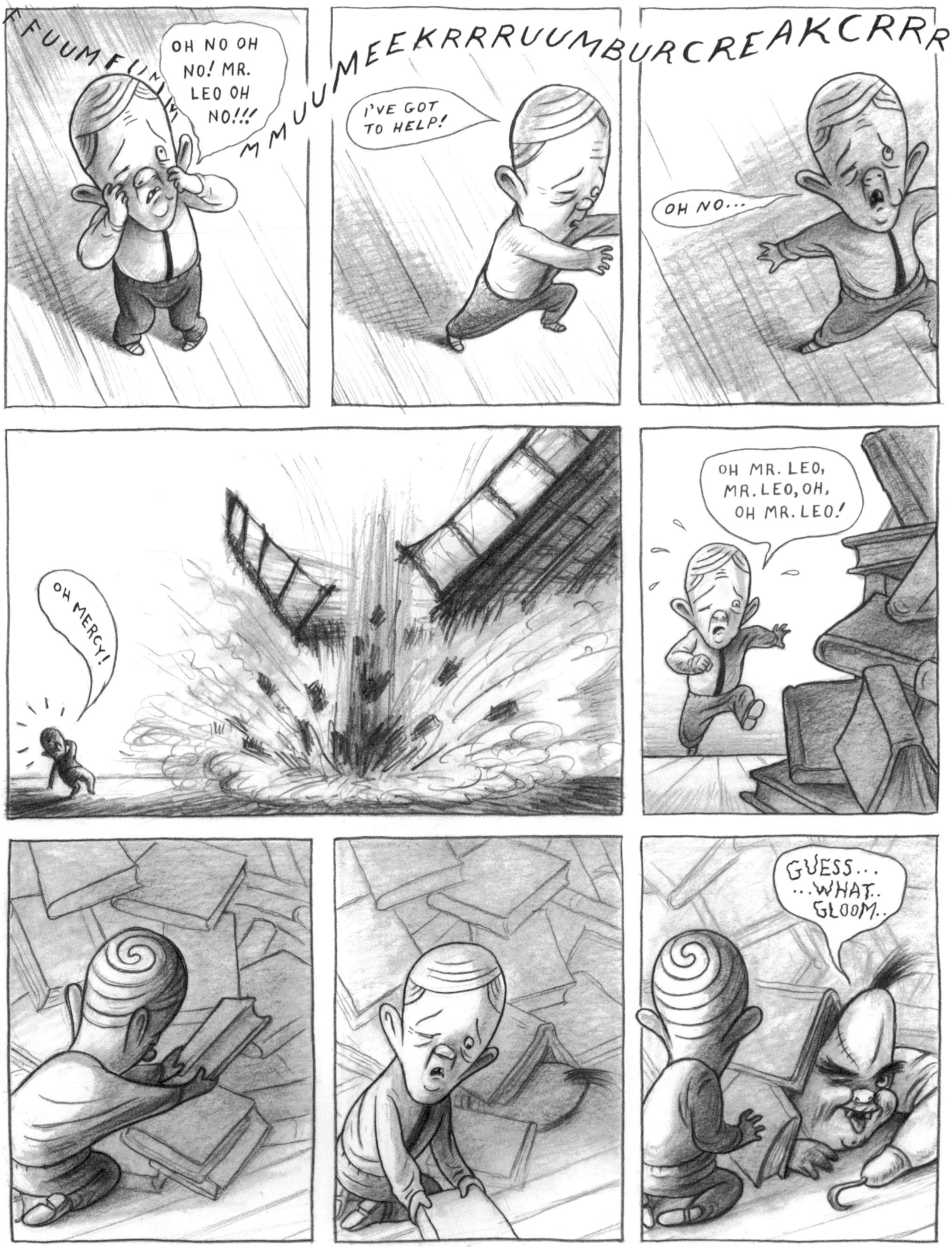
FFUUMF
OH NO OH NO! MR. LEO OH NO!!!
MMUUMEEKRRRUUMBURCREAKCRRR
I'VE GOT TO HELP!
OH NO...
OH MERCY!
OH MR. LEO, MR. LEO, OH, OH MR. LEO!
GUESS... ...WHAT.. GLOOM..

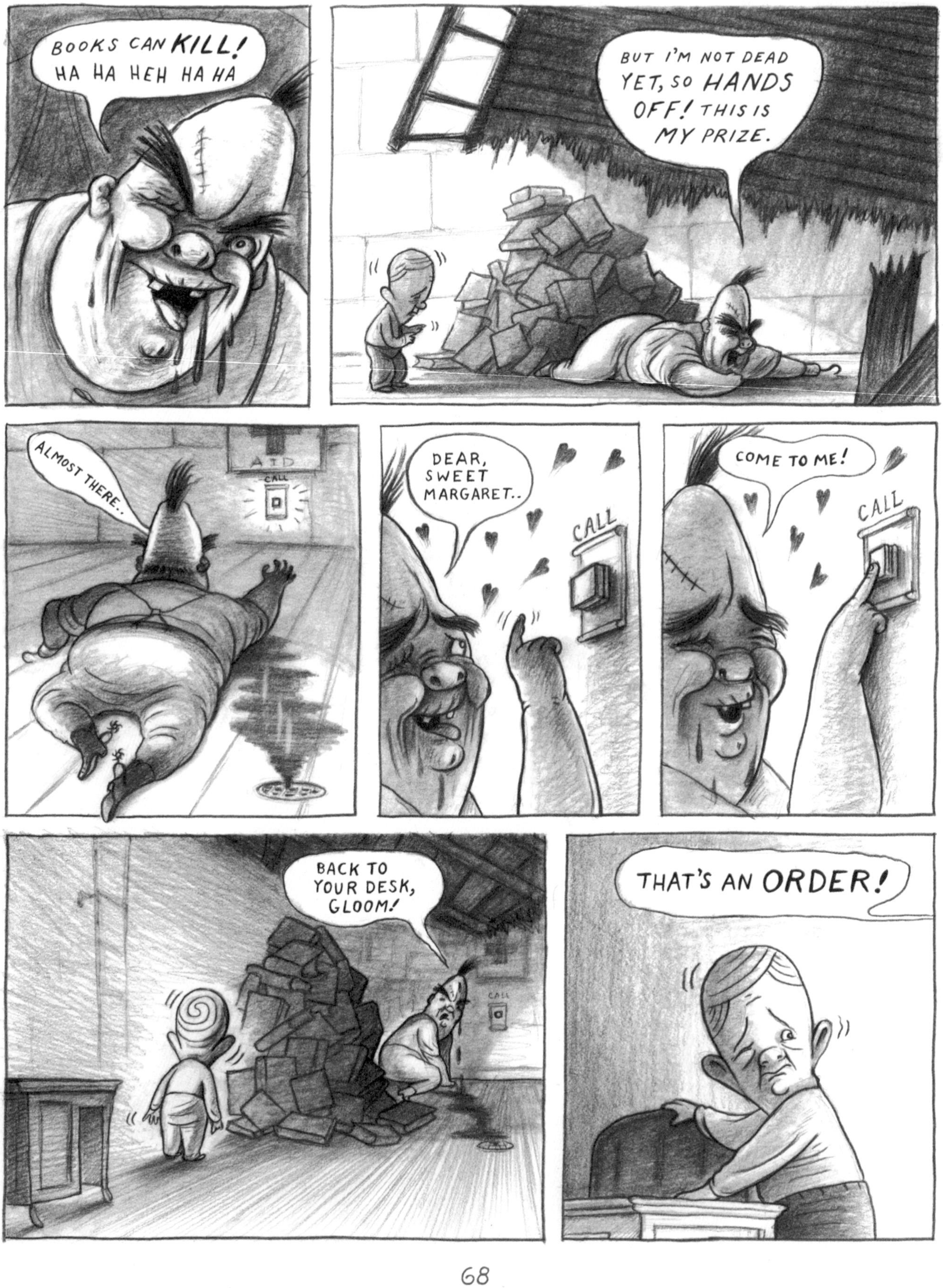

BOOKS CAN KILL! HA HA HEH HA HA
BUT I'M NOT DEAD YET, SO HANDS OFF! THIS IS MY PRIZE.
ALMOST THERE..
AID
CALL
DEAR, SWEET MARGARET..
CALL
COME TO ME!
CALL
BACK TO YOUR DESK, GLOOM!
CALL
THAT'S AN ORDER!

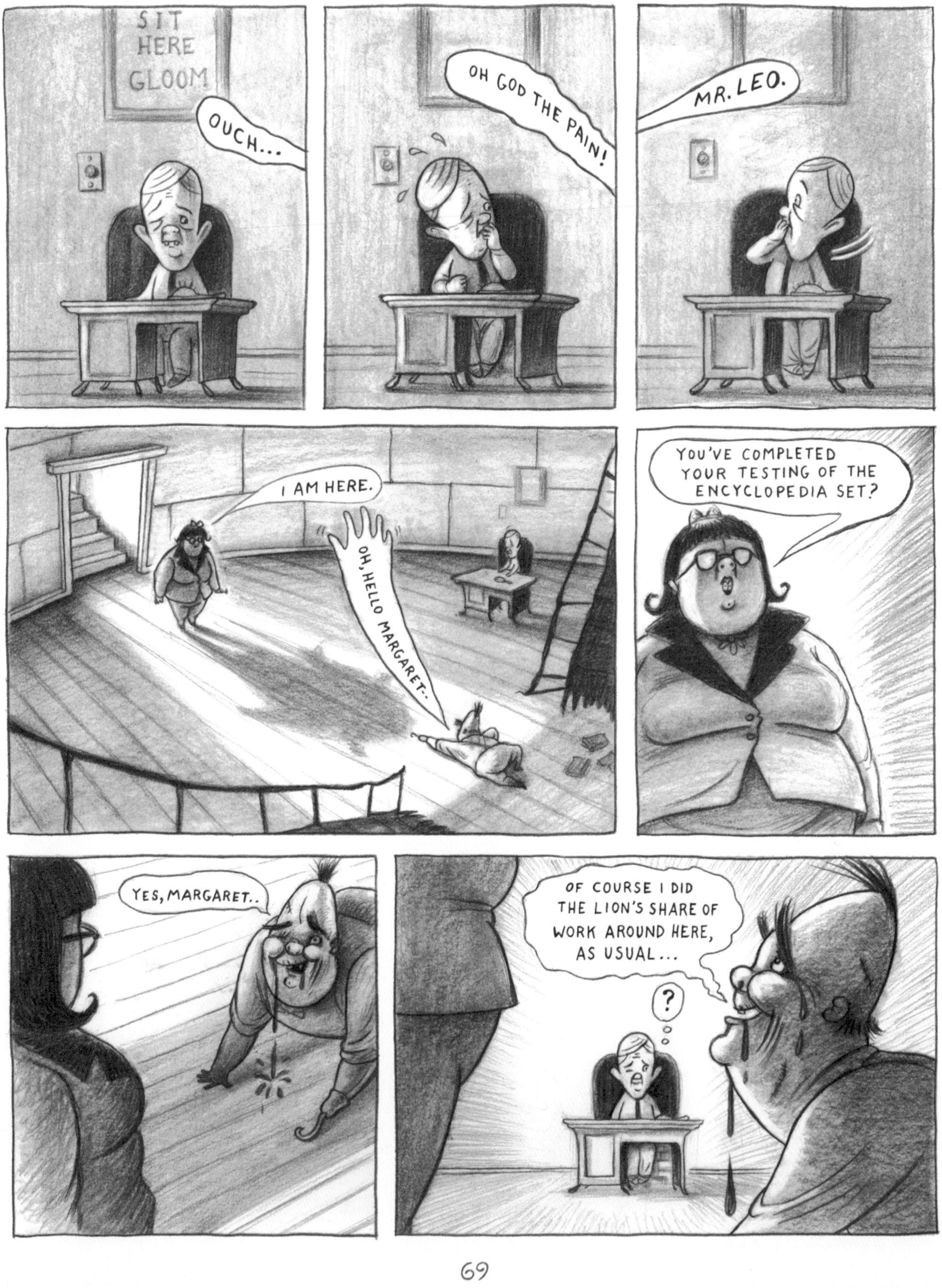
SIT HERE GLOOM
OUCH...
OH GOD THE PAIN!
MR. LEO.
I AM HERE.
OH, HELLO MARGARET..
YOU'VE COMPLETED YOUR TESTING OF THE ENCYCLOPEDIA SET?
YES, MARGARET..
OF COURSE I DID THE LION'S SHARE OF WORK AROUND HERE, AS USUAL...
?

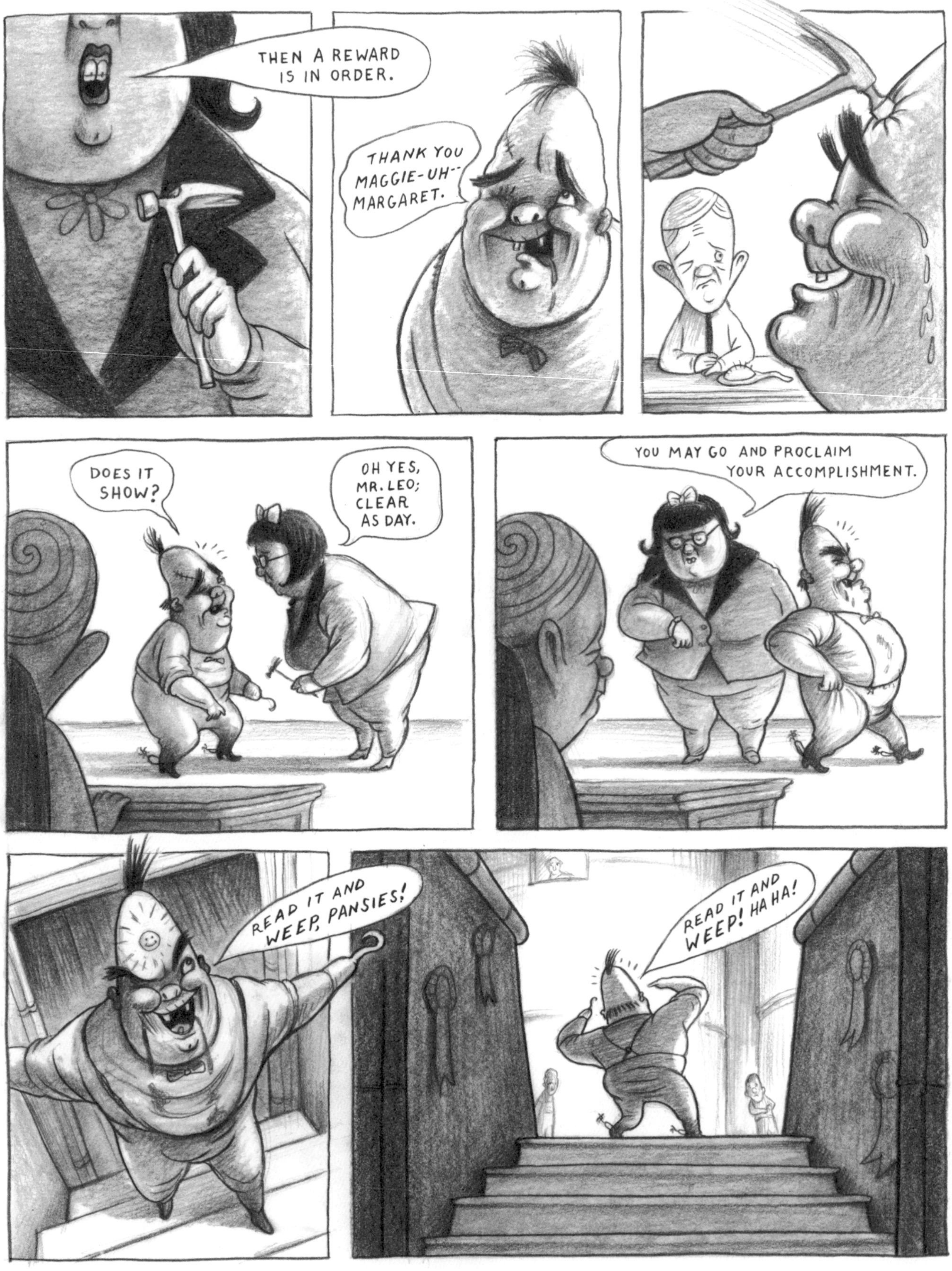

THEN A REWARD IS IN ORDER.
THANK YOU MAGGIE-UH-- MARGARET.
DOES IT SHOW?
OH YES, MR. LEO; CLEAR AS DAY.
YOU MAY GO AND PROCLAIM YOUR ACCOMPLISHMENT.
READ IT AND WEEP, PANSIES!
READ IT AND WEEP! HA HA!

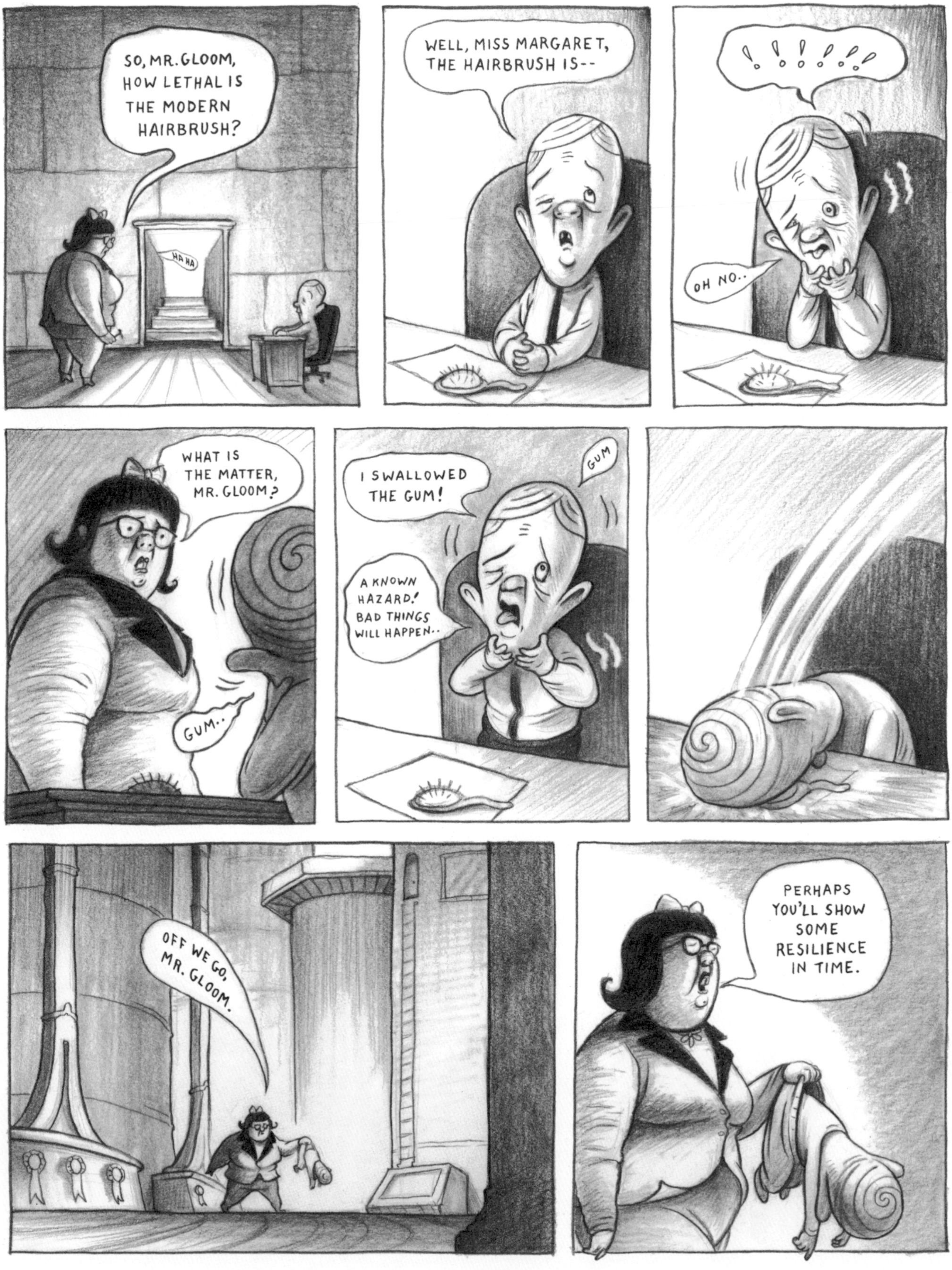
SO, MR. GLOOM, HOW LETHAL IS THE MODERN HAIRBRUSH?
HA HA
WELL, MISS MARGARET, THE HAIRBRUSH IS--
! ! ! ! ! ! !
OH NO..
WHAT IS THE MATTER, MR. GLOOM?
GUM..
I SWALLOWED THE GUM!
GUM
A KNOWN HAZARD! BAD THINGS WILL HAPPEN..
OFF WE GO, MR. GLOOM.
PERHAPS YOU'LL SHOW SOME RESILIENCE IN TIME.

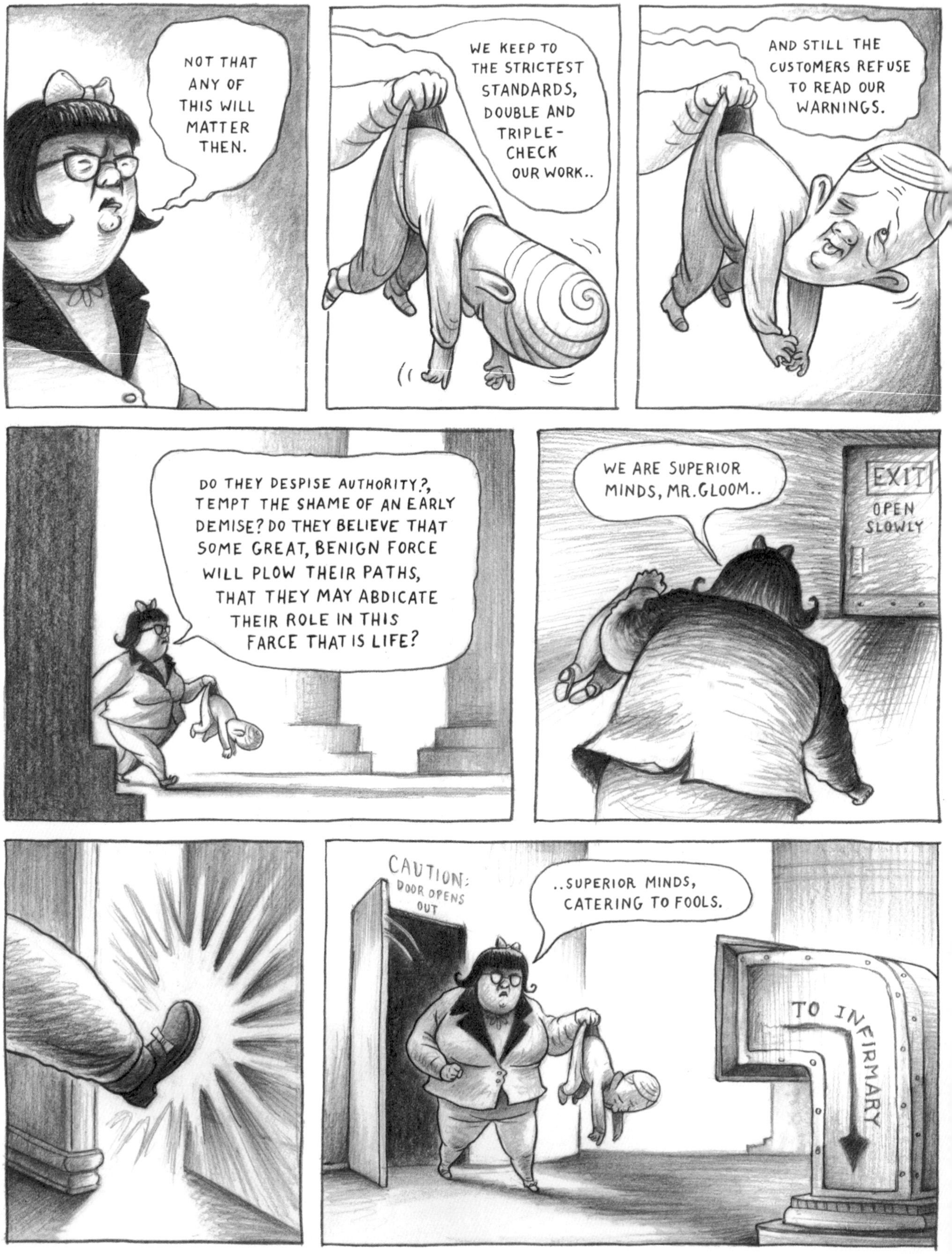
NOT THAT ANY OF THIS WILL MATTER THEN.
WE KEEP TO THE STRICTEST STANDARDS, DOUBLE AND TRIPLE-CHECK OUR WORK..
AND STILL THE CUSTOMERS REFUSE TO READ OUR WARNINGS.
DO THEY DESPISE AUTHORITY.?, TEMPT THE SHAME OF AN EARLY DEMISE? DO THEY BELIEVE THAT SOME GREAT, BENIGN FORCE WILL PLOW THEIR PATHS, THAT THEY MAY ABDICATE THEIR ROLE IN THIS FARCE THAT IS LIFE?
WE ARE SUPERIOR MINDS, MR. GLOOM..
EXIT
OPEN SLOWLY
CAUTION: DOOR OPENS OUT
..SUPERIOR MINDS, CATERING TO FOOLS.
TO INFIRMARY

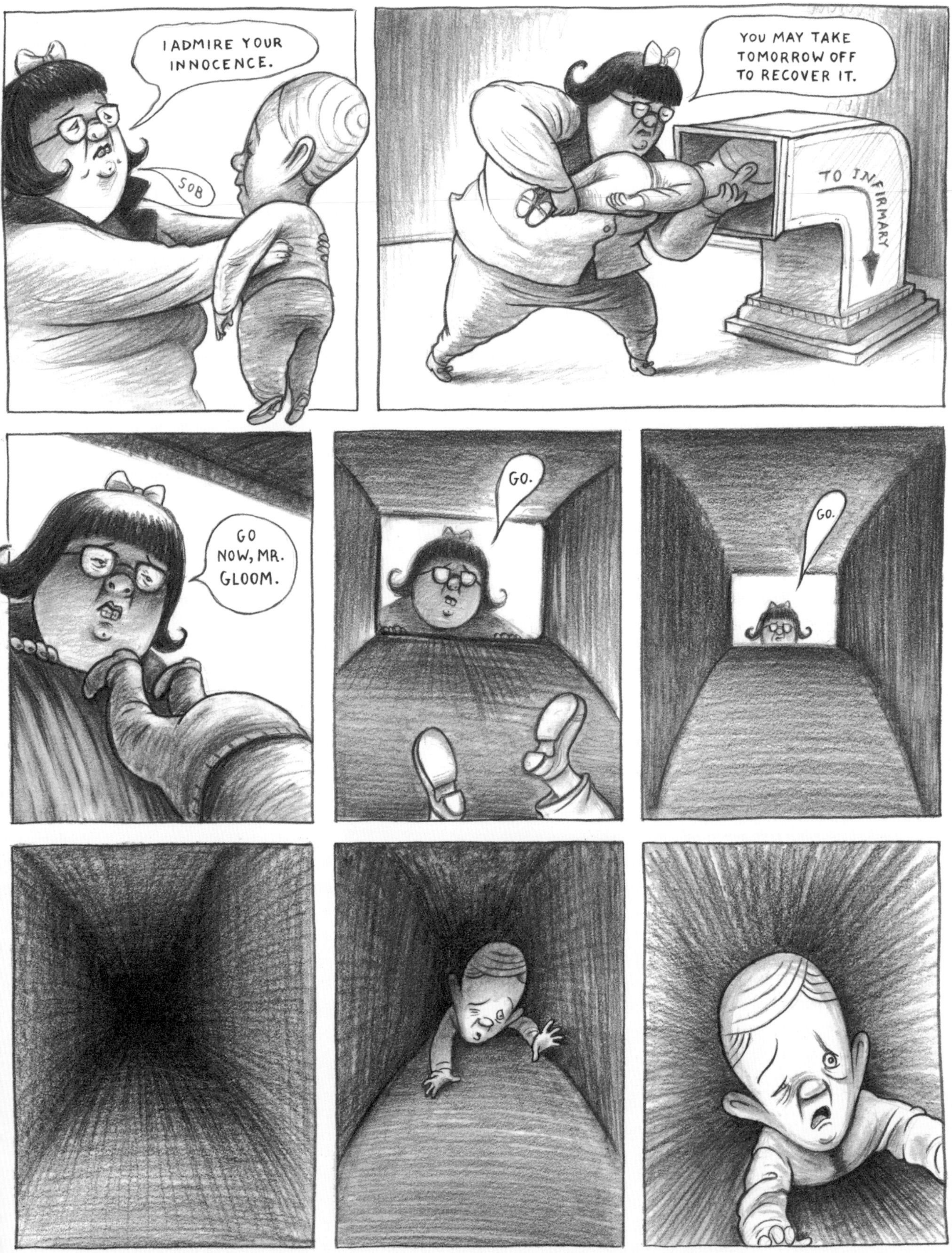
I ADMIRE YOUR INNOCENCE.
SOB
YOU MAY TAKE TOMORROW OFF TO RECOVER IT.
TO INFIRMARY
GO NOW, MR. GLOOM.
GO.
GO.

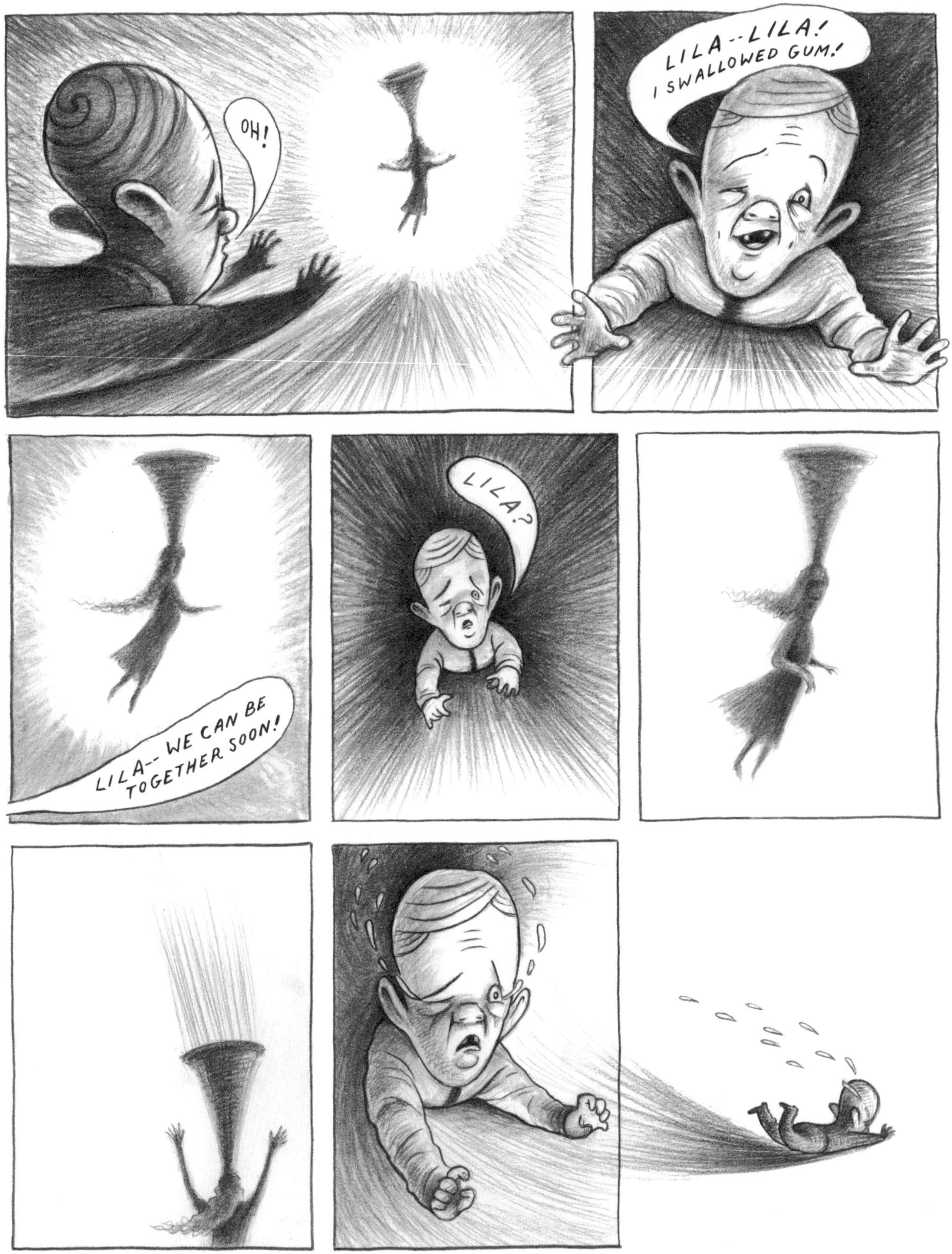
OH!
LILA--LILA! I SWALLOWED GUM!
LILA-- WE CAN BE TOGETHER SOON!
LILA?

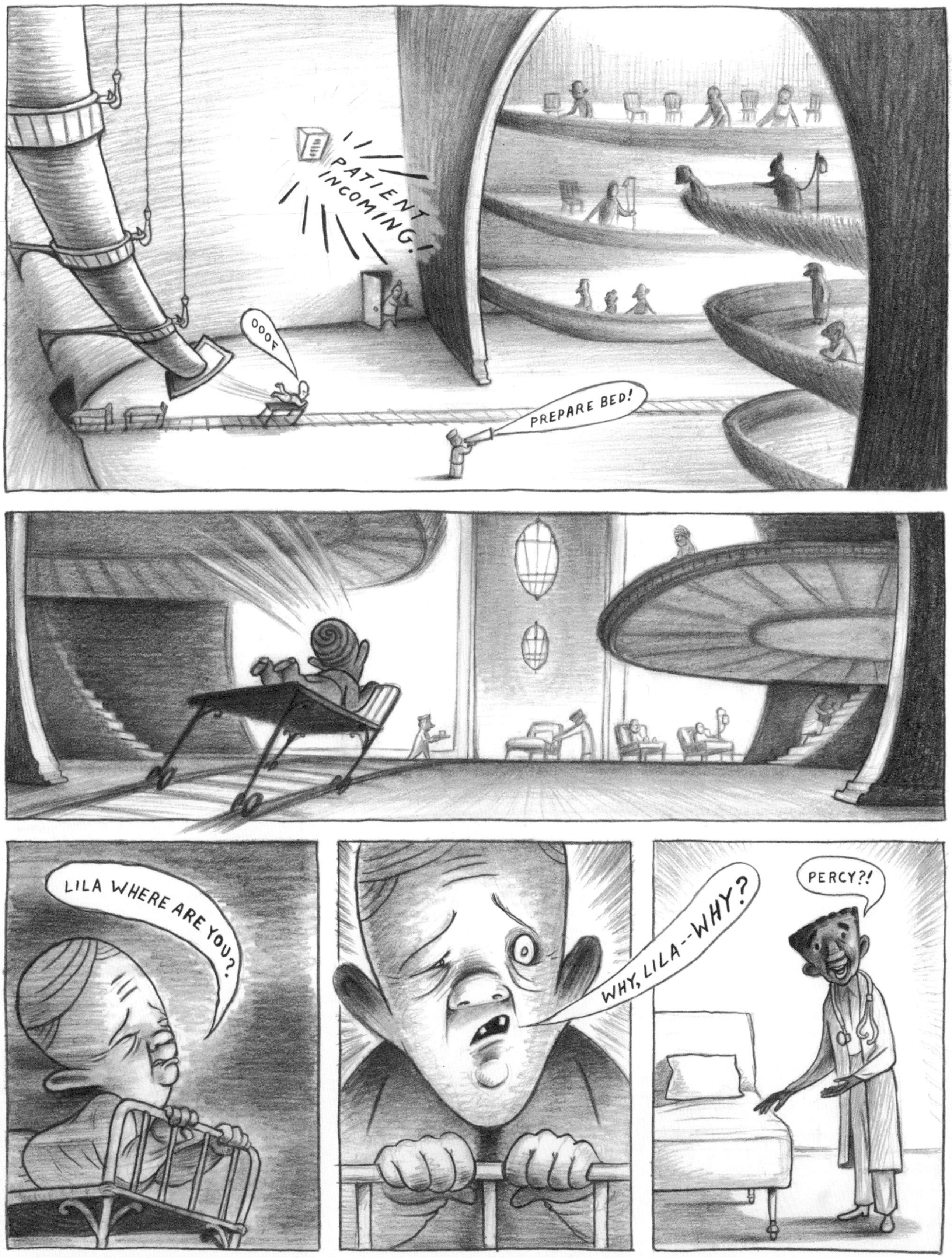
PATIENT INCOMING!
OOOF
PREPARE BED!
LILA WHERE ARE YOU?
WHY, LILA--WHY?
PERCY?!

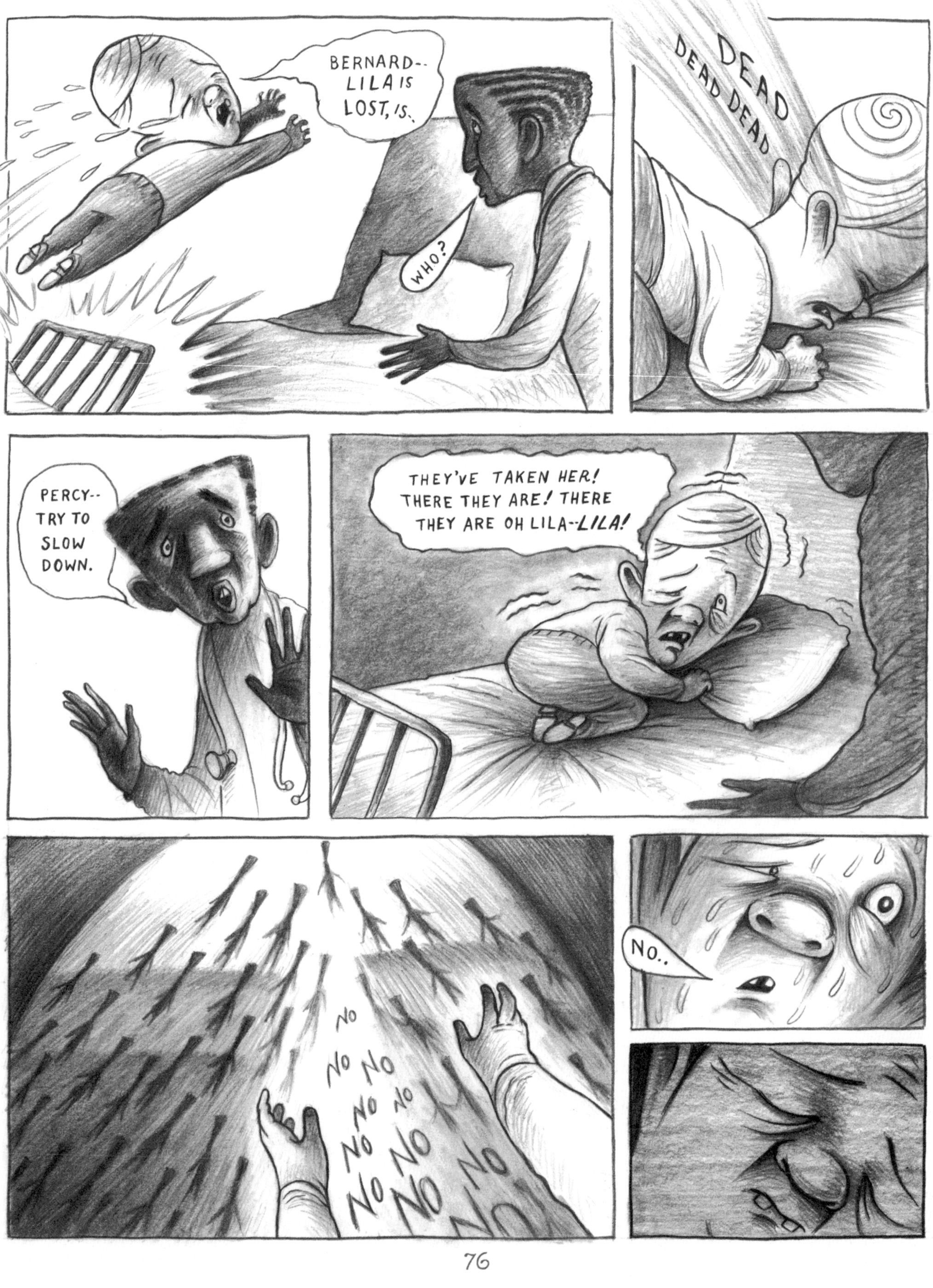
BERNARD--
LILA IS
LOST, IS..
WHO?
DEAD
DEAD DEAD
PERCY--
TRY TO
SLOW
DOWN.
THEY'VE TAKEN HER!
THERE THEY ARE! THERE
THEY ARE OH LILA--LILA!
NO
NO NO
NO NO
NO NO
NO NO NO
NO..

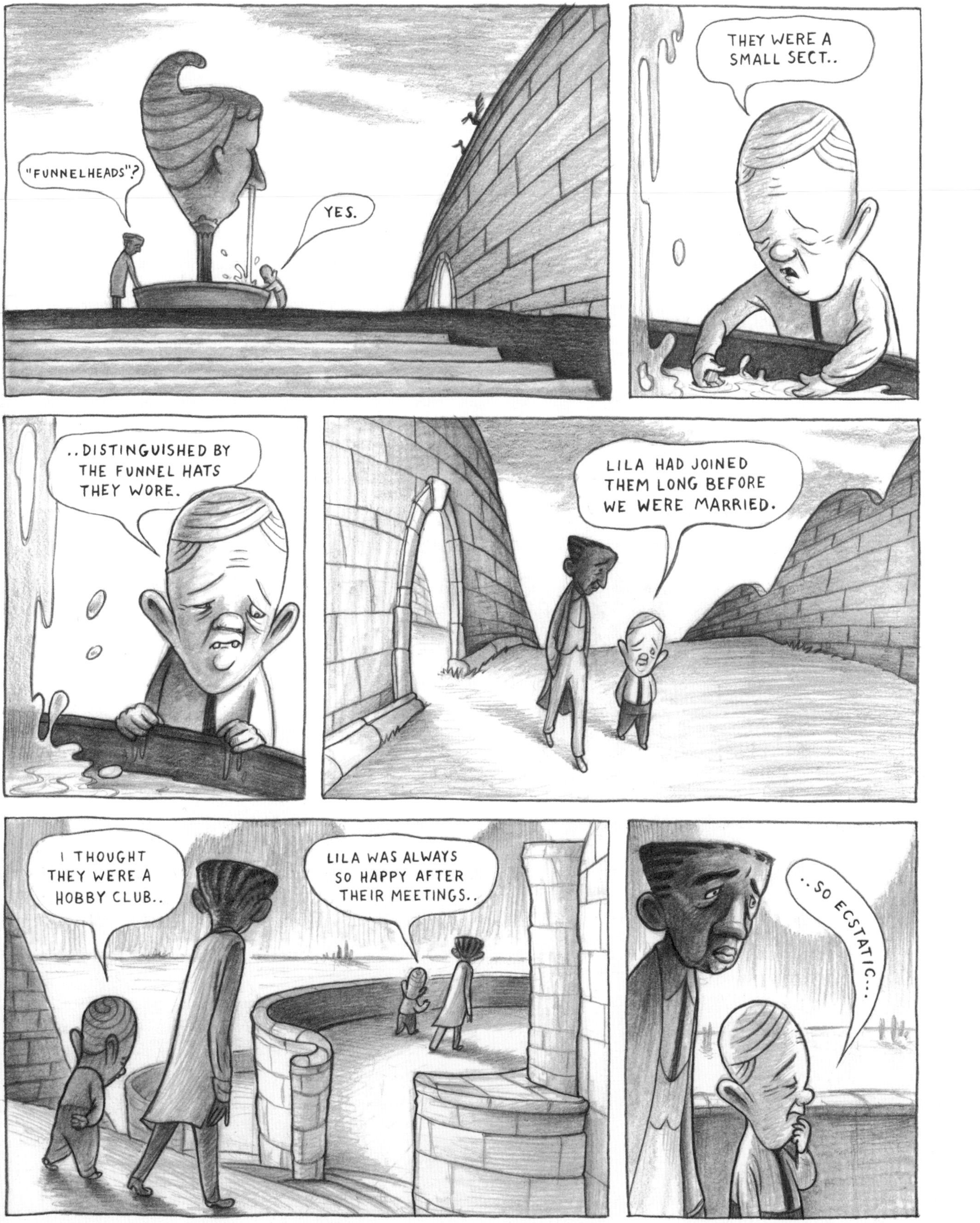
"FUNNELHEADS"?
YES.
THEY WERE A SMALL SECT..
..DISTINGUISHED BY THE FUNNEL HATS THEY WORE.
LILA HAD JOINED THEM LONG BEFORE WE WERE MARRIED.
I THOUGHT THEY WERE A HOBBY CLUB..
LILA WAS ALWAYS SO HAPPY AFTER THEIR MEETINGS..
..SO ECSTATIC...

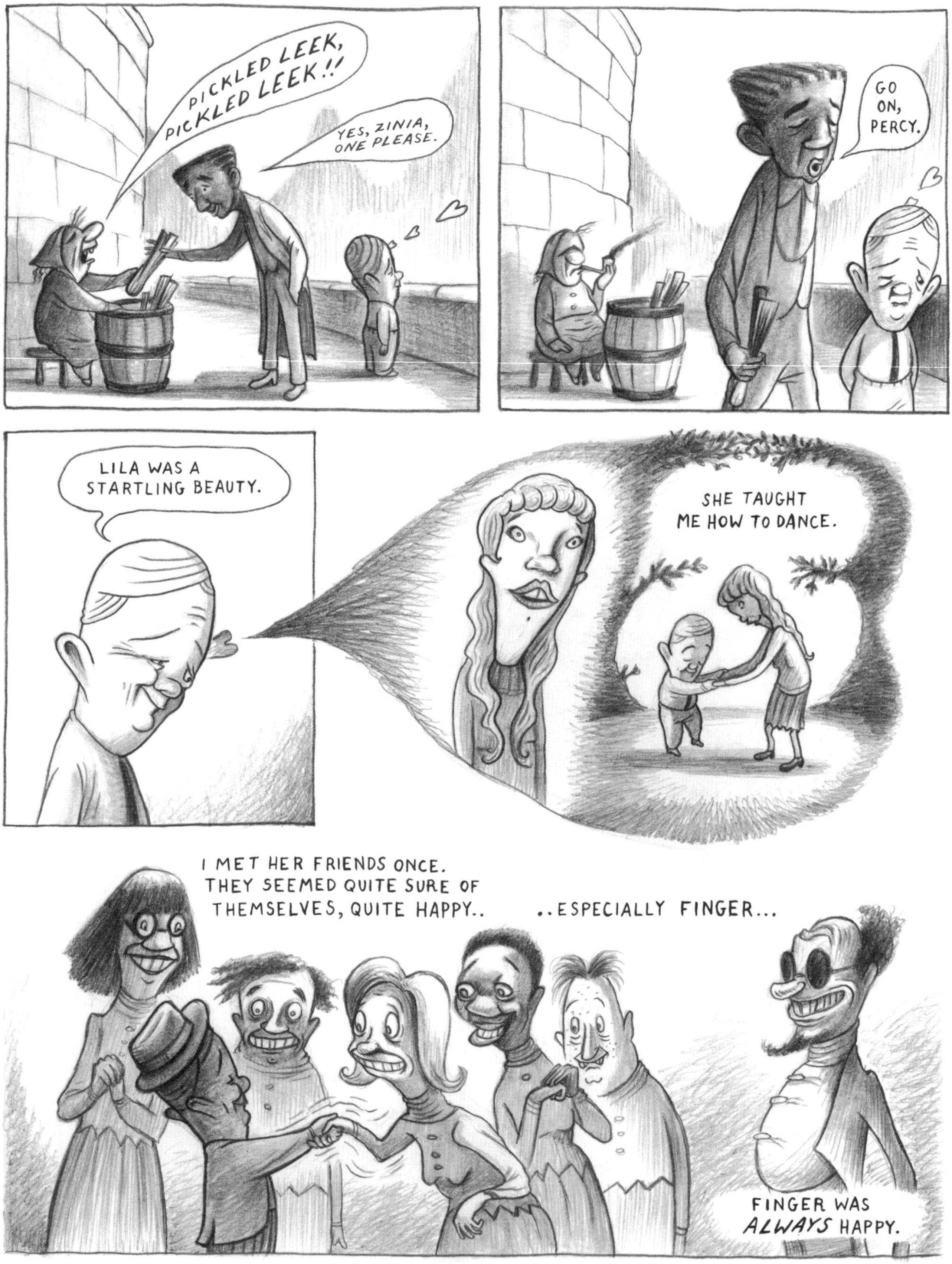
PICKLED LEEK, PICKLED LEEK!!
YES, ZINIA, ONE PLEASE.
GO ON, PERCY.
LILA WAS A STARTLING BEAUTY.
SHE TAUGHT ME HOW TO DANCE.
I MET HER FRIENDS ONCE. THEY SEEMED QUITE SURE OF THEMSELVES, QUITE HAPPY..
..ESPECIALLY FINGER...
FINGER WAS *ALWAYS* HAPPY.

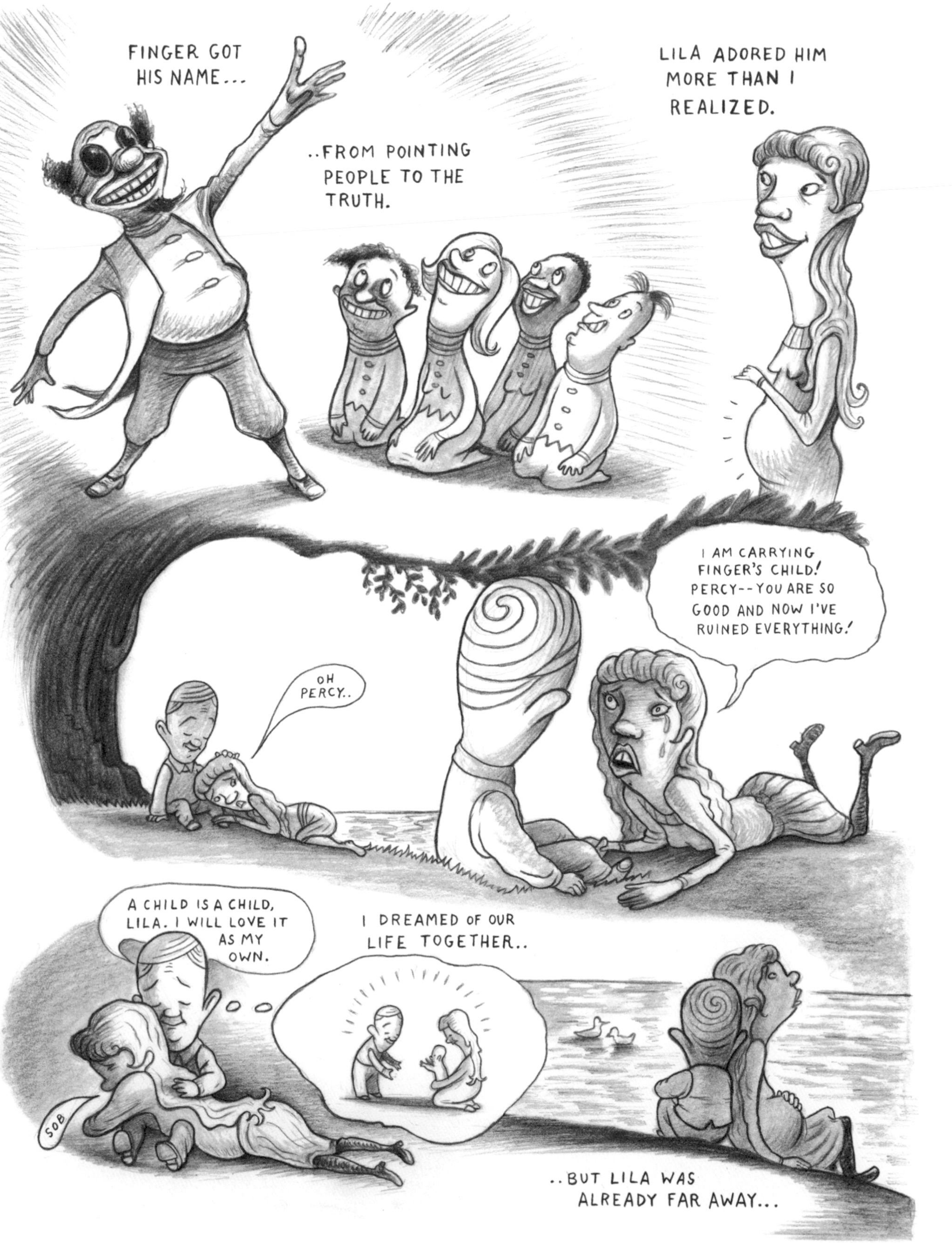

FINGER GOT HIS NAME...
..FROM POINTING PEOPLE TO THE TRUTH.
LILA ADORED HIM MORE THAN I REALIZED.
OH PERCY..
I AM CARRYING FINGER'S CHILD! PERCY--YOU ARE SO GOOD AND NOW I'VE RUINED EVERYTHING!
A CHILD IS A CHILD, LILA. I WILL LOVE IT AS MY OWN.
SOB
I DREAMED OF OUR LIFE TOGETHER..
..BUT LILA WAS ALREADY FAR AWAY...

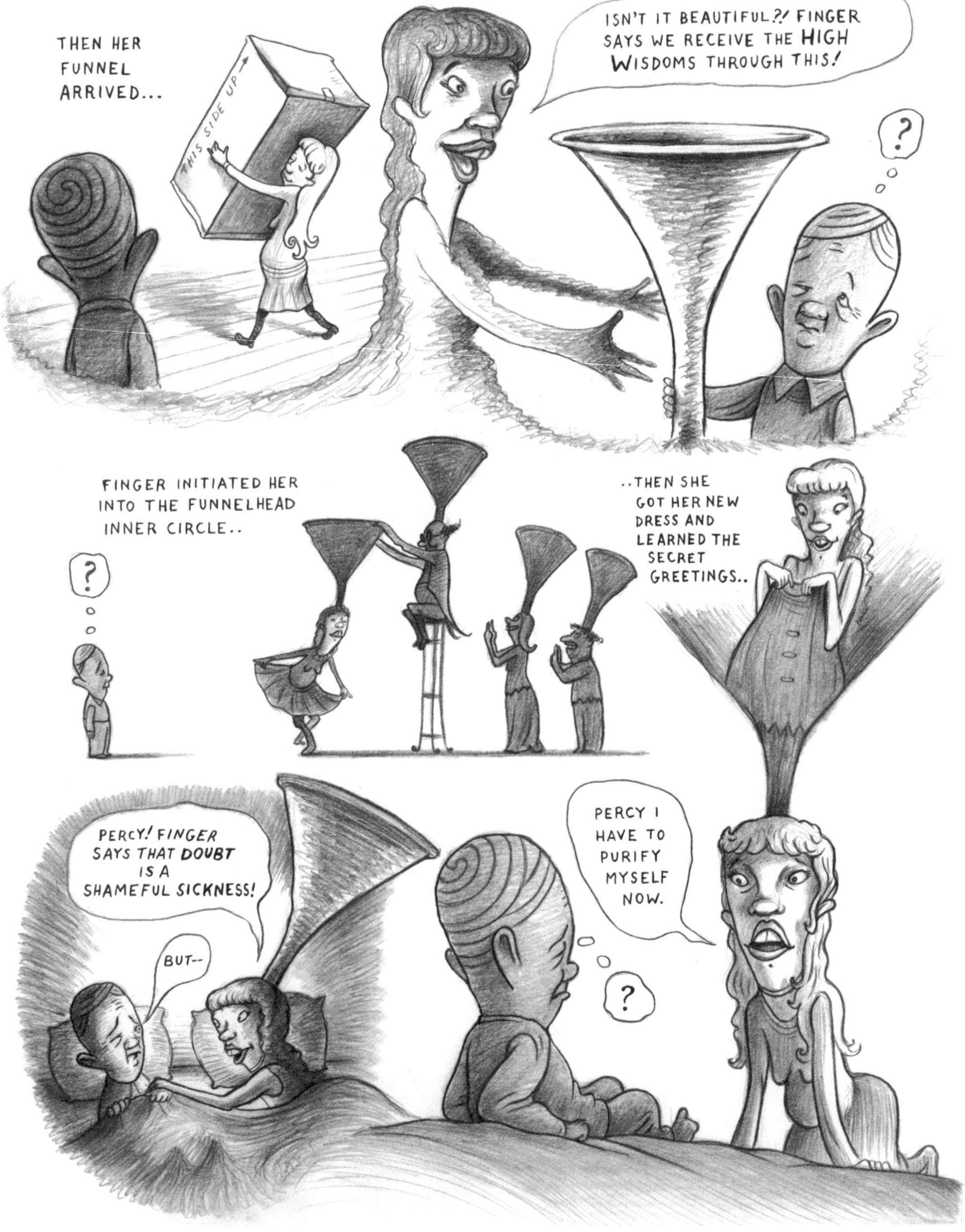
THEN HER FUNNEL ARRIVED...
THIS SIDE UP
ISN'T IT BEAUTIFUL?! FINGER SAYS WE RECEIVE THE HIGH WISDOMS THROUGH THIS!
?
FINGER INITIATED HER INTO THE FUNNELHEAD INNER CIRCLE..
?
..THEN SHE GOT HER NEW DRESS AND LEARNED THE SECRET GREETINGS..
PERCY! FINGER SAYS THAT DOUBT IS A SHAMEFUL SICKNESS!
BUT--
PERCY I HAVE TO PURIFY MYSELF NOW.
?

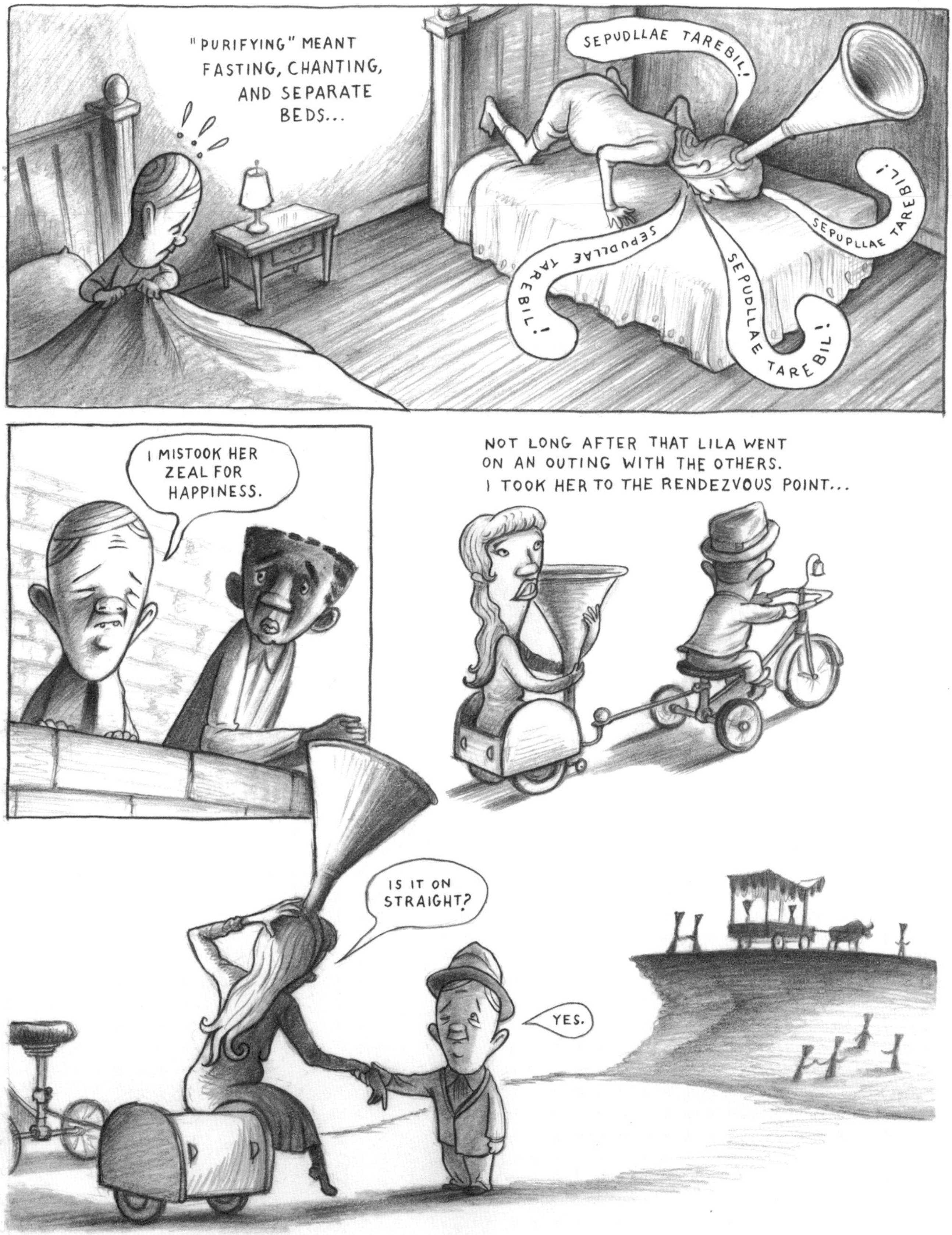
"PURIFYING" MEANT FASTING, CHANTING, AND SEPARATE BEDS...
SEPUDLLAE TAREBIL!
SEPUPLLAE TAREBIL!
SEPUDLLAE TAREBIL!
SEPUDLLAE TAREBIL!
I MISTOOK HER ZEAL FOR HAPPINESS.
NOT LONG AFTER THAT LILA WENT ON AN OUTING WITH THE OTHERS. I TOOK HER TO THE RENDEZVOUS POINT...
IS IT ON STRAIGHT?
YES.

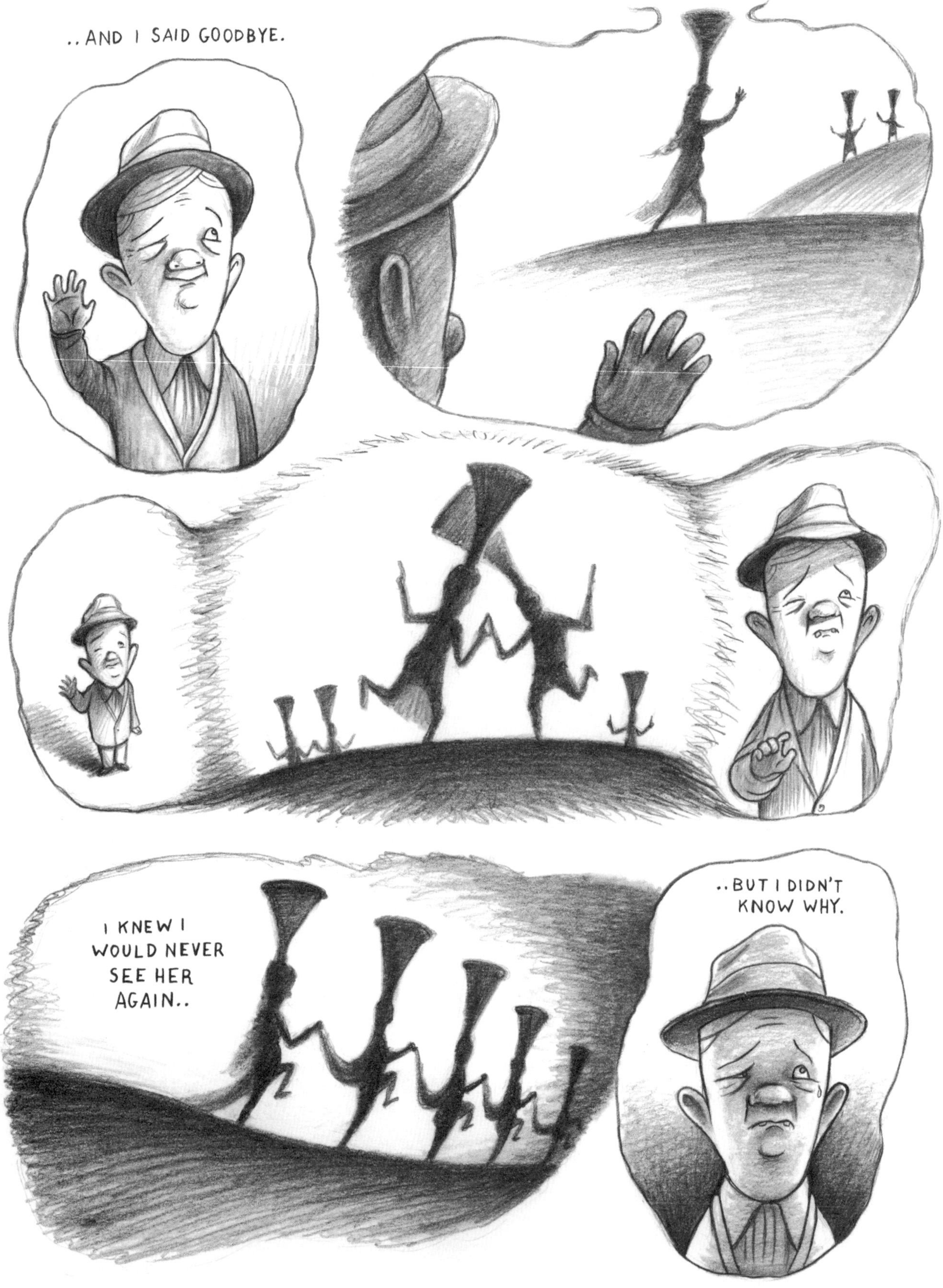
..AND I SAID GOODBYE.
I KNEW I WOULD NEVER SEE HER AGAIN..
..BUT I DIDN'T KNOW WHY.

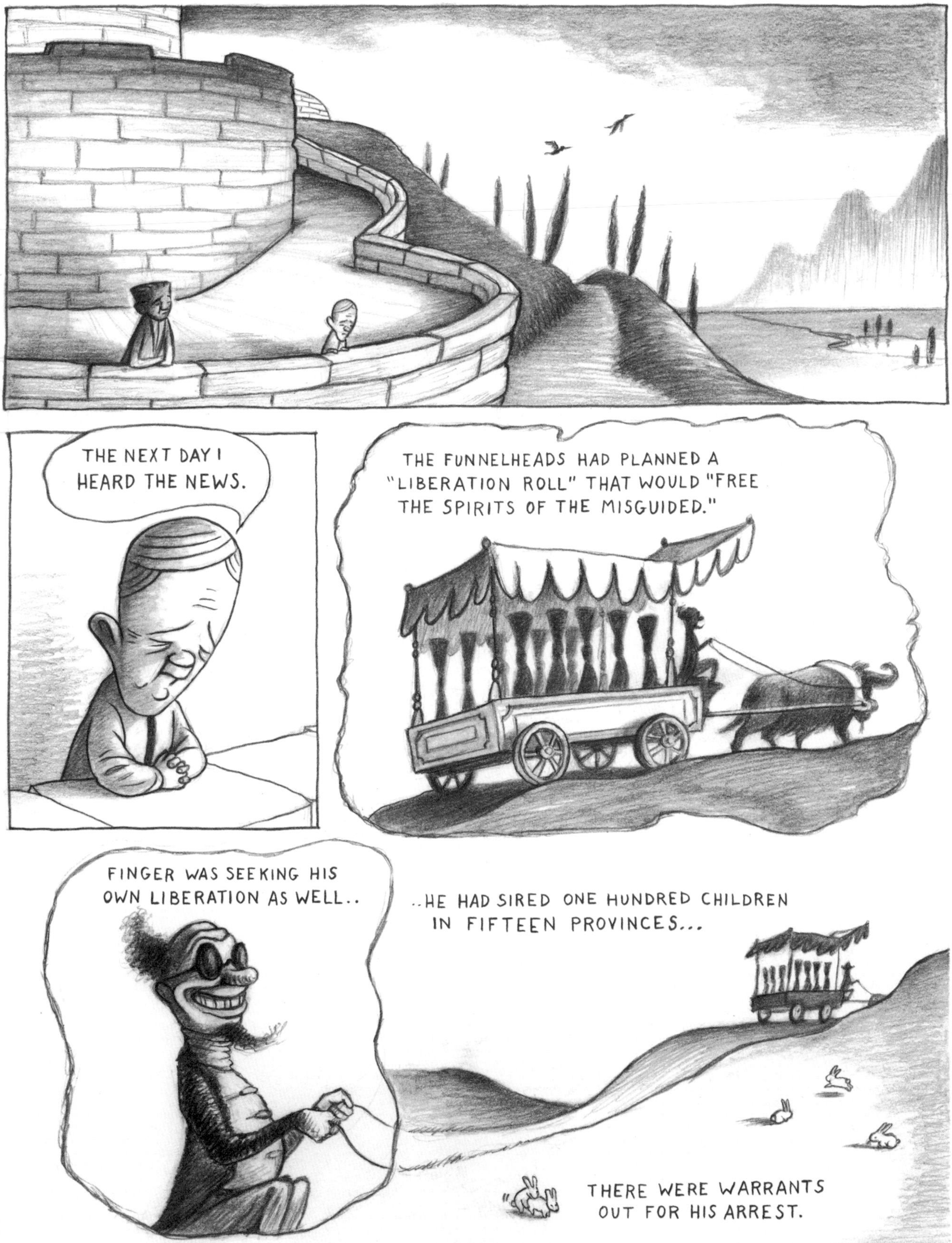
THE NEXT DAY I HEARD THE NEWS.
THE FUNNELHEADS HAD PLANNED A "LIBERATION ROLL" THAT WOULD "FREE THE SPIRITS OF THE MISGUIDED."
FINGER WAS SEEKING HIS OWN LIBERATION AS WELL..
..HE HAD SIRED ONE HUNDRED CHILDREN IN FIFTEEN PROVINCES...
THERE WERE WARRANTS OUT FOR HIS ARREST.

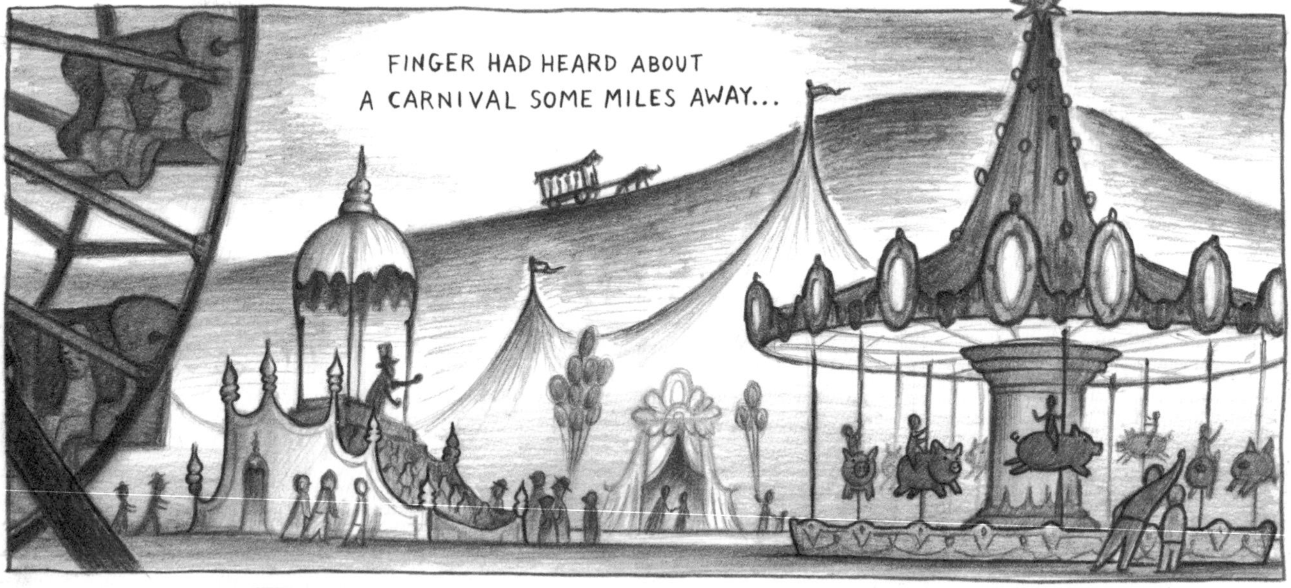
FINGER HAD HEARD ABOUT
A CARNIVAL SOME MILES AWAY...

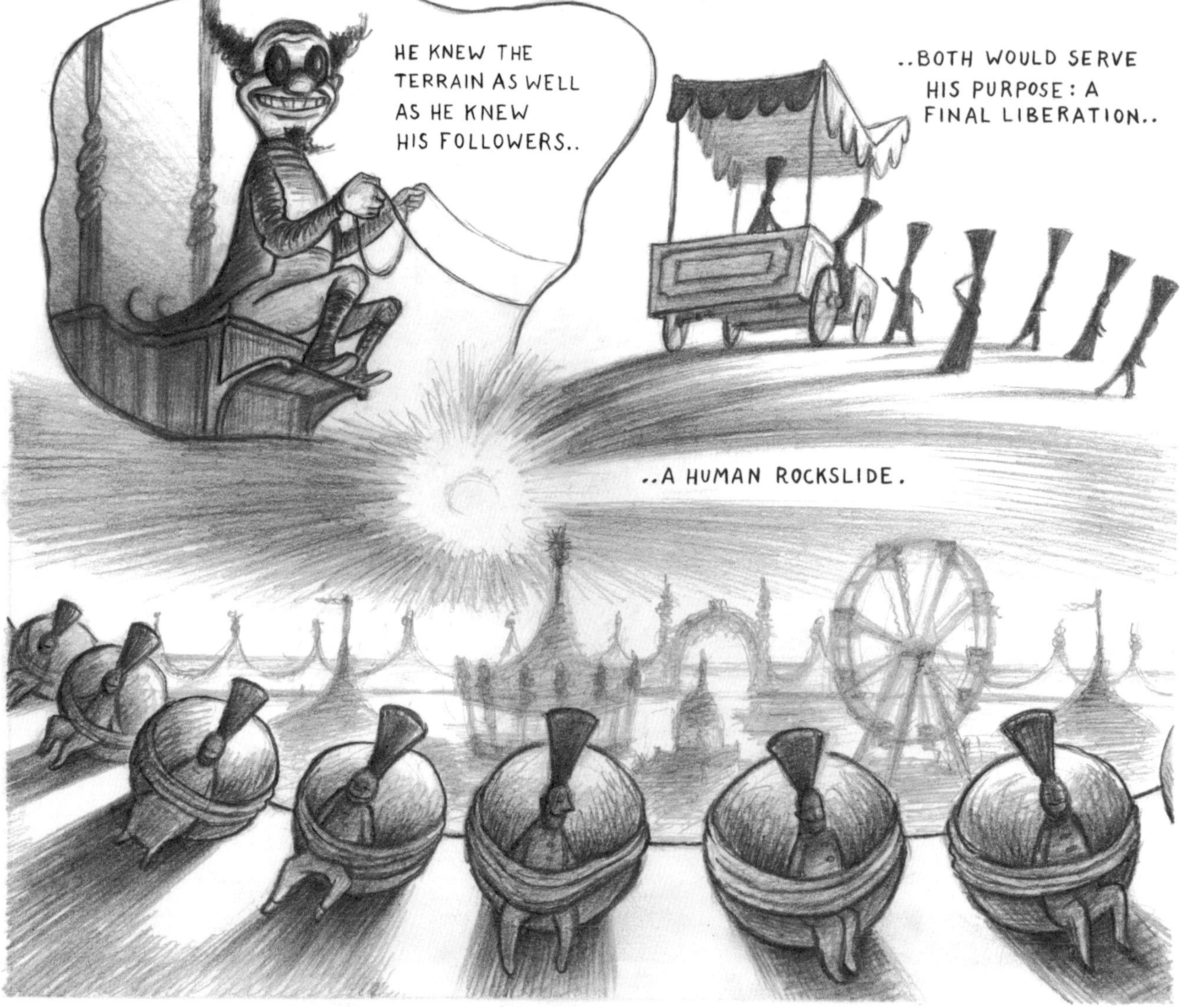
HE KNEW THE
TERRAIN AS WELL
AS HE KNEW
HIS FOLLOWERS..
..BOTH WOULD SERVE
HIS PURPOSE: A
FINAL LIBERATION..
..A HUMAN ROCKSLIDE.

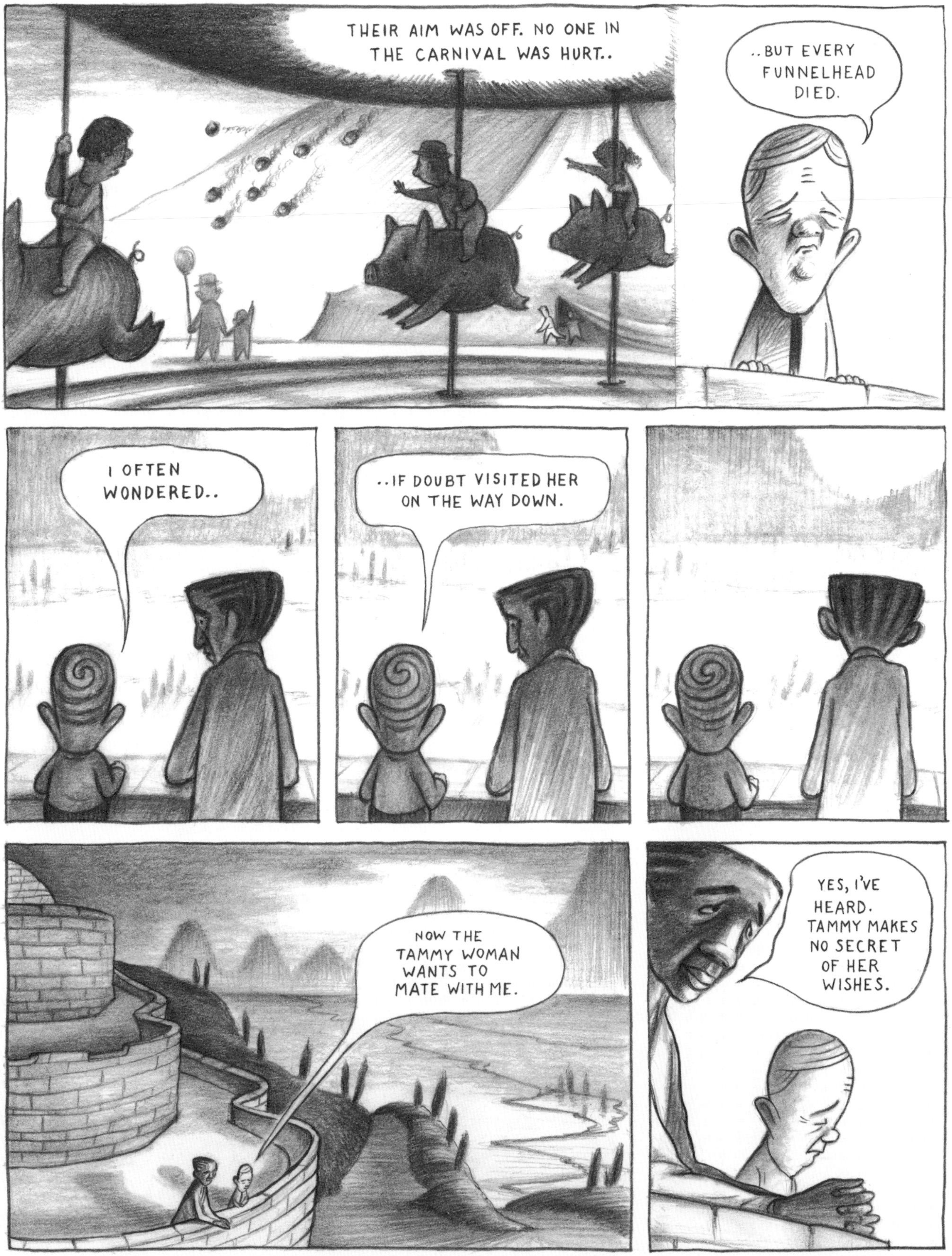
THEIR AIM WAS OFF. NO ONE IN THE CARNIVAL WAS HURT..
..BUT EVERY FUNNELHEAD DIED.
I OFTEN WONDERED..
..IF DOUBT VISITED HER ON THE WAY DOWN.
NOW THE TAMMY WOMAN WANTS TO MATE WITH ME.
YES, I'VE HEARD. TAMMY MAKES NO SECRET OF HER WISHES.

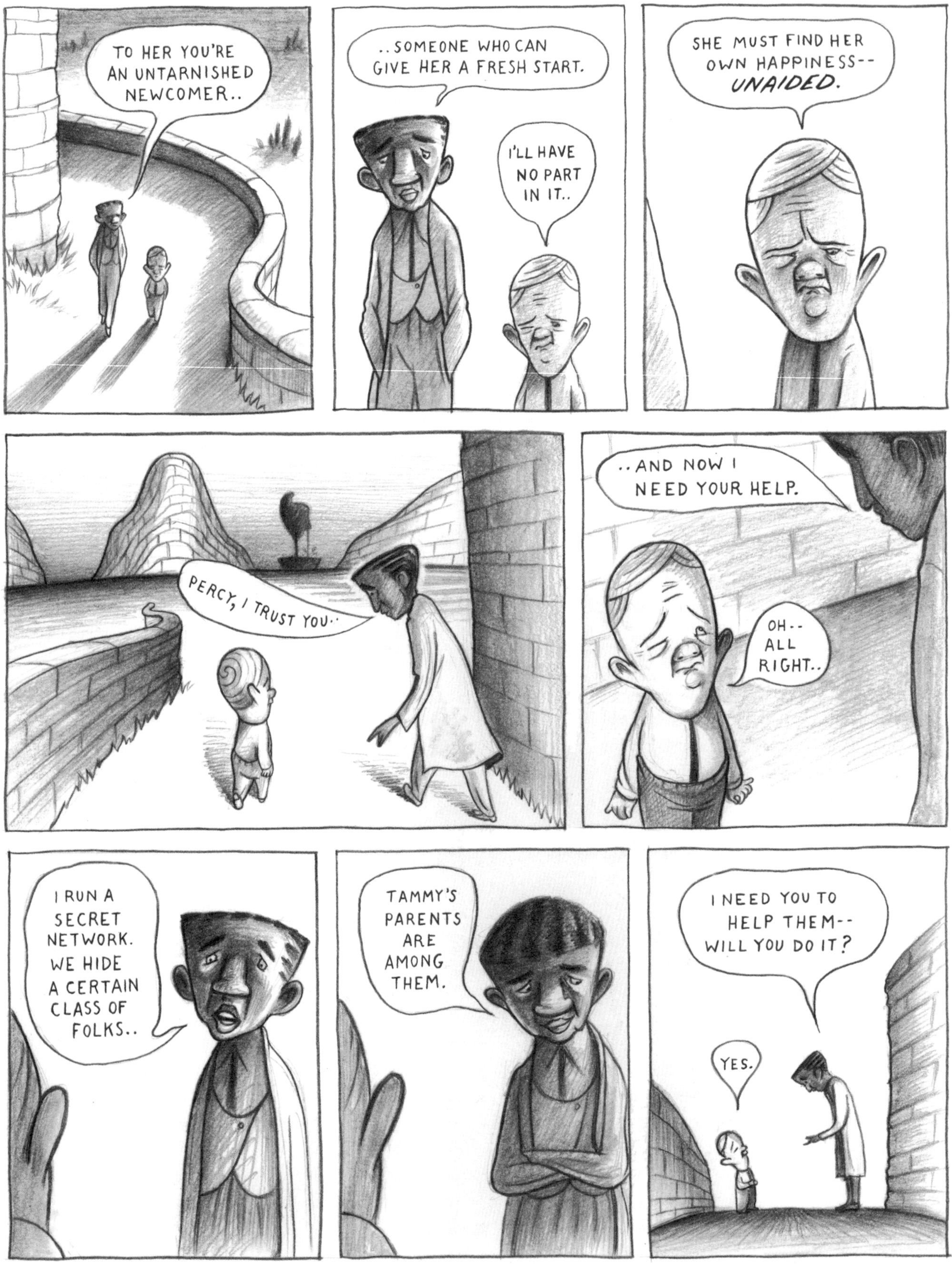
TO HER YOU'RE AN UNTARNISHED NEWCOMER..
..SOMEONE WHO CAN GIVE HER A FRESH START.
I'LL HAVE NO PART IN IT..
SHE MUST FIND HER OWN HAPPINESS-- UNAIDED.
PERCY, I TRUST YOU..
..AND NOW I NEED YOUR HELP.
OH-- ALL RIGHT..
I RUN A SECRET NETWORK. WE HIDE A CERTAIN CLASS OF FOLKS..
TAMMY'S PARENTS ARE AMONG THEM.
I NEED YOU TO HELP THEM-- WILL YOU DO IT?
YES.

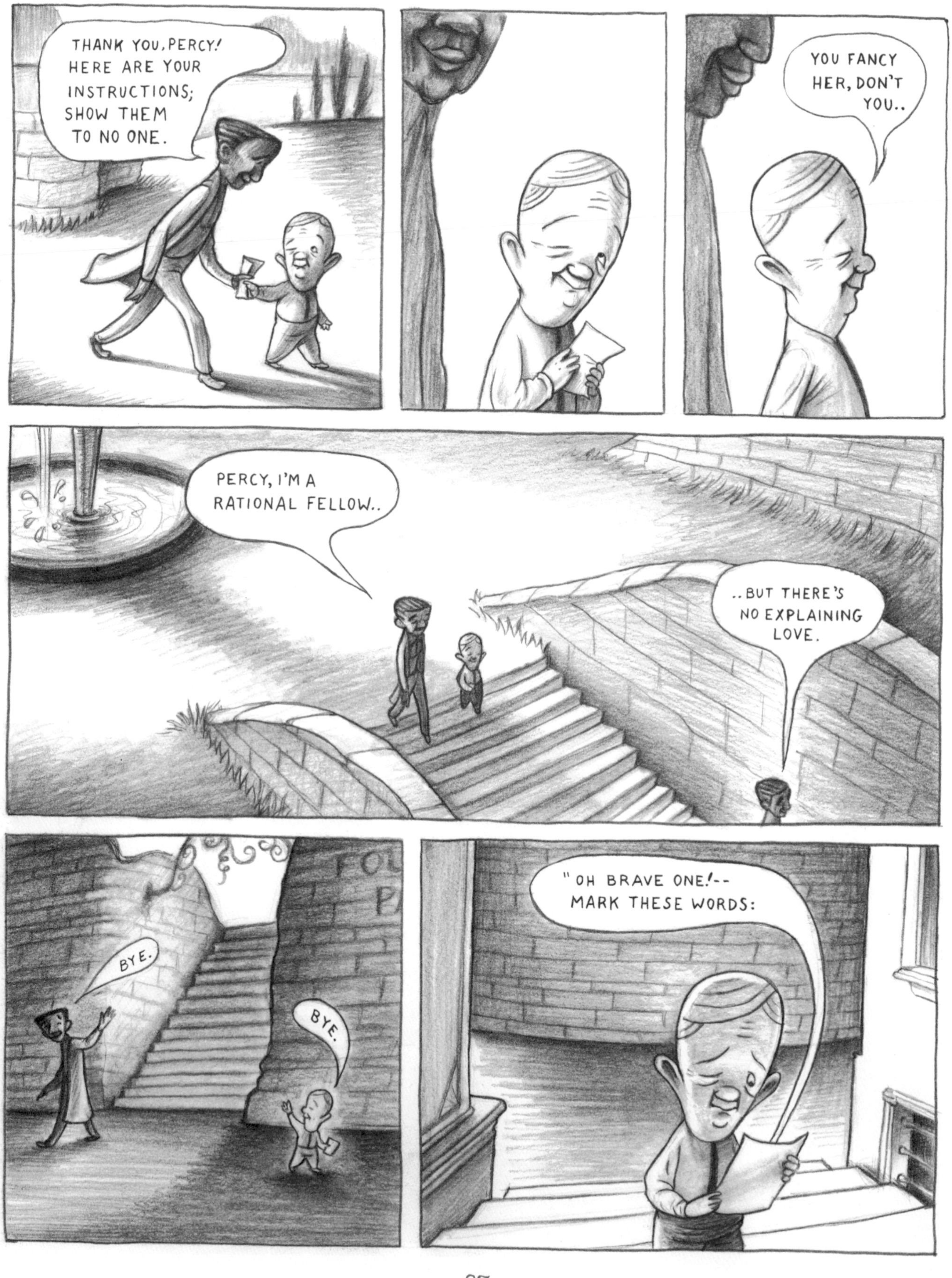
THANK YOU, PERCY! HERE ARE YOUR INSTRUCTIONS; SHOW THEM TO NO ONE.
YOU FANCY HER, DON'T YOU..
PERCY, I'M A RATIONAL FELLOW..
..BUT THERE'S NO EXPLAINING LOVE.
BYE.
BYE.
"OH BRAVE ONE!-- MARK THESE WORDS:

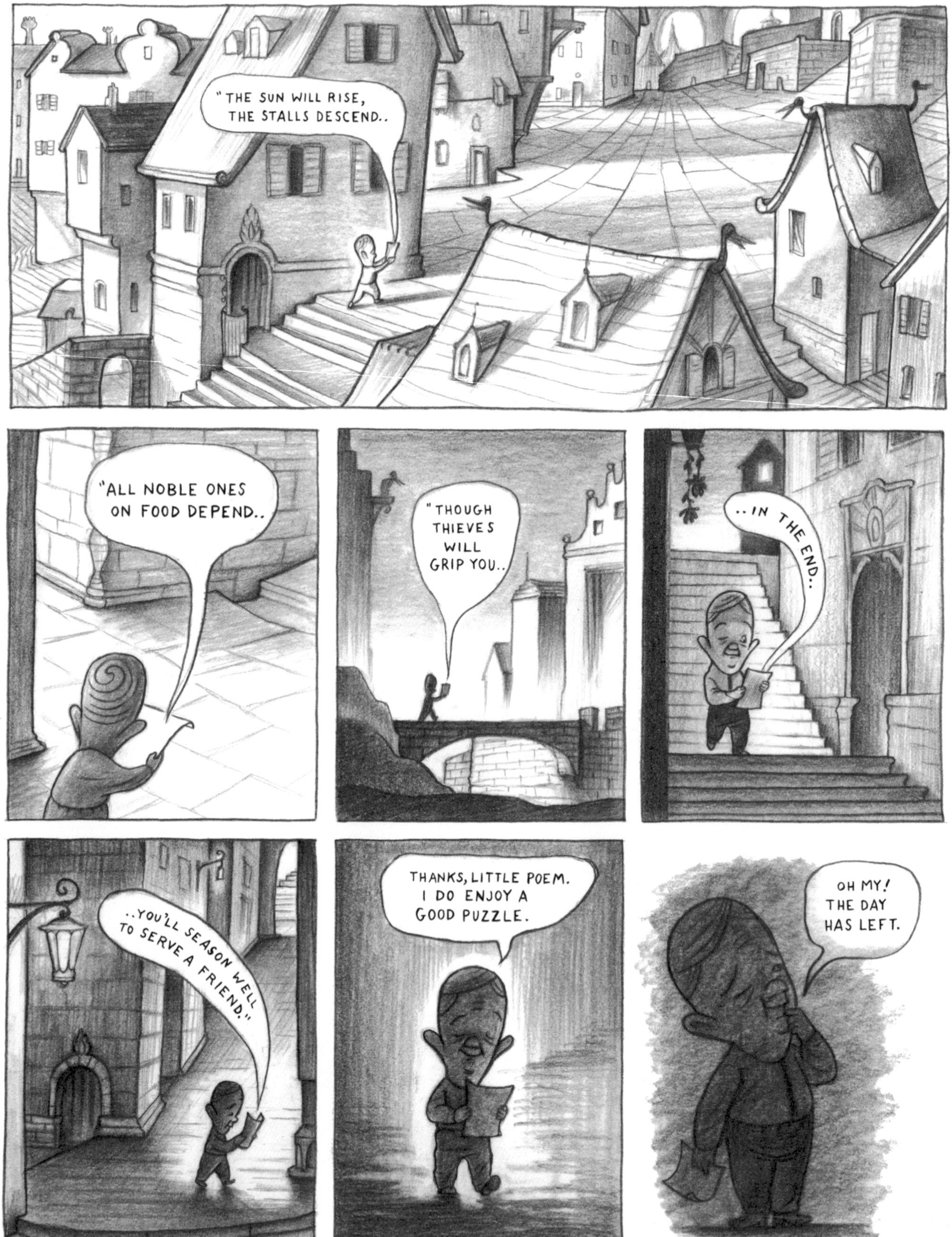
"THE SUN WILL RISE, THE STALLS DESCEND..
"ALL NOBLE ONES ON FOOD DEPEND..
"THOUGH THIEVES WILL GRIP YOU..
..IN THE END..
..YOU'LL SEASON WELL TO SERVE A FRIEND."
THANKS, LITTLE POEM. I DO ENJOY A GOOD PUZZLE.
OH MY! THE DAY HAS LEFT.

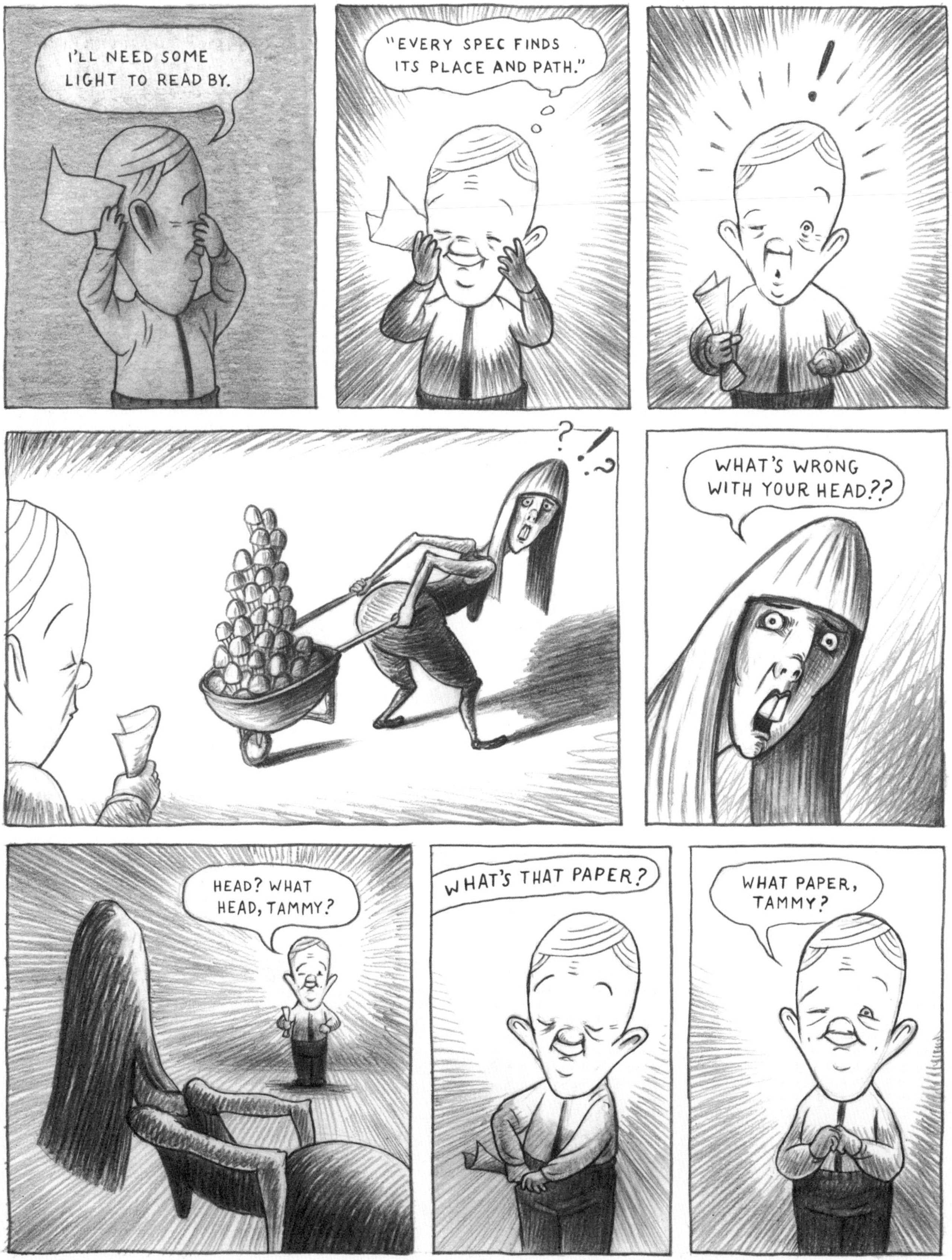
I'LL NEED SOME LIGHT TO READ BY.
"EVERY SPEC FINDS ITS PLACE AND PATH."
!
?!?
WHAT'S WRONG WITH YOUR HEAD??
HEAD? WHAT HEAD, TAMMY?
WHAT'S THAT PAPER?
WHAT PAPER, TAMMY?

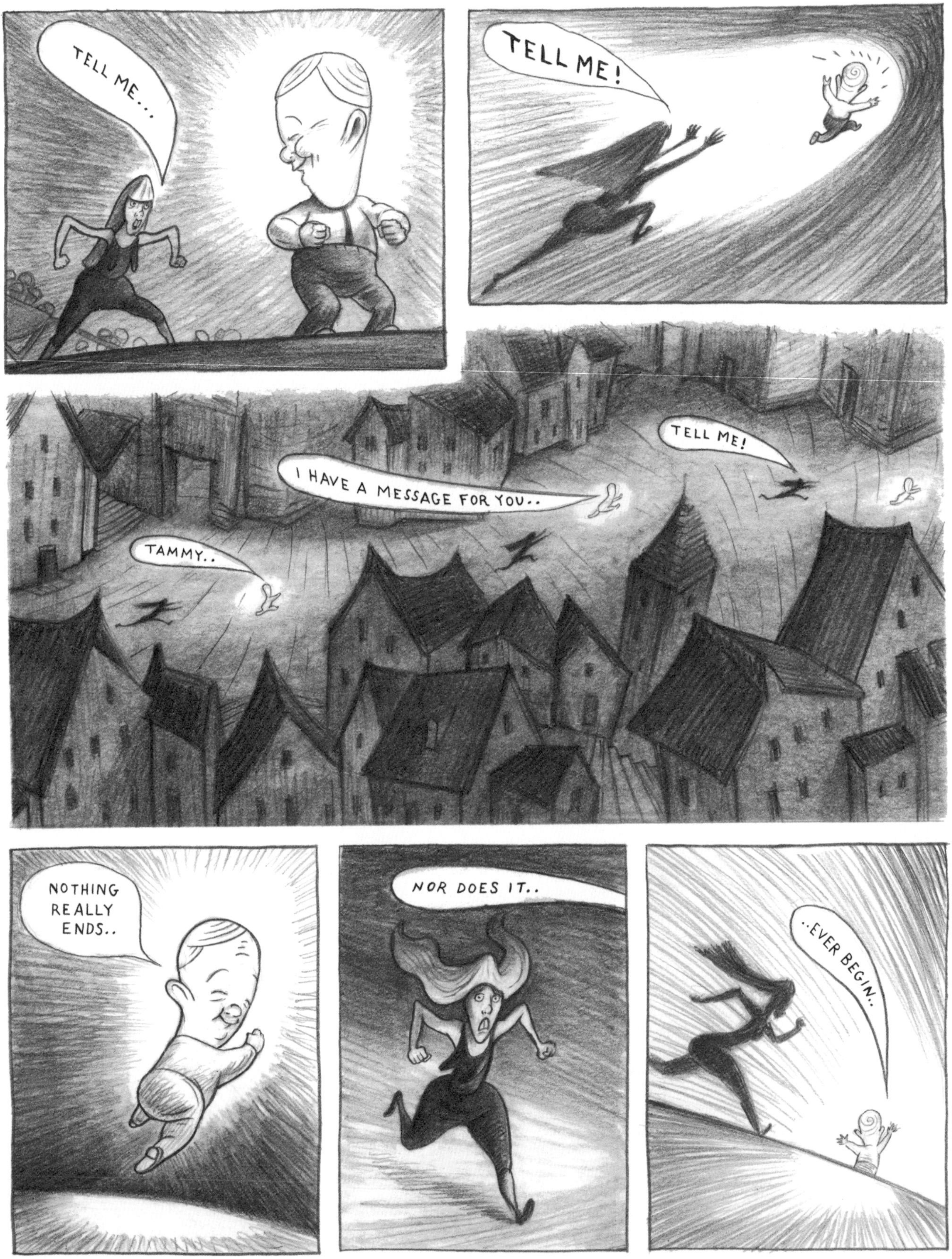
TELL ME...
TELL ME!
TELL ME!
I HAVE A MESSAGE FOR YOU..
TAMMY..
NOTHING REALLY ENDS..
NOR DOES IT..
..EVER BEGIN..

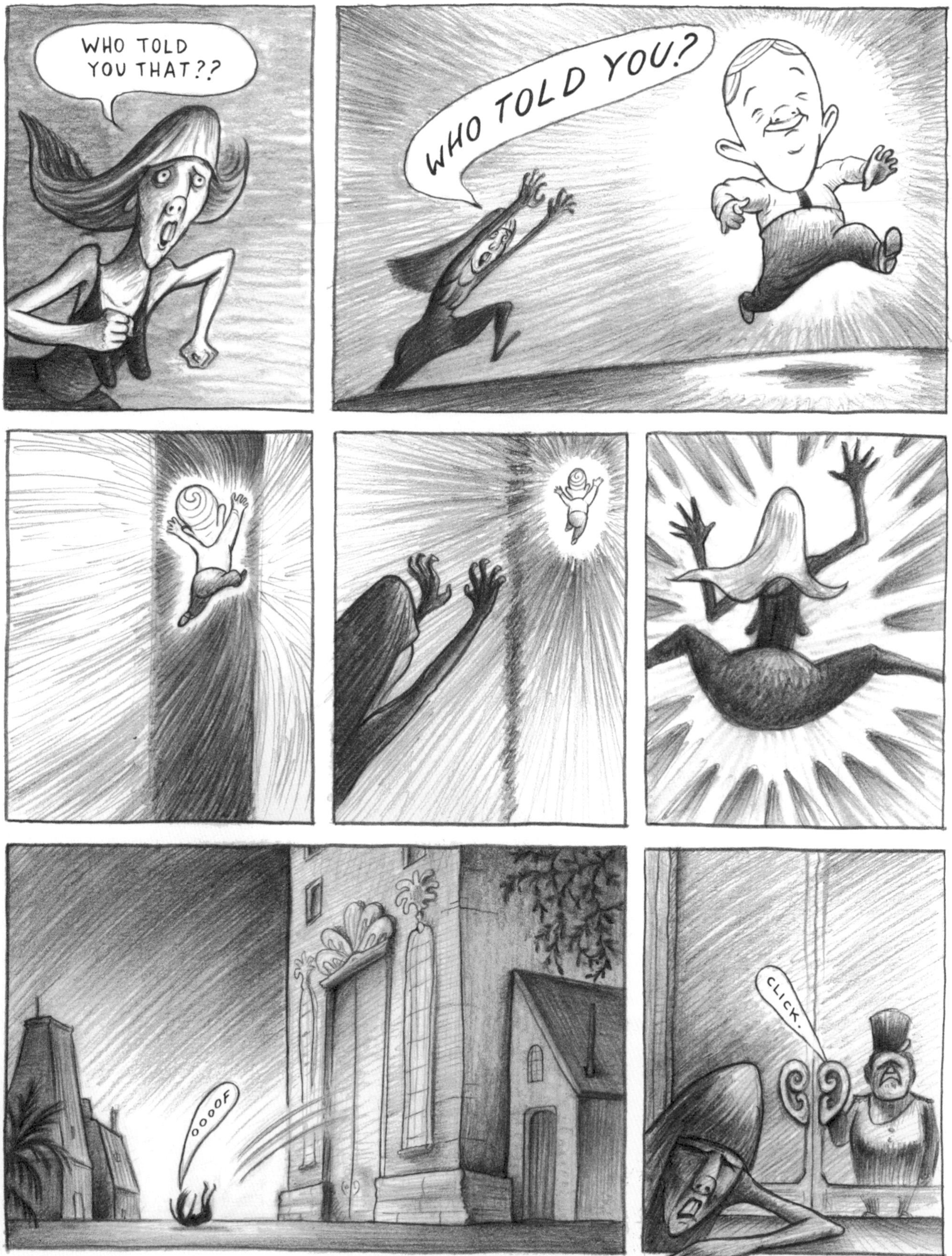
WHO TOLD YOU THAT??
WHO TOLD YOU?
OOOOF
CLICK.

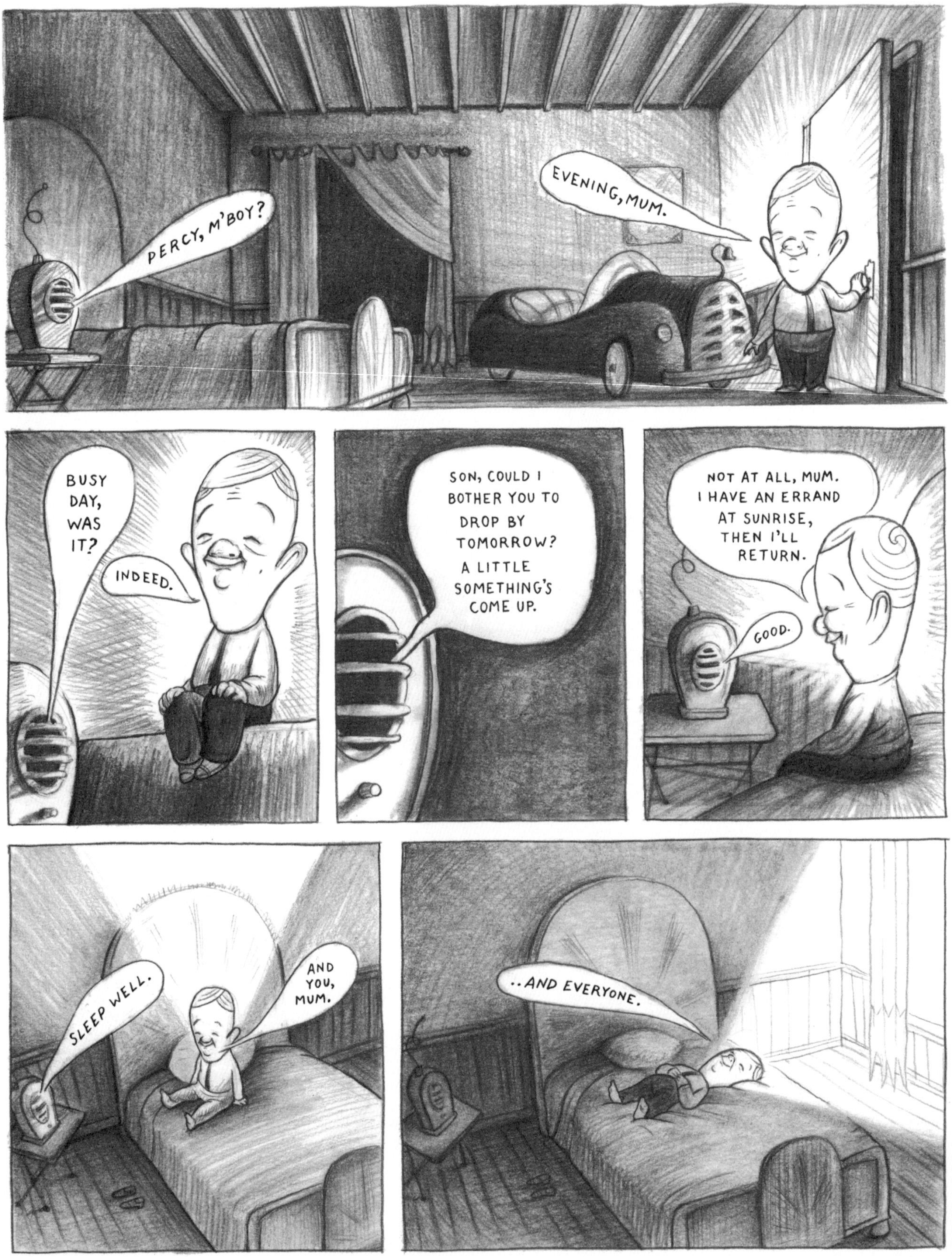
PERCY, M'BOY?
EVENING, MUM.
BUSY DAY, WAS IT?
INDEED.
SON, COULD I BOTHER YOU TO DROP BY TOMORROW? A LITTLE SOMETHING'S COME UP.
NOT AT ALL, MUM. I HAVE AN ERRAND AT SUNRISE, THEN I'LL RETURN.
GOOD.
SLEEP WELL.
AND YOU, MUM.
..AND EVERYONE.

Part Three:
RETURN

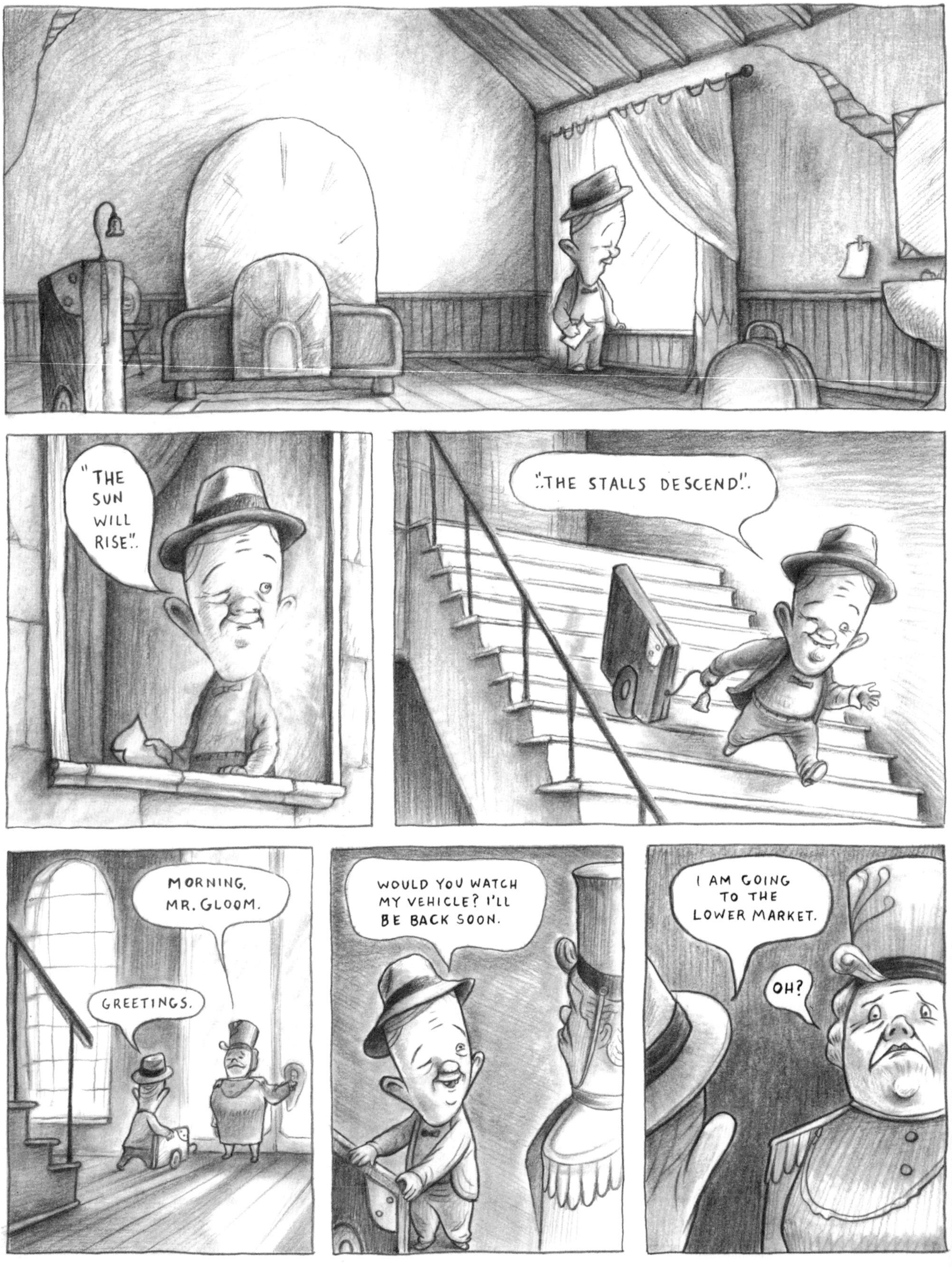
"THE SUN WILL RISE"..
.."THE STALLS DESCEND"..
MORNING, MR. GLOOM.
GREETINGS.
WOULD YOU WATCH MY VEHICLE? I'LL BE BACK SOON.
I AM GOING TO THE LOWER MARKET.
OH?

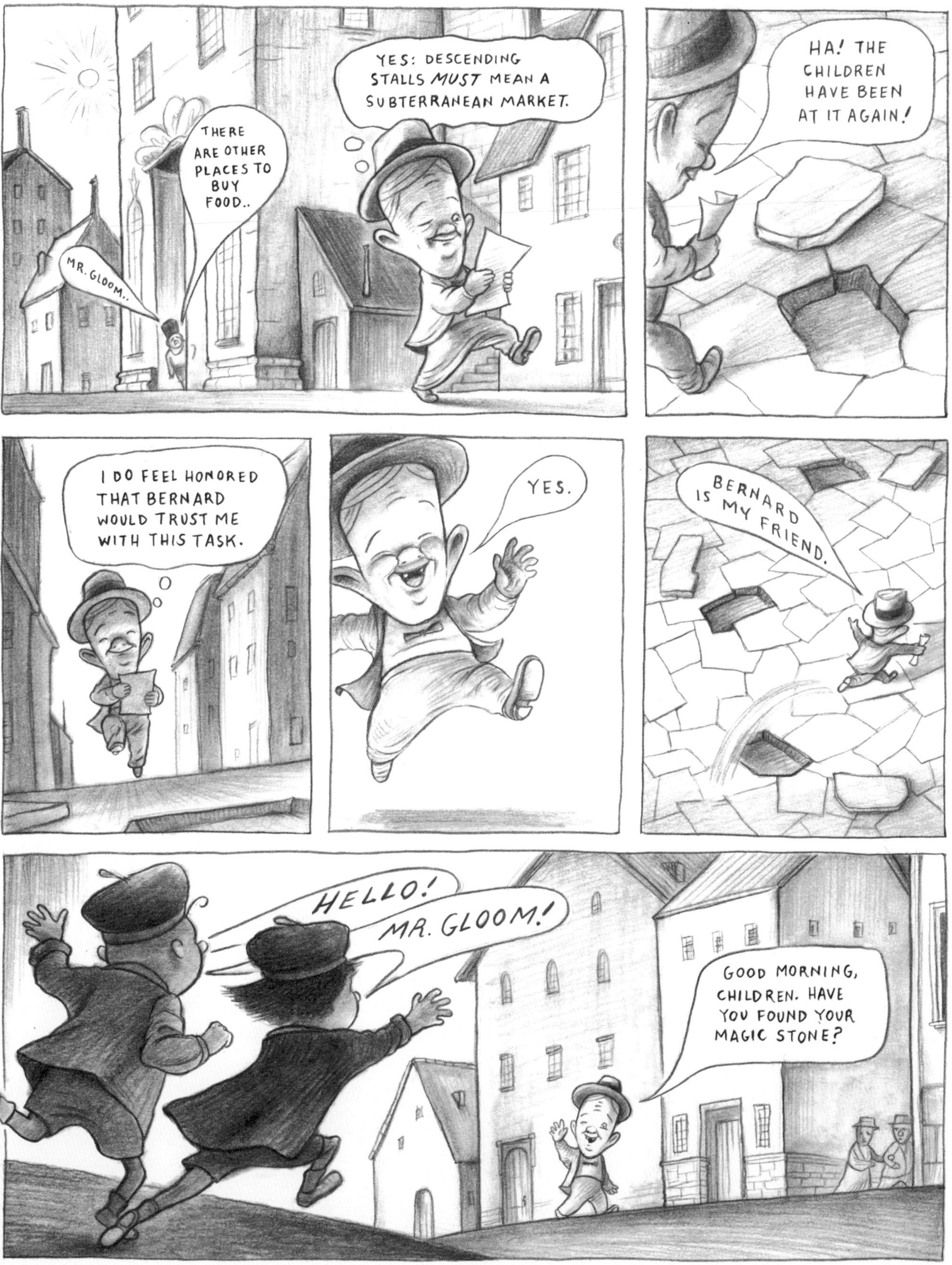
MR. GLOOM..
THERE ARE OTHER PLACES TO BUY FOOD..
YES: DESCENDING STALLS *MUST* MEAN A SUBTERRANEAN MARKET.
HA! THE CHILDREN HAVE BEEN AT IT AGAIN!
I DO FEEL HONORED THAT BERNARD WOULD TRUST ME WITH THIS TASK.
YES.
BERNARD IS MY FRIEND.
HELLO! MR. GLOOM!
GOOD MORNING, CHILDREN. HAVE YOU FOUND YOUR MAGIC STONE?

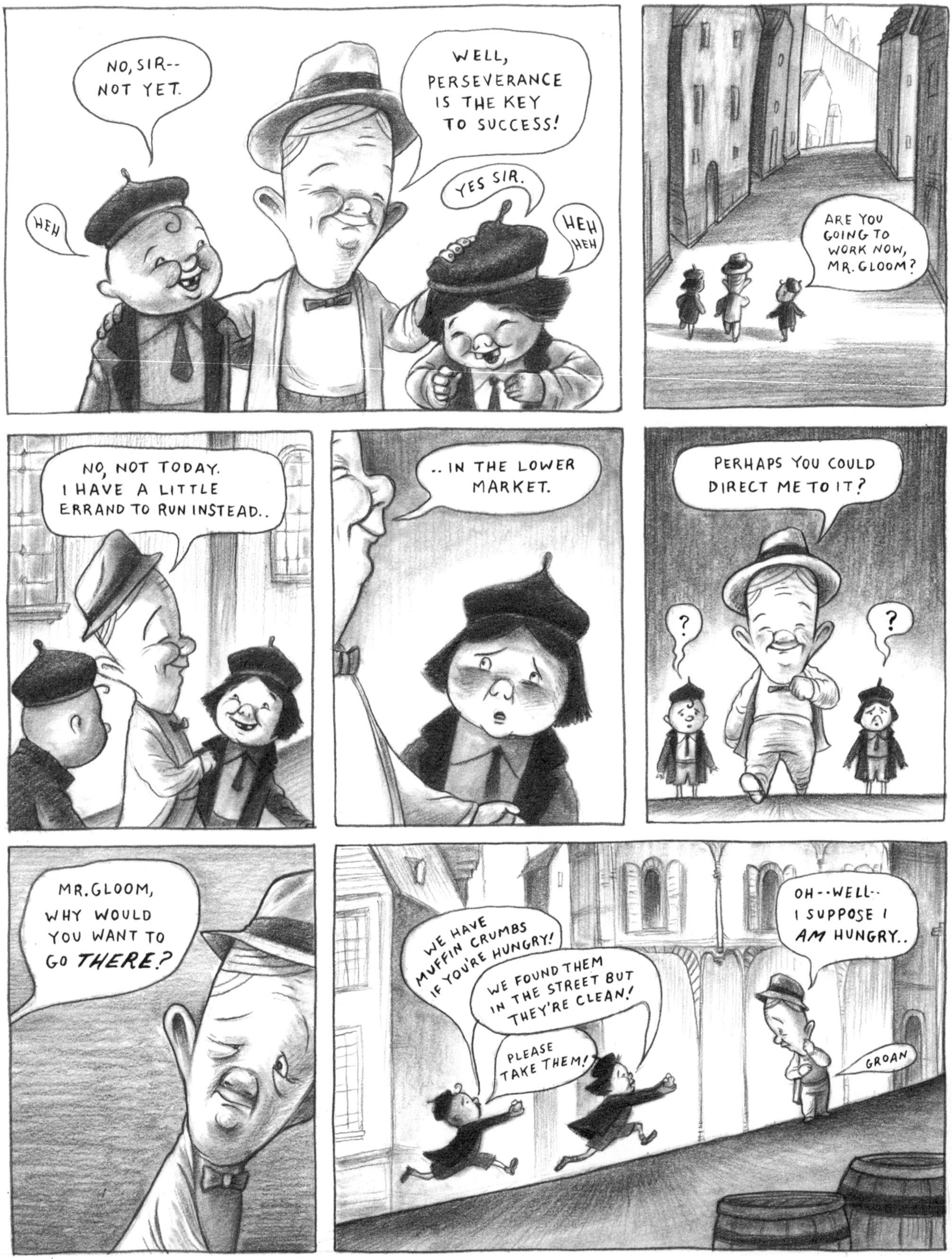
NO, SIR--
NOT YET.
HEH
WELL,
PERSEVERANCE
IS THE KEY
TO SUCCESS!
YES SIR.
HEH HEH
ARE YOU
GOING TO
WORK NOW,
MR. GLOOM?
NO, NOT TODAY.
I HAVE A LITTLE
ERRAND TO RUN INSTEAD..
..IN THE LOWER
MARKET.
PERHAPS YOU COULD
DIRECT ME TO IT?
?
?
MR. GLOOM,
WHY WOULD
YOU WANT TO
GO *THERE*?
WE HAVE
MUFFIN CRUMBS
IF YOU'RE HUNGRY!
WE FOUND THEM
IN THE STREET BUT
THEY'RE CLEAN!
PLEASE
TAKE THEM!
OH--WELL--
I SUPPOSE I
AM HUNGRY..
GROAN

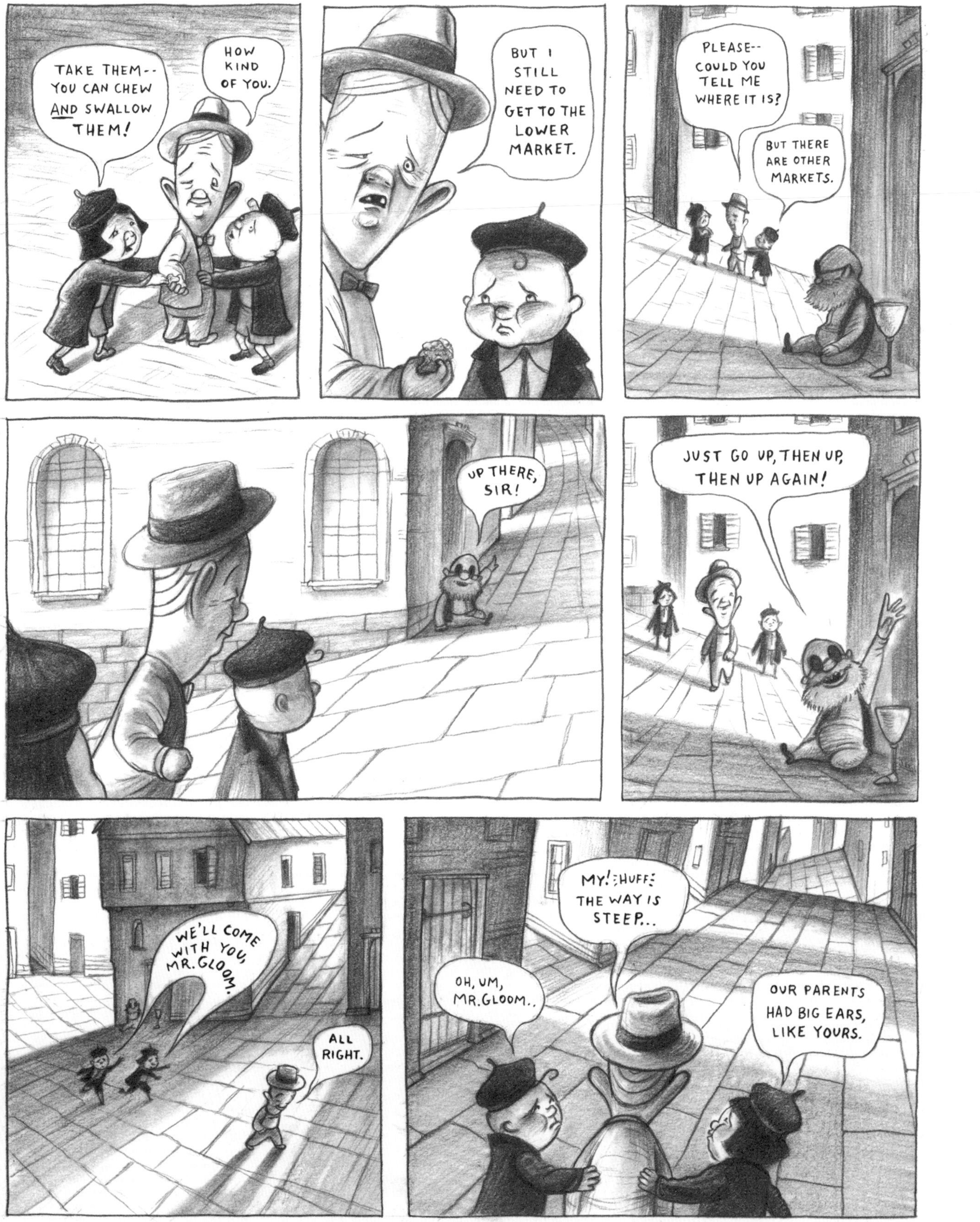

TAKE THEM--
YOU CAN CHEW
AND SWALLOW
THEM!
HOW KIND OF YOU.
BUT I STILL NEED TO GET TO THE LOWER MARKET.
PLEASE--
COULD YOU TELL ME WHERE IT IS?
BUT THERE ARE OTHER MARKETS.
UP THERE, SIR!
JUST GO UP, THEN UP, THEN UP AGAIN!
WE'LL COME WITH YOU, MR. GLOOM.
ALL RIGHT.
MY! :HUFF: THE WAY IS STEEP...
OH, UM, MR. GLOOM..
OUR PARENTS HAD BIG EARS, LIKE YOURS.

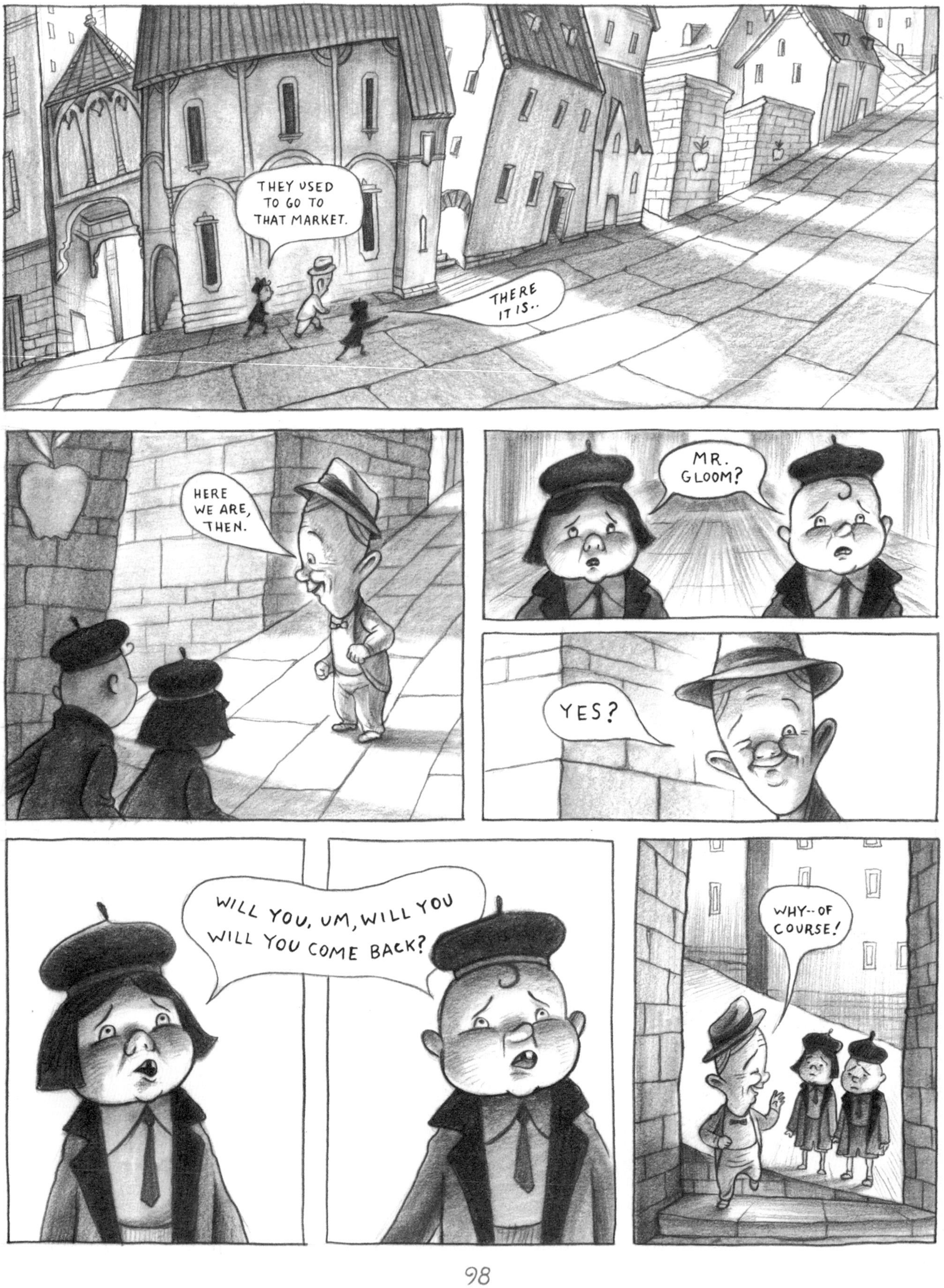
THEY USED TO GO TO THAT MARKET.
THERE IT IS..
HERE WE ARE, THEN.
MR. GLOOM?
YES?
WILL YOU, UM, WILL YOU WILL YOU COME BACK?
WHY--OF COURSE!

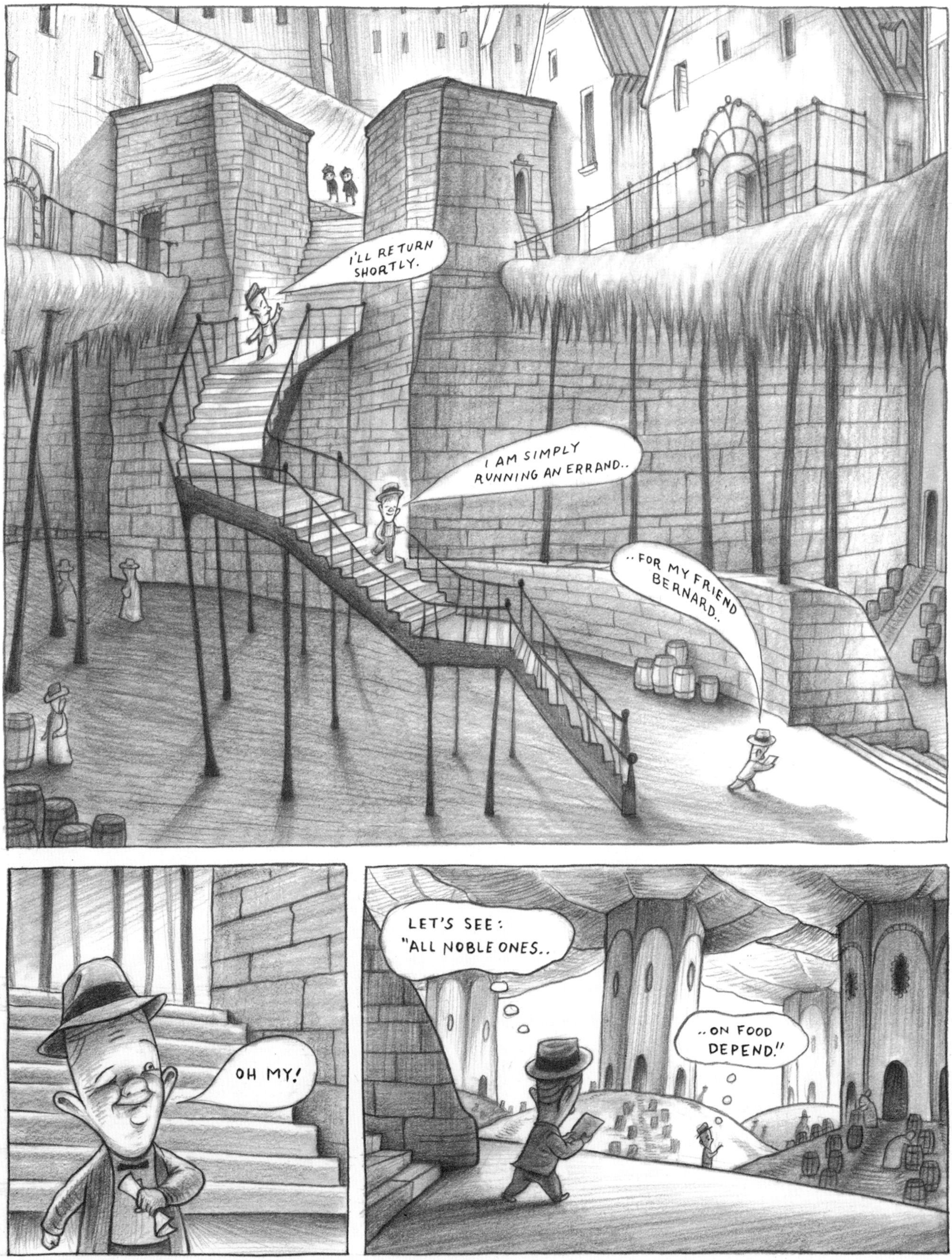
I'LL RETURN SHORTLY.
I AM SIMPLY RUNNING AN ERRAND..
..FOR MY FRIEND BERNARD..
OH MY!
LET'S SEE: "ALL NOBLE ONES..
..ON FOOD DEPEND."

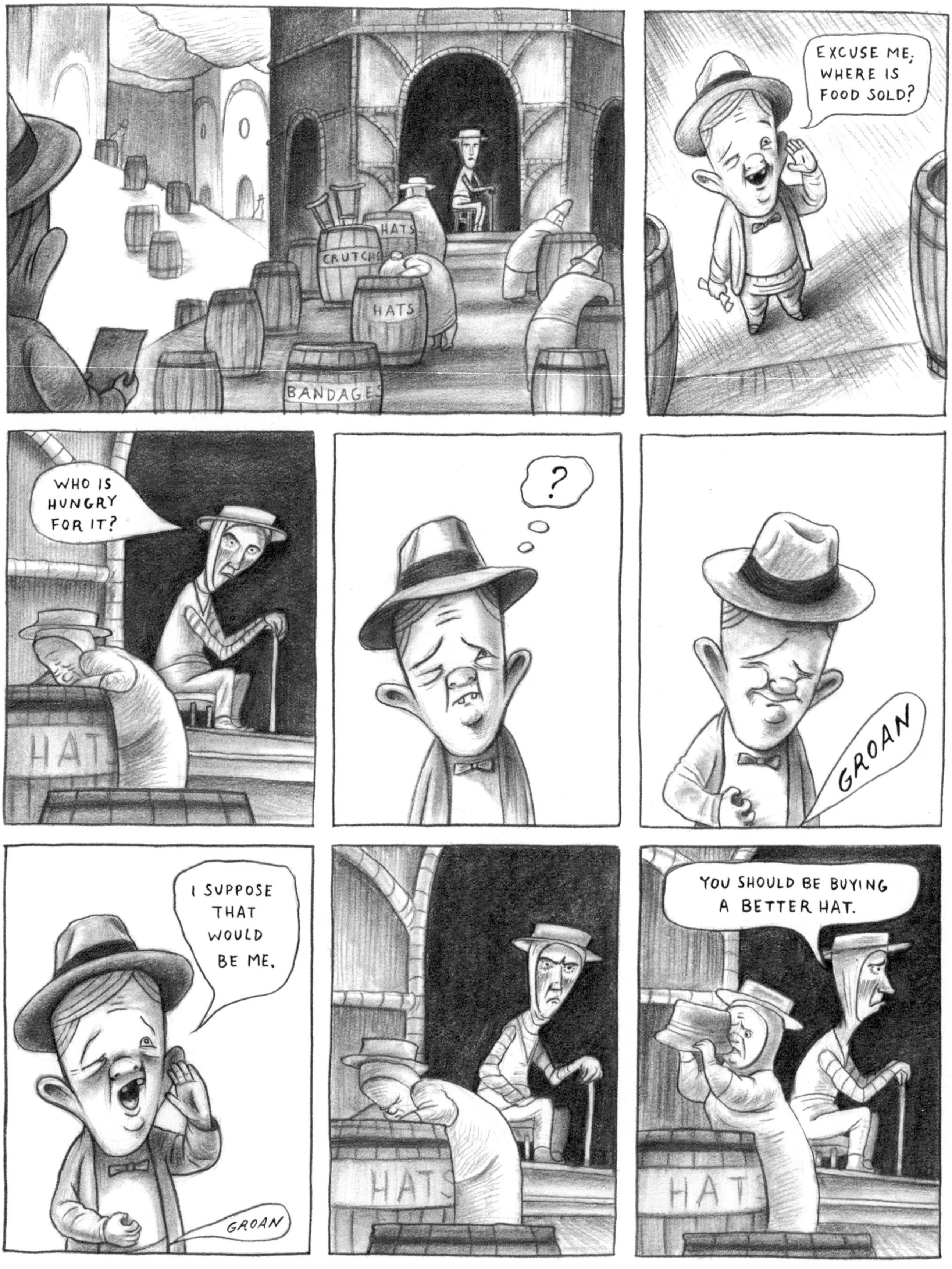
CRUTCHE
HATS
HATS
BANDAGES
EXCUSE ME; WHERE IS FOOD SOLD?
WHO IS HUNGRY FOR IT?
HATS
?
GROAN
I SUPPOSE THAT WOULD BE ME.
GROAN
HATS
YOU SHOULD BE BUYING A BETTER HAT.
HATS

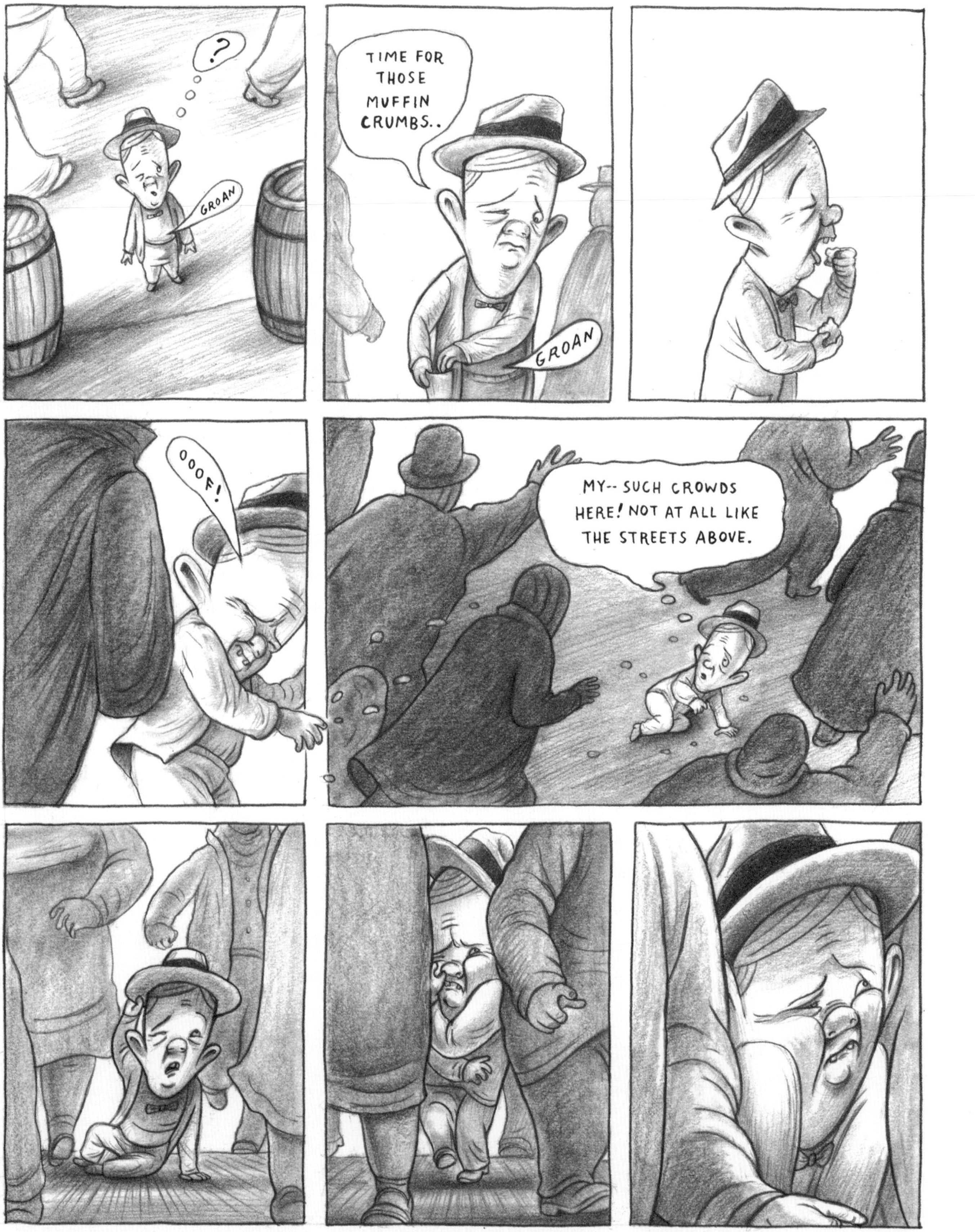
?
GROAN
TIME FOR THOSE MUFFIN CRUMBS..
GROAN
OOOF!
MY-- SUCH CROWDS HERE! NOT AT ALL LIKE THE STREETS ABOVE.

MUSH
P-PUH-PARDON ME.
PLEASE-- ARE WE GOING TOWARD THE FOOD?
?
OOOH
MUSH
MUSH?

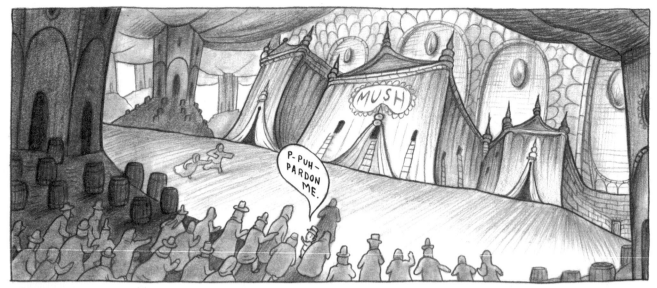

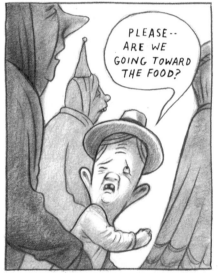

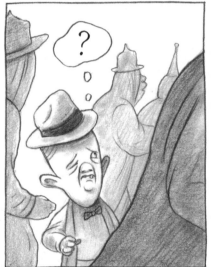

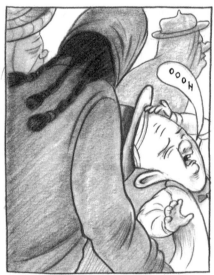

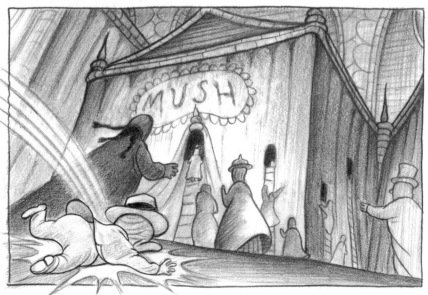

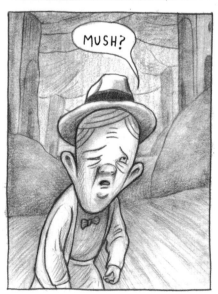

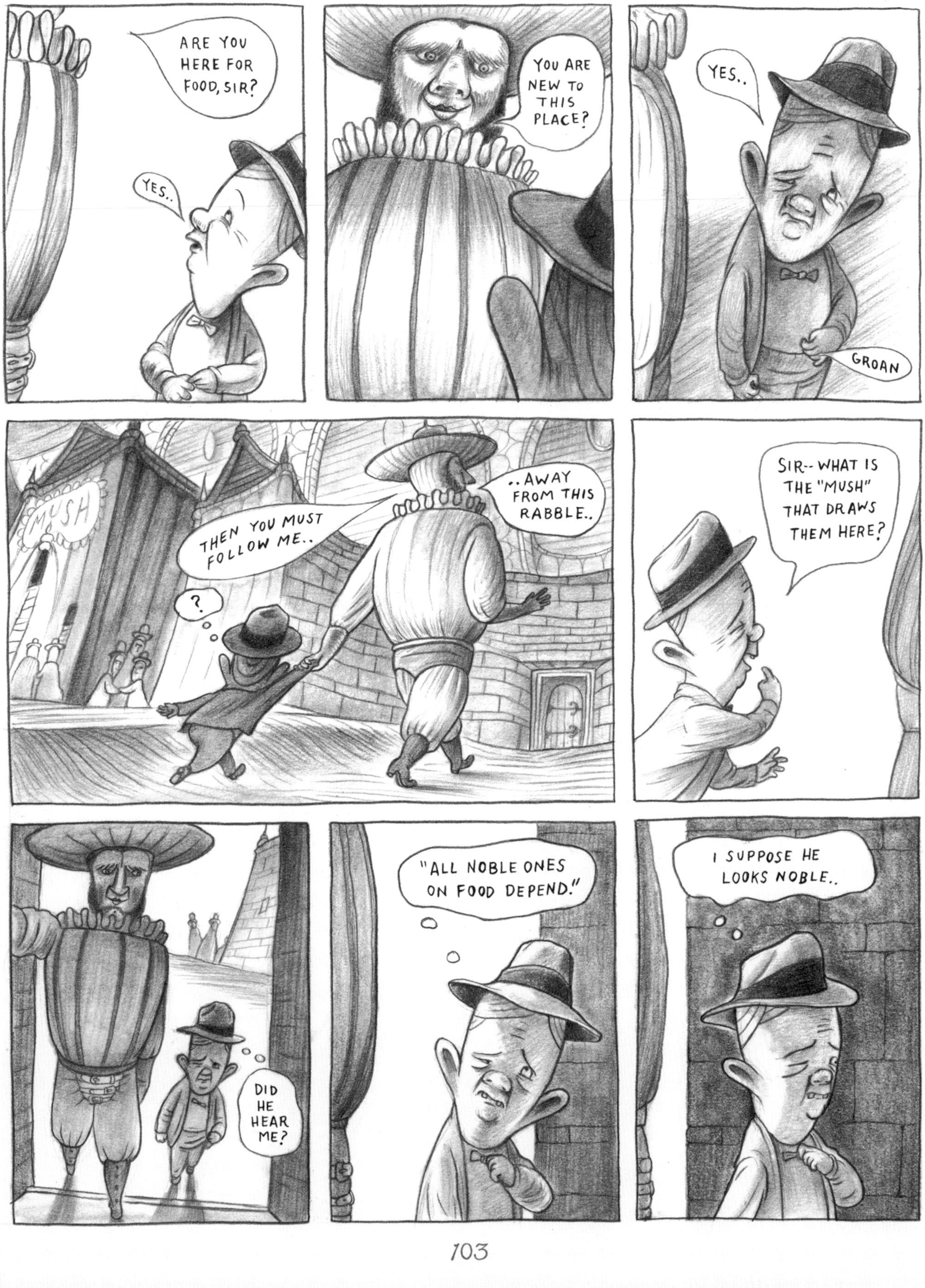
ARE YOU HERE FOR FOOD, SIR?
YES..
YOU ARE NEW TO THIS PLACE?
YES..
GROAN
MUSH
THEN YOU MUST FOLLOW ME..
..AWAY FROM THIS RABBLE..
?
SIR-- WHAT IS THE "MUSH" THAT DRAWS THEM HERE?
DID HE HEAR ME?
"ALL NOBLE ONES ON FOOD DEPEND."
I SUPPOSE HE LOOKS NOBLE..

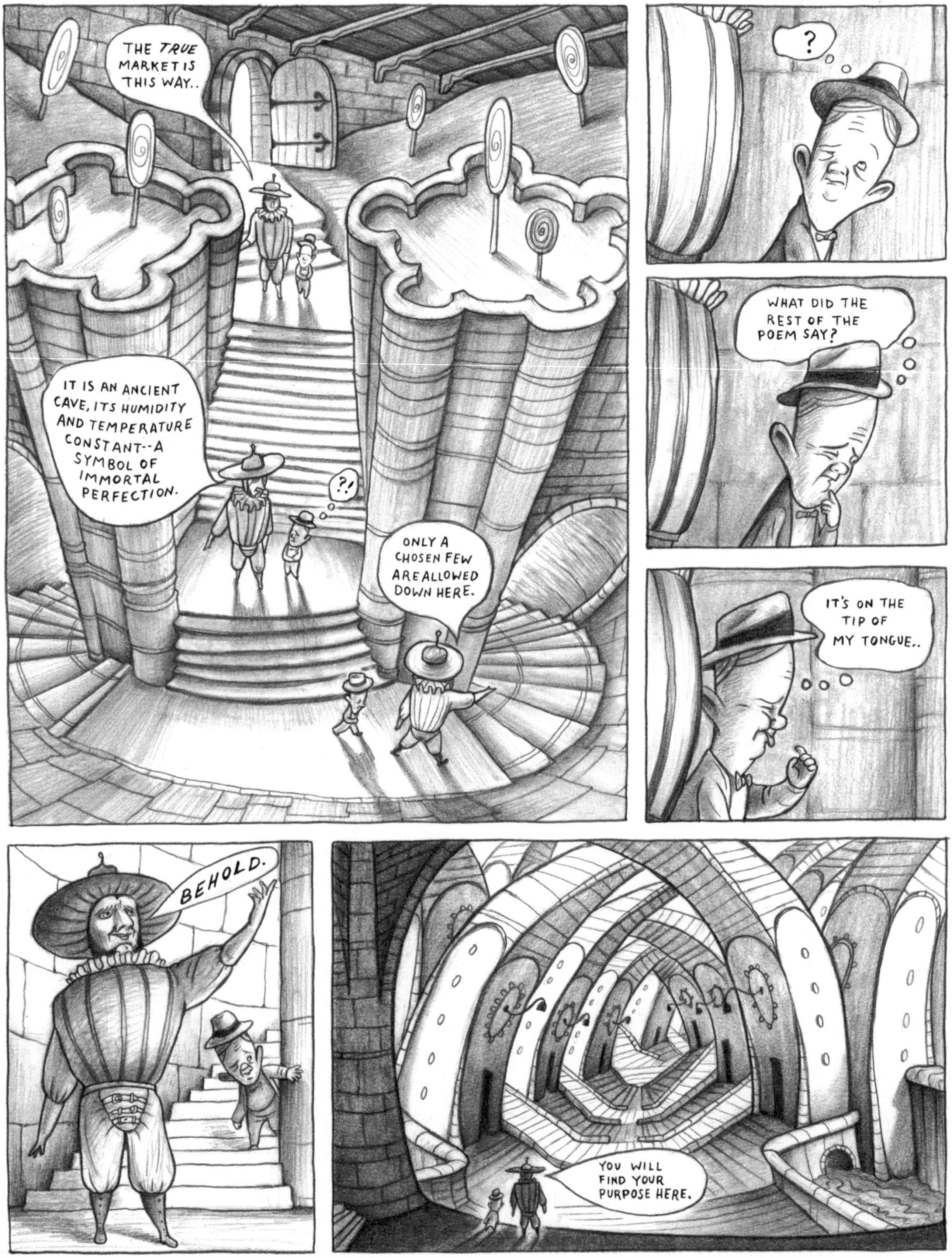
THE TRUE MARKET IS THIS WAY..
IT IS AN ANCIENT CAVE, ITS HUMIDITY AND TEMPERATURE CONSTANT--A SYMBOL OF IMMORTAL PERFECTION.
?!
ONLY A CHOSEN FEW ARE ALLOWED DOWN HERE.
?
WHAT DID THE REST OF THE POEM SAY?
IT'S ON THE TIP OF MY TONGUE..
BEHOLD.
YOU WILL FIND YOUR PURPOSE HERE.

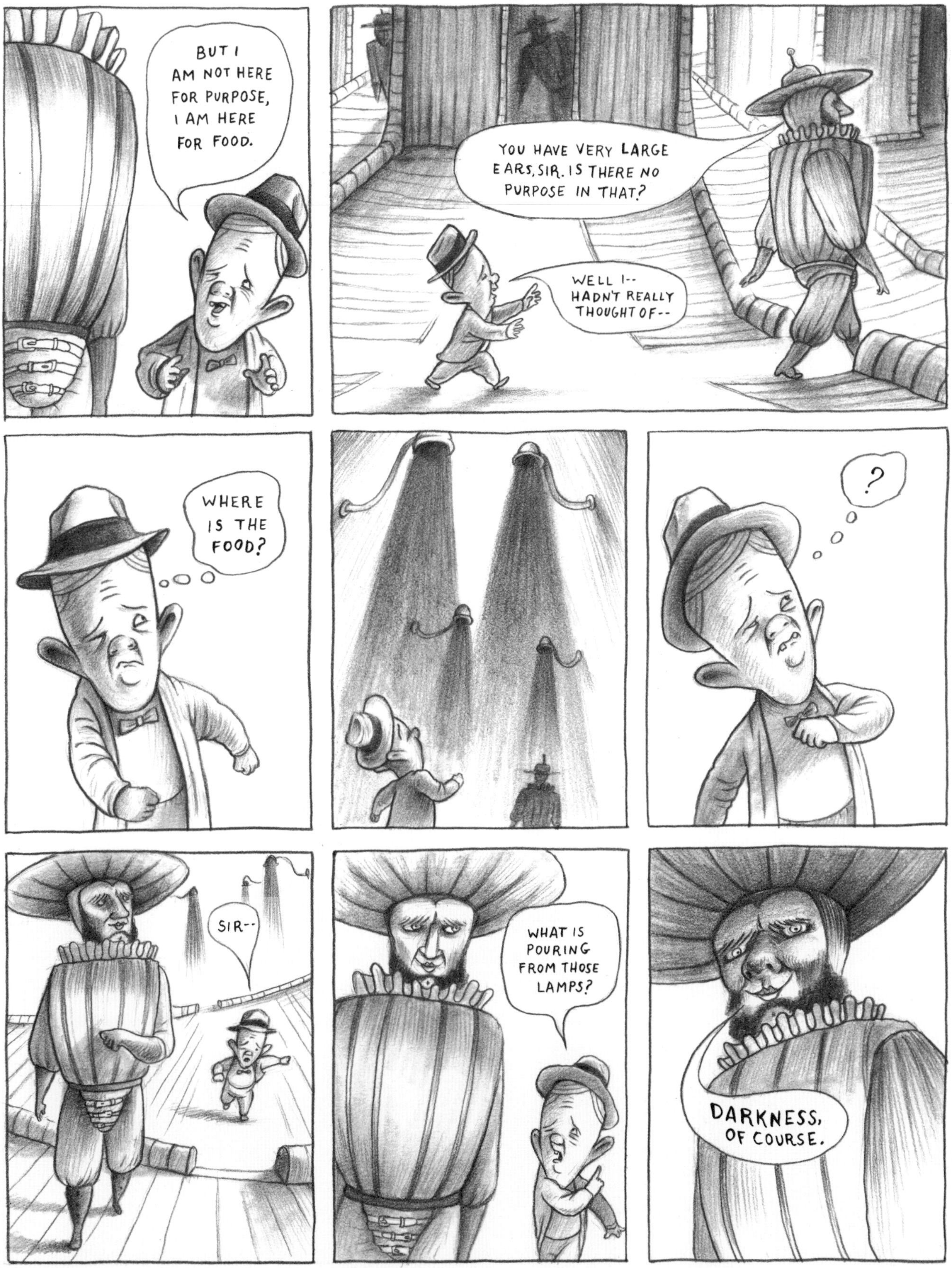
BUT I AM NOT HERE FOR PURPOSE, I AM HERE FOR FOOD.
YOU HAVE VERY LARGE EARS, SIR. IS THERE NO PURPOSE IN THAT?
WELL I-- HADN'T REALLY THOUGHT OF--
WHERE IS THE FOOD?
?
SIR--
WHAT IS POURING FROM THOSE LAMPS?
DARKNESS, OF COURSE.

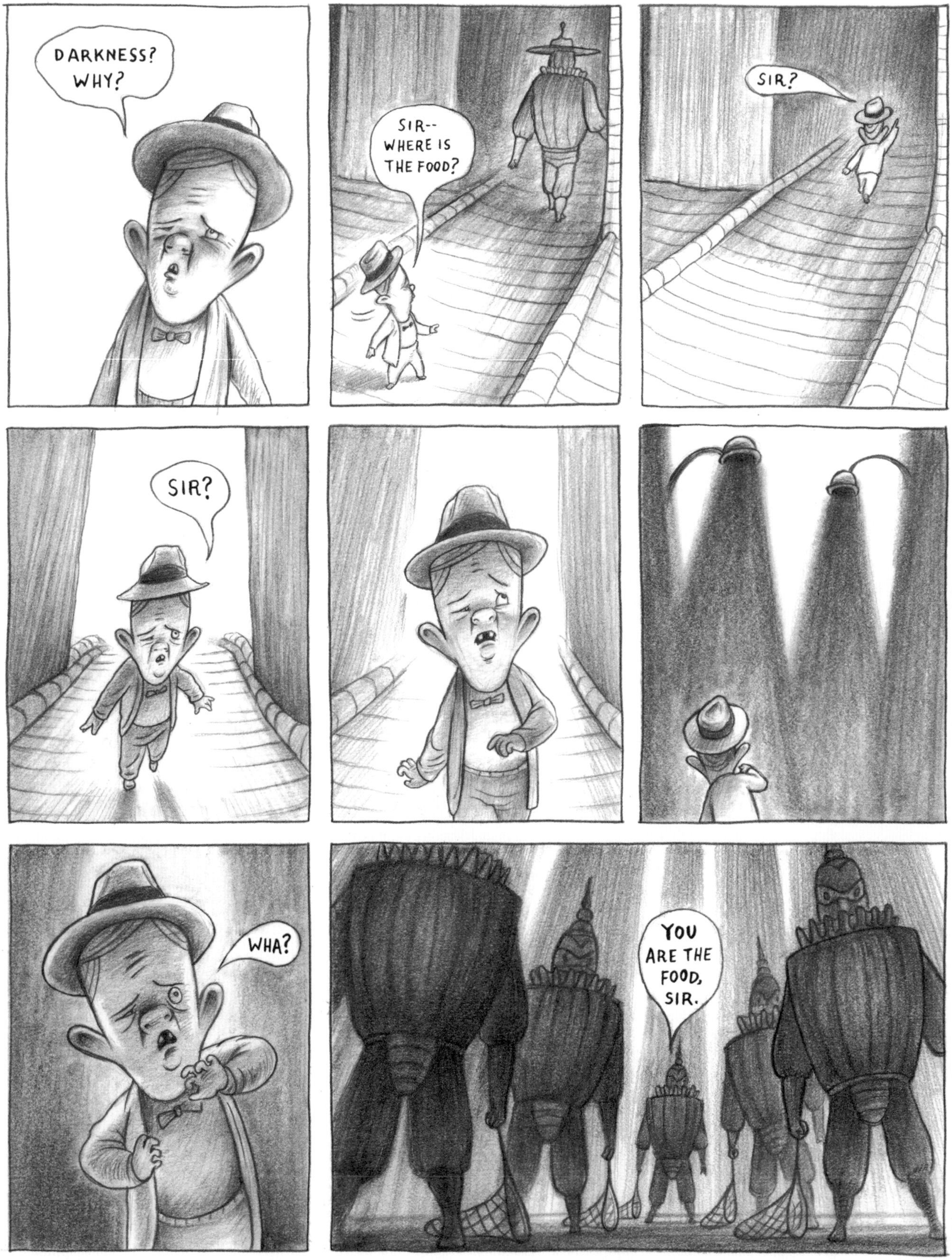
DARKNESS? WHY?
SIR-- WHERE IS THE FOOD?
SIR?
SIR?
WHA?
YOU ARE THE FOOD, SIR.

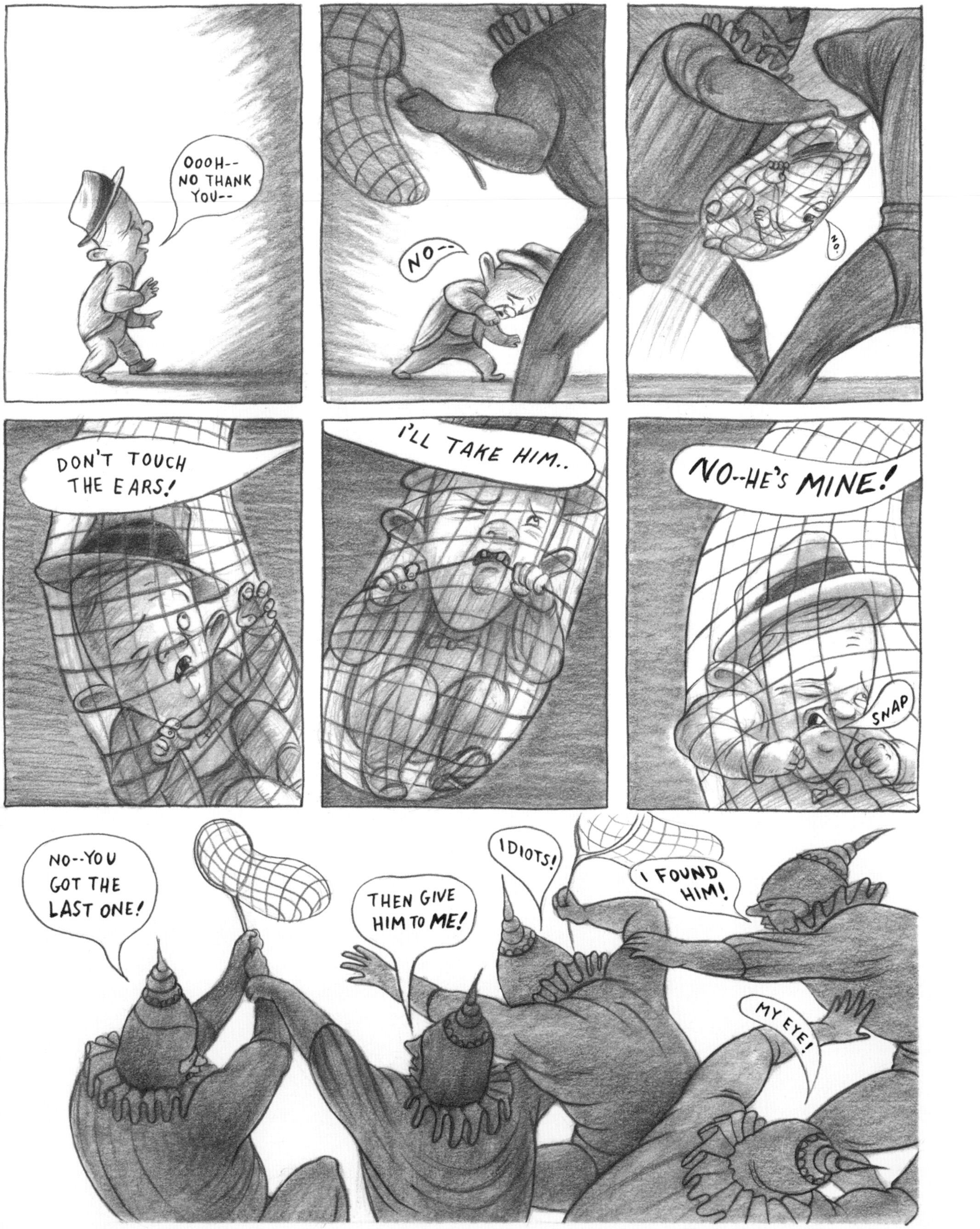
OOOH--
NO THANK
YOU--
NO--
NO.
DON'T TOUCH
THE EARS!
I'LL TAKE HIM..
NO--HE'S MINE!
SNAP
NO--YOU
GOT THE
LAST ONE!
THEN GIVE
HIM TO ME!
IDIOTS!
I FOUND
HIM!
MY EYE!

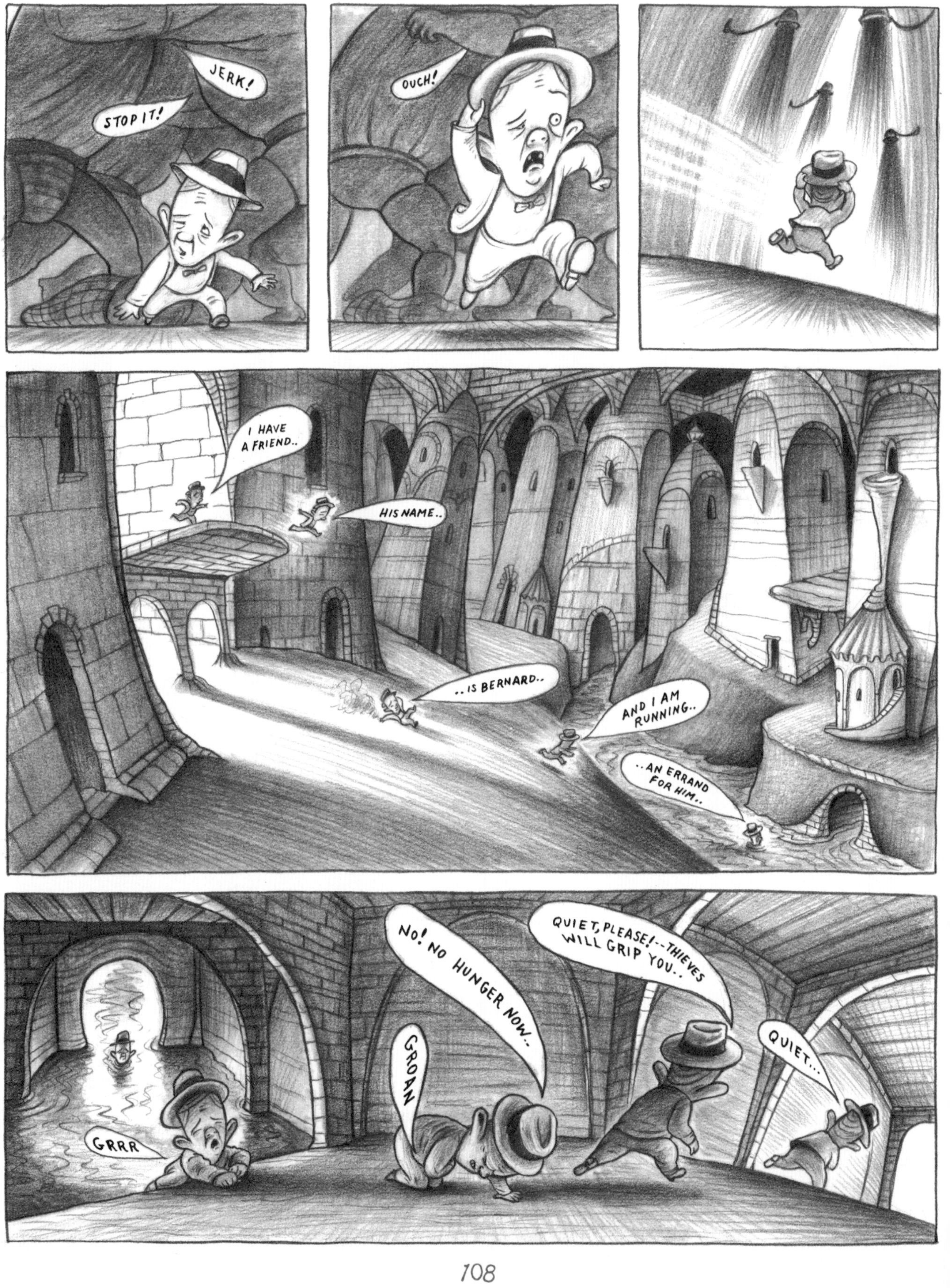
STOP IT!
JERK!
OUCH!
I HAVE A FRIEND..
HIS NAME..
..IS BERNARD..
AND I AM RUNNING..
..AN ERRAND FOR HIM..
GRRR
GROAN
NO! NO HUNGER NOW..
QUIET, PLEASE!--THIEVES WILL GRIP YOU..
QUIET...

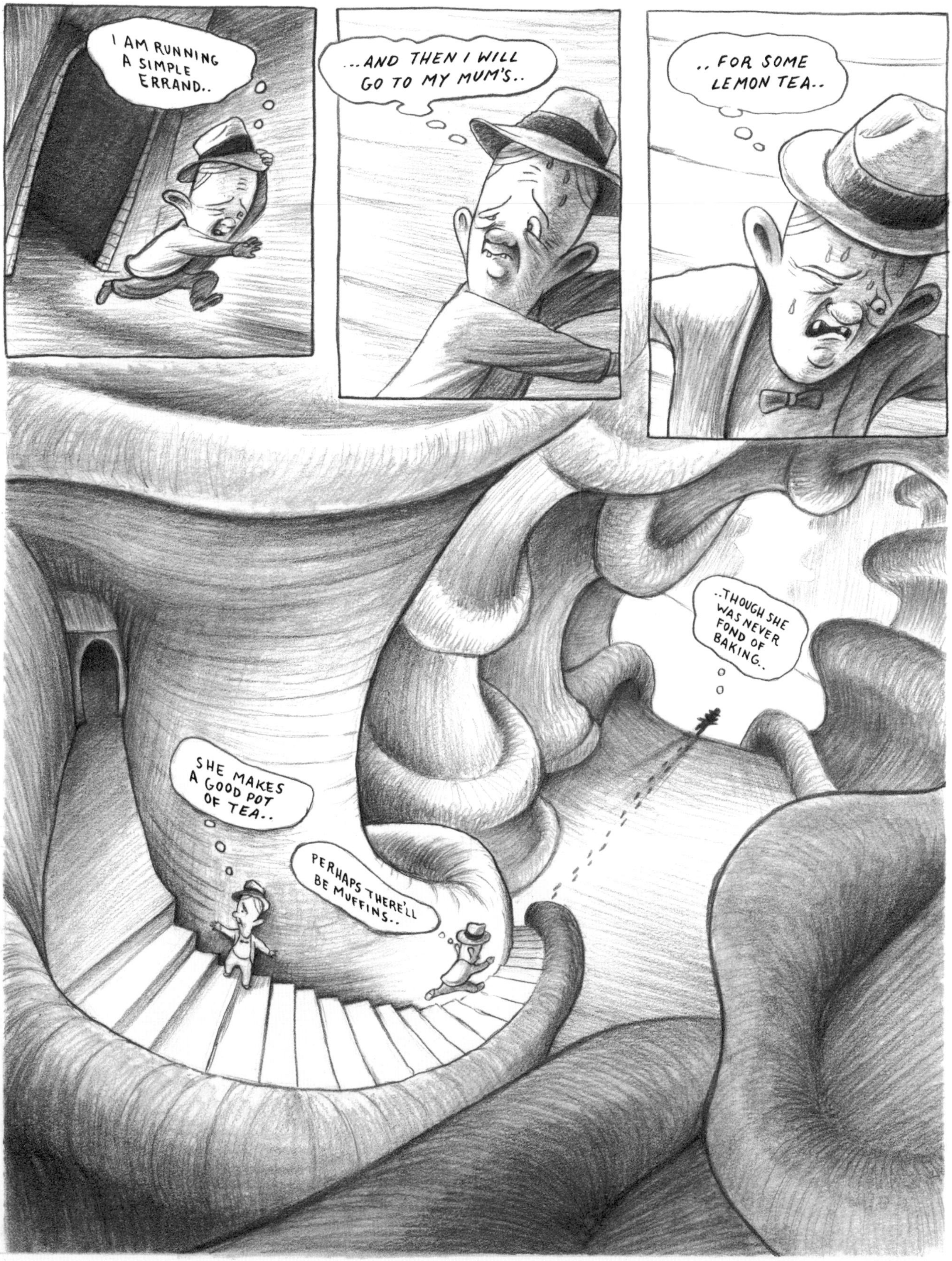
I AM RUNNING A SIMPLE ERRAND..
...AND THEN I WILL GO TO MY MUM'S..
.. FOR SOME LEMON TEA..
SHE MAKES A GOOD POT OF TEA..
PERHAPS THERE'LL BE MUFFINS..
..THOUGH SHE WAS NEVER FOND OF BAKING..

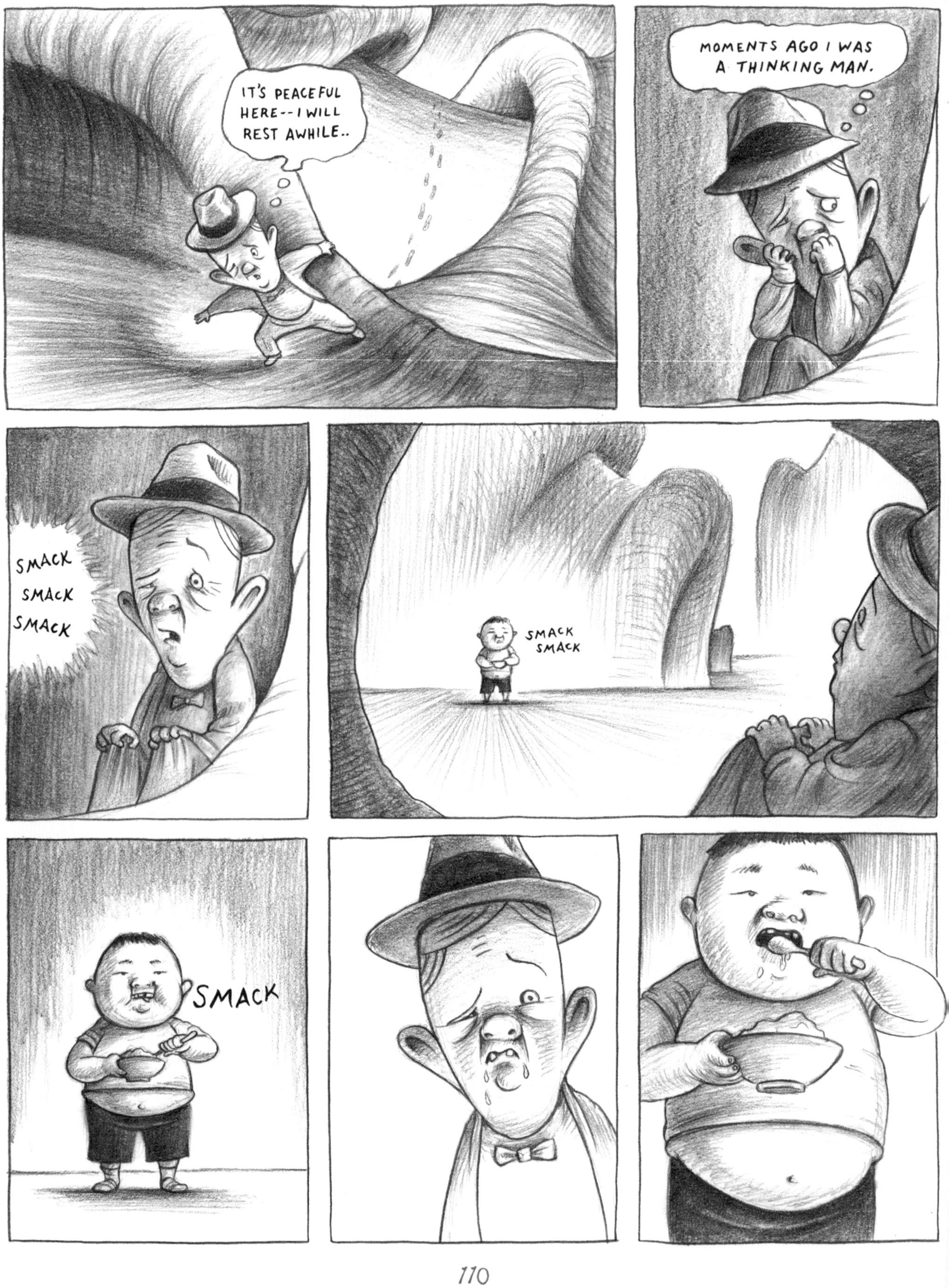
IT'S PEACEFUL HERE--I WILL REST AWHILE..
MOMENTS AGO I WAS A THINKING MAN.
SMACK SMACK SMACK
SMACK SMACK
SMACK

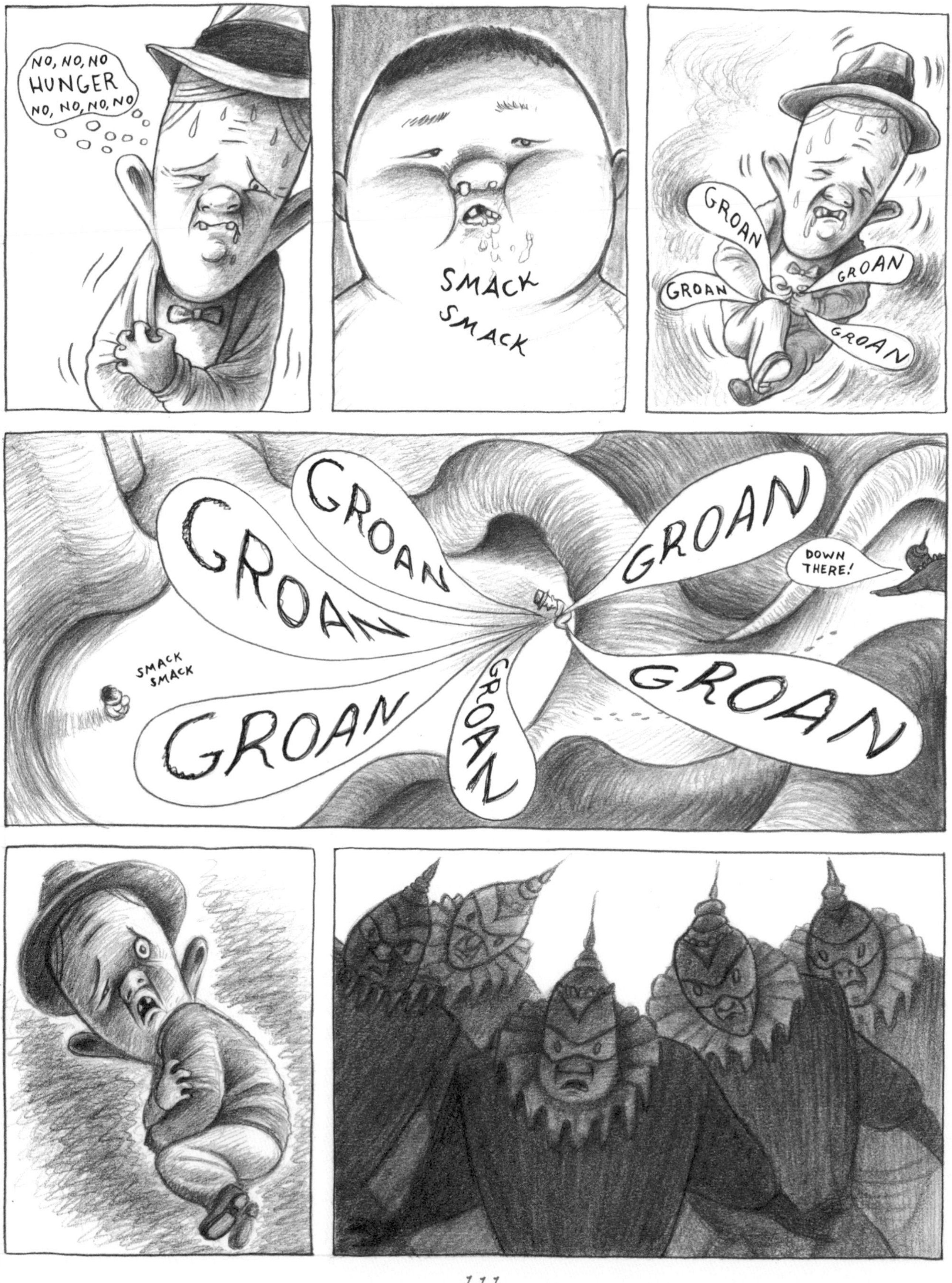
NO, NO, NO
HUNGER
NO, NO, NO, NO
SMACK
SMACK
GROAN
GROAN
GROAN
GROAN
GROAN
GROAN
GROAN
DOWN THERE!
GROAN
SMACK SMACK
GROAN
GROAN
GROAN

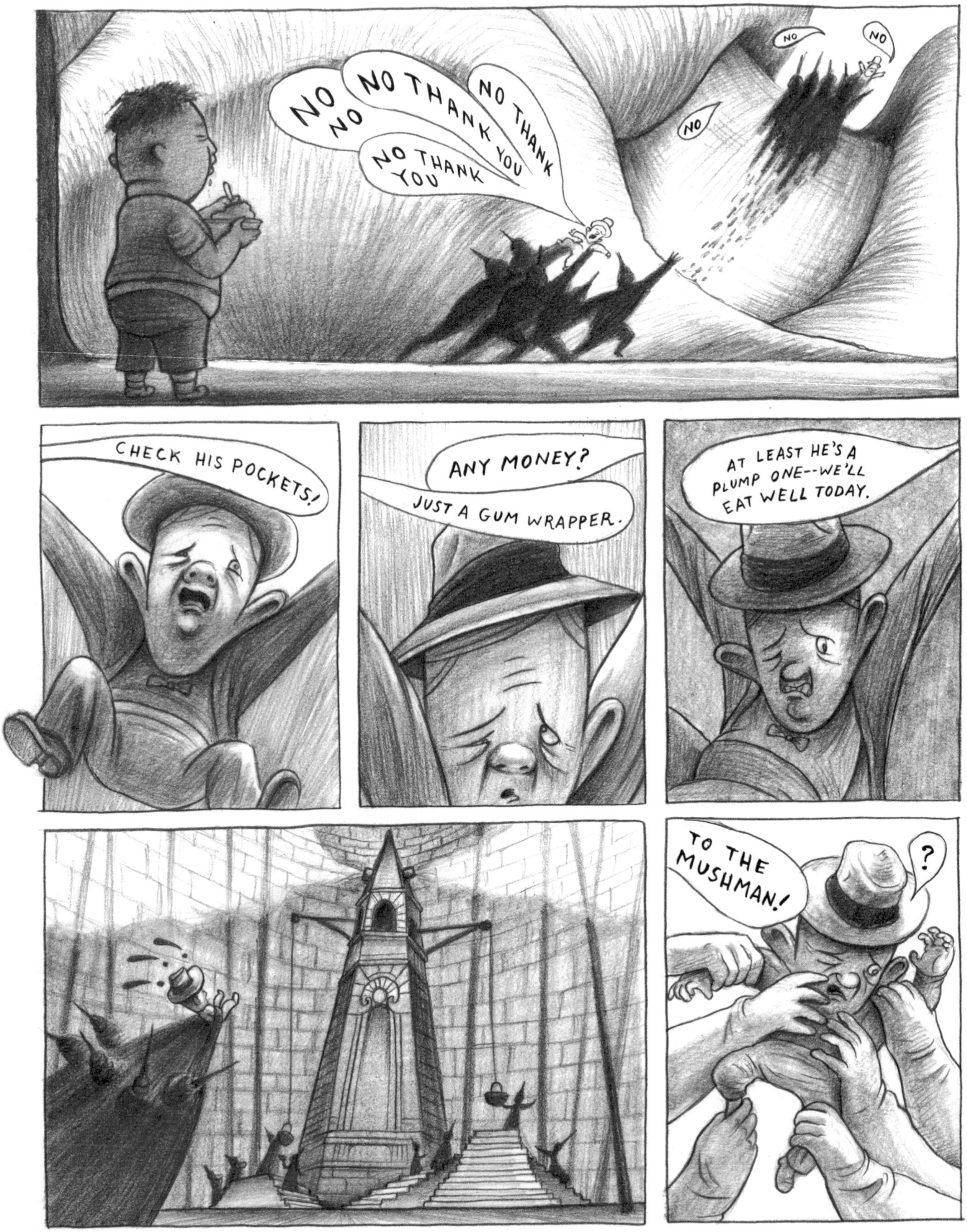

NO
NO
NO THANK YOU
NO THANK YOU
NO THANK YOU
NO
NO
NO
CHECK HIS POCKETS!
ANY MONEY?
JUST A GUM WRAPPER.
AT LEAST HE'S A PLUMP ONE--WE'LL EAT WELL TODAY.
TO THE MUSHMAN!
?

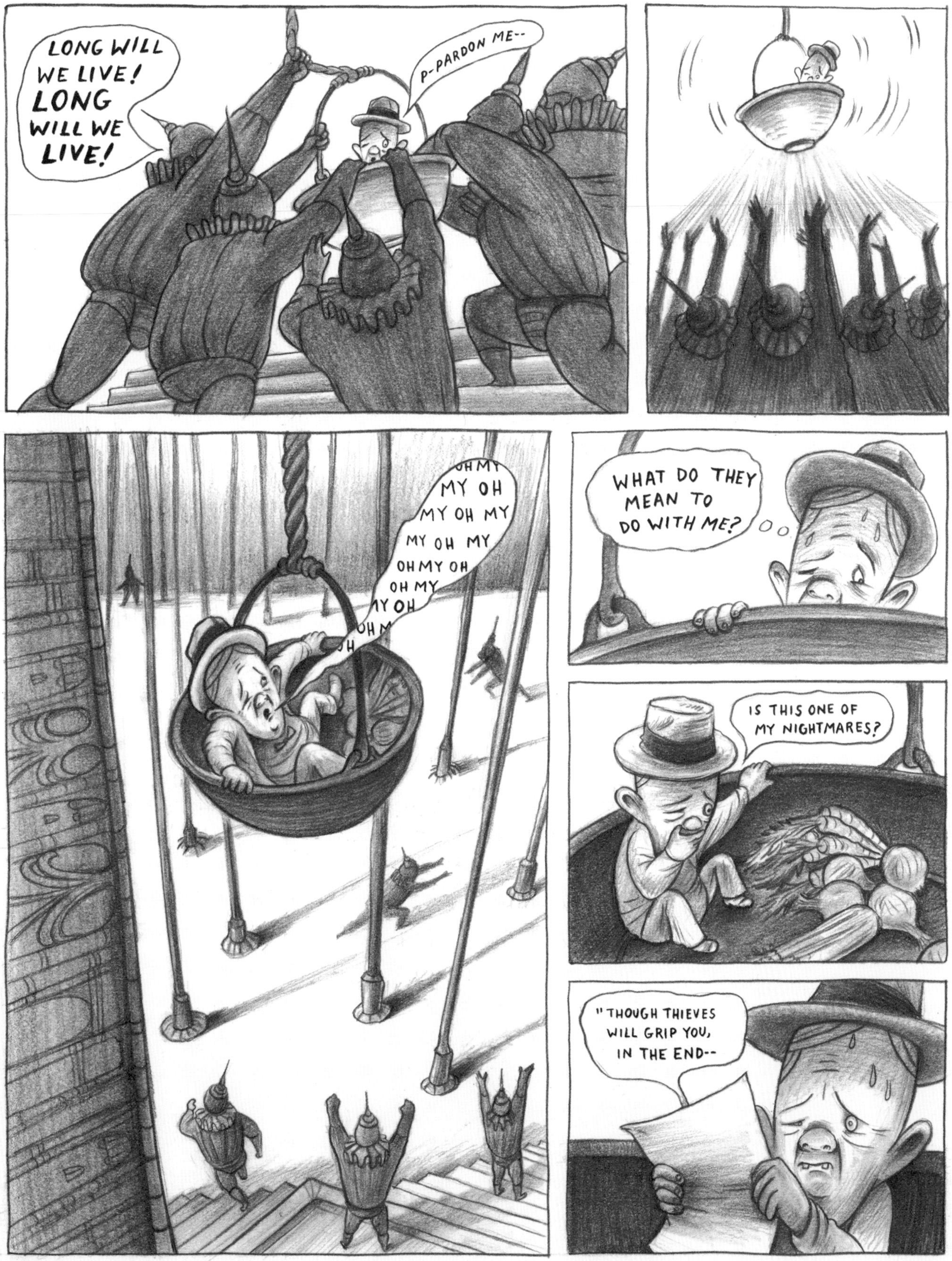

LONG WILL WE LIVE! LONG WILL WE LIVE!
P-PARDON ME--
MY OH MY OH MY OH MY MY OH MY OH MY OH OH MY
WHAT DO THEY MEAN TO DO WITH ME?
IS THIS ONE OF MY NIGHTMARES?
"THOUGH THIEVES WILL GRIP YOU, IN THE END--

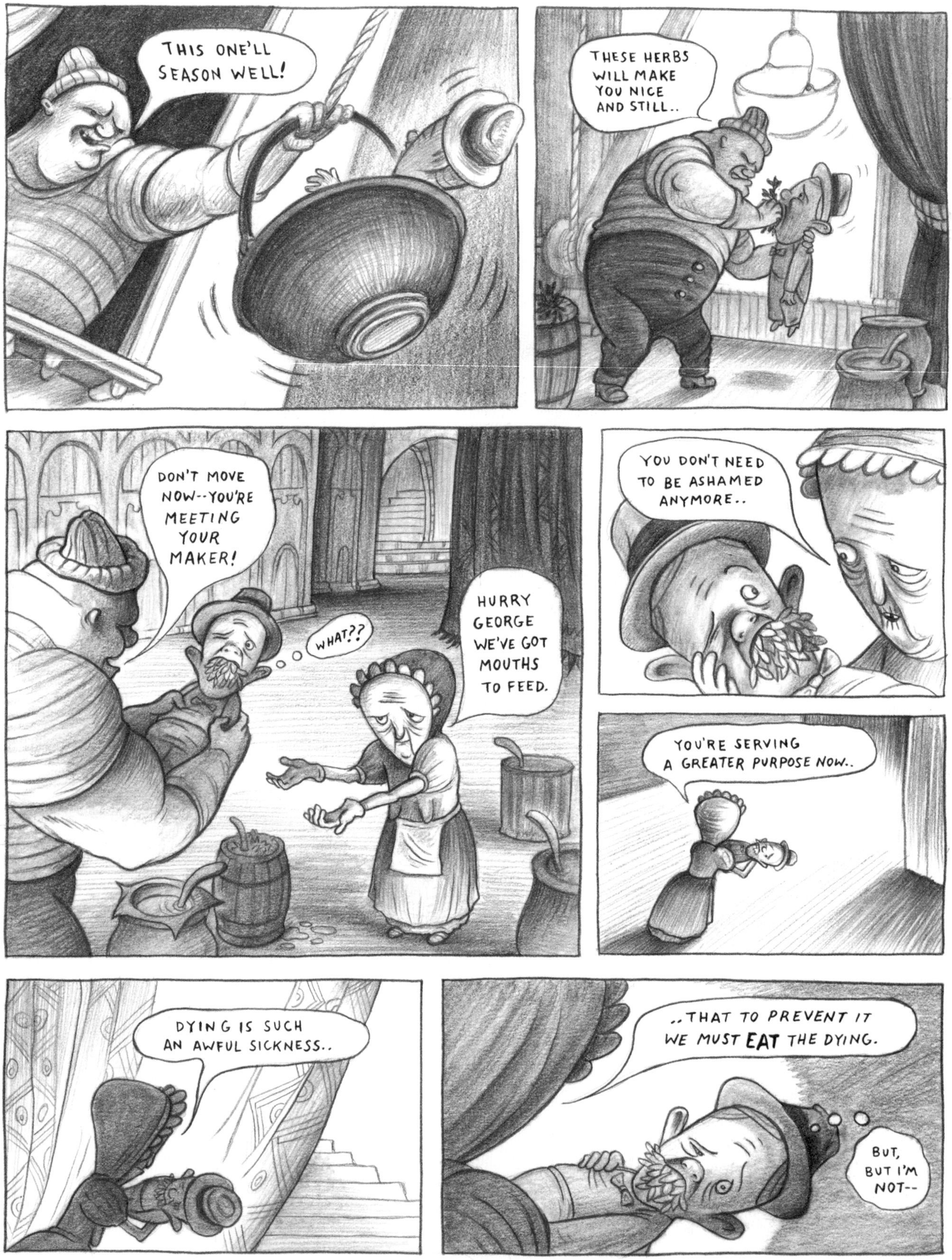
THIS ONE'LL SEASON WELL!
THESE HERBS WILL MAKE YOU NICE AND STILL..
DON'T MOVE NOW--YOU'RE MEETING YOUR MAKER!
WHAT??
HURRY GEORGE WE'VE GOT MOUTHS TO FEED.
YOU DON'T NEED TO BE ASHAMED ANYMORE..
YOU'RE SERVING A GREATER PURPOSE NOW..
DYING IS SUCH AN AWFUL SICKNESS..
..THAT TO PREVENT IT WE MUST EAT THE DYING.
BUT, BUT I'M NOT--

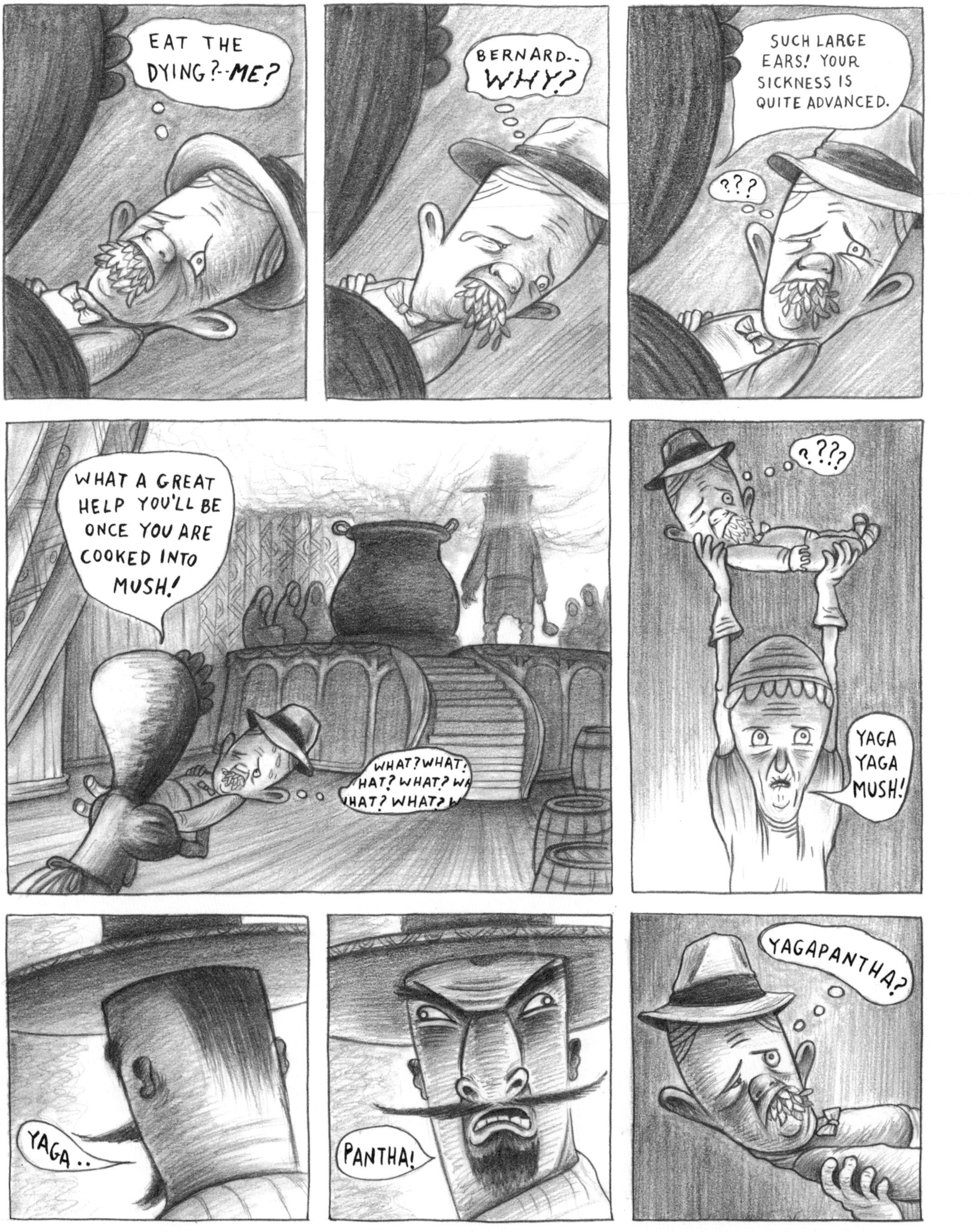
EAT THE DYING?--ME?
BERNARD-- WHY?
SUCH LARGE EARS! YOUR SICKNESS IS QUITE ADVANCED.
???
WHAT A GREAT HELP YOU'LL BE ONCE YOU ARE COOKED INTO MUSH!
WHAT? WHAT? WHAT? WHAT? WHAT? WHAT?
????
YAGA YAGA MUSH!
YAGA..
PANTHA!
YAGAPANTHA?

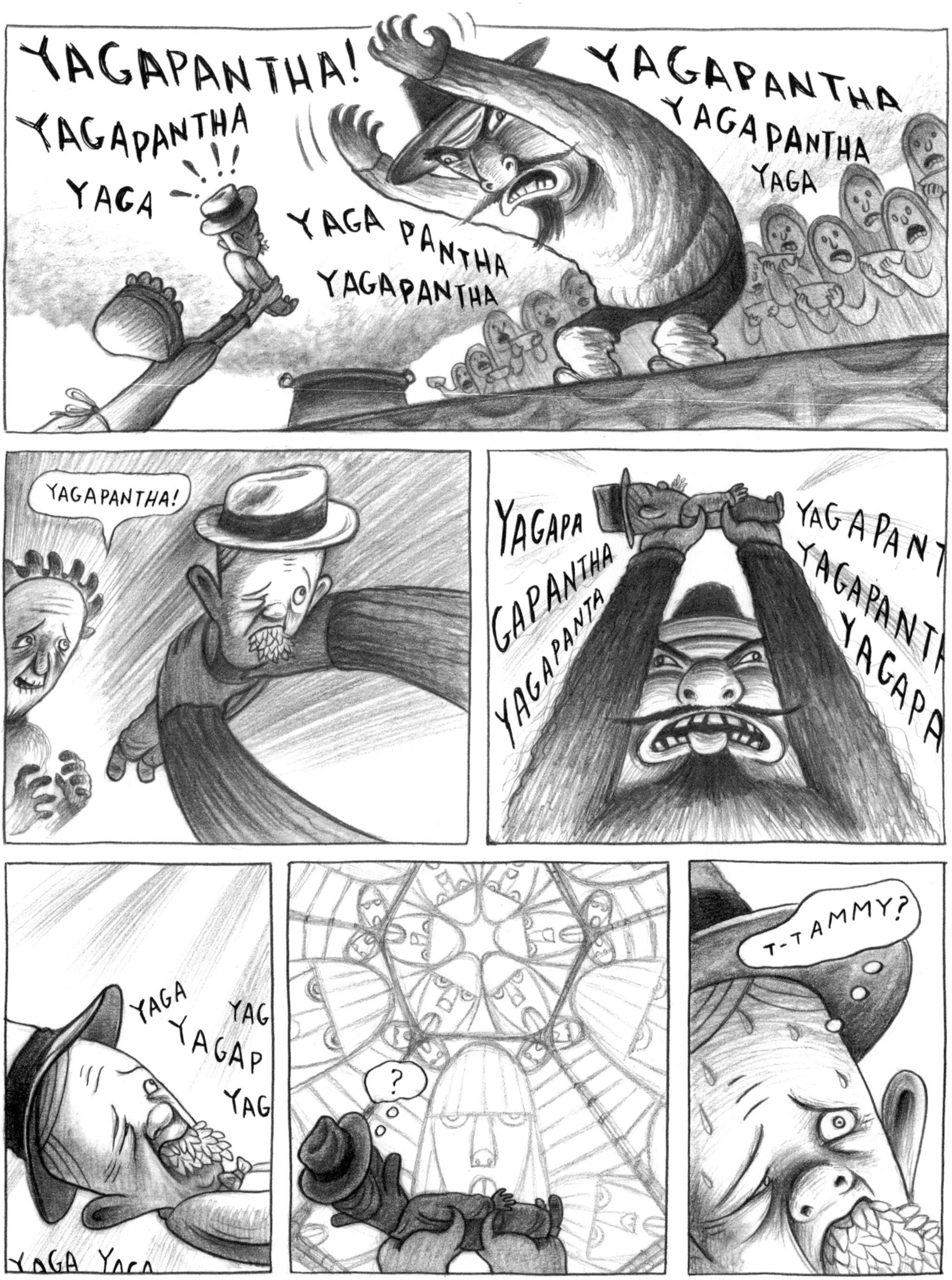
YAGAPANTHA!
YAGAPANTHA
YAGA
YAGA PANTHA
YAGAPANTHA
YAGAPANTHA
YAGAPANTHA
YAGA
YAGAPANTHA!
YAGAPA
GAPANTHA
YAGAPANTA
YAGAPANT
YAGAPANTH
YAGAPA
YAGA
YAG
YAGAP
YAG
?
T-TAMMY?

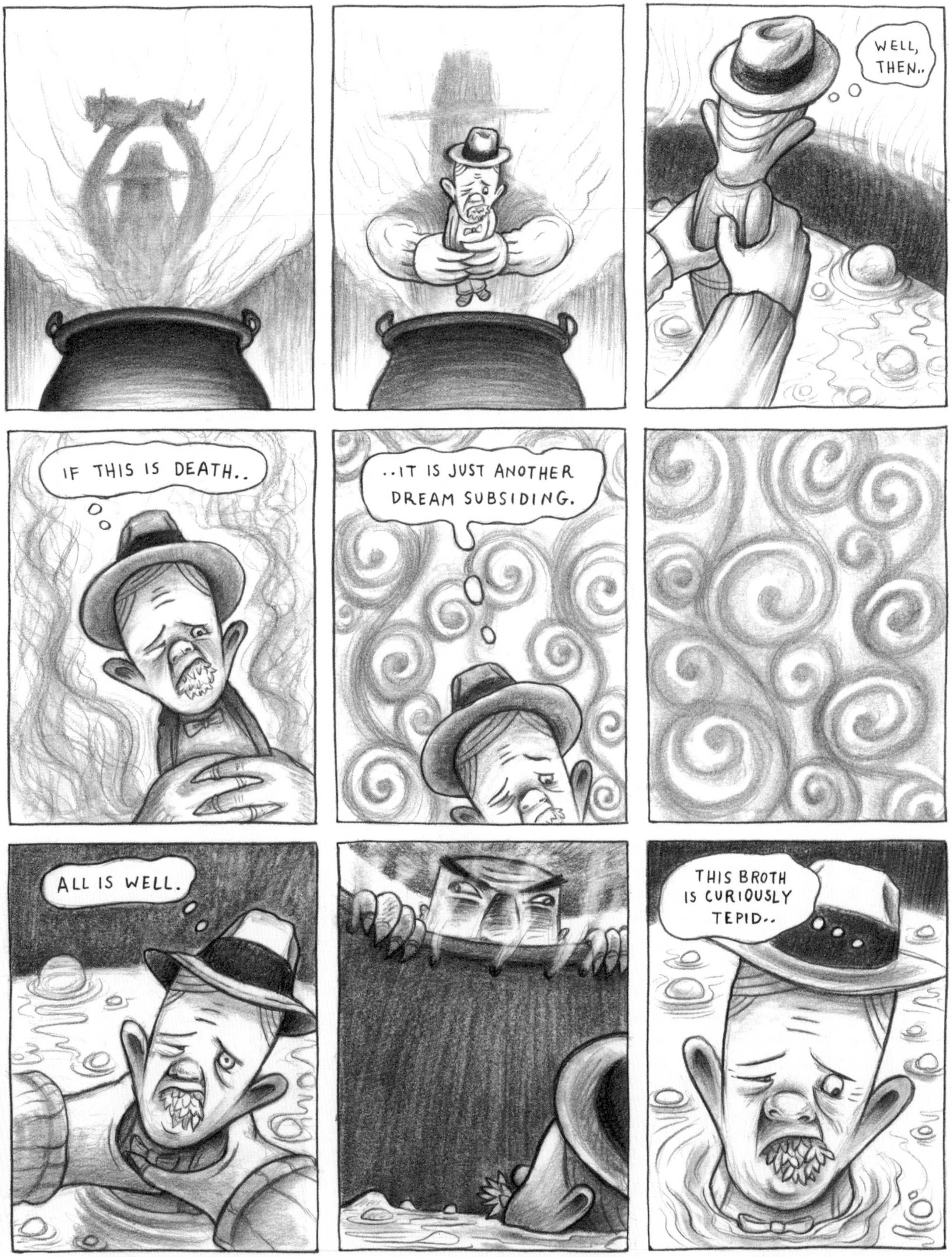
WELL, THEN..
IF THIS IS DEATH..
..IT IS JUST ANOTHER DREAM SUBSIDING.
ALL IS WELL.
THIS BROTH IS CURIOUSLY TEPID..

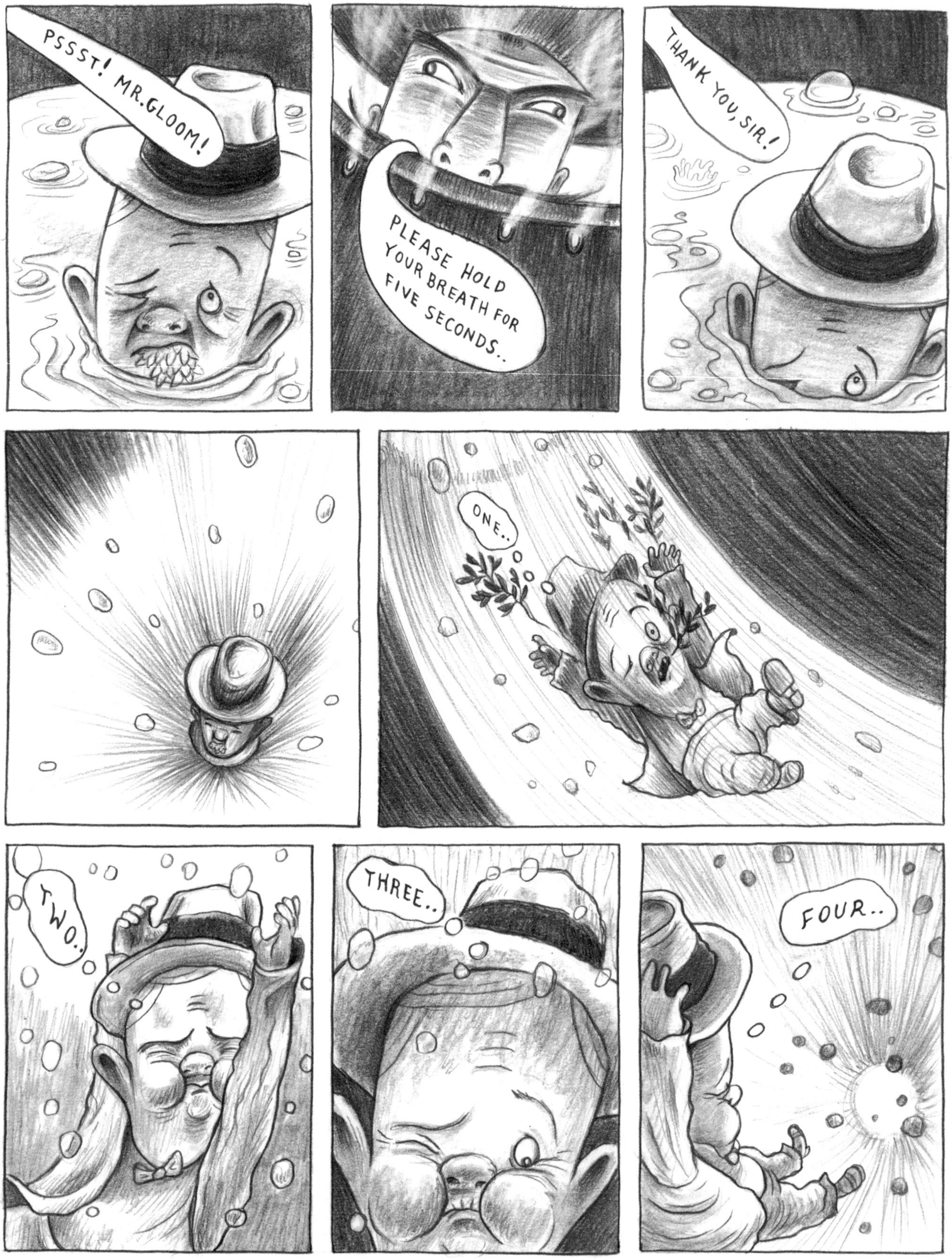
PSSST! MR. GLOOM!
PLEASE HOLD YOUR BREATH FOR FIVE SECONDS..
THANK YOU, SIR!
ONE..
TWO..
THREE..
FOUR..

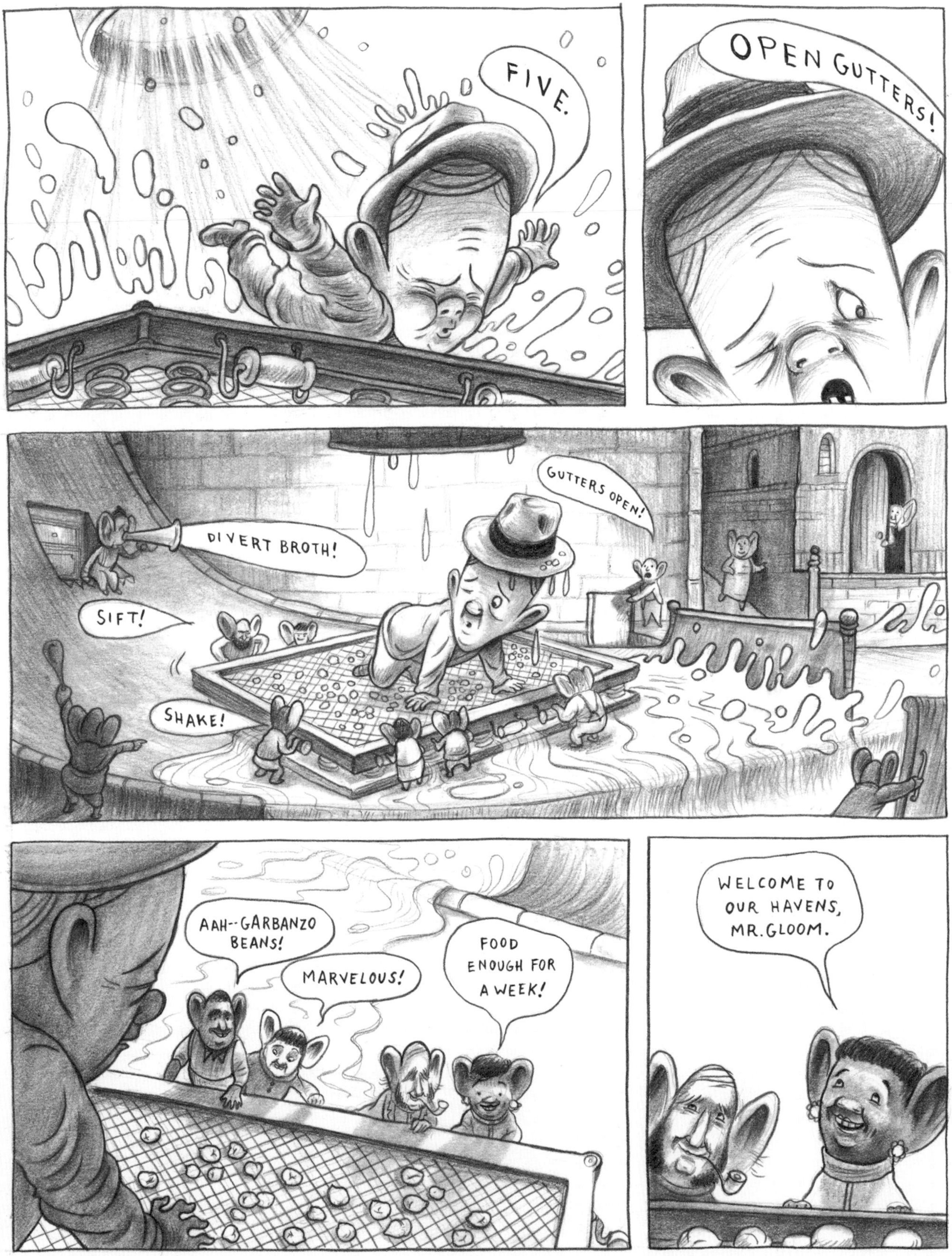

FIVE.
OPEN GUTTERS!
GUTTERS OPEN!
DIVERT BROTH!
SIFT!
SHAKE!
AAH--GARBANZO BEANS!
MARVELOUS!
FOOD ENOUGH FOR A WEEK!
WELCOME TO OUR HAVENS, MR. GLOOM.

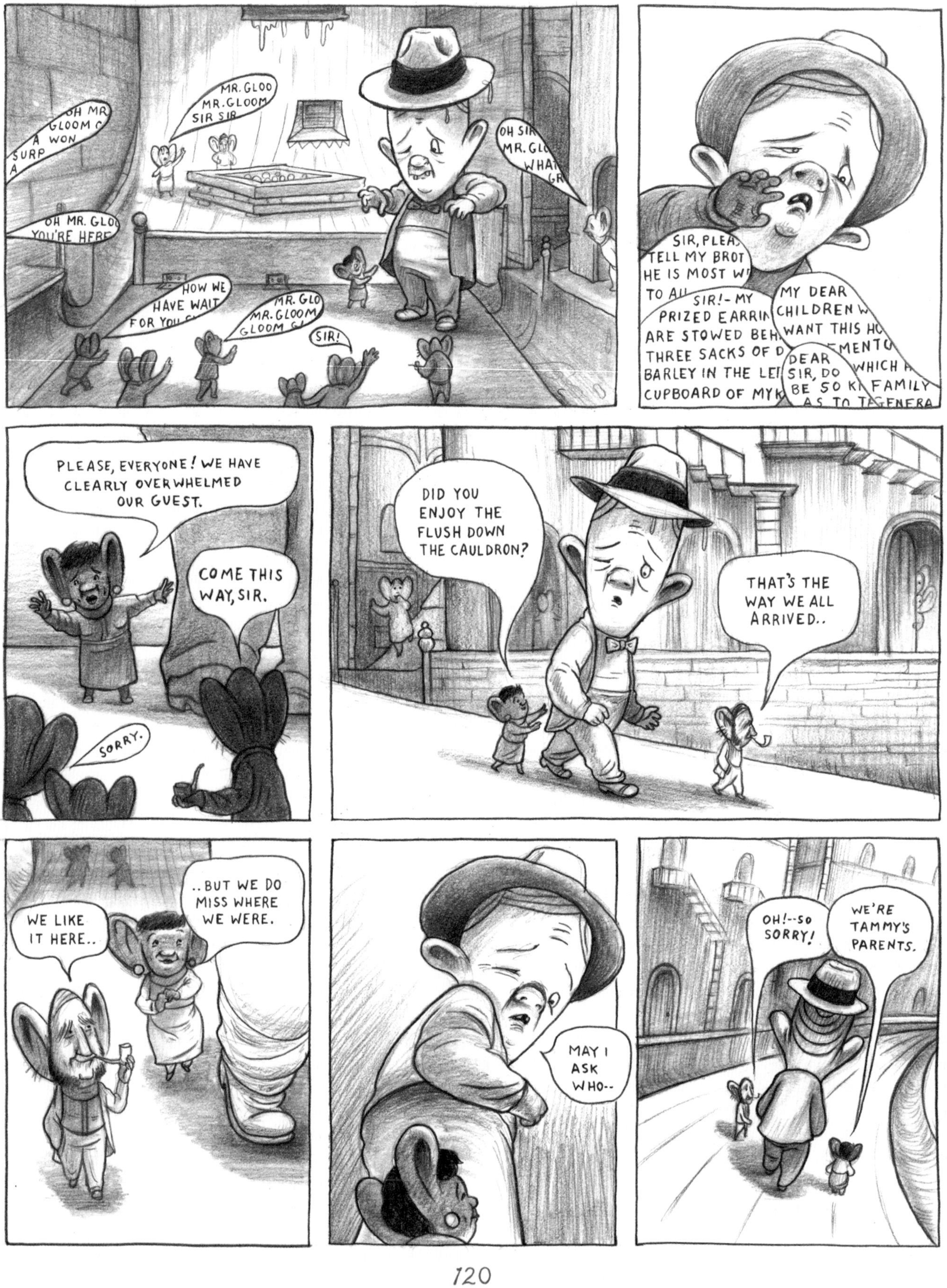
OH MR GLOOM A WON SURP A
MR. GLOO MR. GLOOM SIR SIR
OH SIR MR. GLO WHAT GR
OH MR. GLO YOU'RE HERE
HOW WE HAVE WAIT FOR YOU
MR. GLO MR. GLOOM GLOOM
SIR!
SIR, PLEAS TELL MY BROT HE IS MOST W TO AL
SIR!- MY PRIZED EARRIN ARE STOWED BEH THREE SACKS OF D BARLEY IN THE LE CUPBOARD OF MYK
MY DEAR CHILDREN W WANT THIS HO MEMENTO WHICH H FAMILY
DEAR SIR, DO BE SO K AS TO
PLEASE, EVERYONE! WE HAVE CLEARLY OVERWHELMED OUR GUEST.
COME THIS WAY, SIR.
SORRY.
DID YOU ENJOY THE FLUSH DOWN THE CAULDRON?
THAT'S THE WAY WE ALL ARRIVED..
WE LIKE IT HERE..
..BUT WE DO MISS WHERE WE WERE.
MAY I ASK WHO--
OH!--SO SORRY!
WE'RE TAMMY'S PARENTS.

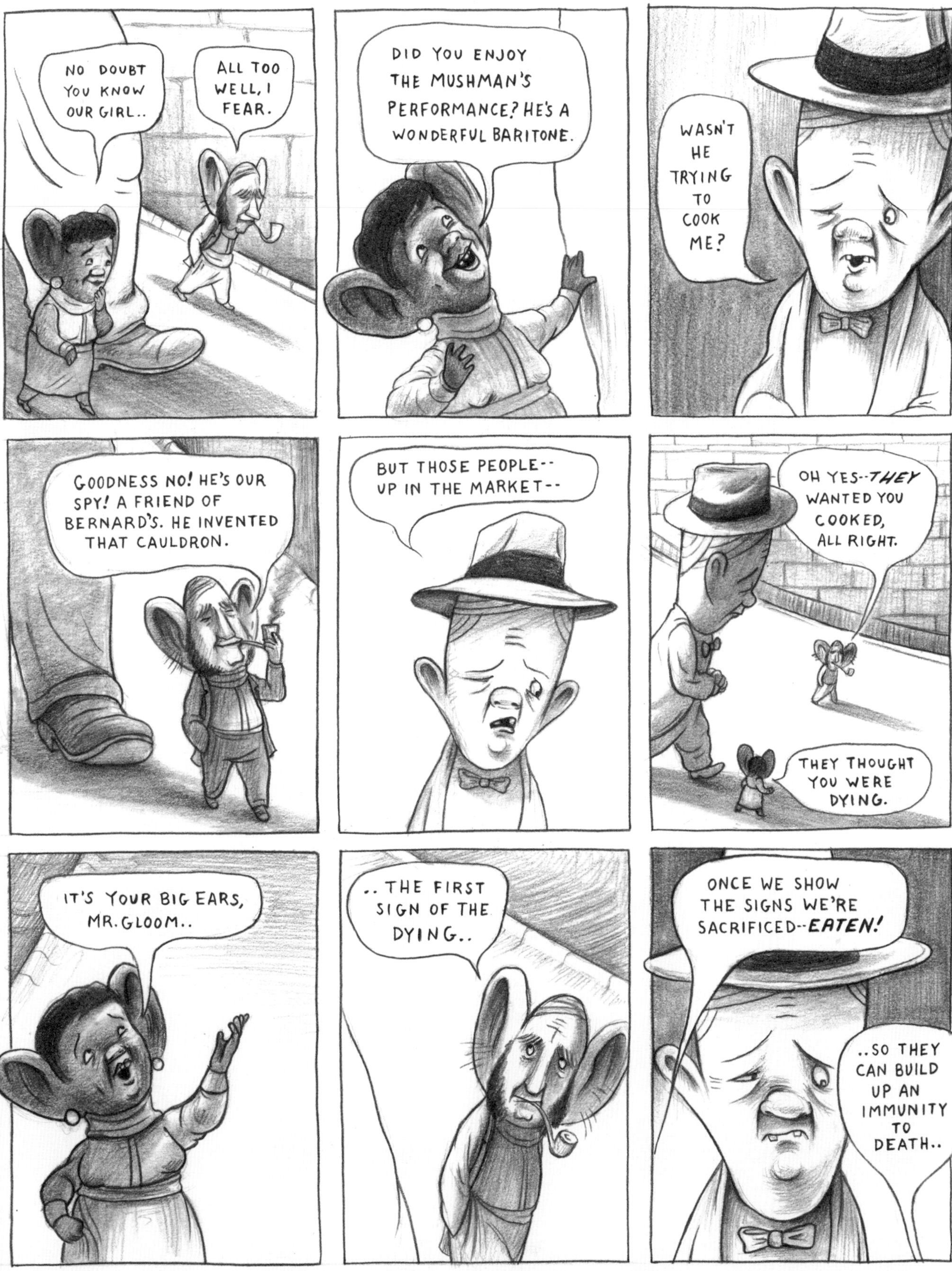
NO DOUBT YOU KNOW OUR GIRL..
ALL TOO WELL, I FEAR.
DID YOU ENJOY THE MUSHMAN'S PERFORMANCE? HE'S A WONDERFUL BARITONE.
WASN'T HE TRYING TO COOK ME?
GOODNESS NO! HE'S OUR SPY! A FRIEND OF BERNARD'S. HE INVENTED THAT CAULDRON.
BUT THOSE PEOPLE-- UP IN THE MARKET--
OH YES--*THEY* WANTED YOU COOKED, ALL RIGHT.
THEY THOUGHT YOU WERE DYING.
IT'S YOUR BIG EARS, MR. GLOOM..
..THE FIRST SIGN OF THE DYING..
ONCE WE SHOW THE SIGNS WE'RE SACRIFICED--*EATEN!*
..SO THEY CAN BUILD UP AN IMMUNITY TO DEATH..

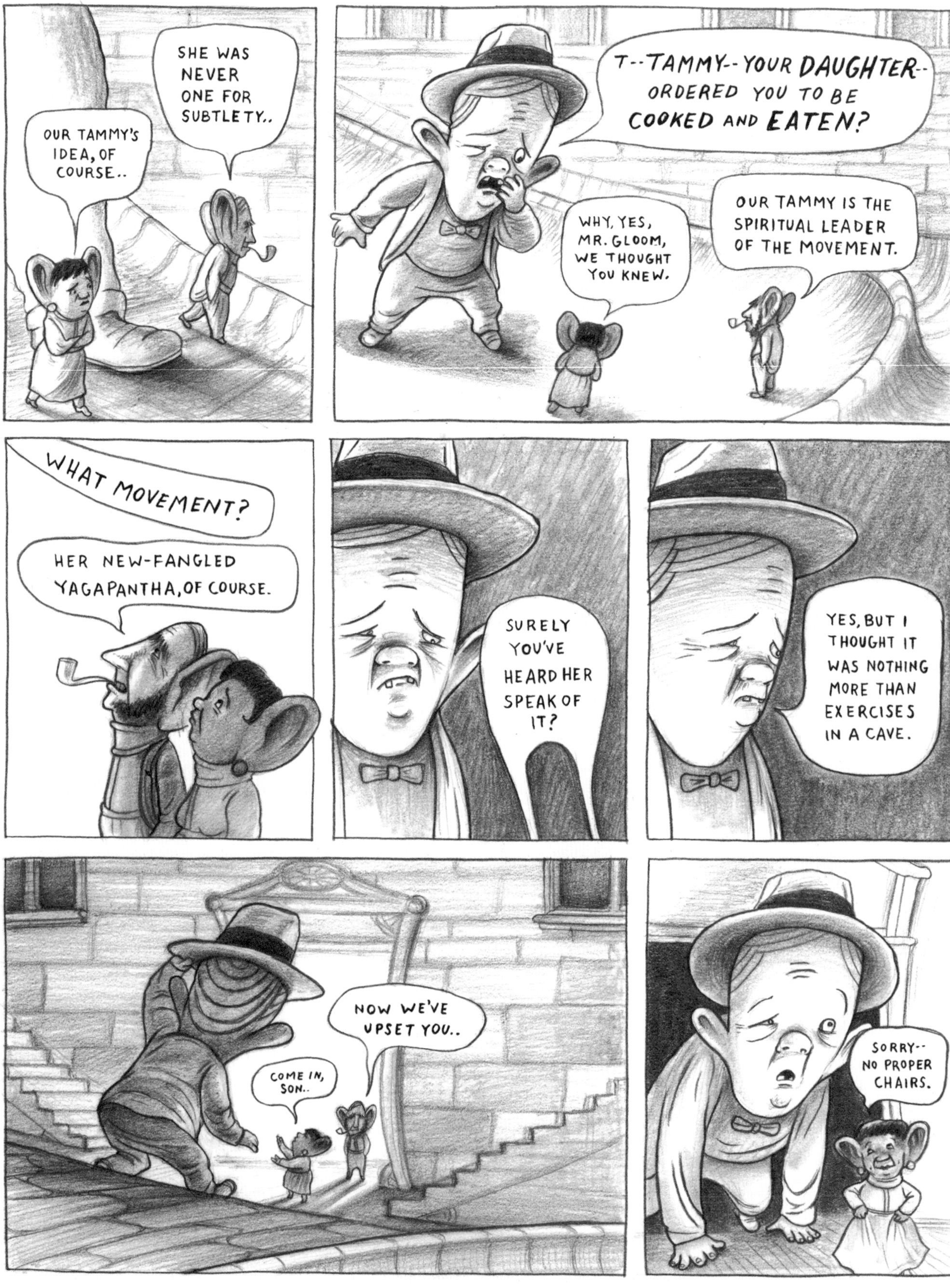

OUR TAMMY'S IDEA, OF COURSE..
SHE WAS NEVER ONE FOR SUBTLETY..
T--TAMMY--YOUR DAUGHTER--ORDERED YOU TO BE COOKED AND EATEN?
WHY, YES, MR. GLOOM, WE THOUGHT YOU KNEW.
OUR TAMMY IS THE SPIRITUAL LEADER OF THE MOVEMENT.
WHAT MOVEMENT?
HER NEW-FANGLED YAGAPANTHA, OF COURSE.
SURELY YOU'VE HEARD HER SPEAK OF IT?
YES, BUT I THOUGHT IT WAS NOTHING MORE THAN EXERCISES IN A CAVE.
NOW WE'VE UPSET YOU..
COME IN, SON..
SORRY--NO PROPER CHAIRS.

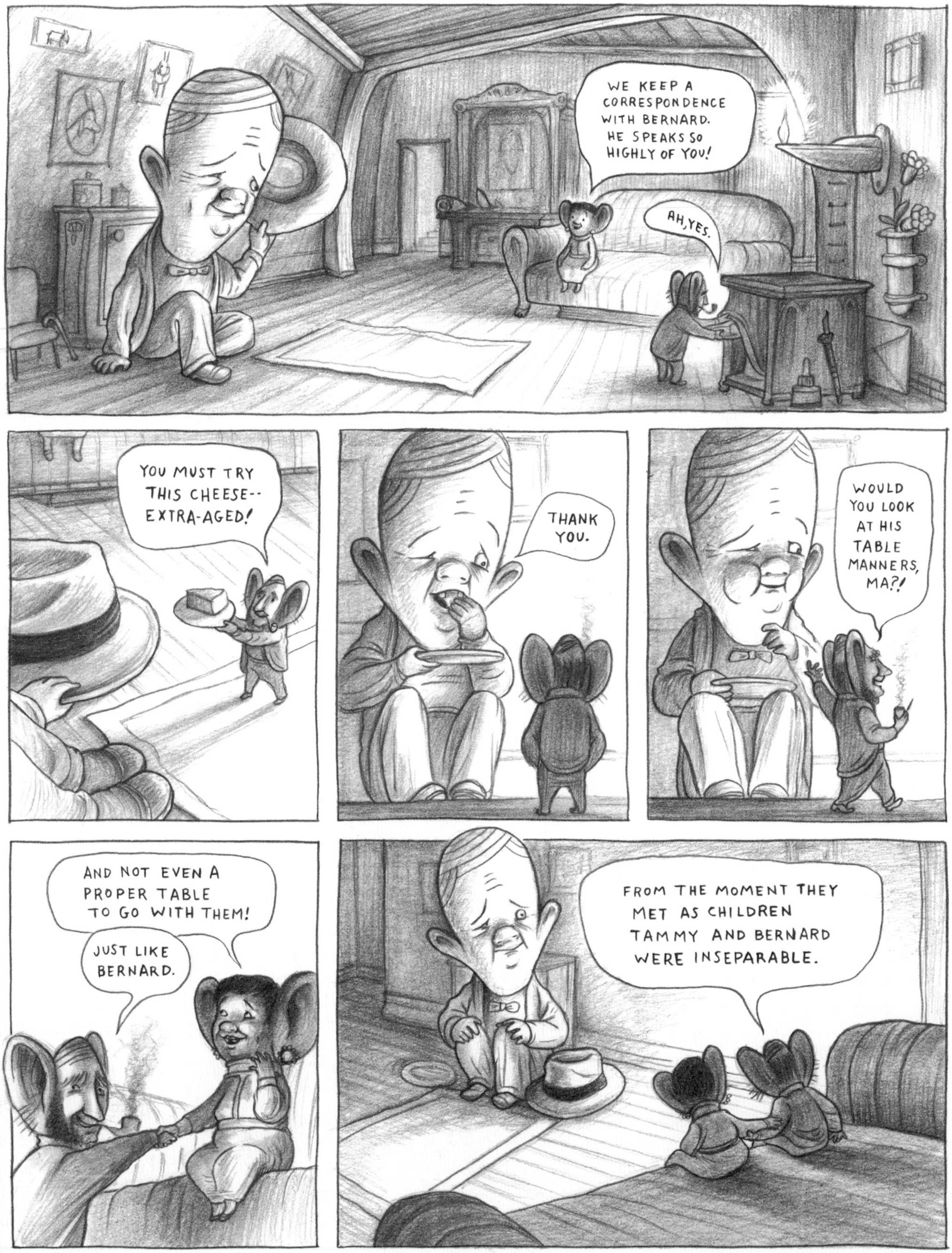
WE KEEP A CORRESPONDENCE WITH BERNARD. HE SPEAKS SO HIGHLY OF YOU!
AH, YES.
YOU MUST TRY THIS CHEESE-- EXTRA-AGED!
THANK YOU.
WOULD YOU LOOK AT HIS TABLE MANNERS, MA?!
AND NOT EVEN A PROPER TABLE TO GO WITH THEM!
JUST LIKE BERNARD.
FROM THE MOMENT THEY MET AS CHILDREN TAMMY AND BERNARD WERE INSEPARABLE.

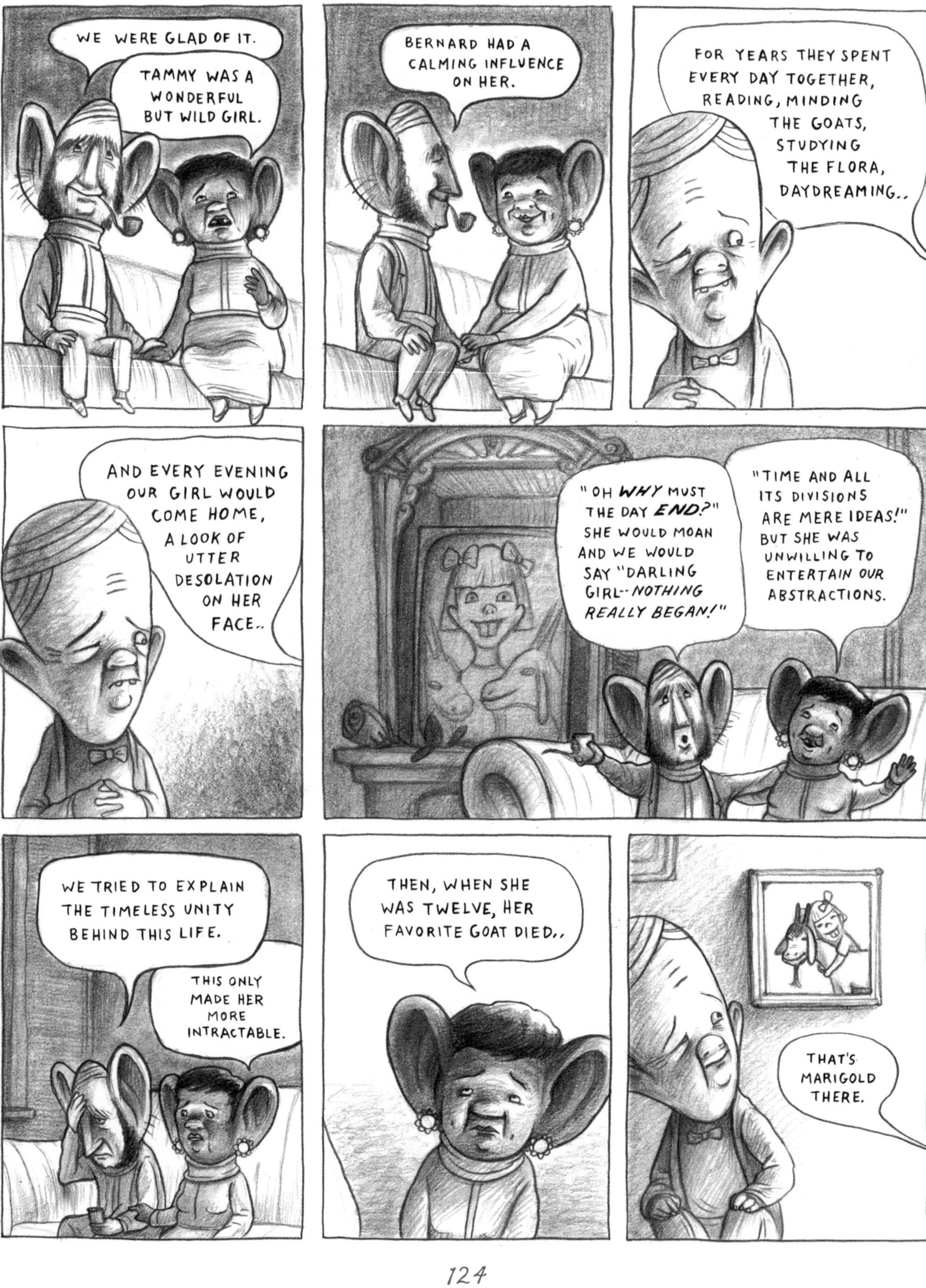
WE WERE GLAD OF IT.
TAMMY WAS A WONDERFUL BUT WILD GIRL.
BERNARD HAD A CALMING INFLUENCE ON HER.
FOR YEARS THEY SPENT EVERY DAY TOGETHER, READING, MINDING THE GOATS, STUDYING THE FLORA, DAYDREAMING..
AND EVERY EVENING OUR GIRL WOULD COME HOME, A LOOK OF UTTER DESOLATION ON HER FACE..
"OH WHY MUST THE DAY END?" SHE WOULD MOAN AND WE WOULD SAY "DARLING GIRL-- NOTHING REALLY BEGAN!"
"TIME AND ALL ITS DIVISIONS ARE MERE IDEAS!" BUT SHE WAS UNWILLING TO ENTERTAIN OUR ABSTRACTIONS.
WE TRIED TO EXPLAIN THE TIMELESS UNITY BEHIND THIS LIFE.
THIS ONLY MADE HER MORE INTRACTABLE.
THEN, WHEN SHE WAS TWELVE, HER FAVORITE GOAT DIED..
THAT'S MARIGOLD THERE.

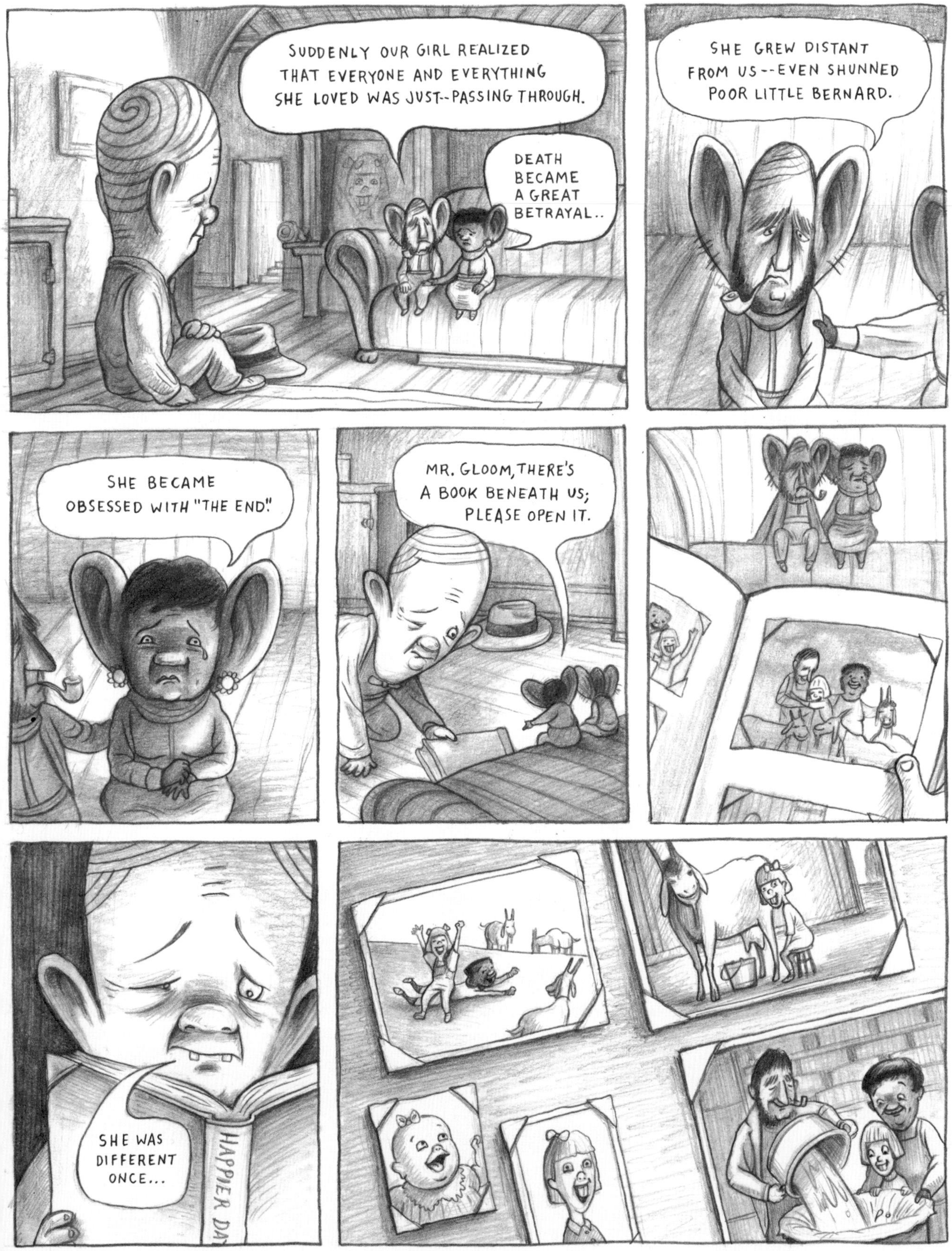
SUDDENLY OUR GIRL REALIZED THAT EVERYONE AND EVERYTHING SHE LOVED WAS JUST--PASSING THROUGH.
DEATH BECAME A GREAT BETRAYAL..
SHE GREW DISTANT FROM US--EVEN SHUNNED POOR LITTLE BERNARD.
SHE BECAME OBSESSED WITH "THE END."
MR. GLOOM, THERE'S A BOOK BENEATH US; PLEASE OPEN IT.
SHE WAS DIFFERENT ONCE...
HAPPIER DA

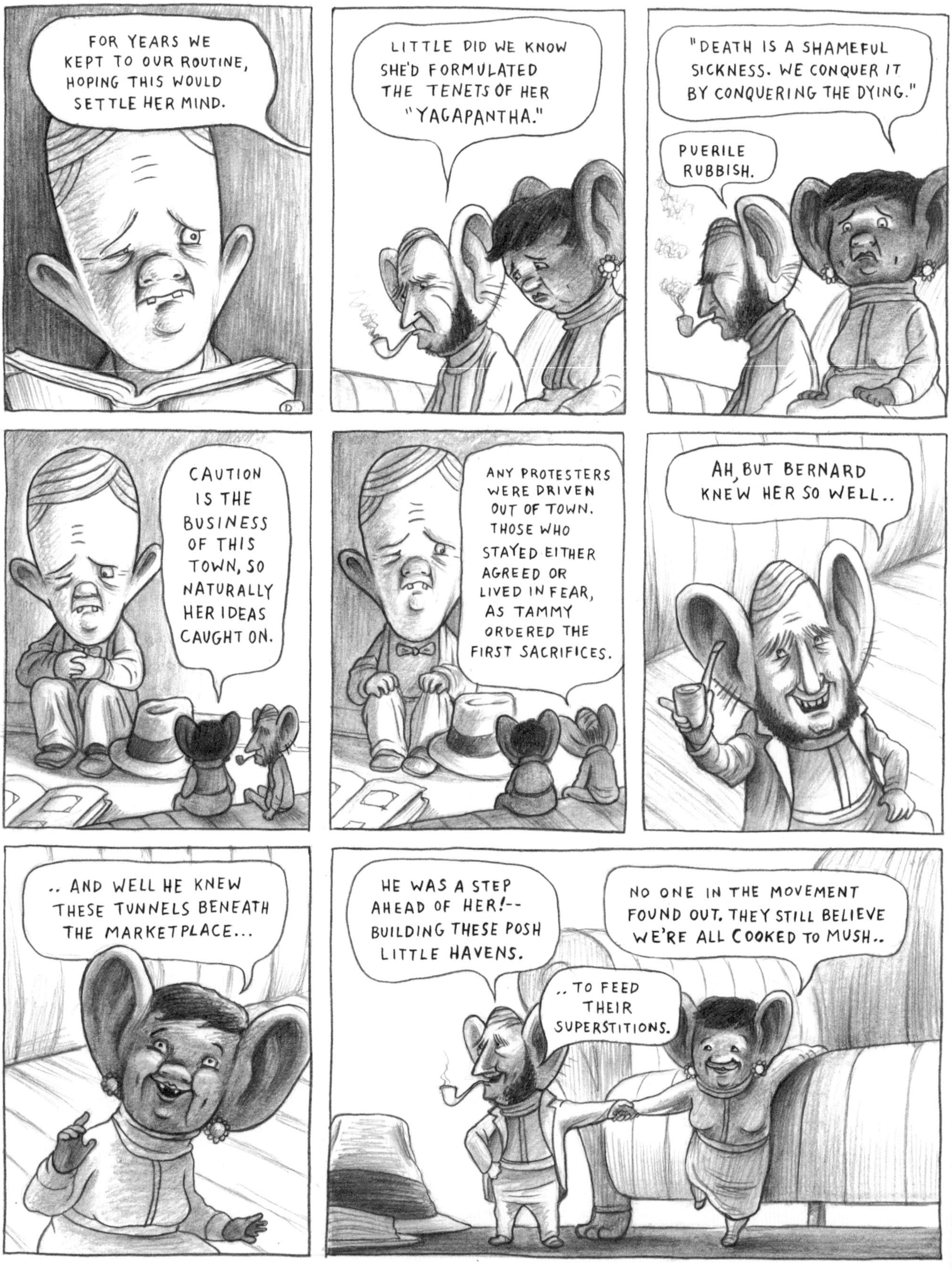
FOR YEARS WE KEPT TO OUR ROUTINE, HOPING THIS WOULD SETTLE HER MIND.
LITTLE DID WE KNOW SHE'D FORMULATED THE TENETS OF HER "YAGAPANTHA."
"DEATH IS A SHAMEFUL SICKNESS. WE CONQUER IT BY CONQUERING THE DYING."
PUERILE RUBBISH.
CAUTION IS THE BUSINESS OF THIS TOWN, SO NATURALLY HER IDEAS CAUGHT ON.
ANY PROTESTERS WERE DRIVEN OUT OF TOWN. THOSE WHO STAYED EITHER AGREED OR LIVED IN FEAR, AS TAMMY ORDERED THE FIRST SACRIFICES.
AH, BUT BERNARD KNEW HER SO WELL..
.. AND WELL HE KNEW THESE TUNNELS BENEATH THE MARKETPLACE...
HE WAS A STEP AHEAD OF HER!-- BUILDING THESE POSH LITTLE HAVENS.
.. TO FEED THEIR SUPERSTITIONS.
NO ONE IN THE MOVEMENT FOUND OUT. THEY STILL BELIEVE WE'RE ALL COOKED TO MUSH..

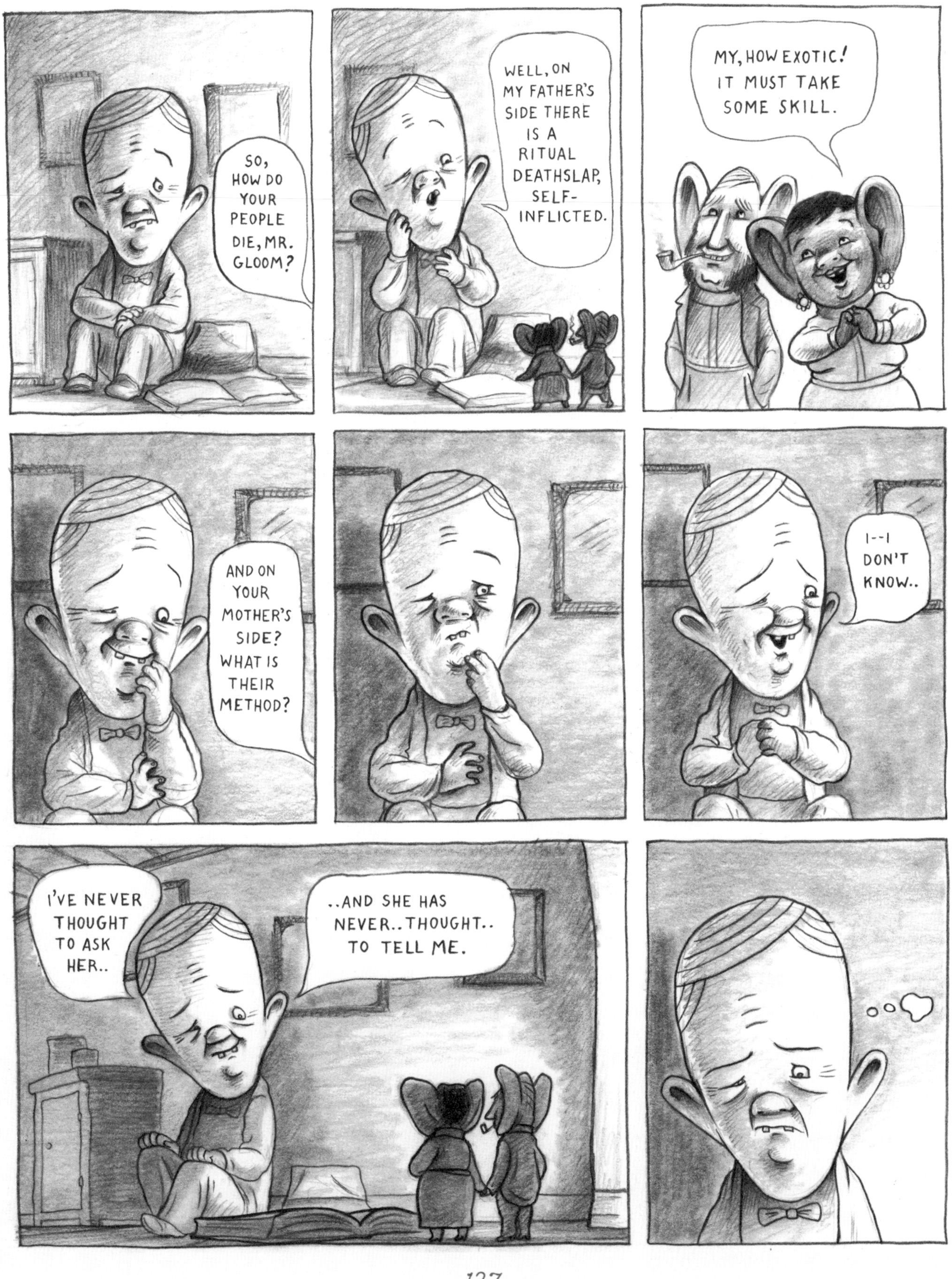
SO, HOW DO YOUR PEOPLE DIE, MR. GLOOM?
WELL, ON MY FATHER'S SIDE THERE IS A RITUAL DEATHSLAP, SELF-INFLICTED.
MY, HOW EXOTIC! IT MUST TAKE SOME SKILL.
AND ON YOUR MOTHER'S SIDE? WHAT IS THEIR METHOD?
I--I DON'T KNOW..
I'VE NEVER THOUGHT TO ASK HER..
..AND SHE HAS NEVER.. THOUGHT.. TO TELL ME.

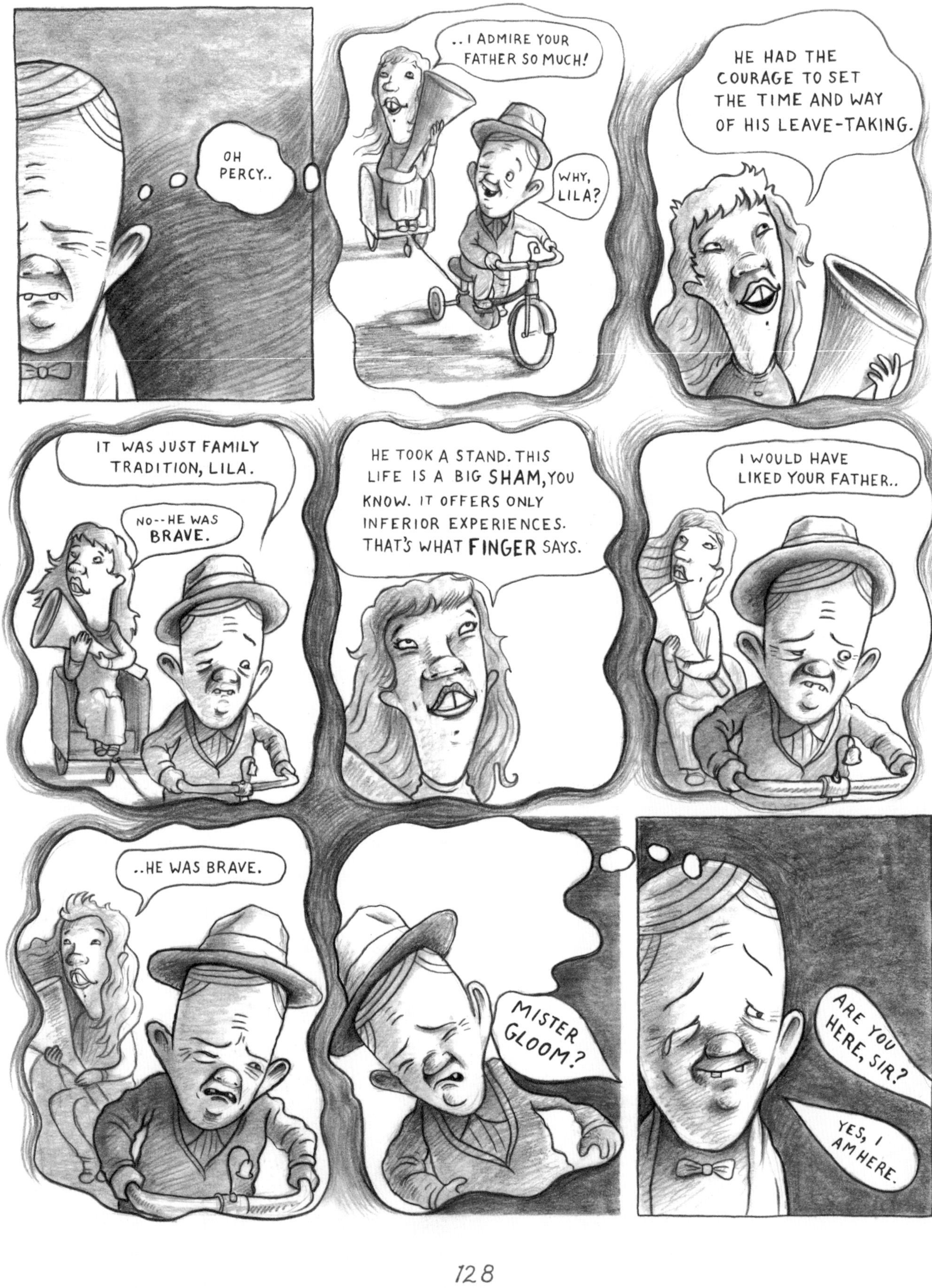
OH PERCY..
..I ADMIRE YOUR FATHER SO MUCH!
WHY, LILA?
HE HAD THE COURAGE TO SET THE TIME AND WAY OF HIS LEAVE-TAKING.
IT WAS JUST FAMILY TRADITION, LILA.
NO--HE WAS BRAVE.
HE TOOK A STAND. THIS LIFE IS A BIG SHAM, YOU KNOW. IT OFFERS ONLY INFERIOR EXPERIENCES. THAT'S WHAT FINGER SAYS.
I WOULD HAVE LIKED YOUR FATHER..
..HE WAS BRAVE.
MISTER GLOOM?
ARE YOU HERE, SIR?
YES, I AM HERE.

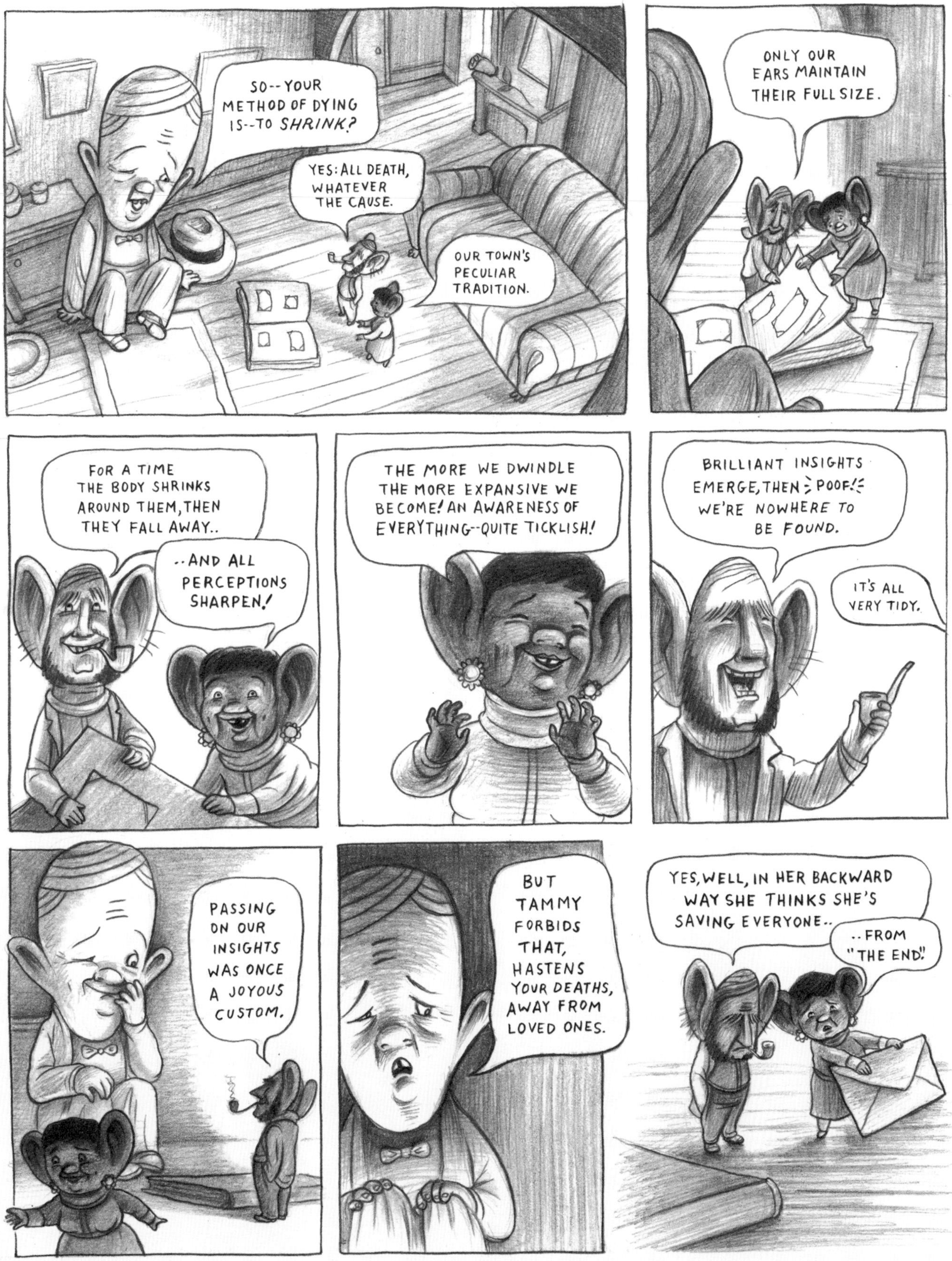

SO--YOUR METHOD OF DYING IS--TO *SHRINK?*
YES: ALL DEATH, WHATEVER THE CAUSE.
OUR TOWN'S PECULIAR TRADITION.
ONLY OUR EARS MAINTAIN THEIR FULL SIZE.
FOR A TIME THE BODY SHRINKS AROUND THEM, THEN THEY FALL AWAY..
..AND ALL PERCEPTIONS SHARPEN!
THE MORE WE DWINDLE THE MORE EXPANSIVE WE BECOME! AN AWARENESS OF EVERYTHING--QUITE TICKLISH!
BRILLIANT INSIGHTS EMERGE, THEN POOF! WE'RE NOWHERE TO BE FOUND.
IT'S ALL VERY TIDY.
PASSING ON OUR INSIGHTS WAS ONCE A JOYOUS CUSTOM.
BUT TAMMY FORBIDS THAT, HASTENS YOUR DEATHS, AWAY FROM LOVED ONES.
YES, WELL, IN HER BACKWARD WAY SHE THINKS SHE'S SAVING EVERYONE..
..FROM "THE END."

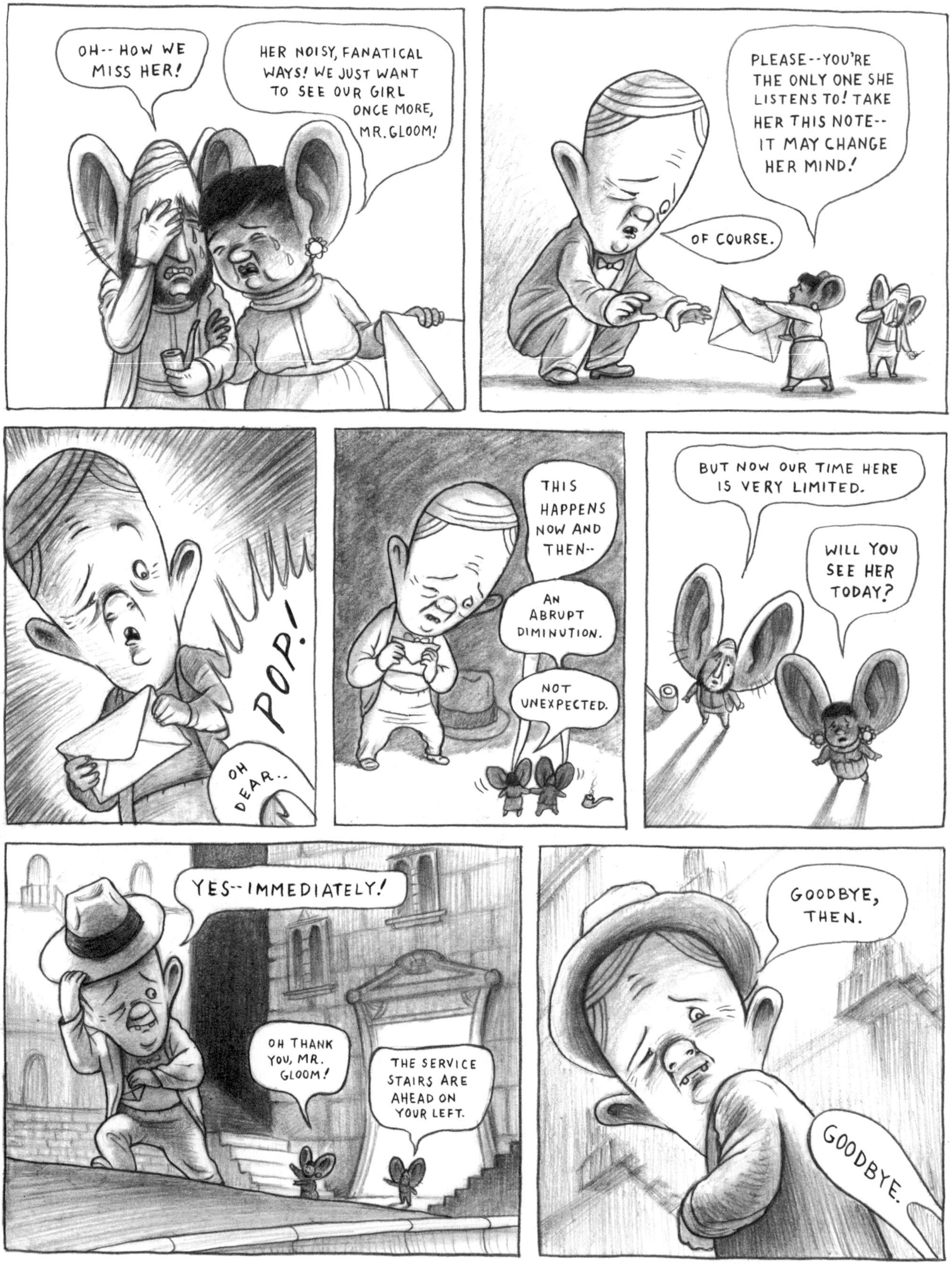
OH-- HOW WE MISS HER!
HER NOISY, FANATICAL WAYS! WE JUST WANT TO SEE OUR GIRL ONCE MORE, MR. GLOOM!
PLEASE--YOU'RE THE ONLY ONE SHE LISTENS TO! TAKE HER THIS NOTE-- IT MAY CHANGE HER MIND!
OF COURSE.
POP!
OH DEAR..
THIS HAPPENS NOW AND THEN--
AN ABRUPT DIMINUTION.
NOT UNEXPECTED.
BUT NOW OUR TIME HERE IS VERY LIMITED.
WILL YOU SEE HER TODAY?
YES--IMMEDIATELY!
OH THANK YOU, MR. GLOOM!
THE SERVICE STAIRS ARE AHEAD ON YOUR LEFT.
GOODBYE, THEN.
GOODBYE.

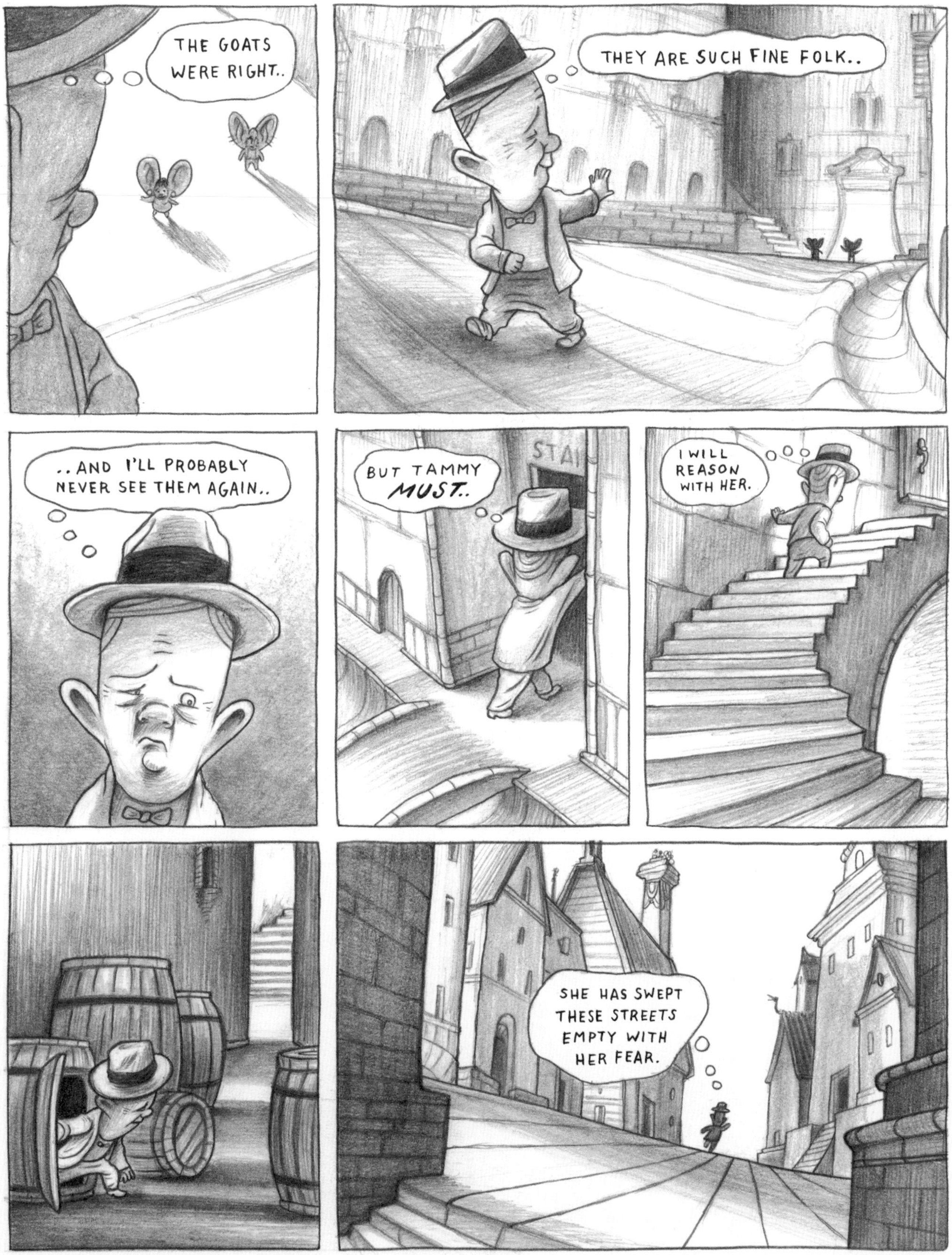
THE GOATS WERE RIGHT..
THEY ARE SUCH FINE FOLK..
..AND I'LL PROBABLY NEVER SEE THEM AGAIN..
STAI
BUT TAMMY MUST..
I WILL REASON WITH HER.
SHE HAS SWEPT THESE STREETS EMPTY WITH HER FEAR.

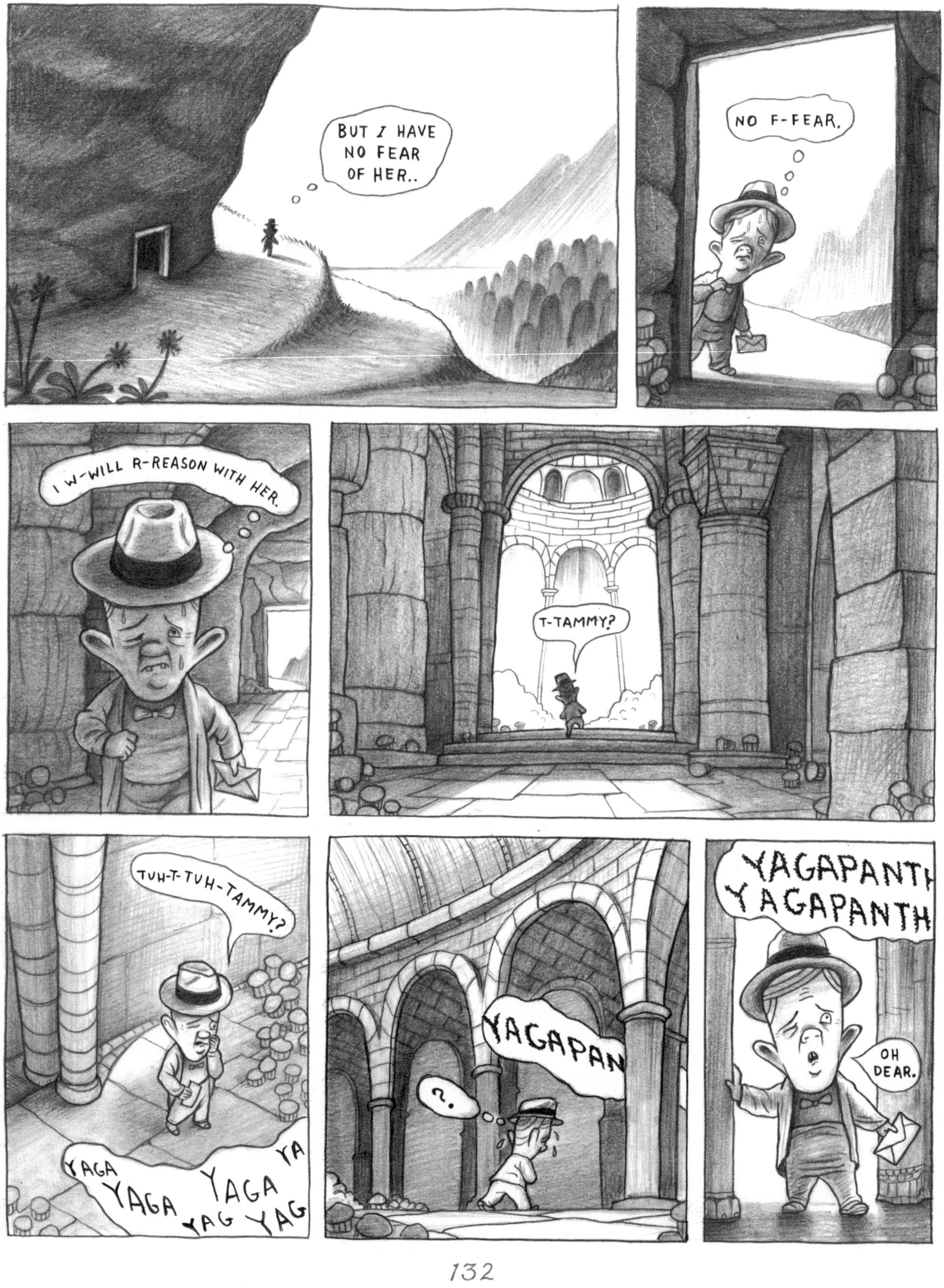
BUT I HAVE NO FEAR OF HER..
NO F-FEAR.
I W-WILL R-REASON WITH HER.
T-TAMMY?
TUH-T-TUH-TAMMY?
YAGA YAGA YAGA YA YAG YAG
YAGAPAN
?
YAGAPANTH YAGAPANTH
OH DEAR.

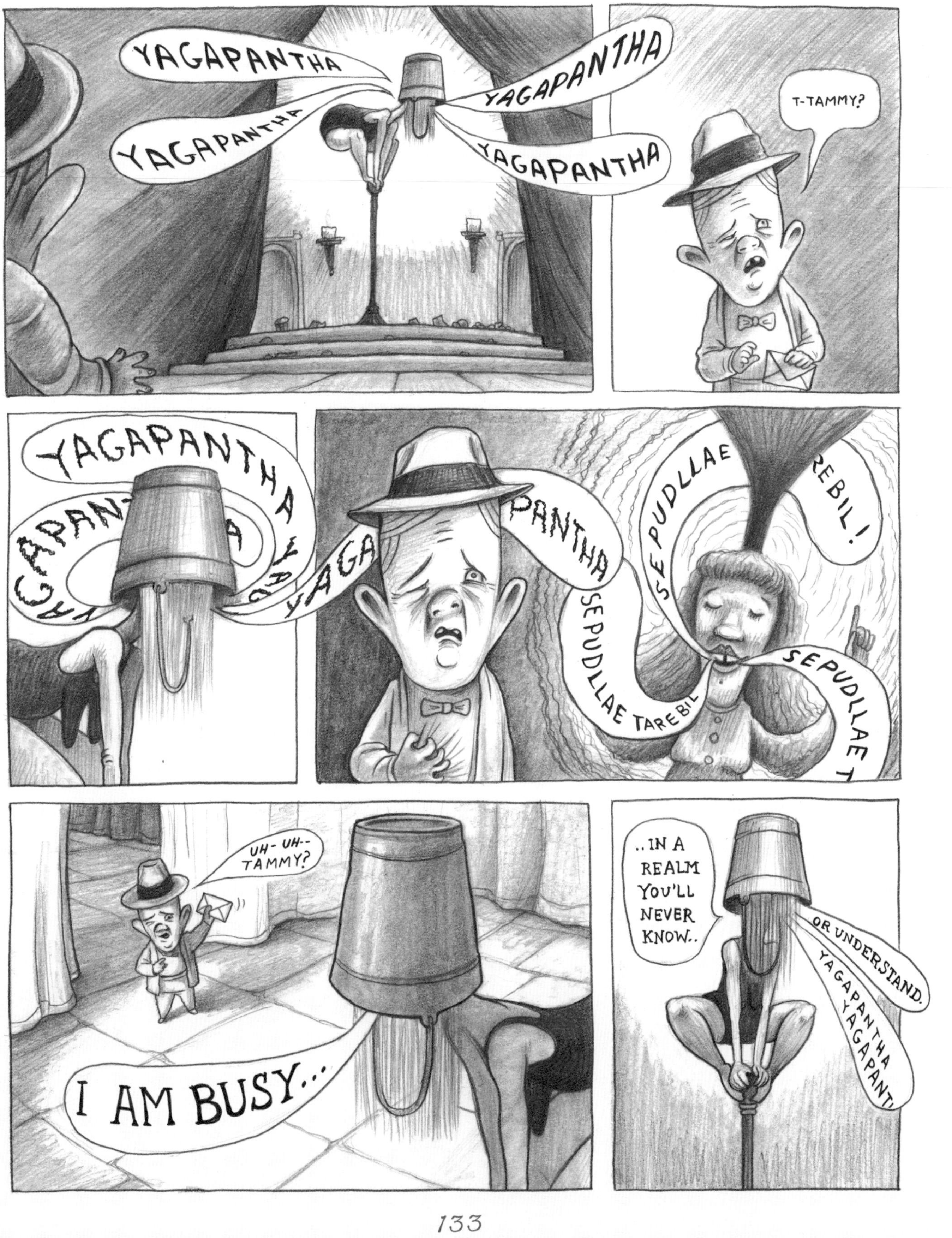
YAGAPANTHA
YAGAPANTHA
YAGAPANTHA
YAGAPANTHA
T-TAMMY?
YAGAPANTHA
YAGAPAN
YAGAPANTHA
SEPUDLLAE TAREBIL!
SEPUDLLAE TAREBIL
SEPUDLLAE T
UH-UH--TAMMY?
I AM BUSY...
..IN A REALM YOU'LL NEVER KNOW..
OR UNDERSTAND.
YAGAPANTHA YAGAPANT

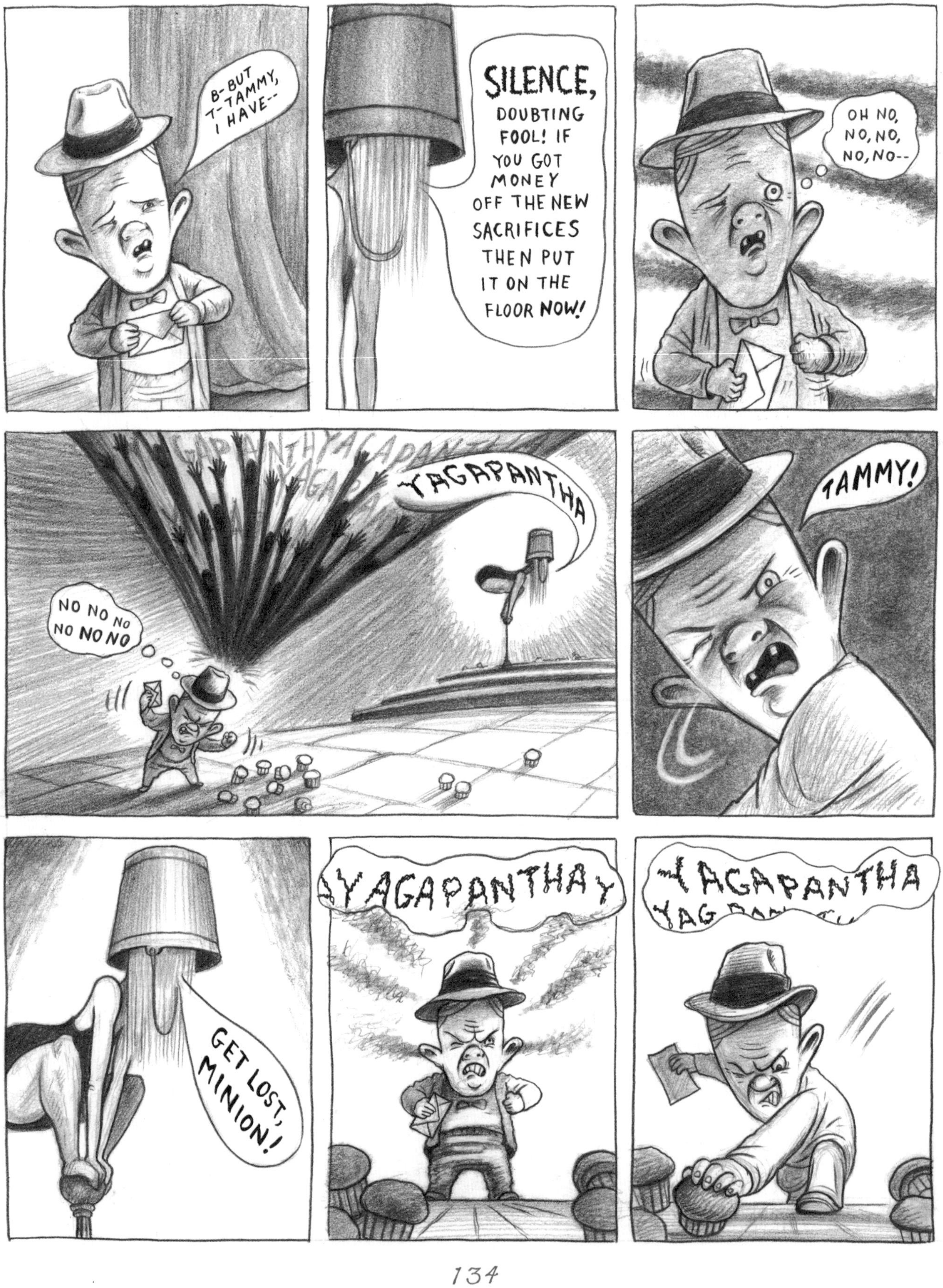
B-BUT T-TAMMY, I HAVE--
SILENCE, DOUBTING FOOL! IF YOU GOT MONEY OFF THE NEW SACRIFICES THEN PUT IT ON THE FLOOR NOW!
OH NO, NO, NO, NO, NO--
YAGAPANTHA
NO NO NO NO NO NO
TAMMY!
GET LOST, MINION!
YAGAPANTHA
YAGAPANTHA

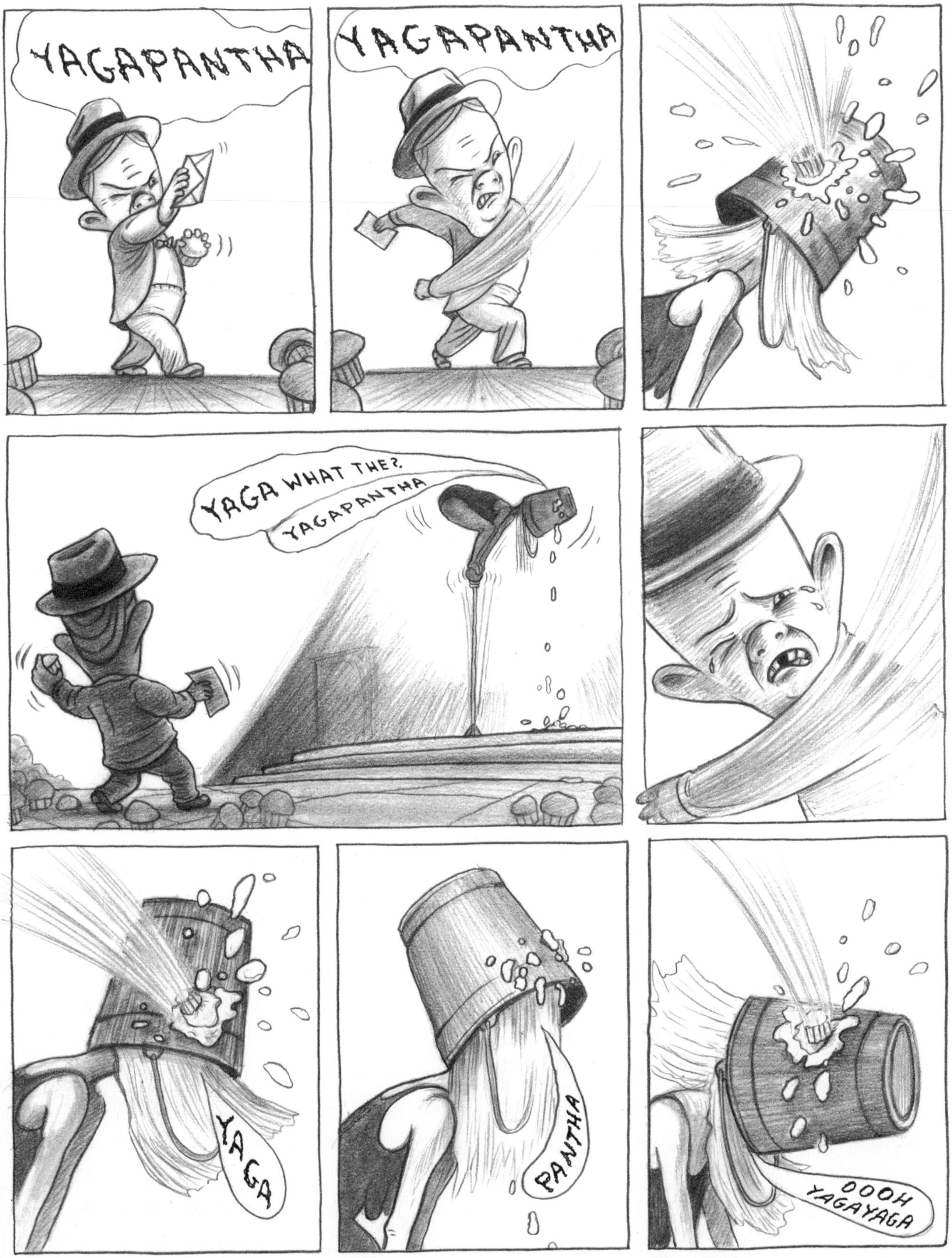
YAGAPANTHA
YAGAPANTHA
YAGA WHAT THE?
YAGAPANTHA
YAGA
PANTHA
OOOH YAGAYAGA

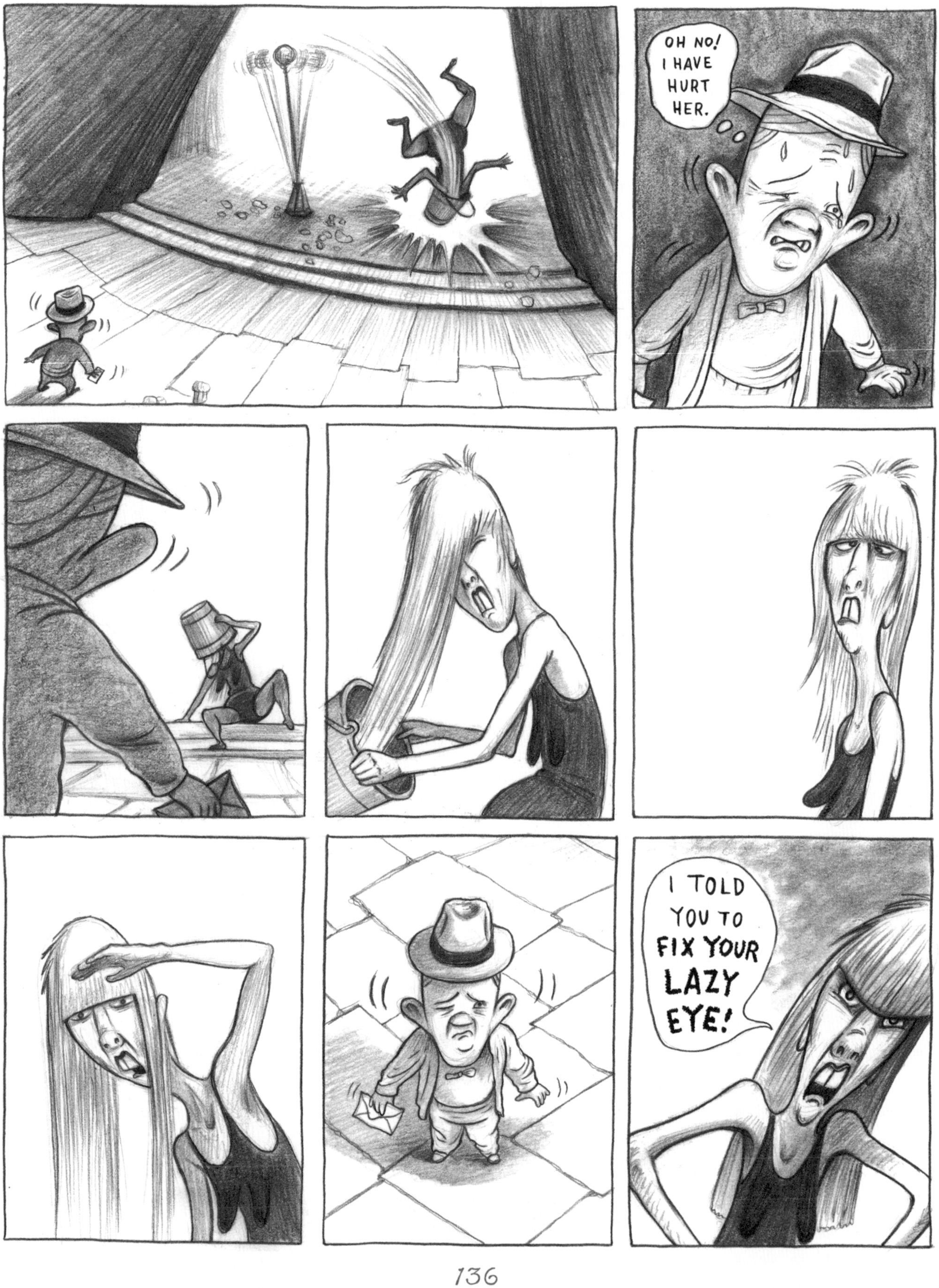
OH NO! I HAVE HURT HER.
I TOLD YOU TO FIX YOUR LAZY EYE!

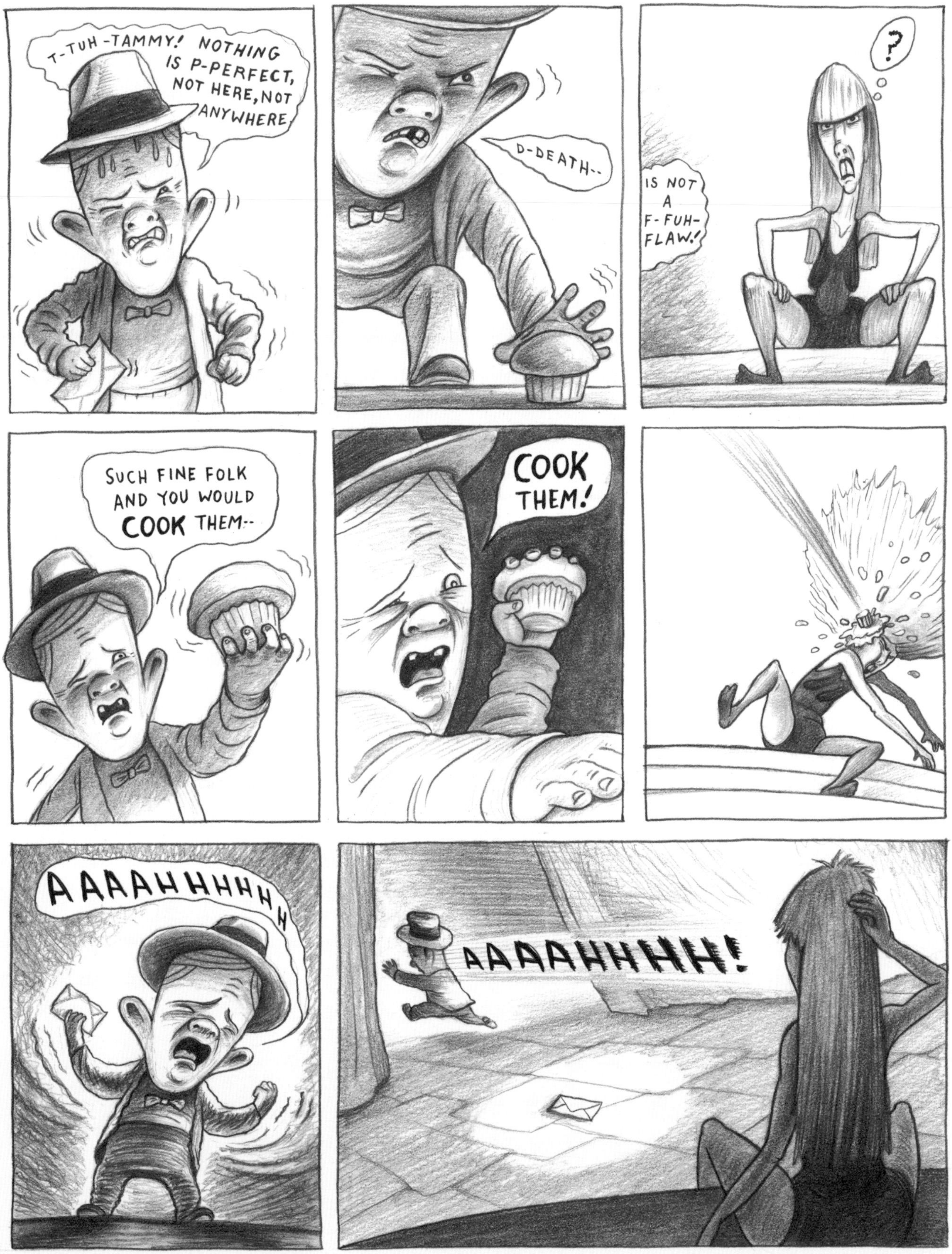

T-TUH-TAMMY! NOTHING IS P-PERFECT, NOT HERE, NOT ANYWHERE.
D-DEATH--
?
IS NOT A F-FUH-FLAW!
SUCH FINE FOLK AND YOU WOULD COOK THEM:--
COOK THEM!
AAAAHHHHHH
AAAAHHHH!

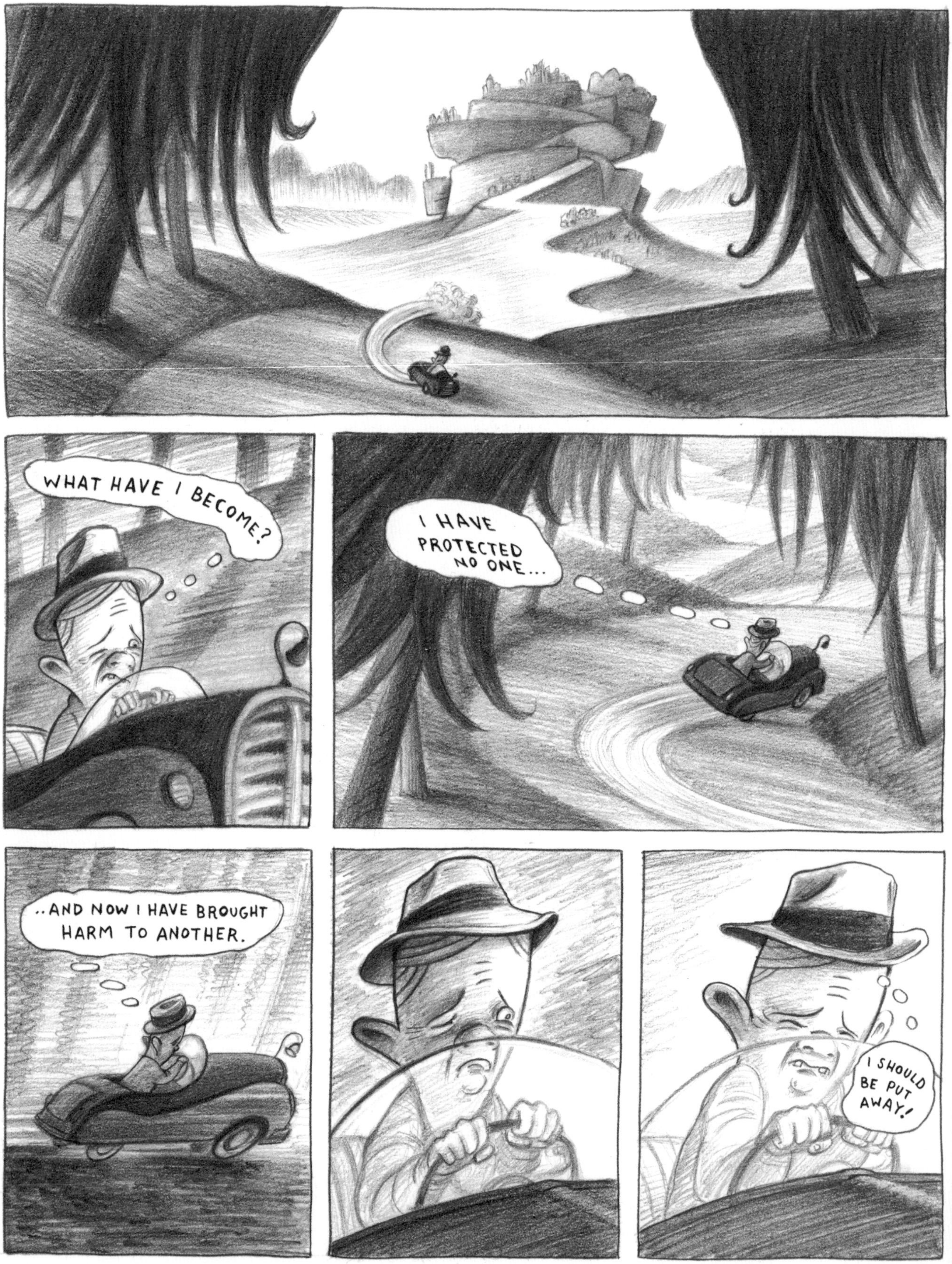
WHAT HAVE I BECOME?
I HAVE PROTECTED NO ONE...
..AND NOW I HAVE BROUGHT HARM TO ANOTHER.
I SHOULD BE PUT AWAY!

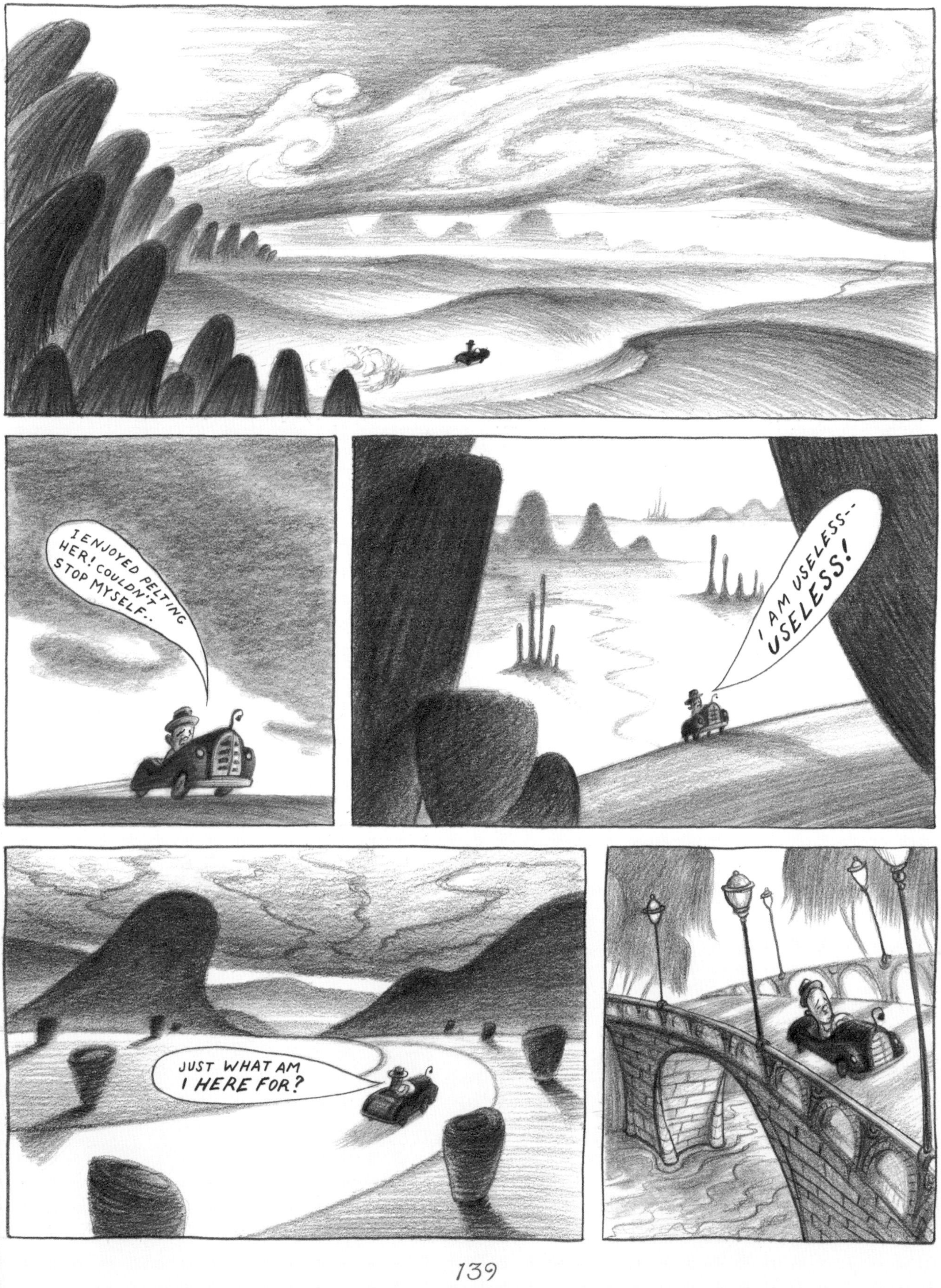
I ENJOYED PELTING HER! COULDN'T STOP MYSELF..
I AM USELESS-- USELESS!
JUST WHAT AM I HERE FOR?

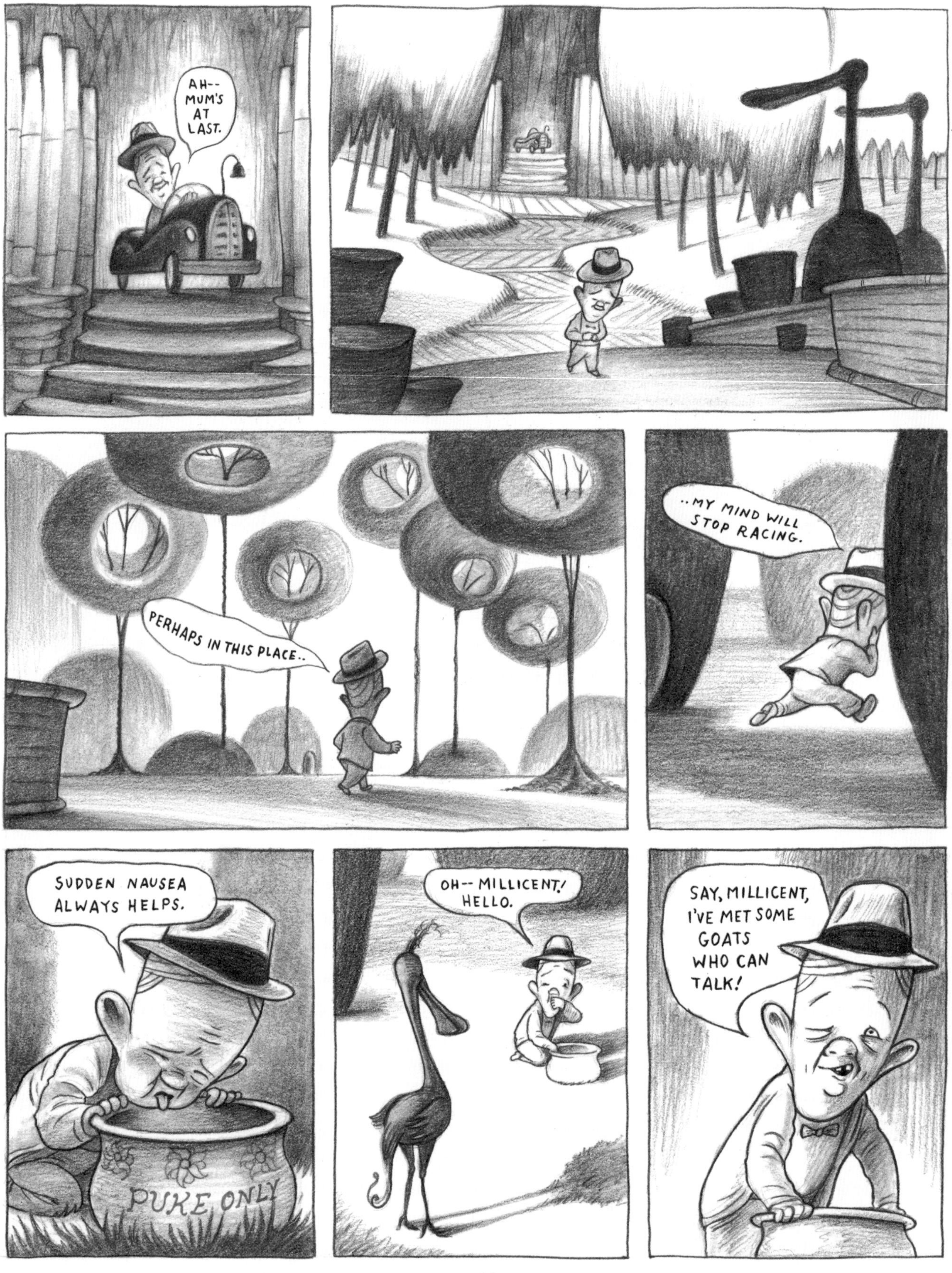
AH-- MUM'S AT LAST.
PERHAPS IN THIS PLACE..
..MY MIND WILL STOP RACING.
SUDDEN NAUSEA ALWAYS HELPS.
PUKE ONLY
OH-- MILLICENT! HELLO.
SAY, MILLICENT, I'VE MET SOME GOATS WHO CAN TALK!

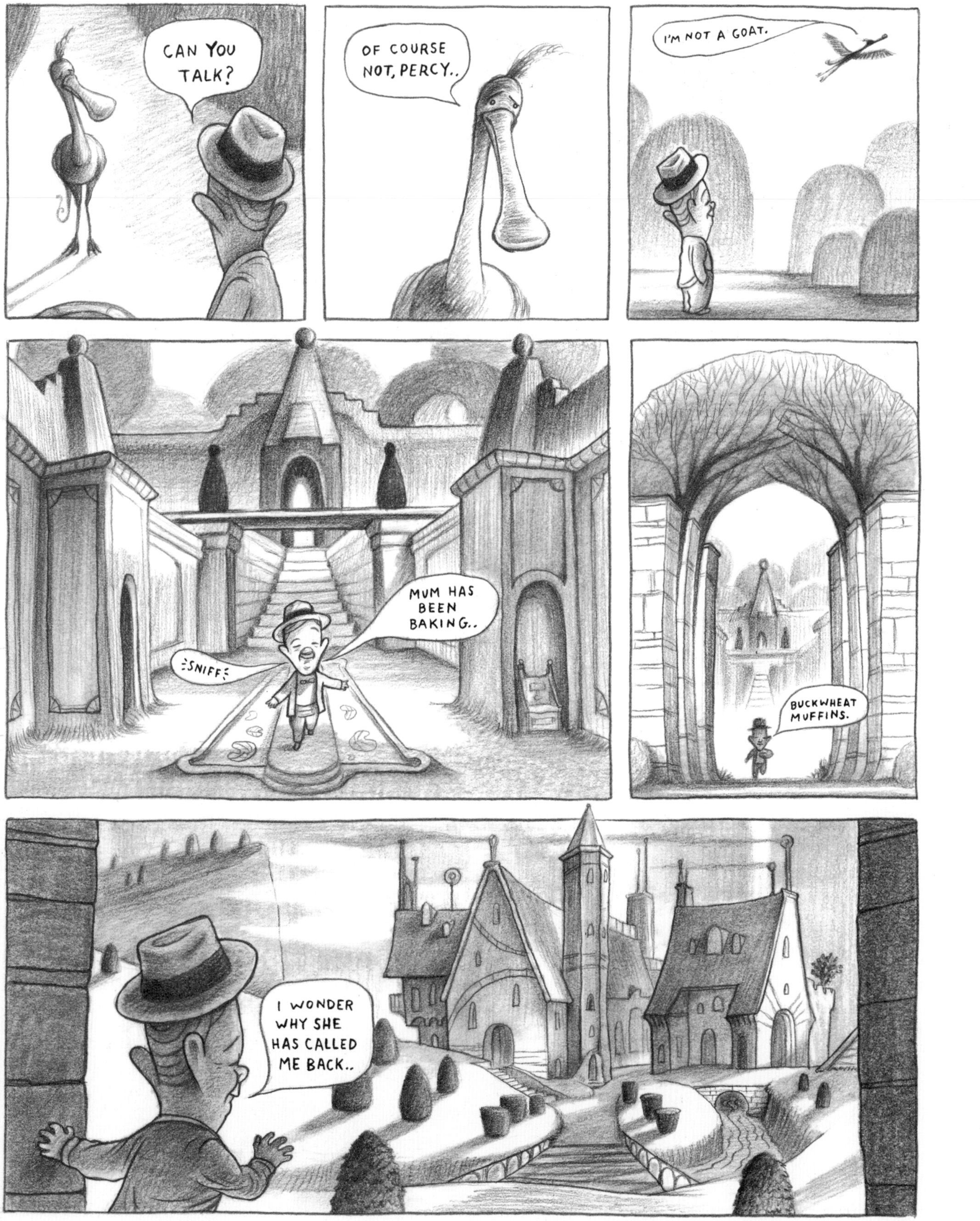
CAN YOU TALK?
OF COURSE NOT, PERCY..
I'M NOT A GOAT.
MUM HAS BEEN BAKING..
SNIFF
BUCKWHEAT MUFFINS.
I WONDER WHY SHE HAS CALLED ME BACK..

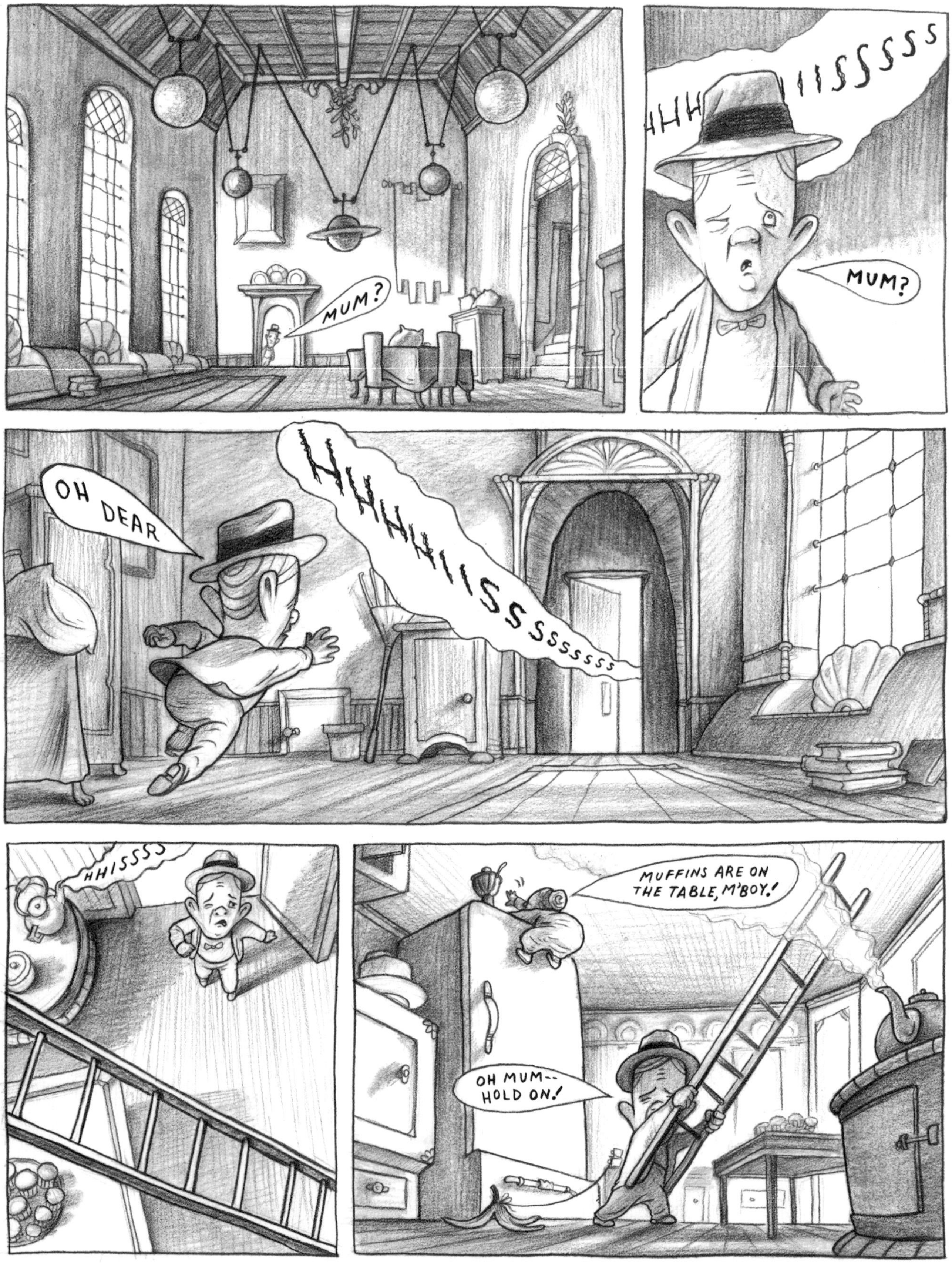
MUM?
HHHIIISSSSSS
MUM?
OH DEAR
HHHHIISSSSSSSSS
HHISSSS
MUFFINS ARE ON THE TABLE, M'BOY!
OH MUM-- HOLD ON!

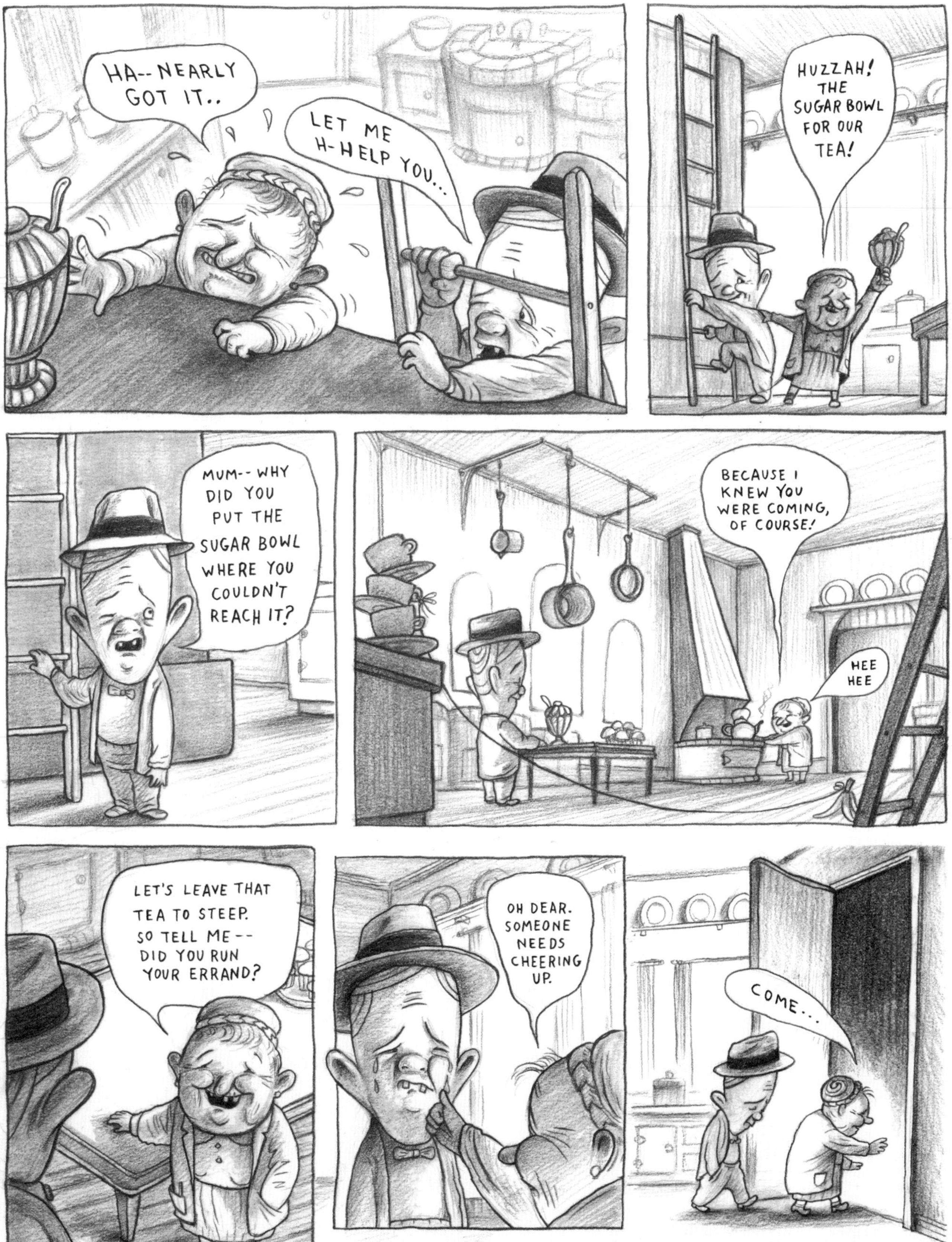
HA-- NEARLY GOT IT..
LET ME H-HELP YOU...
HUZZAH! THE SUGAR BOWL FOR OUR TEA!
MUM-- WHY DID YOU PUT THE SUGAR BOWL WHERE YOU COULDN'T REACH IT?
BECAUSE I KNEW YOU WERE COMING, OF COURSE!
HEE HEE
LET'S LEAVE THAT TEA TO STEEP. SO TELL ME -- DID YOU RUN YOUR ERRAND?
OH DEAR. SOMEONE NEEDS CHEERING UP.
COME...

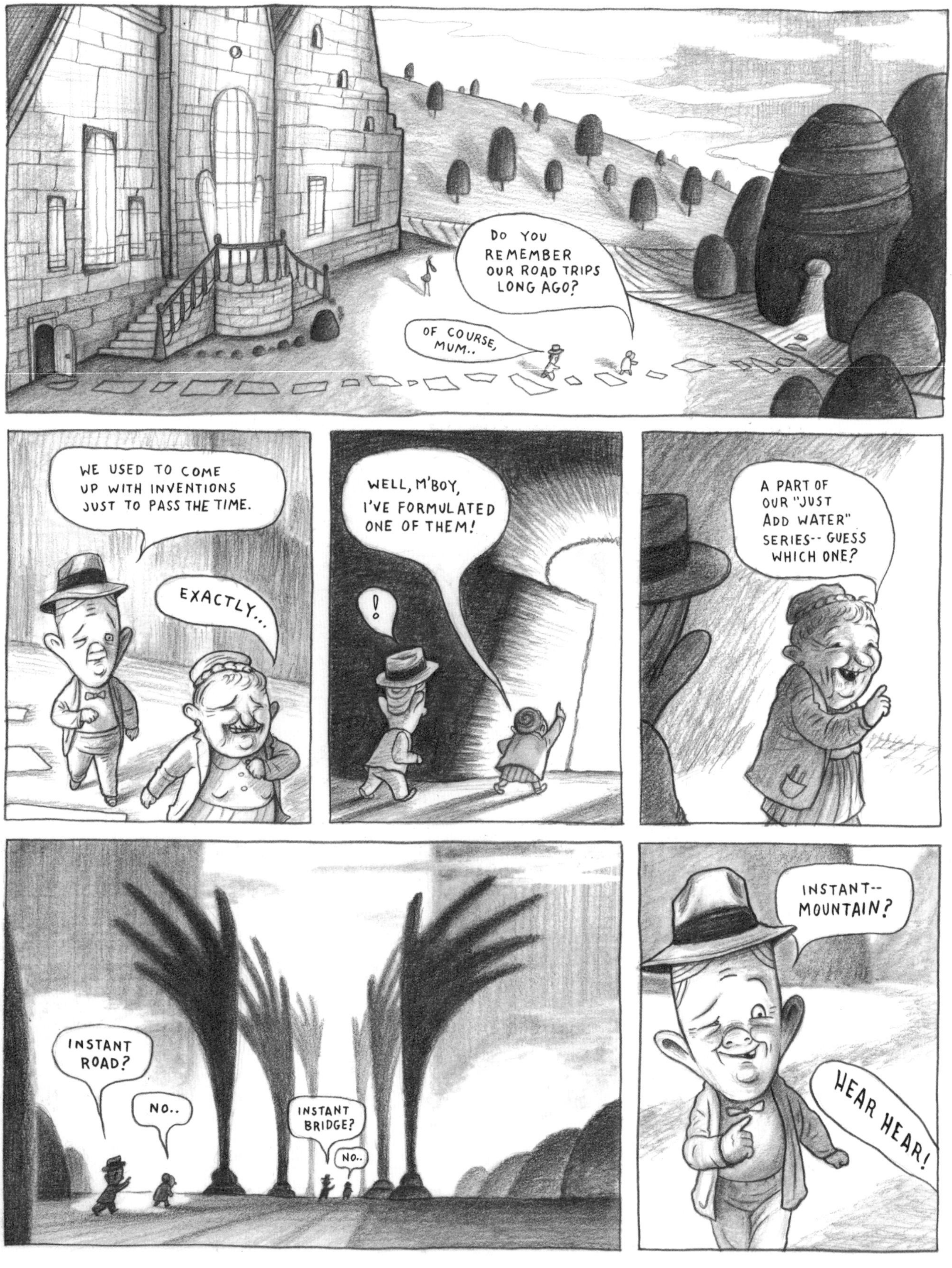
DO YOU REMEMBER OUR ROAD TRIPS LONG AGO?
OF COURSE, MUM..
WE USED TO COME UP WITH INVENTIONS JUST TO PASS THE TIME.
EXACTLY...
WELL, M'BOY, I'VE FORMULATED ONE OF THEM!
!
A PART OF OUR "JUST ADD WATER" SERIES-- GUESS WHICH ONE?
INSTANT ROAD?
NO..
INSTANT BRIDGE?
NO..
INSTANT-- MOUNTAIN?
HEAR HEAR!

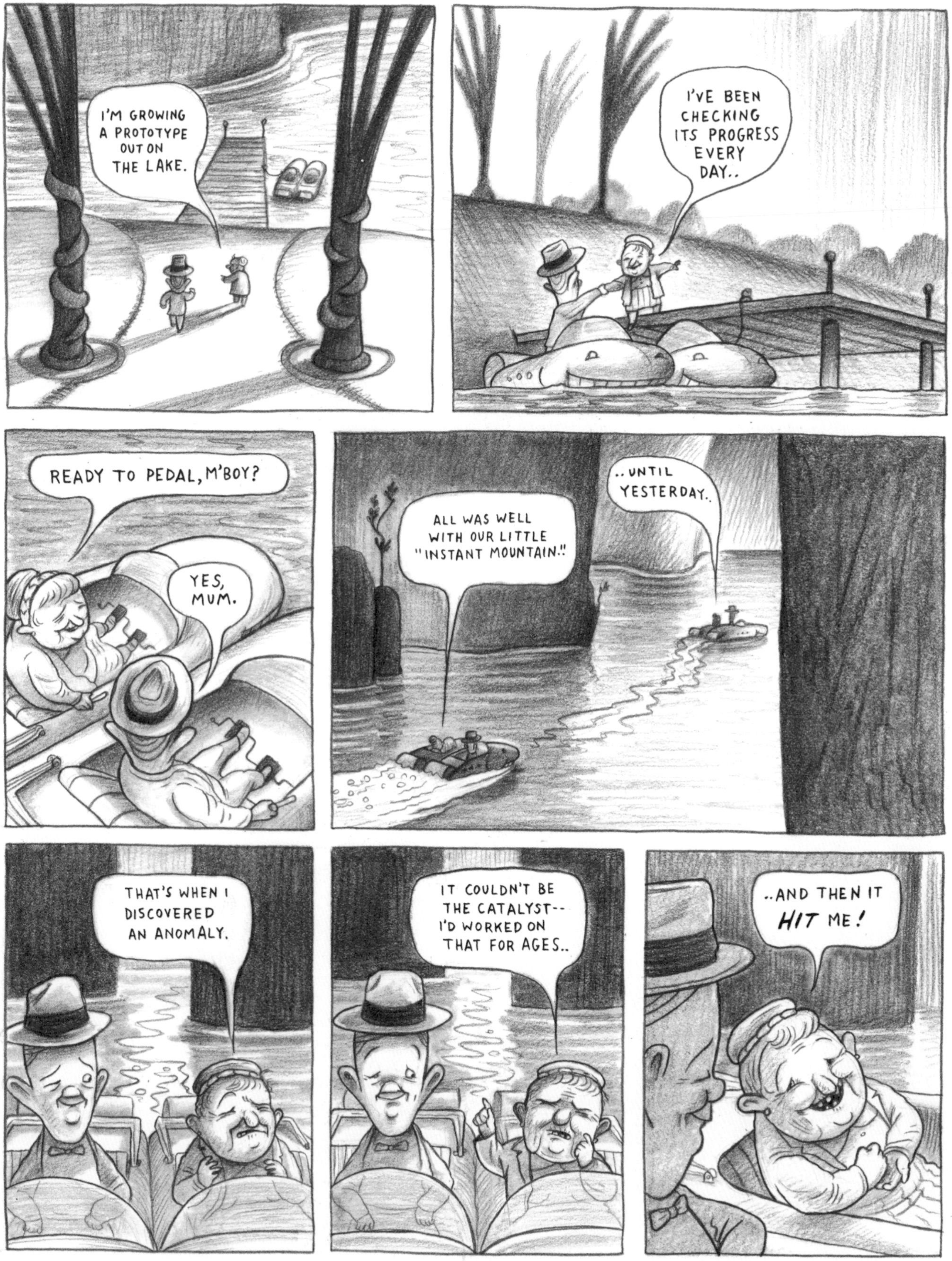
I'M GROWING A PROTOTYPE OUT ON THE LAKE.
I'VE BEEN CHECKING ITS PROGRESS EVERY DAY..
READY TO PEDAL, M'BOY?
YES, MUM.
ALL WAS WELL WITH OUR LITTLE "INSTANT MOUNTAIN."
..UNTIL YESTERDAY..
THAT'S WHEN I DISCOVERED AN ANOMALY.
IT COULDN'T BE THE CATALYST-- I'D WORKED ON THAT FOR AGES..
..AND THEN IT *HIT* ME!

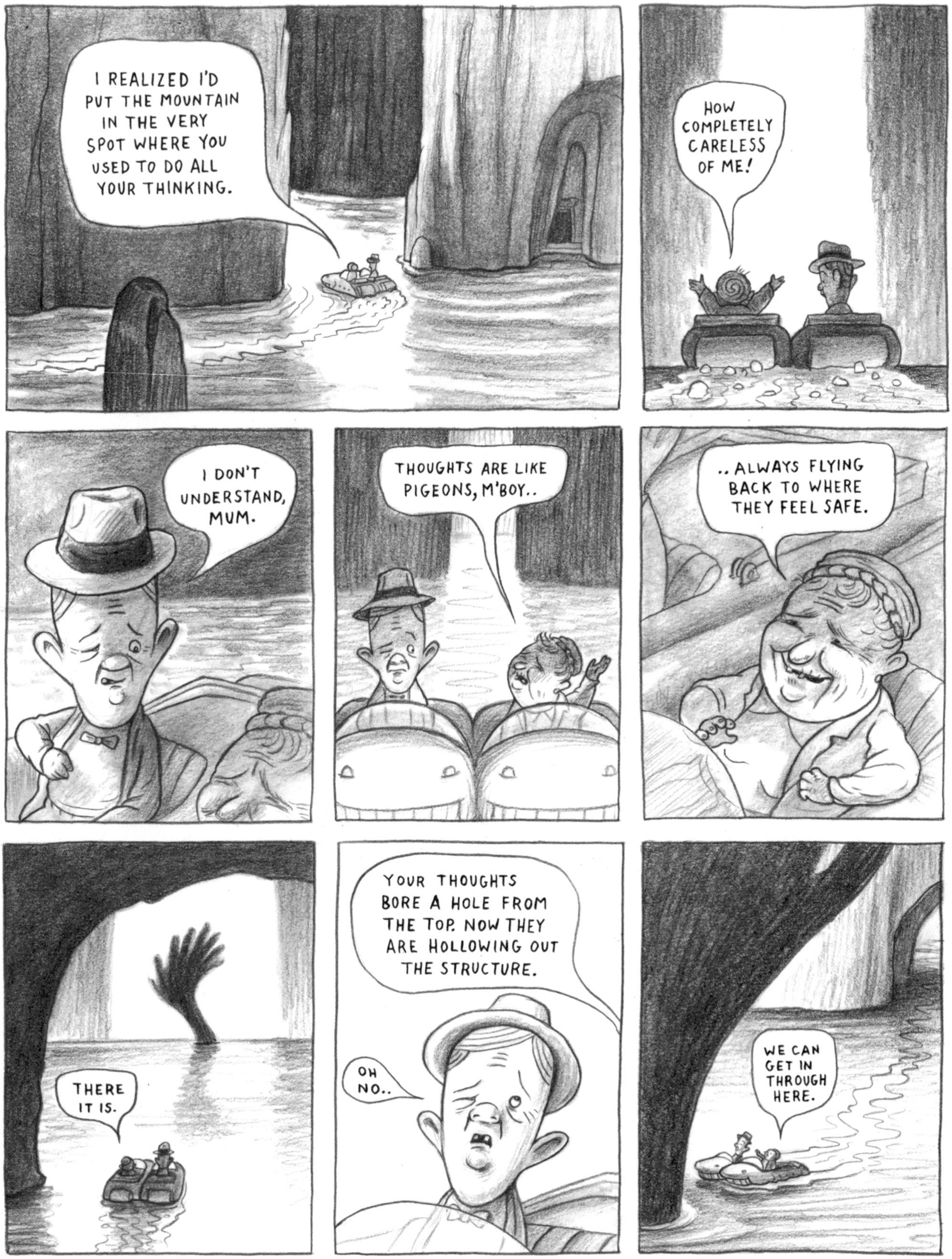
I REALIZED I'D PUT THE MOUNTAIN IN THE VERY SPOT WHERE YOU USED TO DO ALL YOUR THINKING.
HOW COMPLETELY CARELESS OF ME!
I DON'T UNDERSTAND, MUM.
THOUGHTS ARE LIKE PIGEONS, M'BOY..
.. ALWAYS FLYING BACK TO WHERE THEY FEEL SAFE.
THERE IT IS.
YOUR THOUGHTS BORE A HOLE FROM THE TOP. NOW THEY ARE HOLLOWING OUT THE STRUCTURE.
OH NO..
WE CAN GET IN THROUGH HERE.

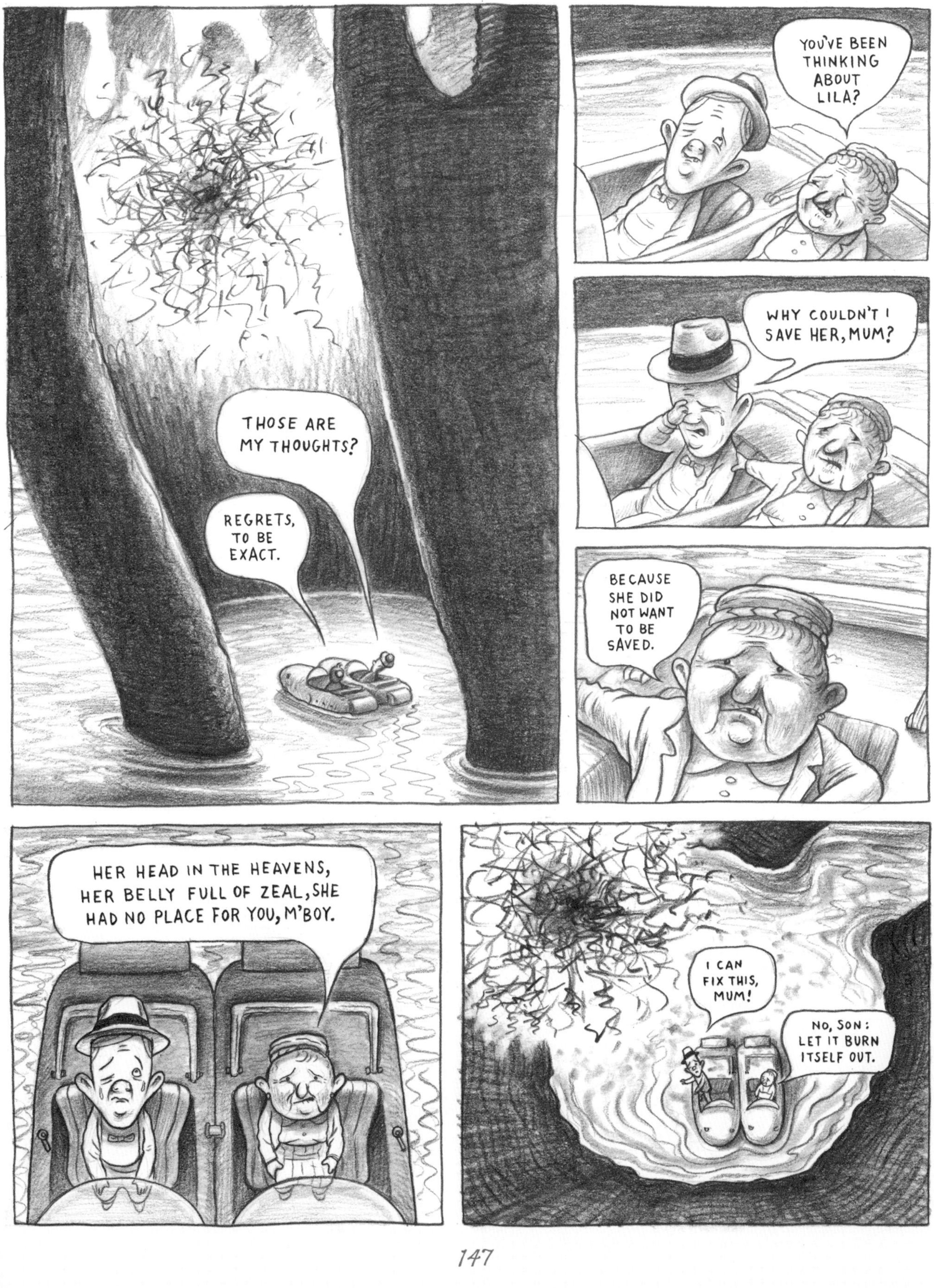
THOSE ARE MY THOUGHTS?
REGRETS, TO BE EXACT.
YOU'VE BEEN THINKING ABOUT LILA?
WHY COULDN'T I SAVE HER, MUM?
BECAUSE SHE DID NOT WANT TO BE SAVED.
HER HEAD IN THE HEAVENS, HER BELLY FULL OF ZEAL, SHE HAD NO PLACE FOR YOU, M'BOY.
I CAN FIX THIS, MUM!
NO, SON: LET IT BURN ITSELF OUT.

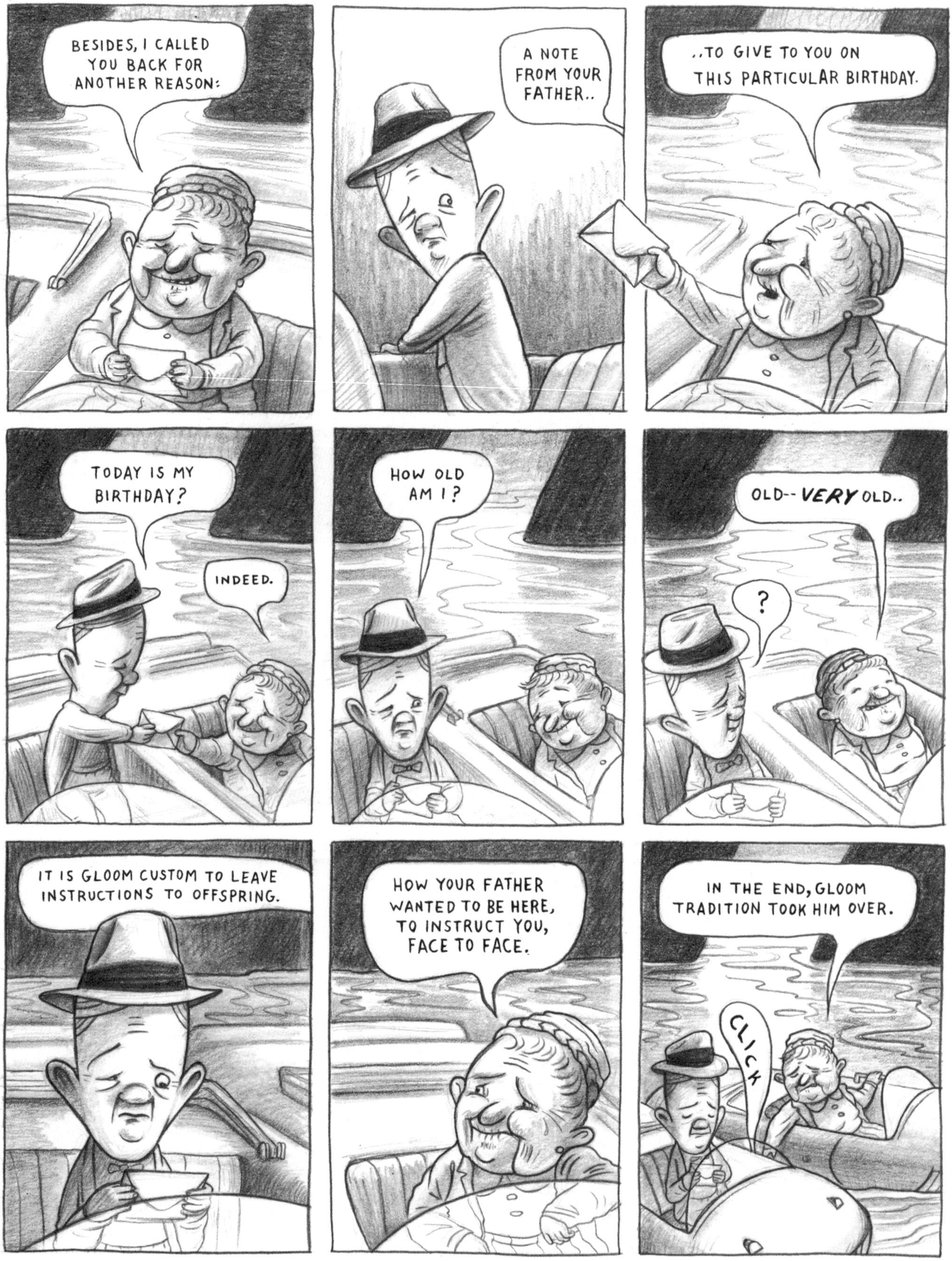
BESIDES, I CALLED YOU BACK FOR ANOTHER REASON:
A NOTE FROM YOUR FATHER..
..TO GIVE TO YOU ON THIS PARTICULAR BIRTHDAY.
TODAY IS MY BIRTHDAY?
INDEED.
HOW OLD AM I?
OLD--VERY OLD..
?
IT IS GLOOM CUSTOM TO LEAVE INSTRUCTIONS TO OFFSPRING.
HOW YOUR FATHER WANTED TO BE HERE, TO INSTRUCT YOU, FACE TO FACE.
IN THE END, GLOOM TRADITION TOOK HIM OVER.
CLICK

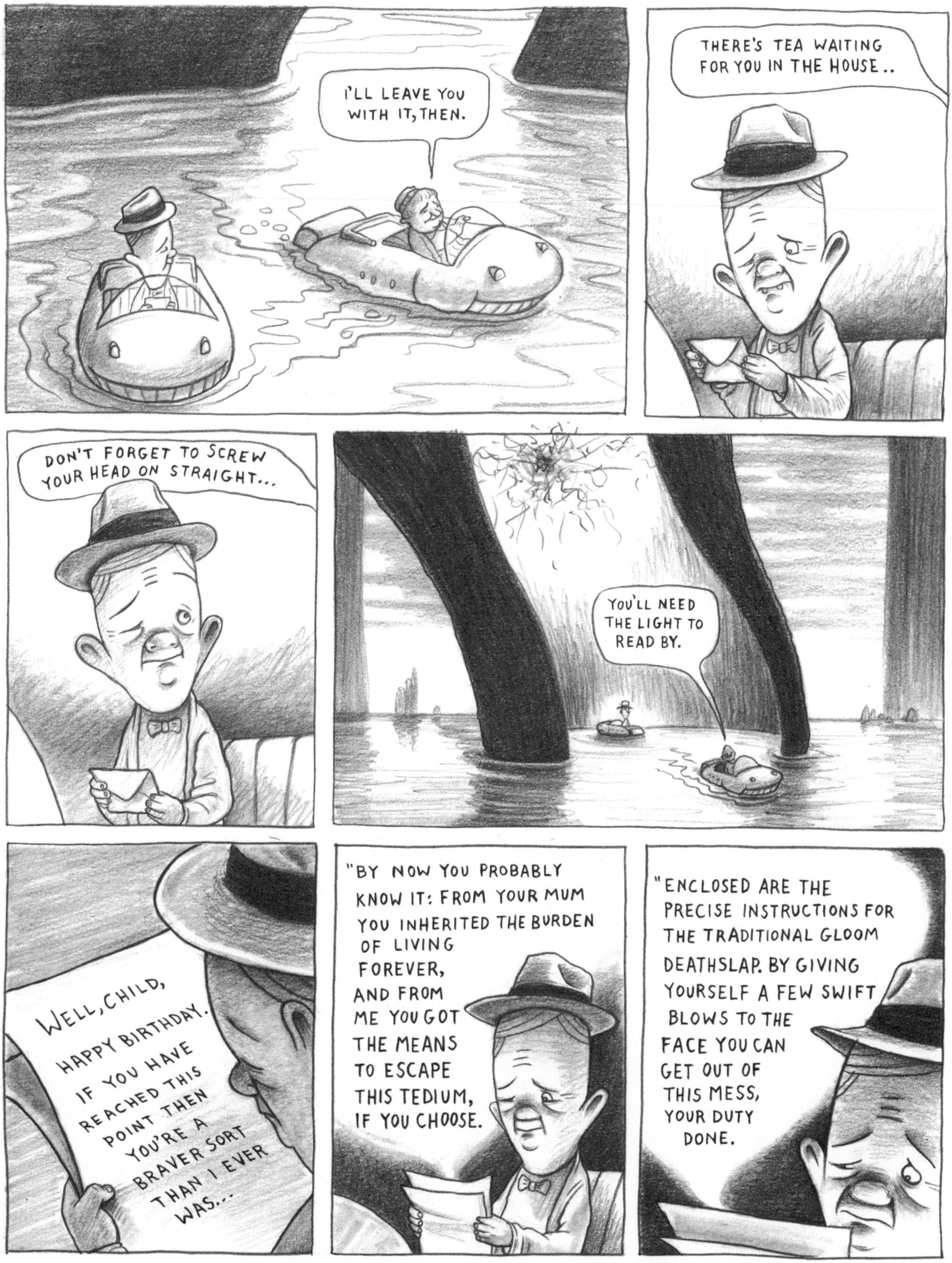
I'LL LEAVE YOU WITH IT, THEN.
THERE'S TEA WAITING FOR YOU IN THE HOUSE..
DON'T FORGET TO SCREW YOUR HEAD ON STRAIGHT...
YOU'LL NEED THE LIGHT TO READ BY.
WELL, CHILD,
HAPPY BIRTHDAY. IF YOU HAVE REACHED THIS POINT THEN YOU'RE A BRAVER SORT THAN I EVER WAS...
"BY NOW YOU PROBABLY KNOW IT: FROM YOUR MUM YOU INHERITED THE BURDEN OF LIVING FOREVER, AND FROM ME YOU GOT THE MEANS TO ESCAPE THIS TEDIUM, IF YOU CHOOSE.
"ENCLOSED ARE THE PRECISE INSTRUCTIONS FOR THE TRADITIONAL GLOOM DEATHSLAP. BY GIVING YOURSELF A FEW SWIFT BLOWS TO THE FACE YOU CAN GET OUT OF THIS MESS, YOUR DUTY DONE.

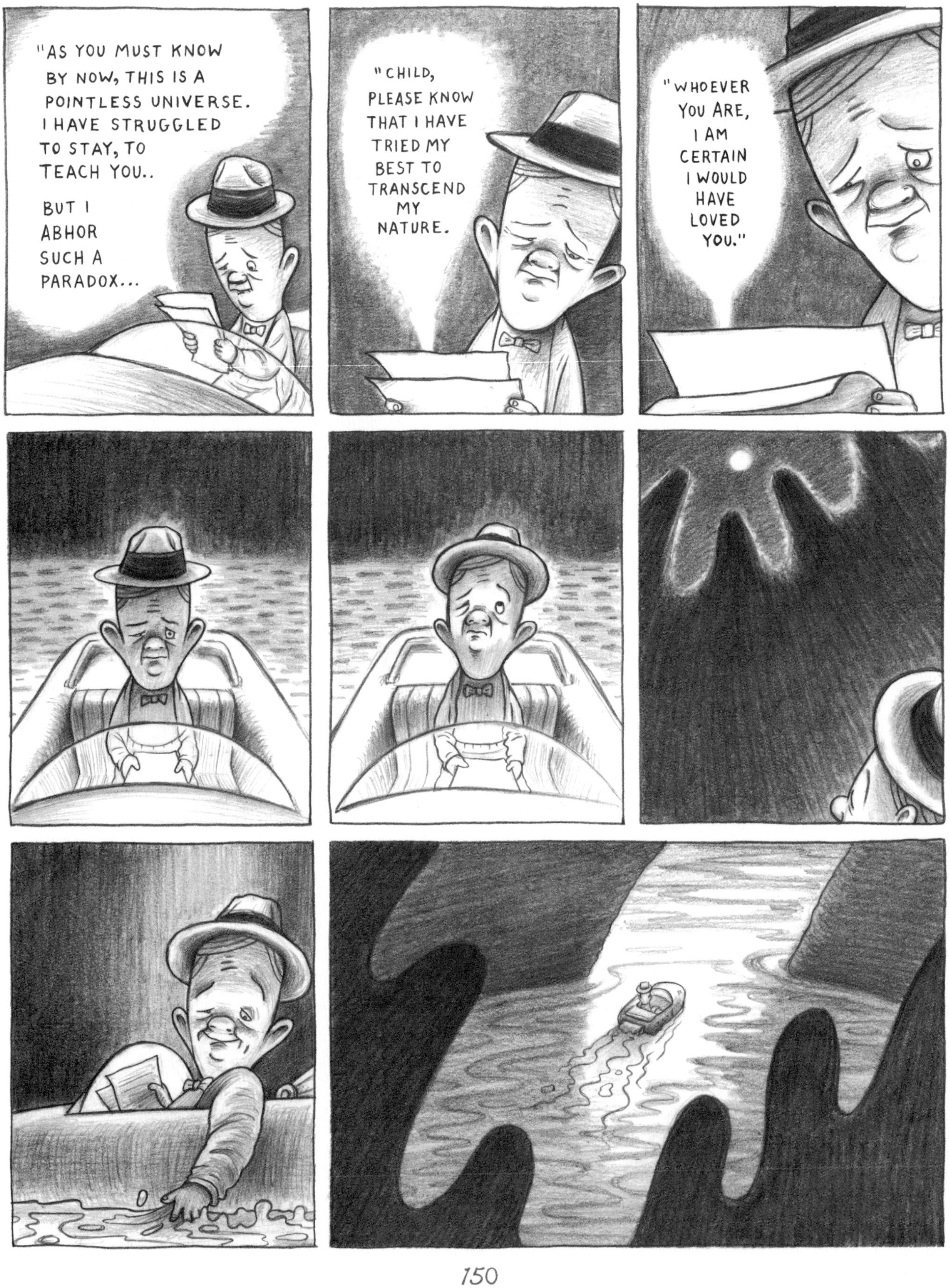
"AS YOU MUST KNOW BY NOW, THIS IS A POINTLESS UNIVERSE. I HAVE STRUGGLED TO STAY, TO TEACH YOU..
BUT I ABHOR SUCH A PARADOX...
"CHILD, PLEASE KNOW THAT I HAVE TRIED MY BEST TO TRANSCEND MY NATURE.
"WHOEVER YOU ARE, I AM CERTAIN I WOULD HAVE LOVED YOU."

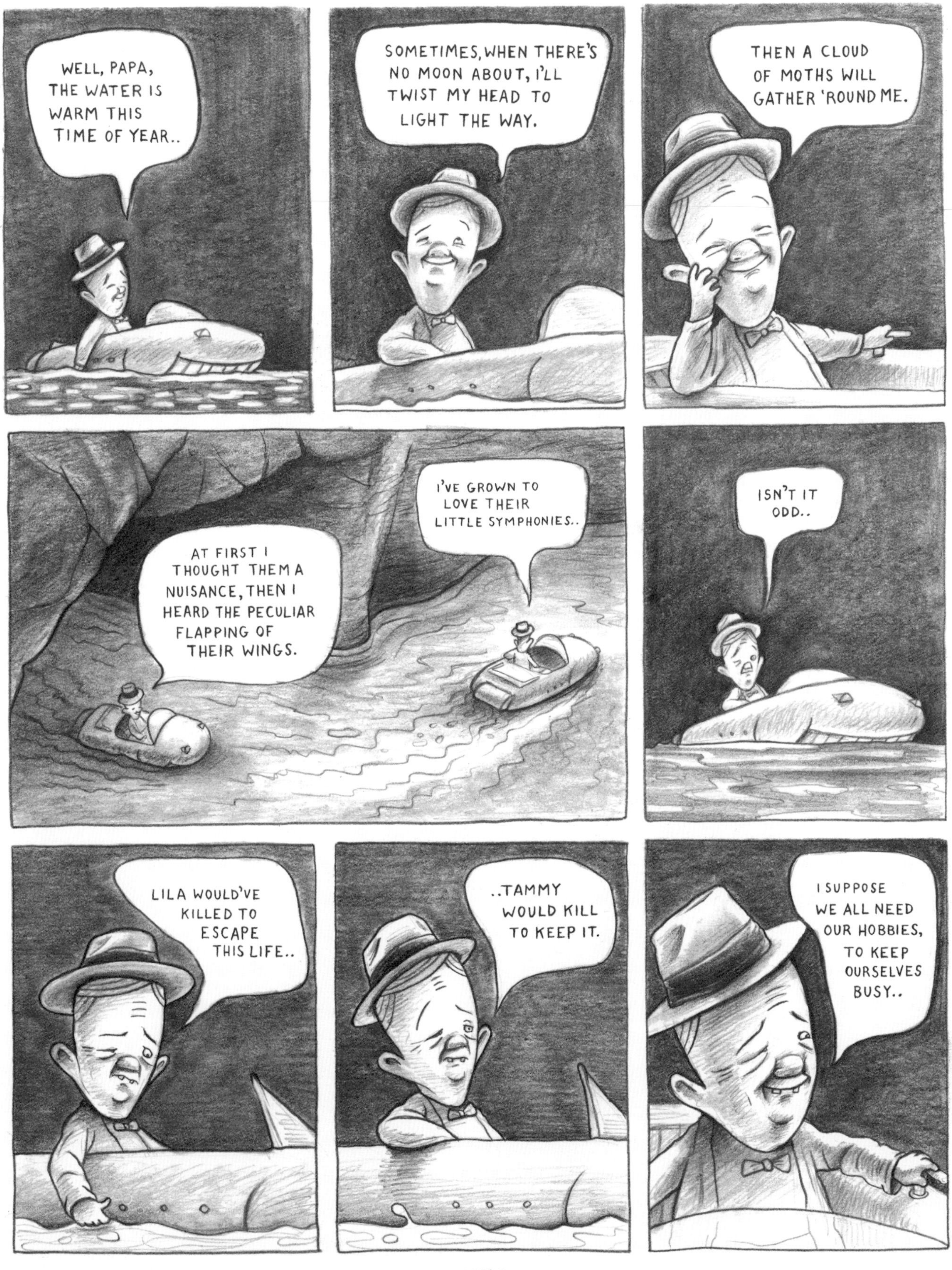
WELL, PAPA, THE WATER IS WARM THIS TIME OF YEAR..
SOMETIMES, WHEN THERE'S NO MOON ABOUT, I'LL TWIST MY HEAD TO LIGHT THE WAY.
THEN A CLOUD OF MOTHS WILL GATHER 'ROUND ME.
AT FIRST I THOUGHT THEM A NUISANCE, THEN I HEARD THE PECULIAR FLAPPING OF THEIR WINGS.
I'VE GROWN TO LOVE THEIR LITTLE SYMPHONIES..
ISN'T IT ODD..
LILA WOULD'VE KILLED TO ESCAPE THIS LIFE..
..TAMMY WOULD KILL TO KEEP IT.
I SUPPOSE WE ALL NEED OUR HOBBIES, TO KEEP OURSELVES BUSY..

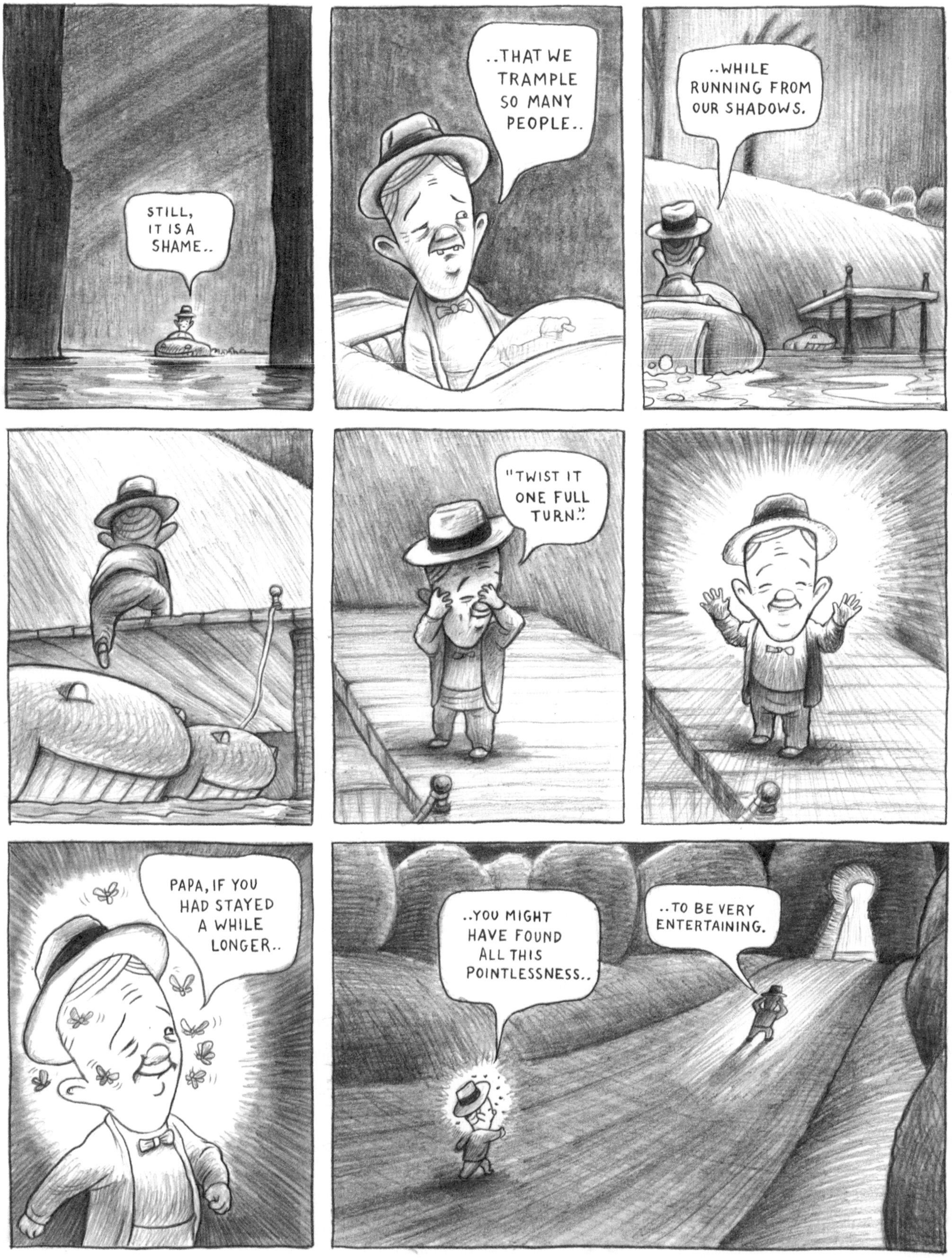
STILL, IT IS A SHAME..
..THAT WE TRAMPLE SO MANY PEOPLE..
..WHILE RUNNING FROM OUR SHADOWS.
"TWIST IT ONE FULL TURN."
PAPA, IF YOU HAD STAYED A WHILE LONGER..
..YOU MIGHT HAVE FOUND ALL THIS POINTLESSNESS..
..TO BE VERY ENTERTAINING.

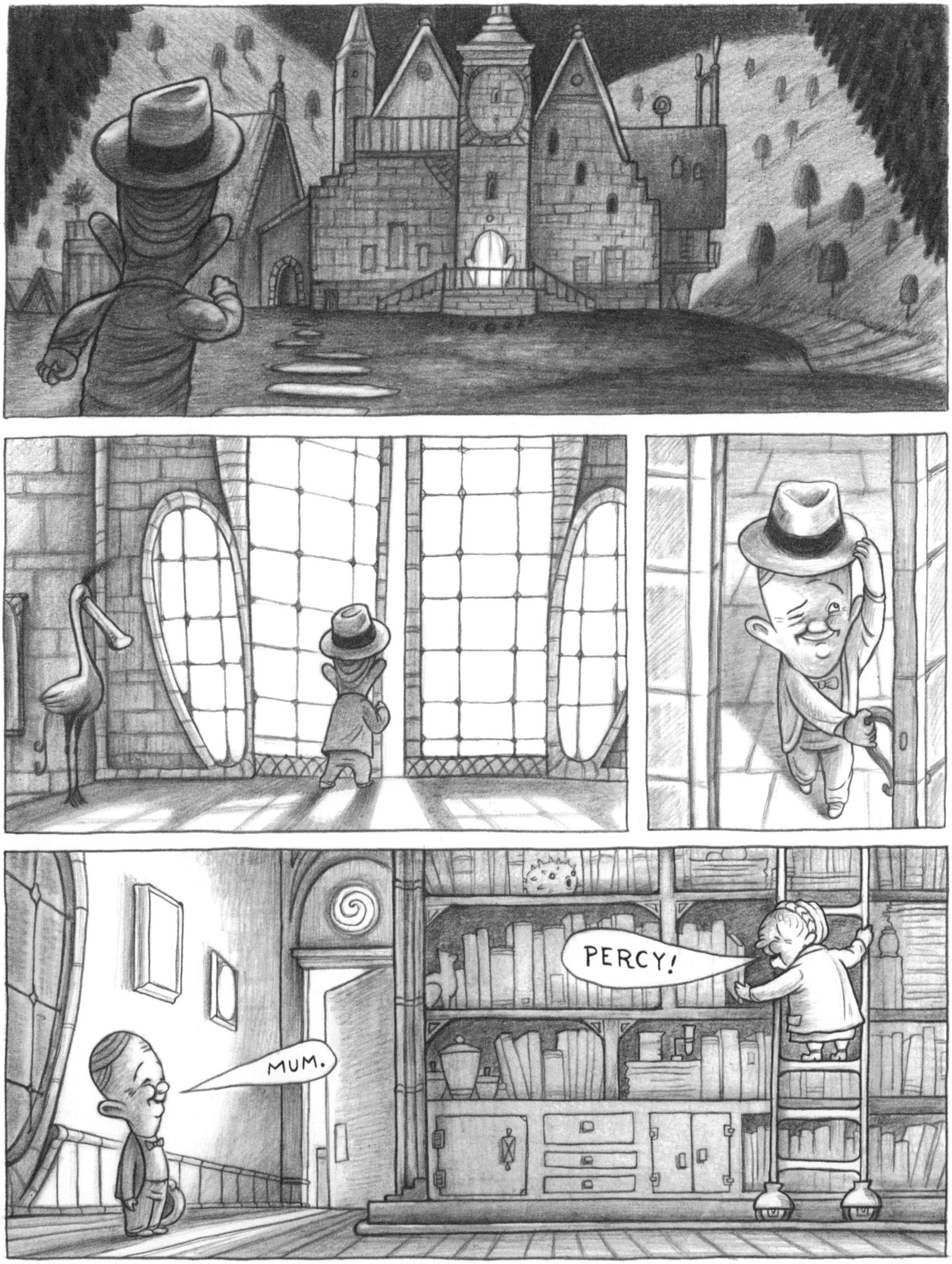
PERCY!
MUM.

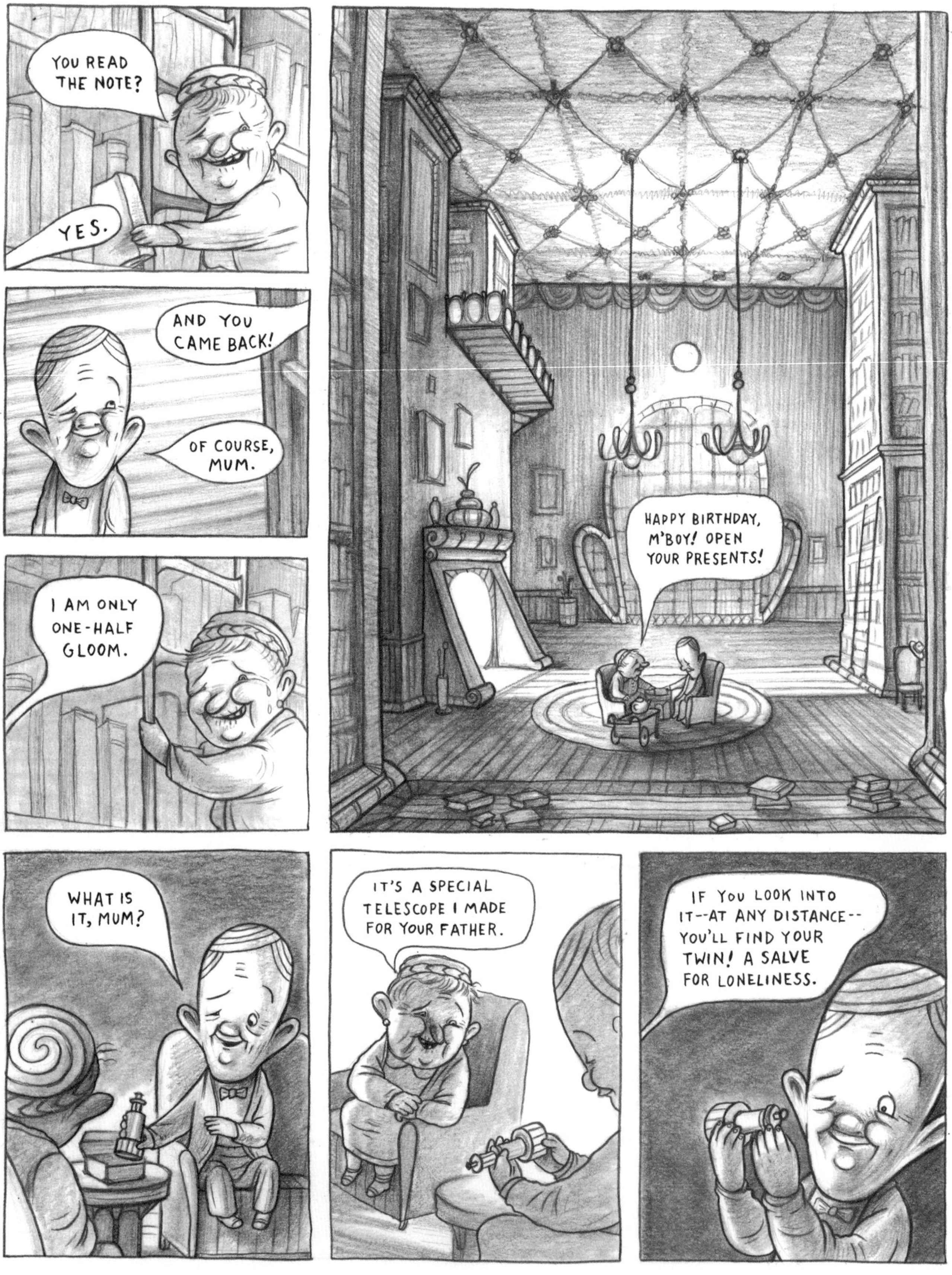
YOU READ THE NOTE?
YES.
AND YOU CAME BACK!
OF COURSE, MUM.
I AM ONLY ONE-HALF GLOOM.
HAPPY BIRTHDAY, M'BOY! OPEN YOUR PRESENTS!
WHAT IS IT, MUM?
IT'S A SPECIAL TELESCOPE I MADE FOR YOUR FATHER.
IF YOU LOOK INTO IT--AT ANY DISTANCE--YOU'LL FIND YOUR TWIN! A SALVE FOR LONELINESS.

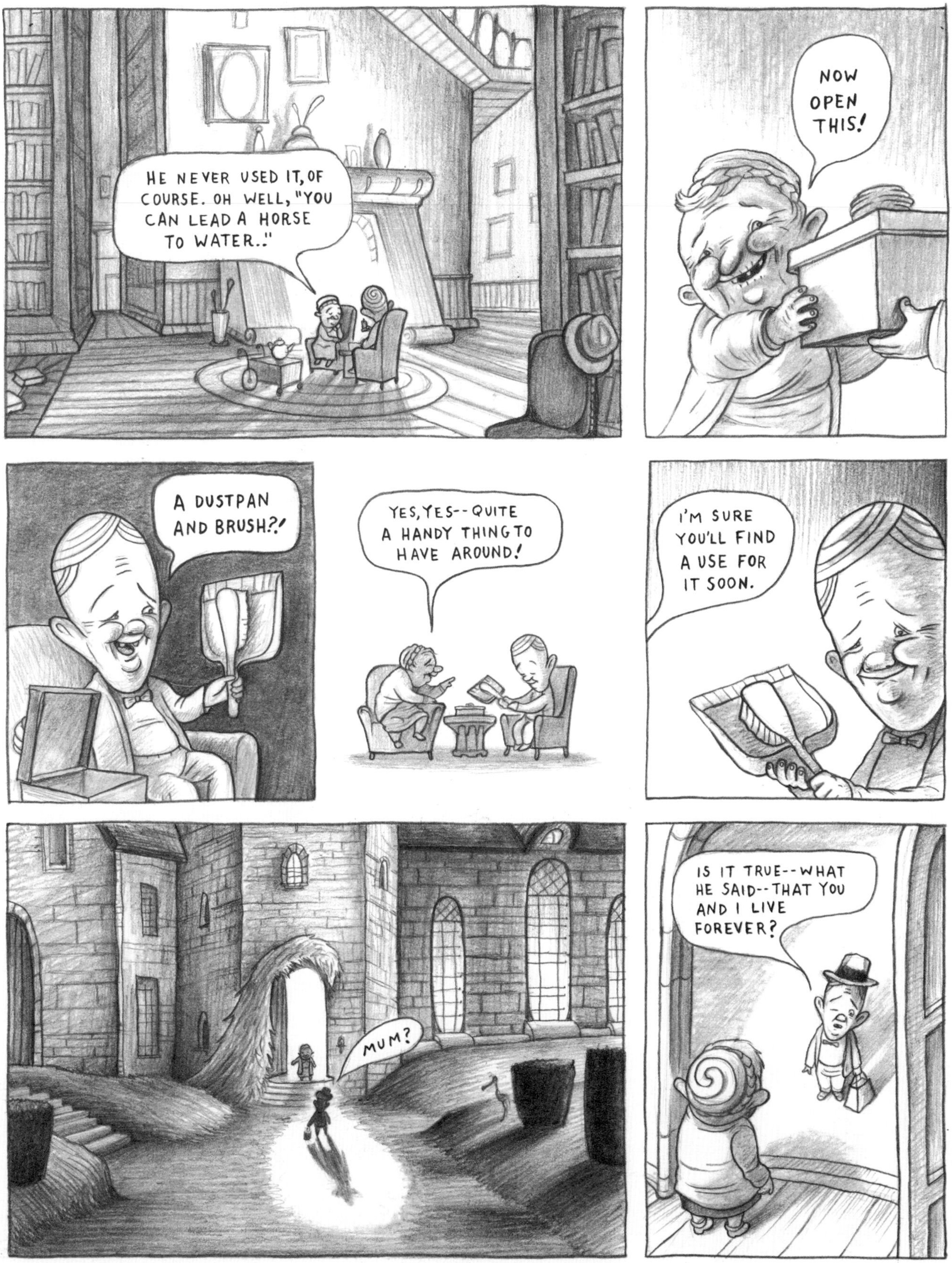
HE NEVER USED IT, OF COURSE. OH WELL, "YOU CAN LEAD A HORSE TO WATER.."
NOW OPEN THIS!
A DUSTPAN AND BRUSH?!
YES, YES--QUITE A HANDY THING TO HAVE AROUND!
I'M SURE YOU'LL FIND A USE FOR IT SOON.
MUM?
IS IT TRUE--WHAT HE SAID--THAT YOU AND I LIVE FOREVER?

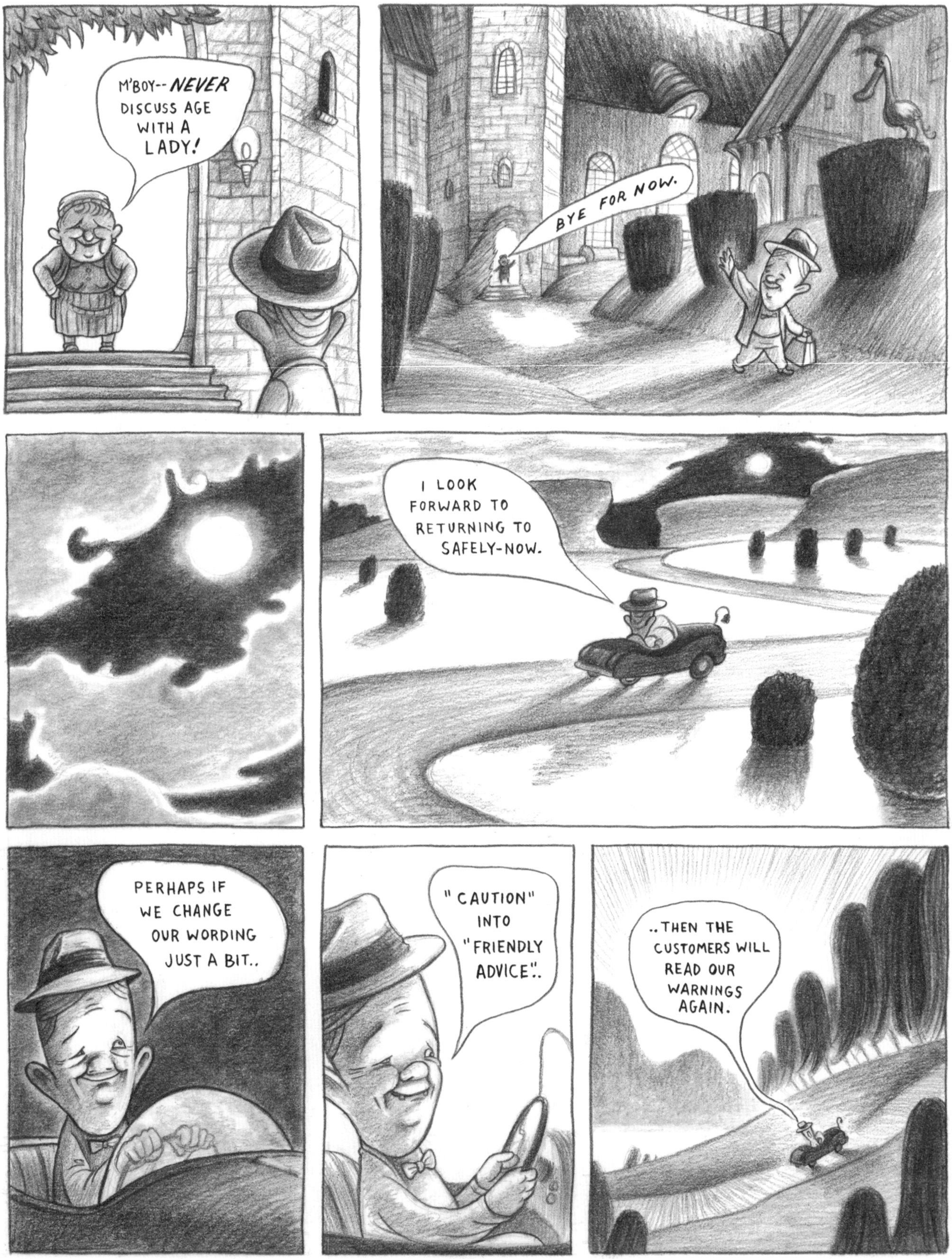
M'BOY-- NEVER DISCUSS AGE WITH A LADY!
BYE FOR NOW.
I LOOK FORWARD TO RETURNING TO SAFELY-NOW.
PERHAPS IF WE CHANGE OUR WORDING JUST A BIT..
"CAUTION" INTO "FRIENDLY ADVICE"..
..THEN THE CUSTOMERS WILL READ OUR WARNINGS AGAIN.

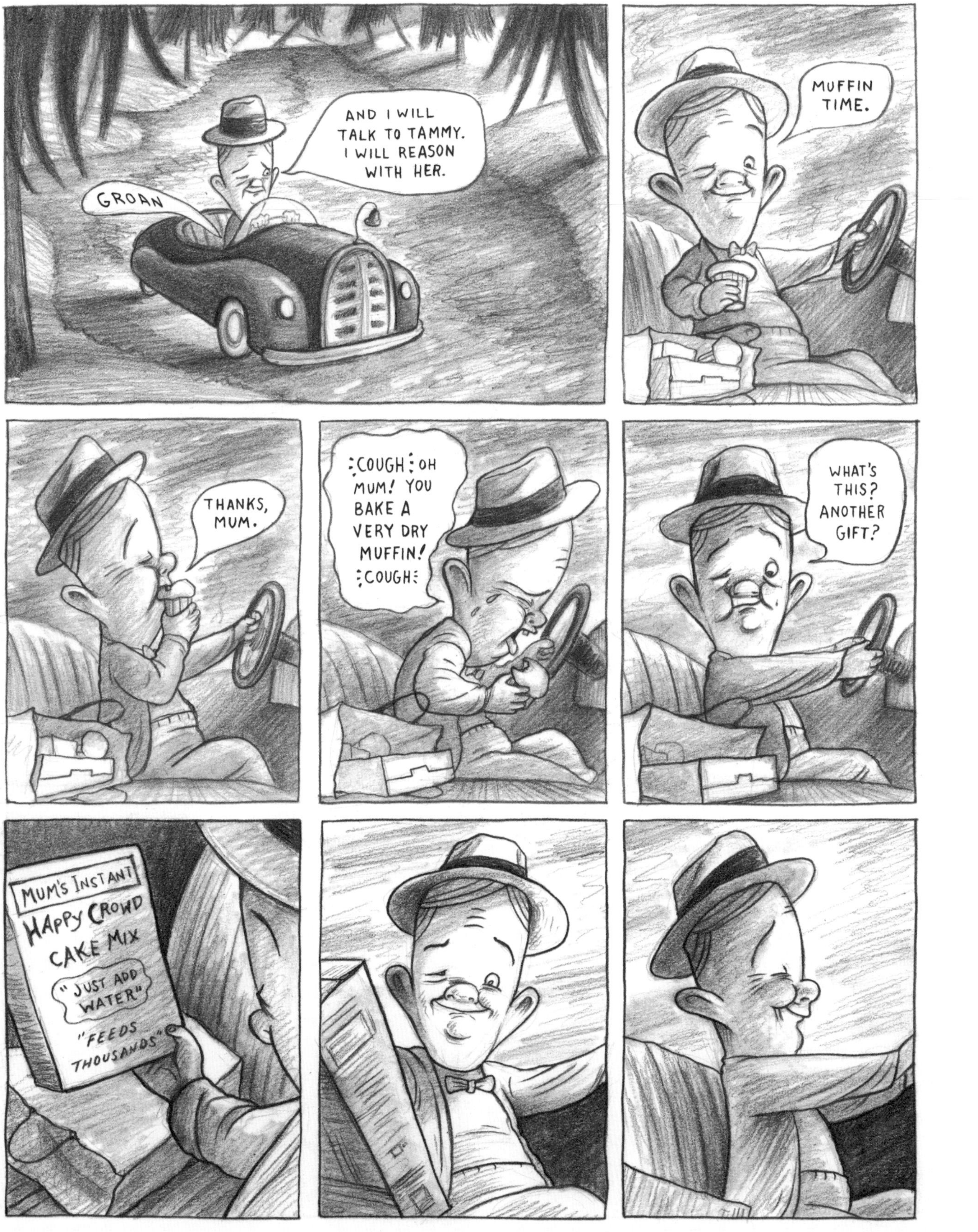
AND I WILL TALK TO TAMMY. I WILL REASON WITH HER.
GROAN
MUFFIN TIME.
THANKS, MUM.
COUGH OH MUM! YOU BAKE A VERY DRY MUFFIN! COUGH
WHAT'S THIS? ANOTHER GIFT?
MUM'S INSTANT
HAPPY CROWD CAKE MIX
"JUST ADD WATER"
"FEEDS THOUSANDS"

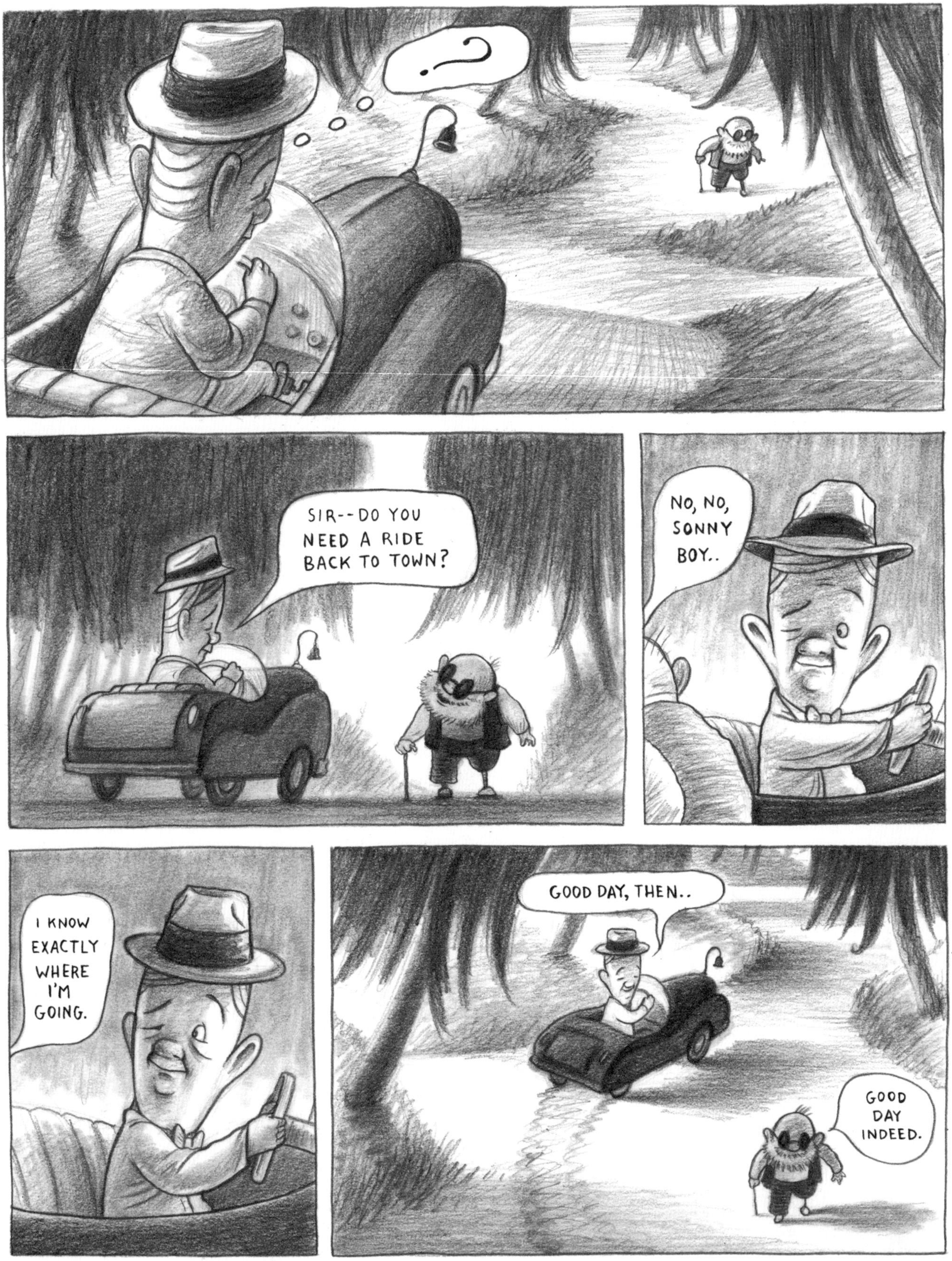
?
SIR--DO YOU NEED A RIDE BACK TO TOWN?
NO, NO, SONNY BOY..
I KNOW EXACTLY WHERE I'M GOING.
GOOD DAY, THEN..
GOOD DAY INDEED.

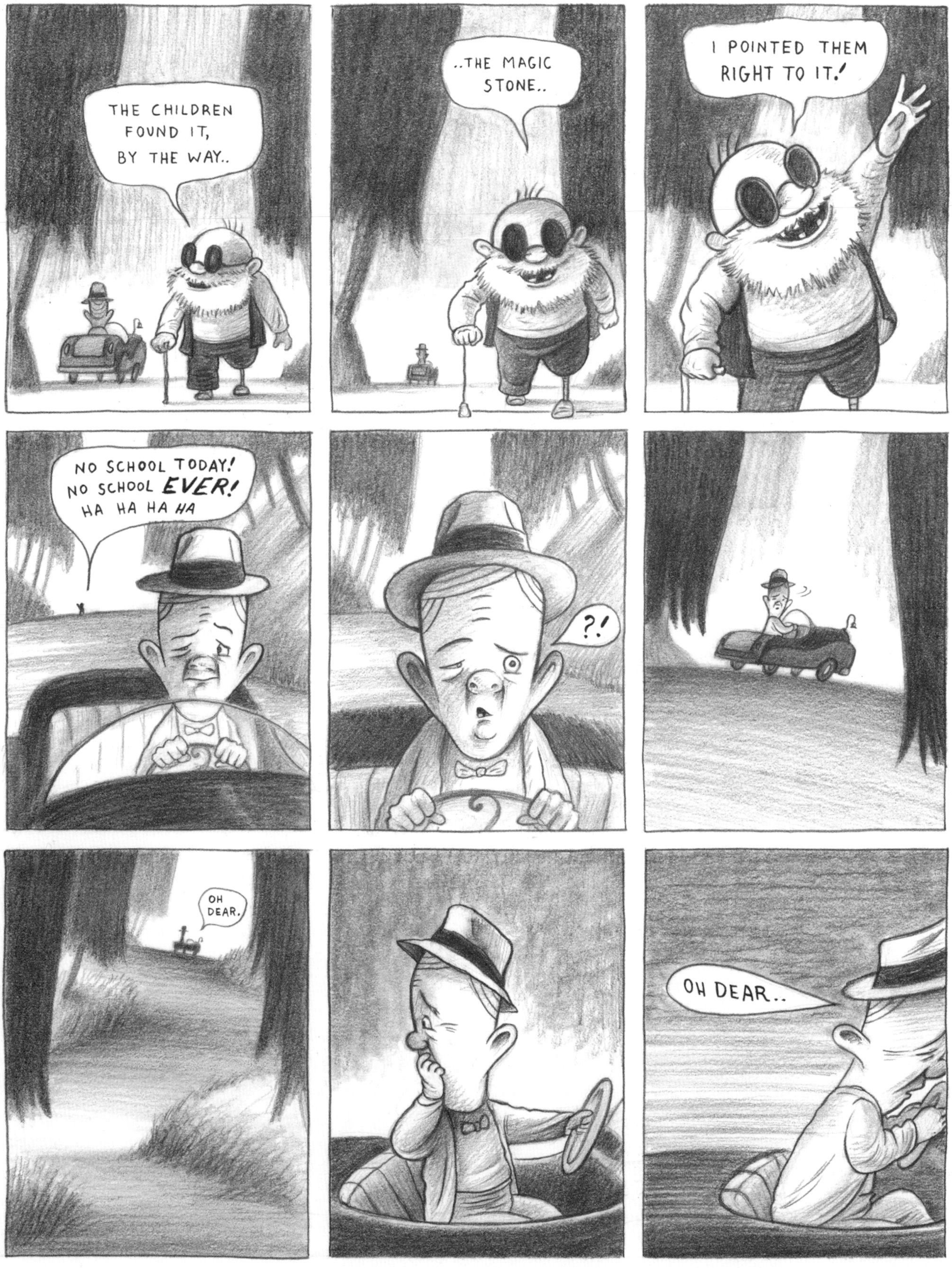
THE CHILDREN FOUND IT, BY THE WAY..
..THE MAGIC STONE..
I POINTED THEM RIGHT TO IT!
NO SCHOOL TODAY! NO SCHOOL EVER! HA HA HA HA
?!
OH DEAR.
OH DEAR..

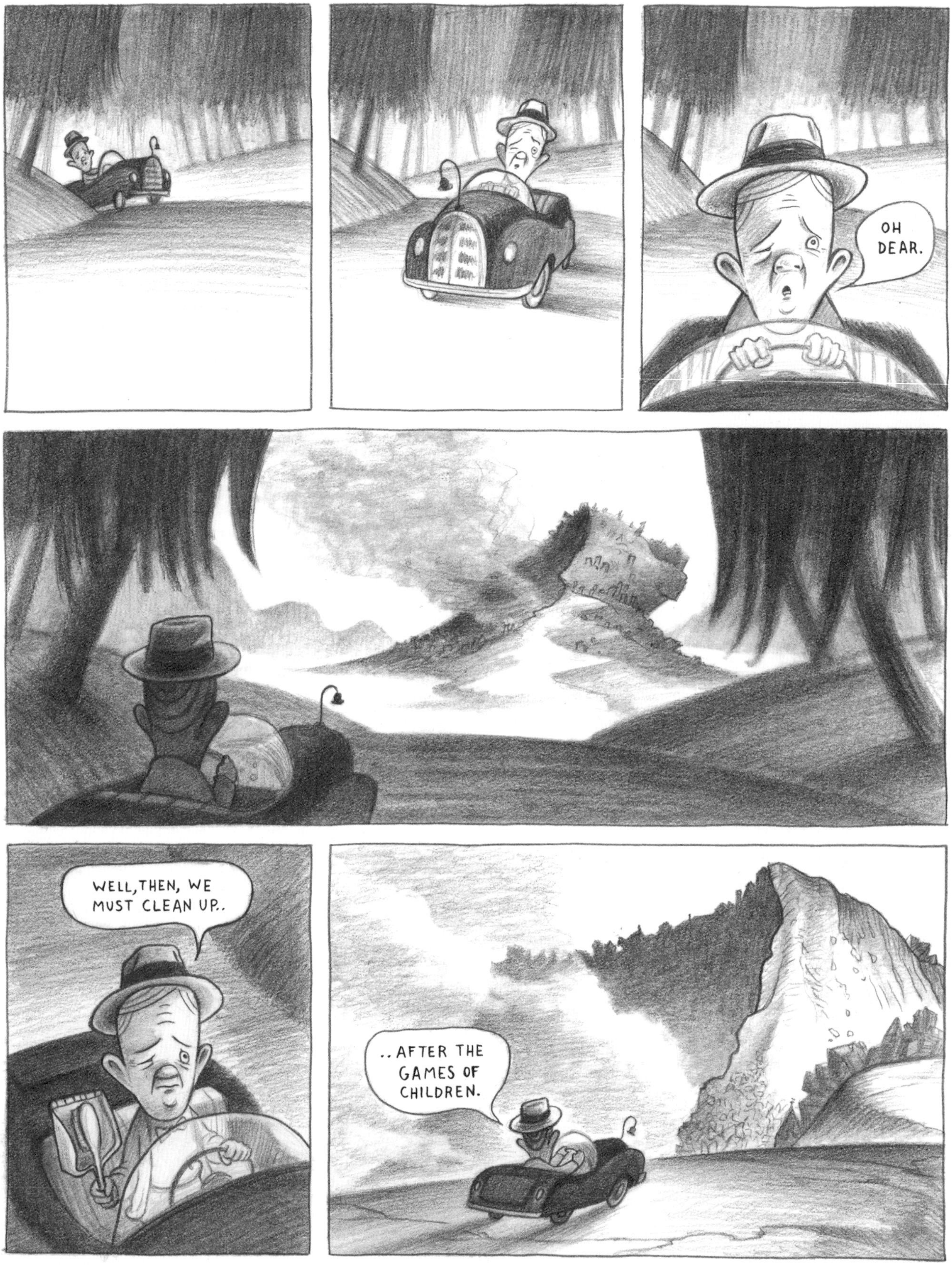
OH DEAR.
WELL, THEN, WE MUST CLEAN UP..
..AFTER THE GAMES OF CHILDREN.

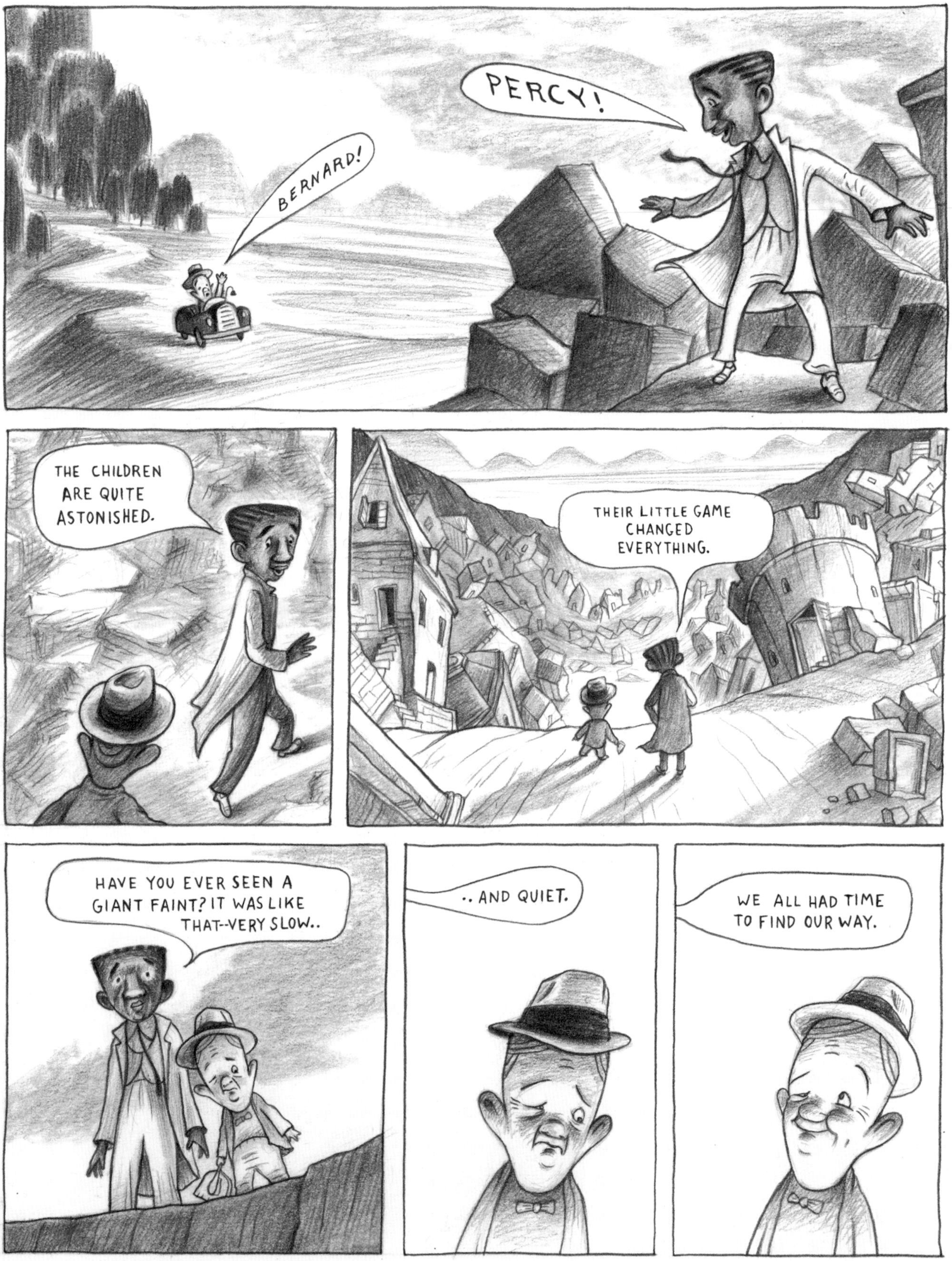
BERNARD!
PERCY!
THE CHILDREN ARE QUITE ASTONISHED.
THEIR LITTLE GAME CHANGED EVERYTHING.
HAVE YOU EVER SEEN A GIANT FAINT? IT WAS LIKE THAT--VERY SLOW..
.. AND QUIET.
WE ALL HAD TIME TO FIND OUR WAY.

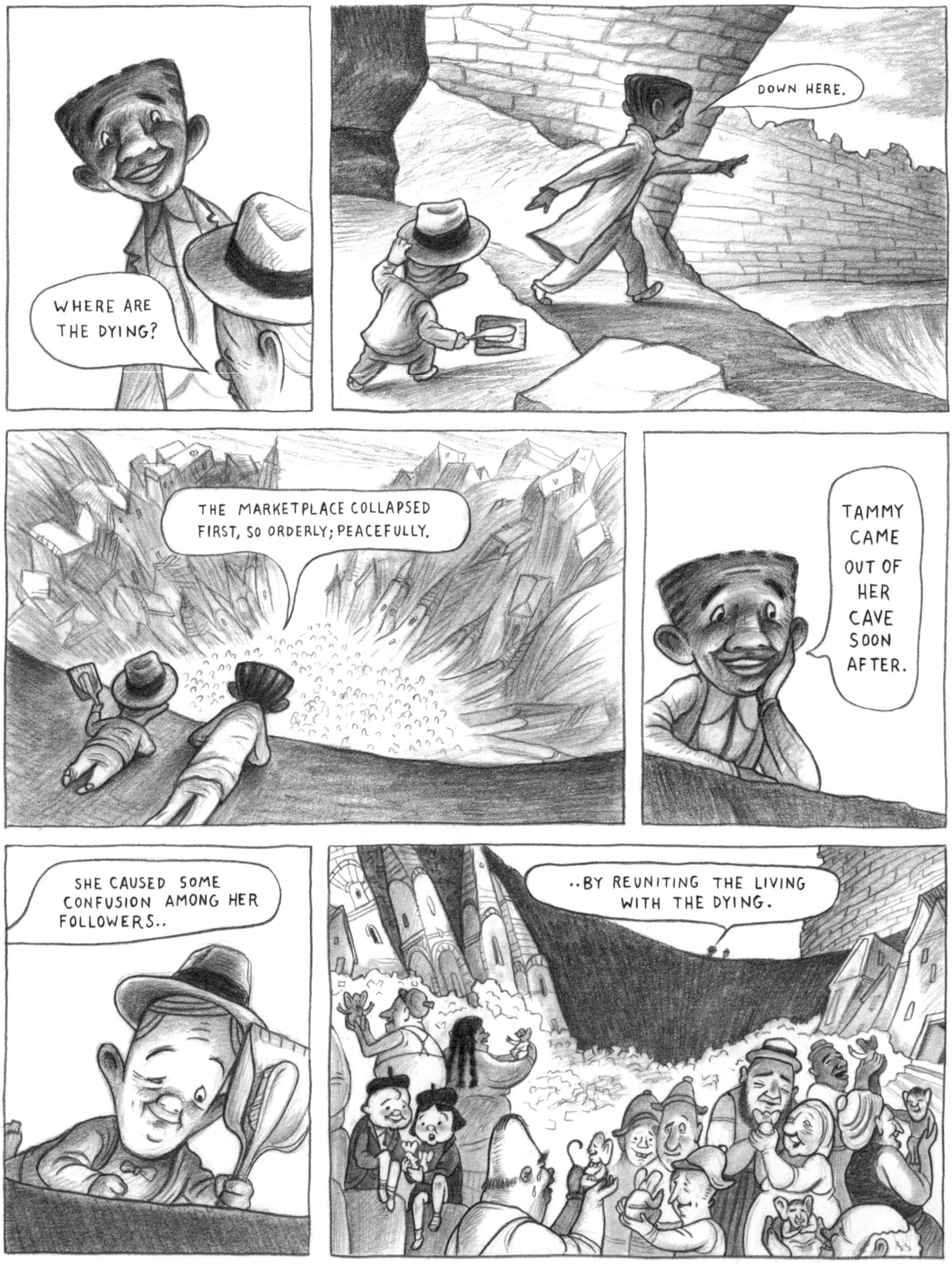
WHERE ARE THE DYING?
DOWN HERE.
THE MARKETPLACE COLLAPSED FIRST, SO ORDERLY; PEACEFULLY.
TAMMY CAME OUT OF HER CAVE SOON AFTER.
SHE CAUSED SOME CONFUSION AMONG HER FOLLOWERS..
..BY REUNITING THE LIVING WITH THE DYING.

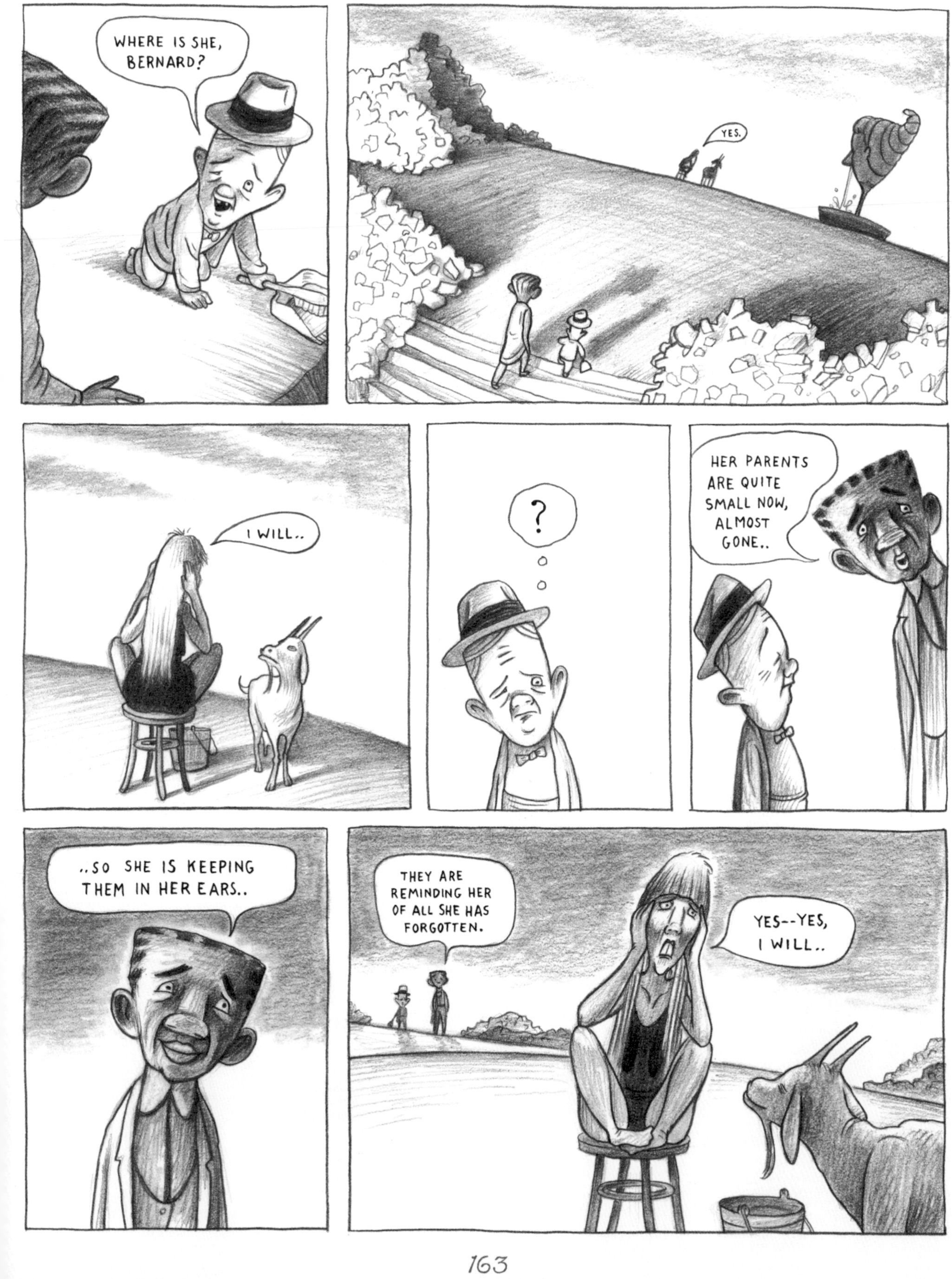
WHERE IS SHE, BERNARD?
YES.
I WILL..
?
HER PARENTS ARE QUITE SMALL NOW, ALMOST GONE..
..SO SHE IS KEEPING THEM IN HER EARS..
THEY ARE REMINDING HER OF ALL SHE HAS FORGOTTEN.
YES--YES, I WILL..

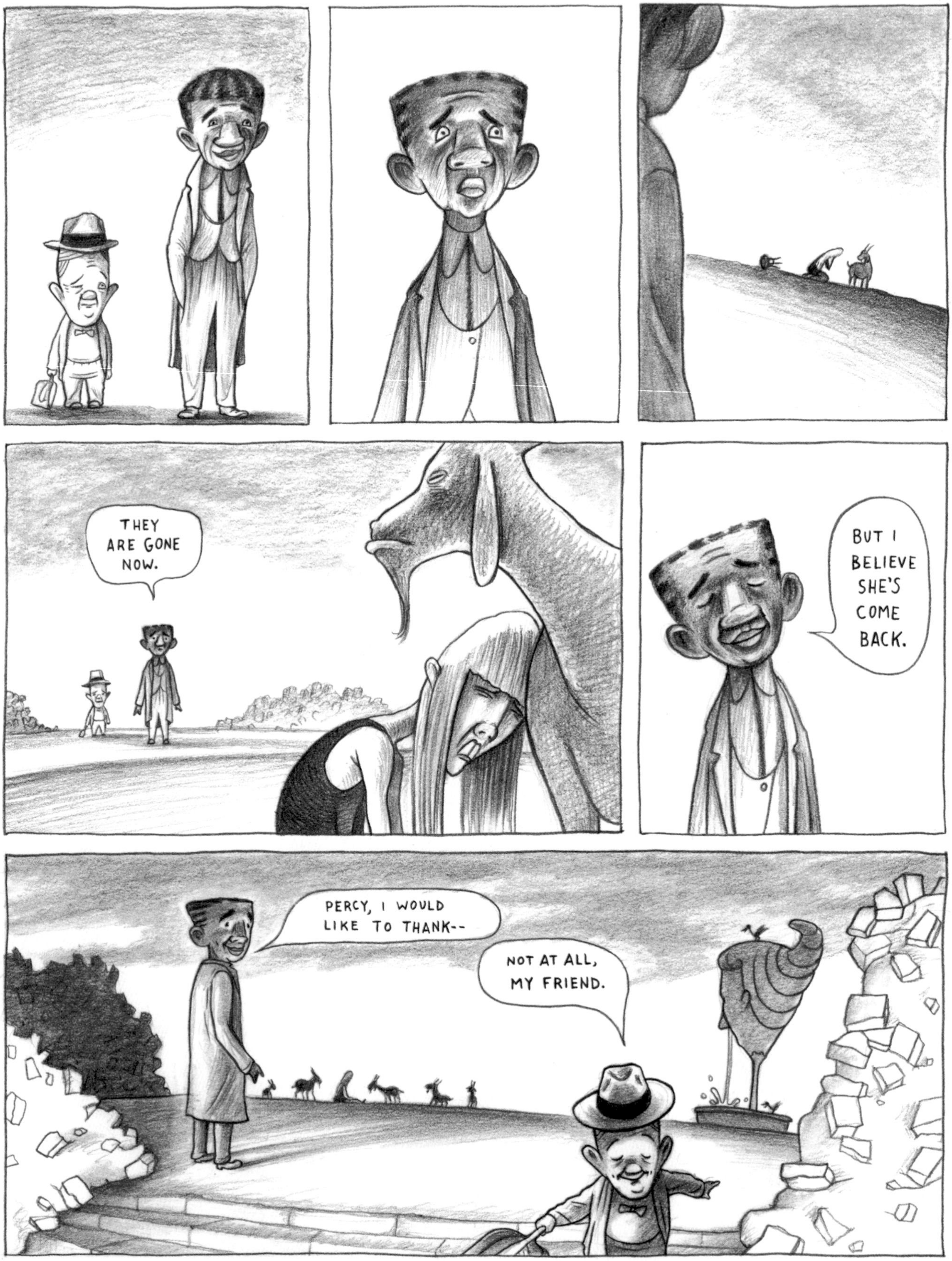
THEY ARE GONE NOW.
BUT I BELIEVE SHE'S COME BACK.
PERCY, I WOULD LIKE TO THANK--
NOT AT ALL, MY FRIEND.

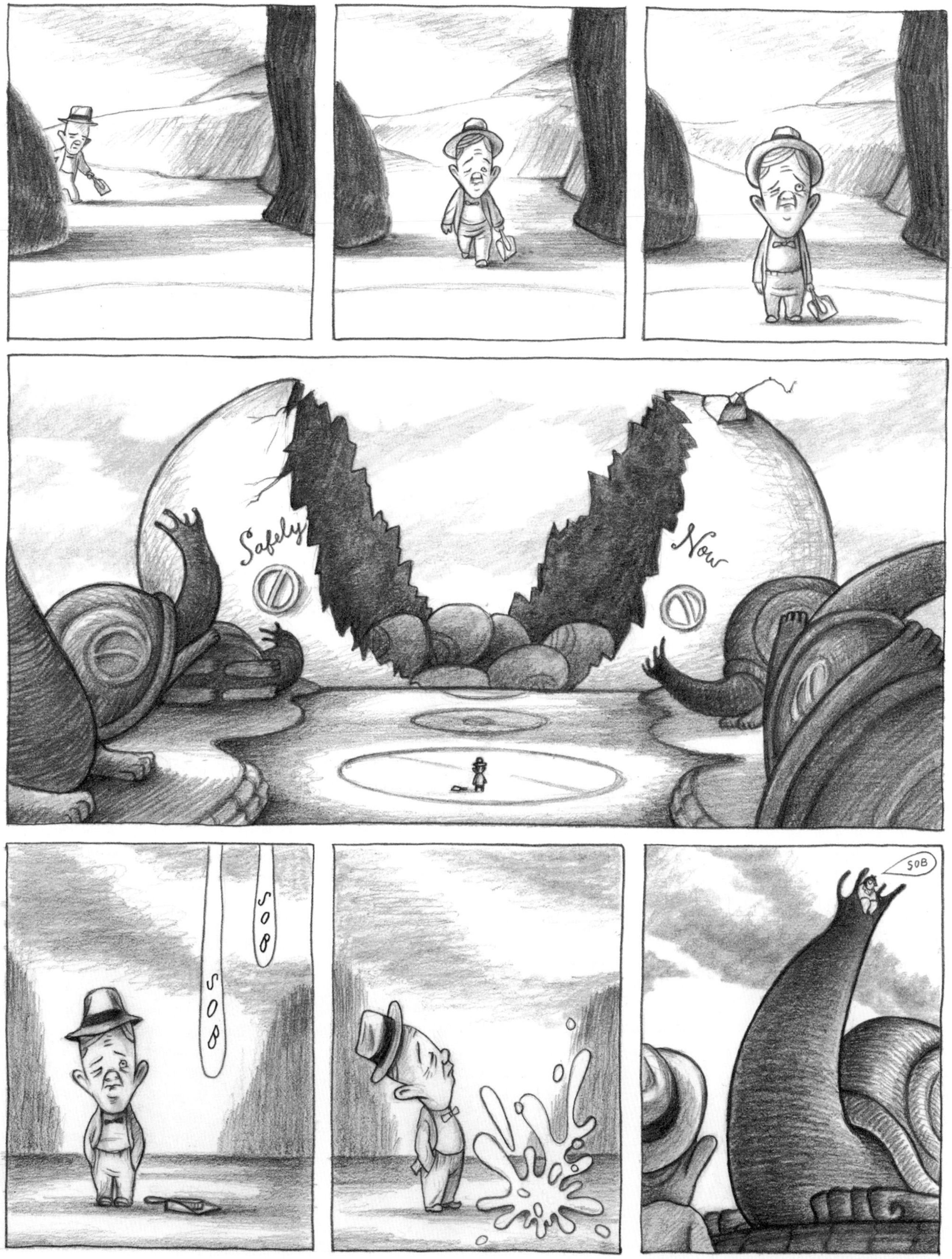
Safely
Now
SOB
SOB
SOB

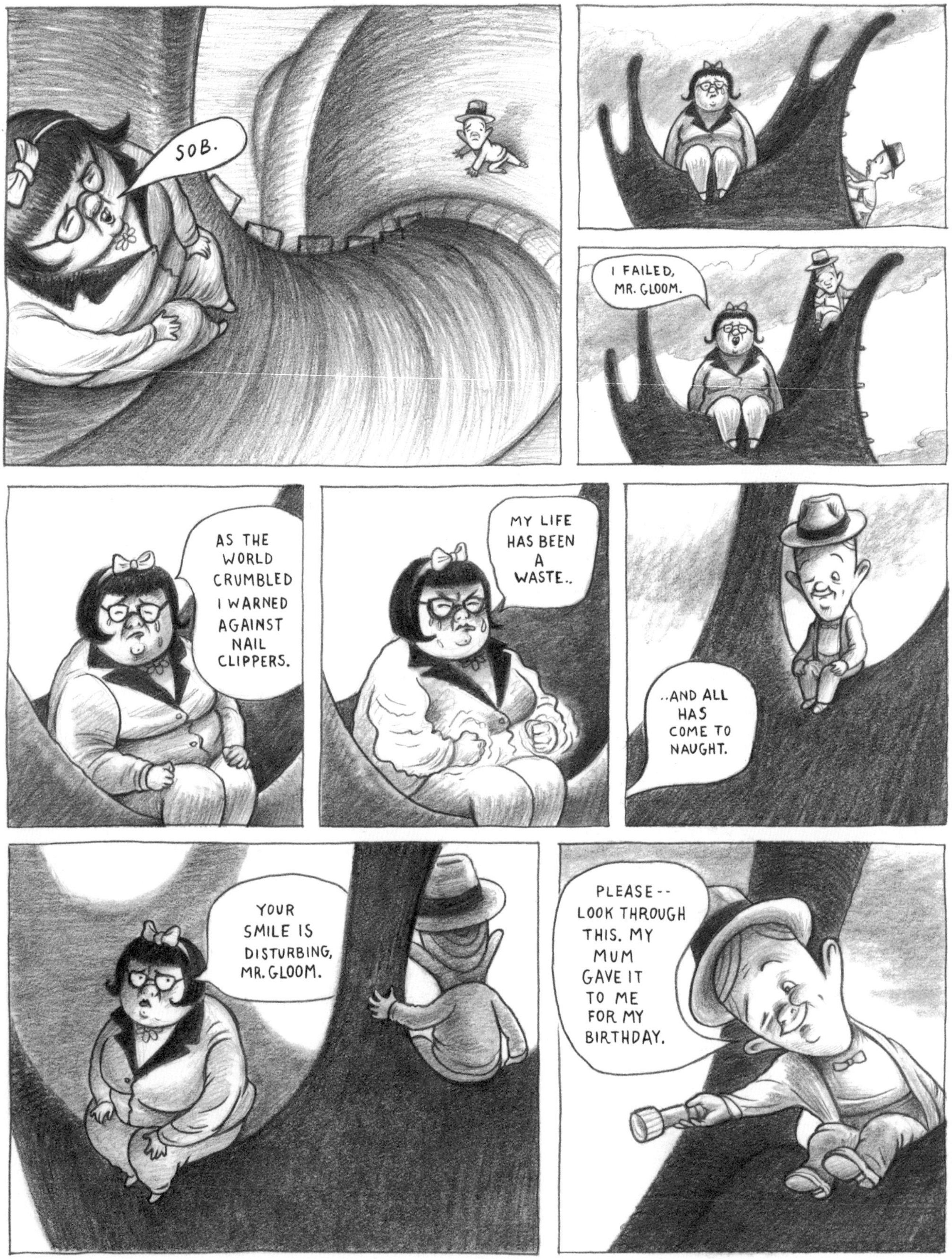
SOB.
I FAILED, MR. GLOOM.
AS THE WORLD CRUMBLED I WARNED AGAINST NAIL CLIPPERS.
MY LIFE HAS BEEN A WASTE..
..AND ALL HAS COME TO NAUGHT.
YOUR SMILE IS DISTURBING, MR. GLOOM.
PLEASE-- LOOK THROUGH THIS. MY MUM GAVE IT TO ME FOR MY BIRTHDAY.

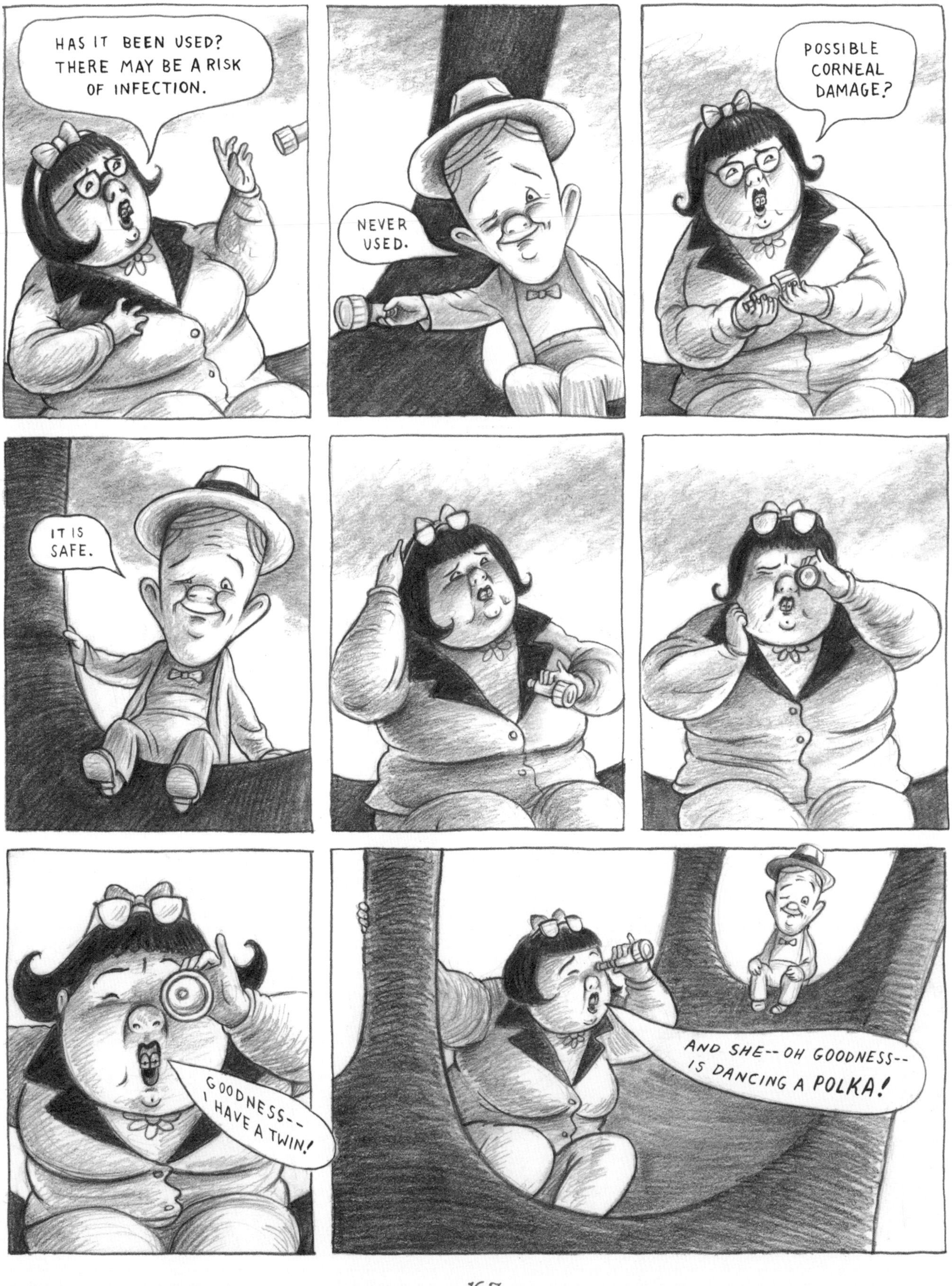
HAS IT BEEN USED? THERE MAY BE A RISK OF INFECTION.
NEVER USED.
POSSIBLE CORNEAL DAMAGE?
IT IS SAFE.
GOODNESS-- I HAVE A TWIN!
AND SHE--OH GOODNESS-- IS DANCING A POLKA!

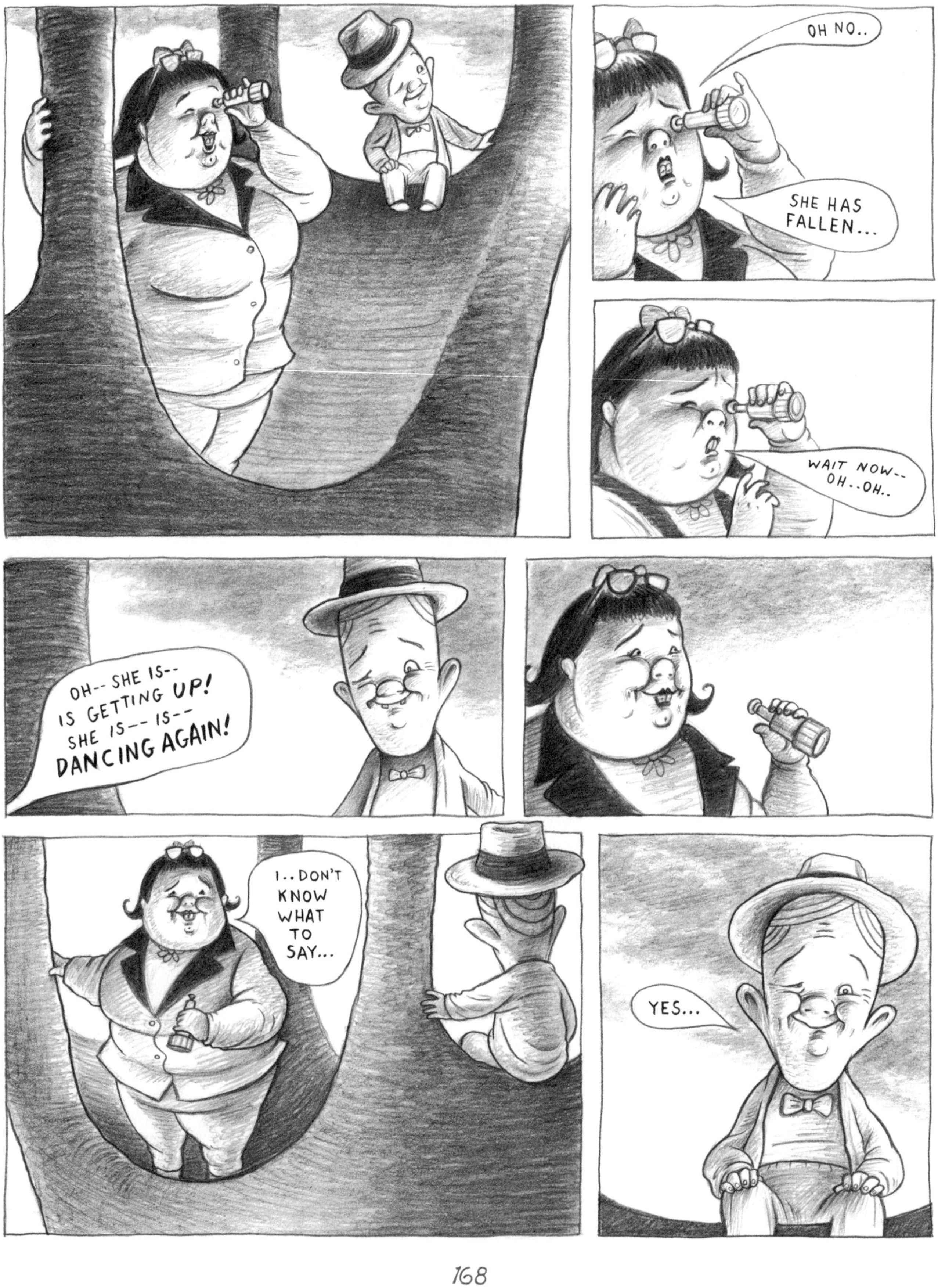
OH NO..
SHE HAS FALLEN...
WAIT NOW-- OH..OH..
OH-- SHE IS-- IS GETTING UP! SHE IS-- IS-- DANCING AGAIN!
I..DON'T KNOW WHAT TO SAY...
YES...

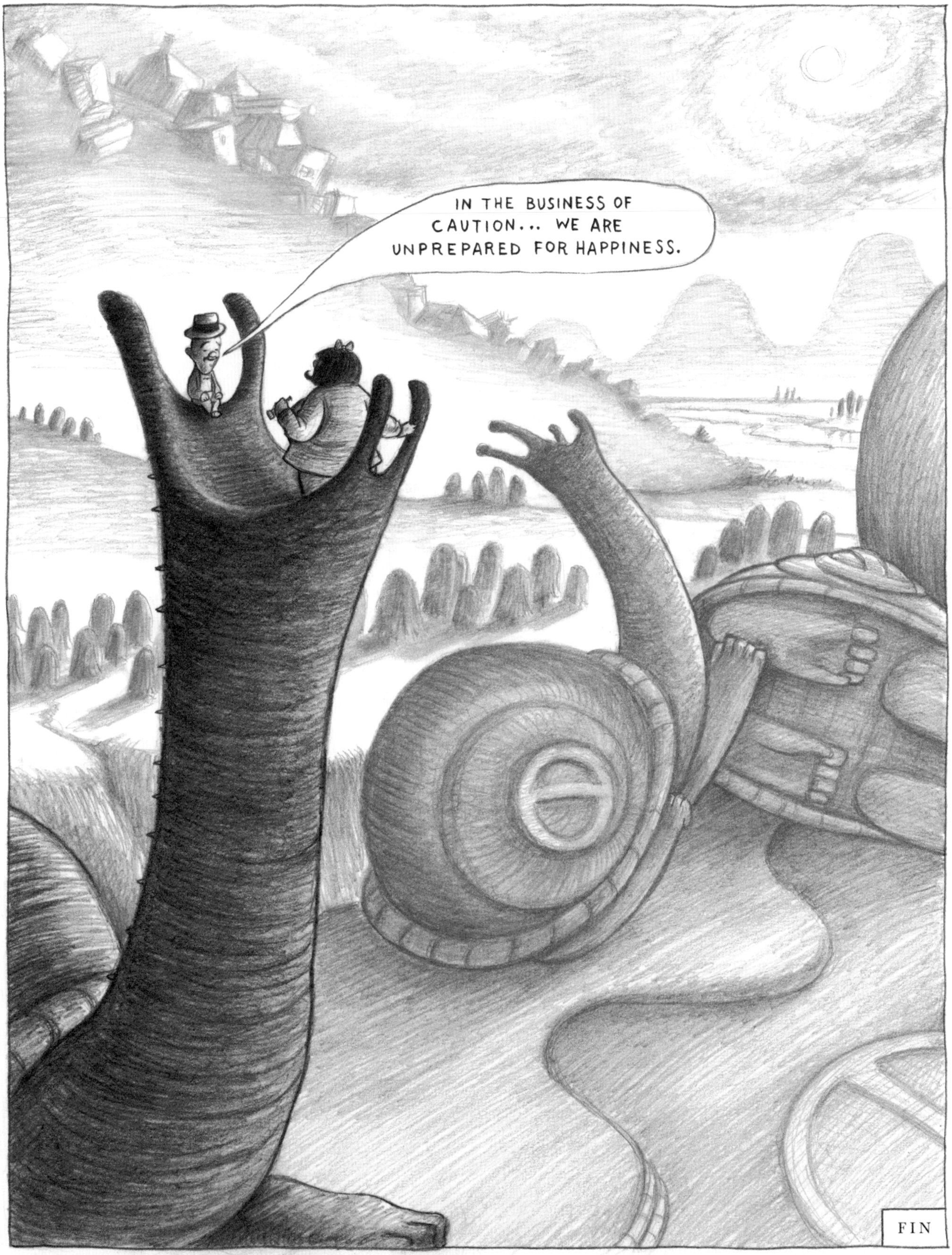
IN THE BUSINESS OF CAUTION... WE ARE UNPREPARED FOR HAPPINESS.
FIN

♩ = 112
Nu- lla è nuo- vo so- tto il so- le.

Appendix:

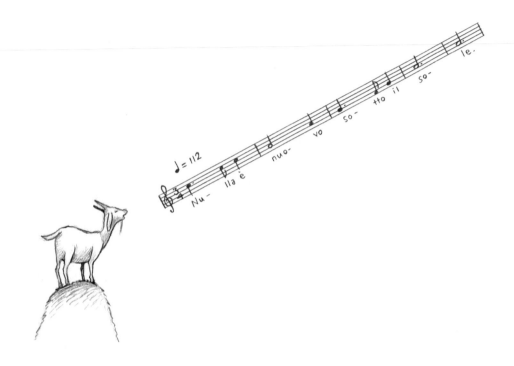

“NULLA È NUOVO”

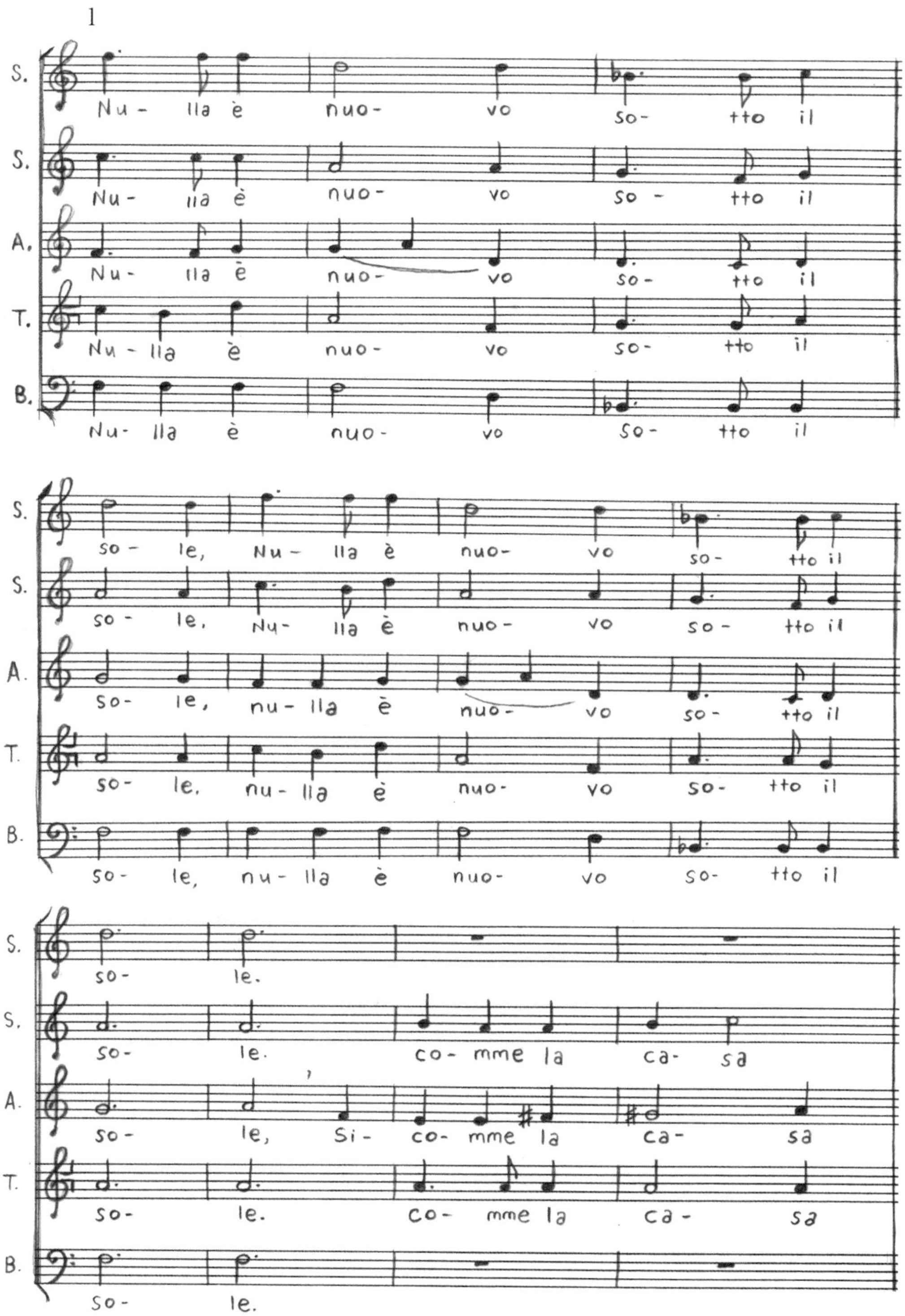
1
S. Nu- lla è nuo- vo so- tto il
S. Nu- lla è nuo- vo so - tto il
A. Nu- lla è nuo- vo so- tto il
T. Nu - lla è nuo- vo so- tto il
B. Nu- lla è nuo- vo so- tto il
S. so - le, Nu - lla è nuo- vo so- tto il
S. so - le. Nu- lla è nuo - vo so - tto il
A. so- le, nu - lla è nuo- vo so- tto il
T. so- le. nu - lla è nuo- vo so- tto il
B. so- le, nu - lla è nuo- vo so- tto il
S. so- le.
S. so- le. co- mme la ca- sa
A. so- le, Si- co- mme la ca- sa
T. so- le. co- mme la ca - sa
B. so- le.

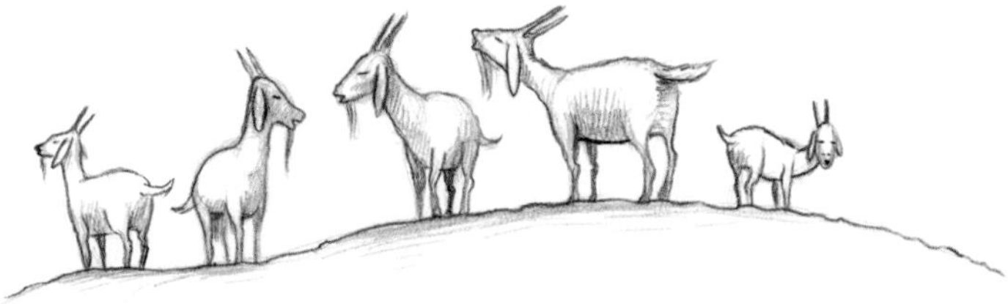

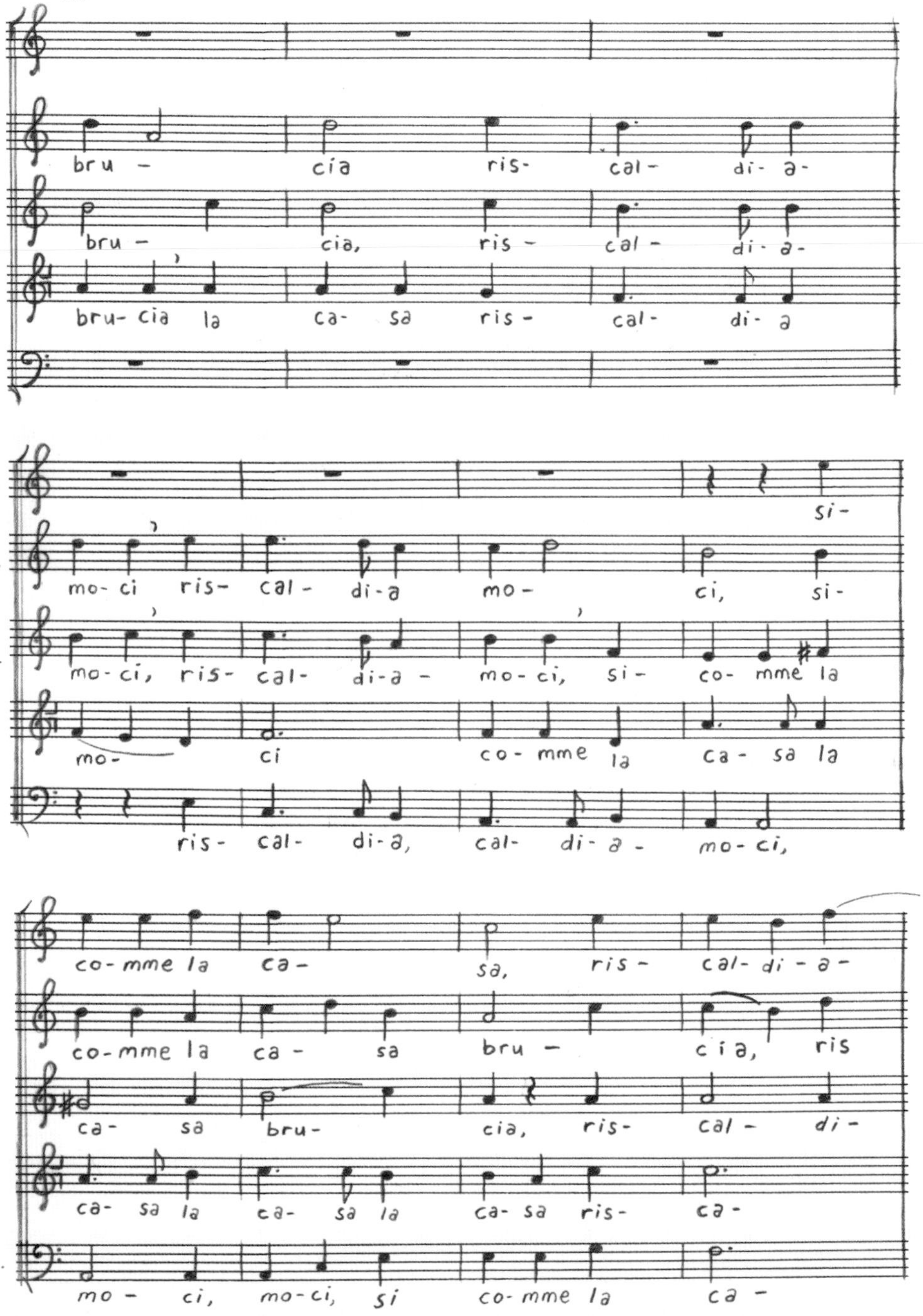
S.
S.
bru – cia ris- cal- di- a-
A.
bru – cia, ris – cal – di- a-
T.
bru- cia la ca- sa ris – cal- di- a
B.
S.
si-
S.
mo- ci ris- cal- di-a mo – ci, si-
A.
mo- ci, ris- cal- di-a – mo- ci, si – co- mme la
T.
mo- ci co- mme la ca – sa la
B.
ris- cal- di-a, cal- di- a – mo- ci,
S.
co- mme la ca – sa, ris – cal- di – a-
S.
co- mme la ca – sa bru – c i a, ris
A.
ca- sa bru- cia, ris- cal – di-
T.
ca- sa la ca- sa la ca- sa ris- ca-
B.
mo – ci, mo- ci, si co- mme la ca –

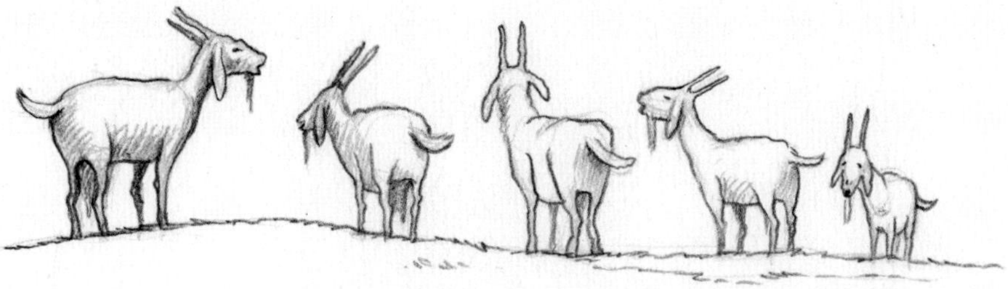

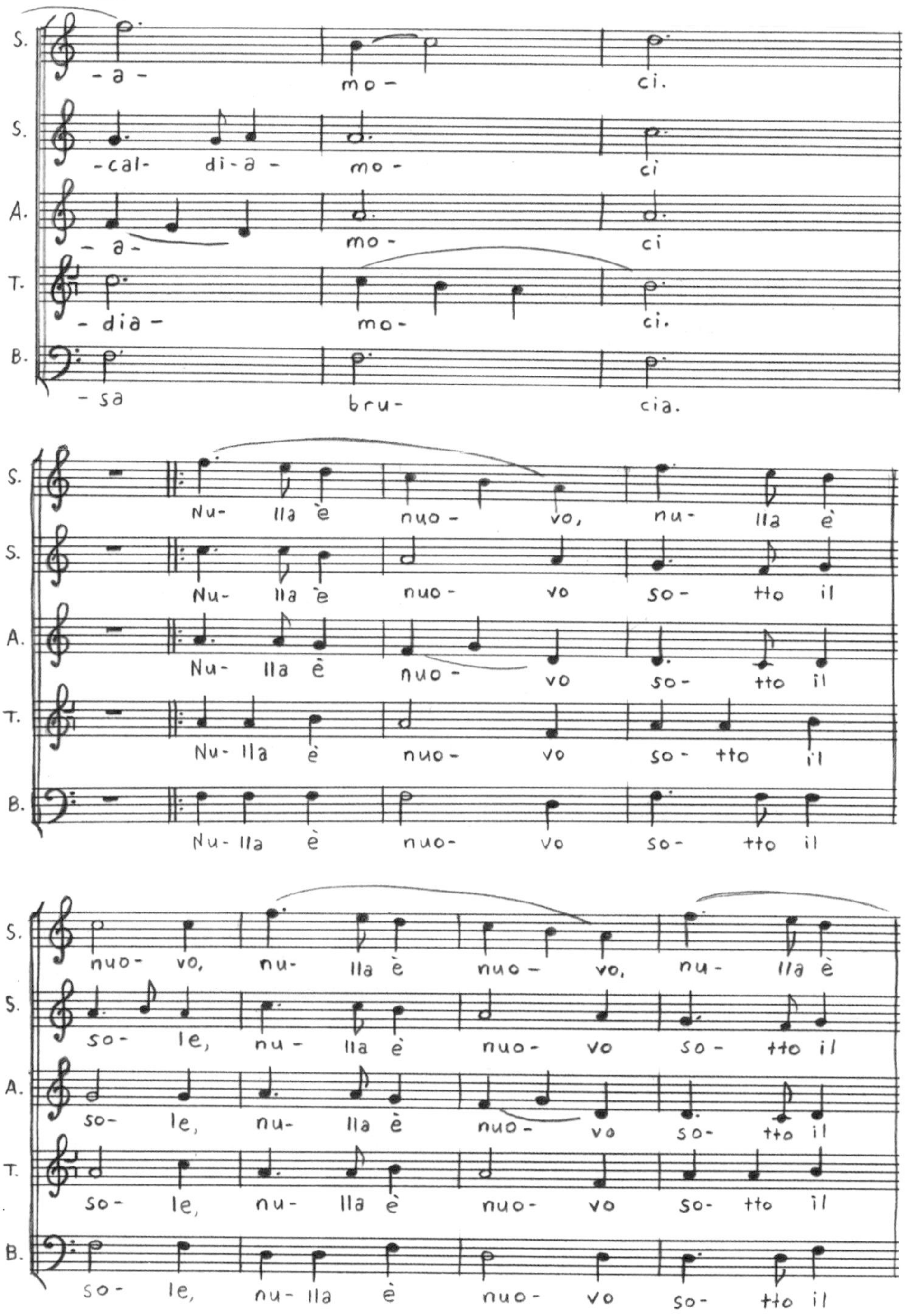
S. -a- mo- ci.
S. -cal- di-a- mo- ci
A. -a- mo- ci
T. -dia- mo- ci.
B. -sa bru- cia.
S. Nu- lla è nuo- vo, nu- lla è
S. Nu- lla è nuo- vo so- tto il
A. Nu- lla è nuo- vo so- tto il
T. Nu- lla è nuo- vo so- tto il
B. Nu- lla è nuo- vo so- tto il
S. nuo- vo, nu- lla è nuo- vo, nu- lla è
S. so- le, nu- lla è nuo- vo so- tto il
A. so- le, nu- lla è nuo- vo so- tto il
T. so- le, nu- lla è nuo- vo so- tto il
B. so- le, nu- lla è nuo- vo so- tto il

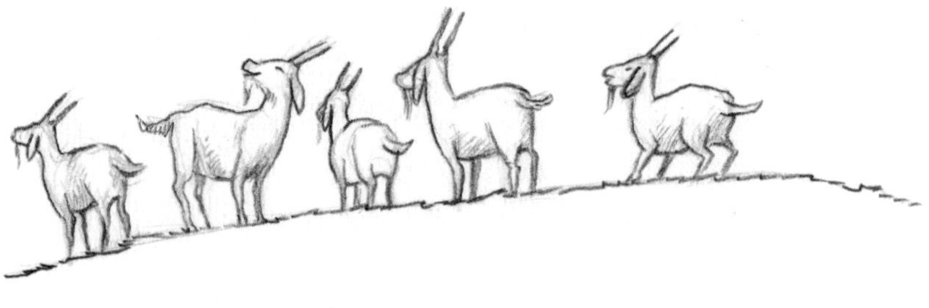

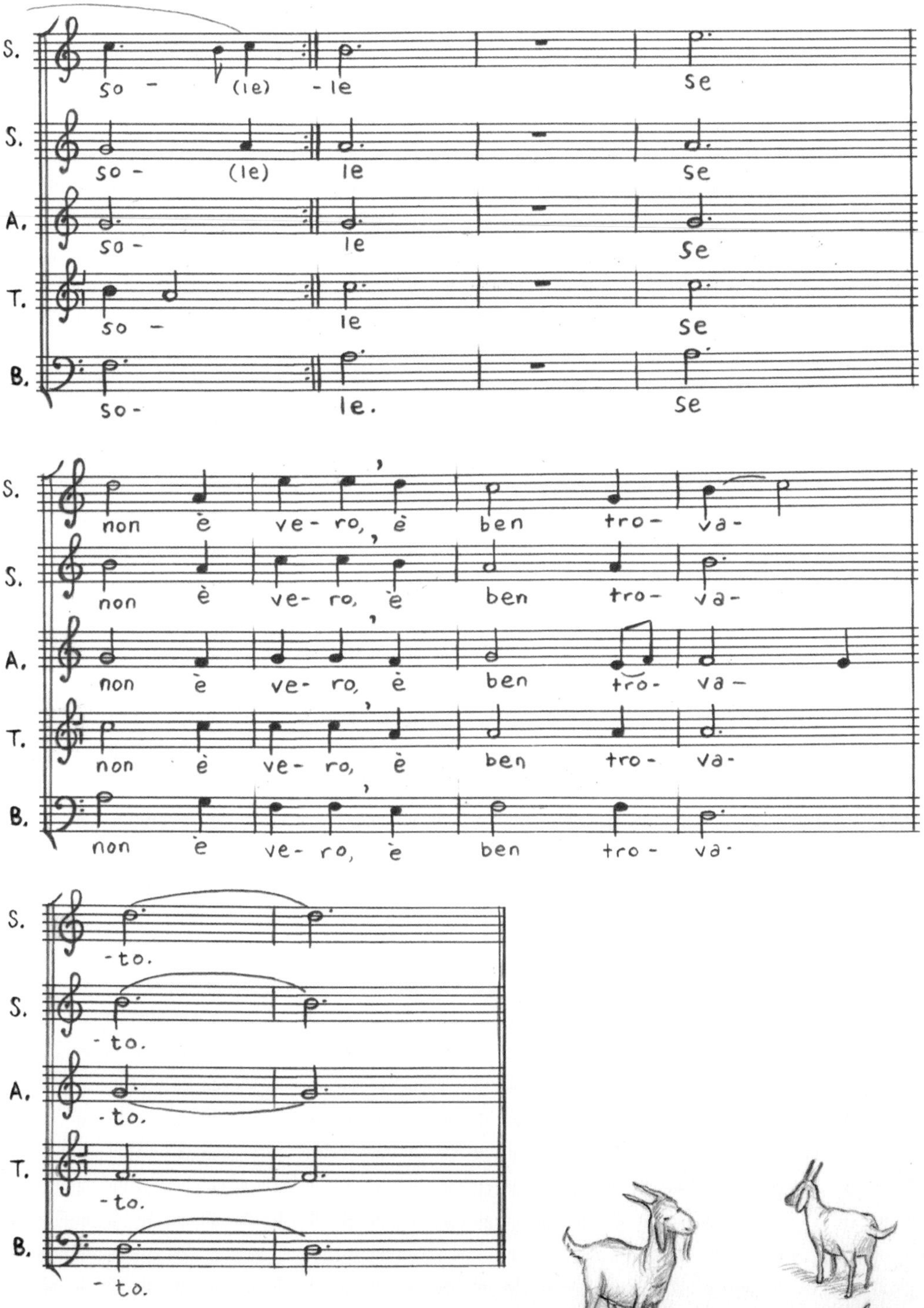
S.
so – (le) – le se
S.
so – (le) le se
A.
so – le se
T.
so – le se
B.
so- le. se
non è ve- ro, è ben tro- va-
non è ve- ro, è ben tro- va-
non è ve- ro, è ben tro- va –
non è ve- ro, è ben tro- va-
non è ve- ro, è ben tro- va-
-to.
-to.
-to.
-to.
-to.

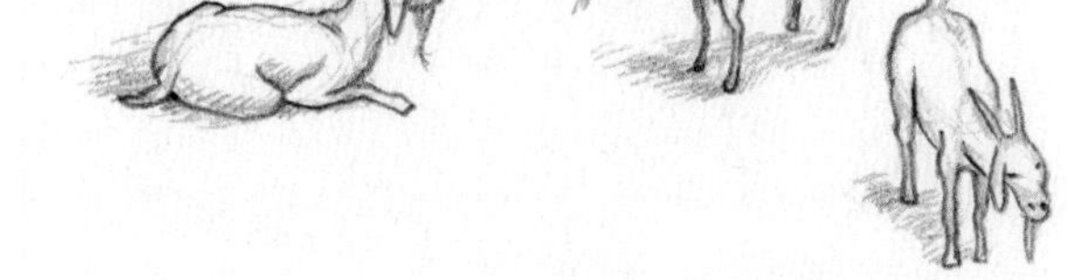

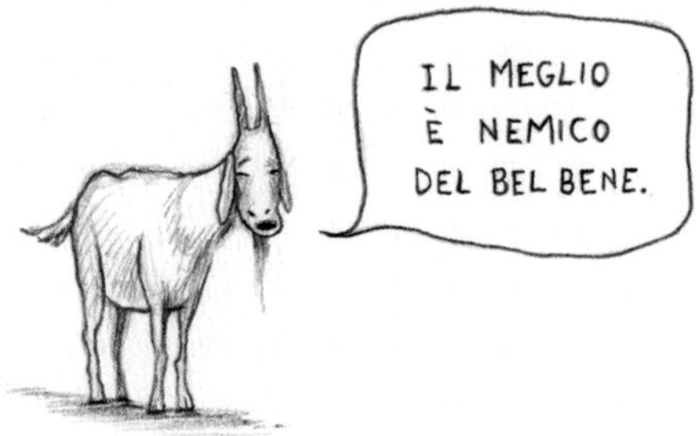
IL MEGLIO
È NEMICO
DEL BEL BENE.